KIDS IN CAGES

KIDS IN CAGES

Surviving and Resisting Child Migrant Detention

EDITED BY EMILY RUEHS-NAVARRO,
LINA CASWELL MUÑOZ, AND SARAH J. DIAZ

THE UNIVERSITY OF
ARIZONA PRESS
TUCSON

The University of Arizona Press
www.uapress.arizona.edu

We respectfully acknowledge the University of Arizona is on the land and territories of Indigenous peoples. Today, Arizona is home to twenty-two federally recognized tribes, with Tucson being home to the O'odham and the Yaqui. Committed to diversity and inclusion, the University strives to build sustainable relationships with sovereign Native Nations and Indigenous communities through education offerings, partnerships, and community service.

© 2024 by The Arizona Board of Regents
All rights reserved. Published 2024

ISBN-13: 978-0-8165-5381-5 (hardcover)
ISBN-13: 978-0-8165-5380-8 (paperback)
ISBN-13: 978-0-8165-5382-2 (ebook)

Cover design by Leigh McDonald
Typeset by Sara Thaxton in 10/14 Warnock Pro with PF Fuel and Avenir LT Std

Publication of this book is made possible in part by the proceeds of a permanent endowment created with the assistance of a Challenge Grant from the National Endowment for the Humanities, a federal agency.

Library of Congress Cataloging-in-Publication Data
Names: Ruehs-Navarro, Emily, editor. | Caswell Muñoz, Lina, 1980– editor. | Diaz, Sarah J., 1979– editor.
Title: Kids in cages : surviving and resisting child migrant detention / edited by Emily Ruehs-Navarro, Lina Caswell Muñoz, and Sarah J. Diaz.
Description: Tucson : University of Arizona Press, 2024. | Includes bibliographical references and index.
Identifiers: LCCN 2024005288 (print) | LCCN 2024005289 (ebook) | ISBN 9780816553815 (hardcover) | ISBN 9780816553808 (paperback) | ISBN 9780816553822 (ebook)
Subjects: LCSH: Immigrant children—Effect of imprisonment on—United States. | Juvenile detention—United States.
Classification: LCC JV6600 .K54 2024 (print) | LCC JV6600 (ebook) | DDC 305.23086/9120973—dc23/eng/20240710
LC record available at https://lccn.loc.gov/2024005288
LC ebook record available at https://lccn.loc.gov/2024005289

Printed in the United States of America
♾ This paper meets the requirements of ANSI/NISO Z39.48-1992 (Permanence of Paper).

CONTENTS

Acknowledgments — vii

Introduction — 3
EMILY RUEHS-NAVARRO AND LINA CASWELL MUÑOZ

Cages: Contextualizing the Violence of Child Migrant Detention

1. "Not 'Our' Children": The Othering of Migrant Children and Youth and the Concomitant Use of State-Sanctioned Violence Through Immigration Law and Policy — 31
   SARAH J. DIAZ, KATHERINE KAUFKA WALTS, AND LISA JACOBS

2. Kids, Paperwork, and Cages: An Analysis of the Unseen Representations of Immigrant Minors in the Key Documents and Legal Resources of the Unaccompanied Children Program — 59
   AIREEN GRACE ANDAL

3. Centering Children's Experiences: Lessons for Advocates — 87
   MARISA CHUMIL AND JENNIFER NAGDA

Survival: Voices of Resilience

4. "She Took Care of Me, and I Don't Even Remember Her Name": Relational Ruptures in Detention Settings — 117
   CORINNE KENTOR

5. "I'm Not an Animal. I'm a Girl.": Recognizing Resistance in Latinx Migrant Youths' *Testimonios* of Being Detained by Customs and Border Protection — 143
   JENN M. LILLY

6. Detained Homemaking: The Liminal Homemaking of Sexual and Gender Minority Central American Unaccompanied Youth — 173
LUIS EDWARD TENORIO

7. Emerging into Darkness: Coming of Age in the American Immigration Detention System — 189
JAJAH WU AND VIDA OPOKU

Resistance: A People's Response

8. Reimagining Treatment for Children Caged at the Border: From Therapy to Liberation — 221
SANDRA ESPINOZA, IMAN DADRAS, JACQUELINE FLORIAN, AND HERLIN SOTO-MATUTE

9. Alternatives to Detention: A Faith-Based Response — 245
REVEREND DR. SAMUEL ARROYO

Part 1. Watching Unaccompanied Minors Flourish: Hospitality as an Alternative to Detention — 255
FATHER COREY BROST AND BROTHER MICHAEL GOSCH

Part 2. What About the Women? — 270
SISTER PATRICIA CROWLEY, SISTER KATHLYN MULCAHY, DARLENE GRAMIGNA, SISTER STELLA AKELLO, JESSICA ALANIZ, AND EMILY RUEHS-NAVARRO

10. A Practitioner's Case Study of Immigrant Children's Artistic Narratives of Resistance — 283
SILVIA RODRIGUEZ VEGA

Conclusion. Toward a Decarceral Future: Reflections on the Practicability of Abolishing Migrant Child Detention — 307
SARAH J. DIAZ

Contributors — 325
Index — 335

ACKNOWLEDGMENTS

First, and most importantly, we would like to thank the children and youth about whom this book was written for being experts on their own experiences, for sharing those experiences with us, and for allowing all the authors to help facilitate their journey in whatever small ways that we have. We would also like to thank the following individuals for their time and helpful insights on this project: Emily Bartholomew, Stephanie Canizales, Diana Cedeña, Chiara Galli, Catherine Gaze, Ilaria Giglioli, Lauren Heidbrink, Kelly Kribs, Nancy Lee, Derek Loh, Diana Leon Boys, Erika McCombs, and Kate Swanson. In addition, we are particularly grateful to the anonymous reviewers who have provided useful feedback in the various iterations of this project. Finally, this project came to fruition through the financial support of Elmhurst University and Loyola University Chicago School of Law, and we are grateful for these contributions.

KIDS IN CAGES

Introduction

EMILY RUEHS-NAVARRO AND LINA CASWELL MUÑOZ

In the early summer of 2019, installations began popping up across New York City. In front of the American Museum of Natural History, at a Williamsburg subway stop, and near the Google building in Manhattan, small chain-linked cages appeared overnight. Inside of them, mannequins laid supine and in fetal positions, covered by foil blankets, with tennis shoes sticking out of the bottoms. Passersby could hear the wails of children coming from the cages, real audio that had been secretly taken in a Customs and Border Protection (CBP) facility. On top of the installations was a hashtag reading #NoKidsin-Cages (Bekiempis 2019).

These installations, promptly removed by city police, were part of an activist campaign, mobilized to decry a range of anti-immigrant policies put in place by the Donald Trump administration, not least of these the practice of holding migrant children in detention facilities and the zero-tolerance immigration enforcement policy, which separated migrant children from their parents. These activists were part of a diverse coalition that had been mobilized from across the country. In fact, in the previous summer, more than seven hundred demonstrations took place across the United States on June 30, 2018, with slogans such as "#EndFamilyDetention" and "Jails Are Not for Children." From Huntsville, Alabama, to Chicago to Los Angeles, thousands of people took to the streets, admonishing the administration that "Families Belong Together" and decrying the fact that "ICE [Immigration and Customs Enforcement] Cages Children." It was a life-affirming demonstration, organizer Marj Halperin told a reporter with the *Chicago Tribune*:

"Lives are truly at stake in this case . . . and the outpouring of people today around the country affirms that this nation supports immigrants" (Mahr, Briscoe, and Olumhense 2018).

It was certainly true that the Trump administration's anti-immigrant policies prompted a groundswell of support for immigrants, and it was an inspiring reminder that many Americans cared passionately about the government's treatment of immigrants and the welfare of children. But it was also a deeply ahistorical moment of protest, focused almost entirely on Trump and his administration, with little understanding of the history of child migration, the use of detention as a form of deterrence, and the culpability of various administrations, Republican and Democrat alike, in the inhumane treatment of immigrants. It is telling, in fact, that national backlash against Trump policies has all but disappeared during the Joe Biden administration, although the plight of immigrant children in the United States has not improved in meaningful ways.[1] Indeed, from Ronald Reagan to Joe Biden, the administrations of the past four decades have implemented and cemented a convoluted and utterly dehumanizing system of child migrant detention that has swept up hundreds of thousands of young migrants. And, as is explored in chapter 1 of this volume, it was centuries of dehumanizing and racist policies and ideologies, which "othered" Black, Brown, and Native children, that laid the groundwork for this modern system.

Despite the fact that the public outcry in recent years has decreased significantly, it would be disingenuous to suggest that no one cares about child migrant detention today. In fact, throughout the construction and maintenance of the modern system of detention, there has been a steady push of activists, attorneys, and practitioners who have witnessed the harms done to migrant children and have worked to heal the traumas of detention and push back against the practice altogether. From attorneys who work to close detention centers, to psychologists who attempt to provide mental health care to young people who are detained, to religious leaders who rally their communities to create hospitality homes as alternatives to detention, there is a passionate cohort of people who care and actively engage in finding solutions. However, these individuals do not always agree on a way forward: On the one hand, some argue that the system of detention is so entrenched in larger national policies that, seeing no change in the immediate future, the best way forward is through harm reduction. That is, the goal of these advocates is to make detention child-friendly and trauma-informed. On the other hand, many activists and scholars argue that detention is so fundamentally destructive that there is no way forward in harm reduction. That is, the goal must be to pursue abolition from the system entirely.

It would be easy to engage this conversation on a theoretical level, but the reality is that there are young people today experiencing the humiliations, indignities, and violences of detention. As discussed throughout this volume, it is clear that detention does tremendous harm to these children, and they will bear the scars of their experiences throughout their lives. However, young migrants also find ways to survive. They build relationships with one another, even forging chosen families. They resist indignities, finding spaces and moments in which they might exert power against an overwhelming system. And they find compassion in those around them, surviving off the kindness of strangers. A conversation about the way forward would not be complete without the active centering of their stories and their voices.

In this volume, we present the voices, ideas, and experiences of young migrants and those who have fought with them and for them. Collectively, we agree that the system of child migrant detention is an unjust and dehumanizing institution and we believe in working toward a future in which migrant children are treated with dignity, humanity, and compassion.

Children and Youth as Migrants: Alone and with Families

Children have been migrating to the United States alone, and with families, for centuries. Specific waves of child migrants have included European children in the late nineteenth century, Mexican children through the early twentieth century, and groups of refugee children throughout the twentieth century from countries ranging from Vietnam to Sudan. However, since the early 2010s, the United States saw a significant change in child migration at the U.S.-Mexico border, with the arrival of young migrants from El Salvador, Guatemala, and Honduras. The numbers of unaccompanied young people crossing the border from these countries had been stable throughout the early twenty-first century, with CBP reporting the apprehension of 3,304 unaccompanied minors in 2009. However, the numbers began to increase, and in 2014 the nation took notice as CBP reported an astounding 51,705 apprehensions of unaccompanied minors from this region (U.S. Customs and Border Protection n.d.-c). The numbers remained high, and although there was a significant drop in border encounters in 2020, record numbers of young people were recorded in the following years with 146,925 encounters in FY 2021 and 152,057 in FY 2022 (U.S. Customs and Border Protection n.d.-b). At the same time, the number of children and youth migrating with family members also increased. CBP reported a total of 68,684 individuals apprehended with a family member in fiscal year 2014 and 560,646 in 2022 (U.S. Customs and Border Protection n.d.-b, n.d.-c). In the past few years, there has also been a notable increase in migration from several other countries, including Venezuela, Cuba, and Nicaragua.

Like adults, children and youth migrate due to a variety of push and pull factors that are often overlapping and deeply rooted in global economics and political history. Indeed, the increase of migration from Central America coincides with a variety of shocks experienced in these countries. On the one hand, global climate change has brought severe droughts, pests, and other natural disasters to the region, destabilizing the agricultural base, which has led to an increase in poverty and food instability, especially in rural communities (World Food Programme 2017). This has had a particularly destabilizing effect on the food systems of Indigenous communities. Simultaneously, the global economic system of neoliberal capitalism has deepened inequality for both urban and rural citizens. In addition, community and political violence, rooted in a history of U.S. government interventions and the supply of weapons, and further exacerbated by local corruption, creates tremendous fear and uncertainty among residents (Menjívar and Rodríguez 2005; Zilberg 2007; Gonzalez 2011; United Nations Development Programme 2013; Leónova 2019). These various pressures have converged to create a veritable crisis, prompting significant increases of emigration.

In addition to these reasons for increased migration generally, there are also specific reasons that a young person might migrate alone that are unique to the experience of childhood and adolescence, and connected to the intersectional identities of these migrants. For example, young men who live in communities with high rates of violence may experience gang recruitment, and young women may experience gang-related, gender-based violence specifically during their teen years (Kids in Need of Defense n.d.). Young people may seek better educational opportunities, thus prompting solitary or family migration (Tucker et al. 2012; Ruehs-Navarro 2022). Adolescent boys may seek to use migration as a part of the coming-of-age process (Hernández

Hernández 2012; Ruehs 2016). Children and youth who experience violence in the home may use migration as a way of escaping this abuse. Furthermore, Indigenous youth face a range of oppressive conditions that mediate migration decisions (Heidbrink 2020) and LGBTQ-identified young people might flee violence that is linked to their identity (Luibhéid and Chávez 2020). And, finally, children and youth may seek family reunification with parents or other relatives who had migrated, a reality that is made worse by the United States' restrictive immigration and border policies (Dreby 2010; Abrego 2014).

A Note on Terminology

The terminology used to describe young people who migrate has evolved over recent years, and in this volume we have been mindful to consider the importance and precision of legal terms but also recognize the critiques that youth studies scholars have waged against an array of frequently used terminology. In U.S. statutes, young people who enter the United States without immigration status and without a parent or legal guardian, under the age of eighteen, have been designated as "unaccompanied alien children" (UAC). This term was used throughout government agencies until quite recently. While the term remains consistent in statute, President Biden issued a memo in July 2021 for government agencies to replace the use of *alien* and *illegal* with other terms, including *noncitizen* and *undocumented* (King 2021). Immigration agencies have followed suit, and on its website, CBP uses "unaccompanied children" in most titles and text on its website, although other terminology appears throughout its documents. Similarly, the Office of Refugee Resettlement (ORR) Unaccompanied Children Program uses "unaccompanied children" throughout most of its public-facing information, although UAC still appears on some official forms.

Although *child* is used throughout much of the public relations media by these departments as a blanket term for all minors, age designation becomes important in placement and service determination while in ORR custody and in the ORR release process. The ORR guide "Children Entering the United States Unaccompanied" uses the term *children* for ages 0–13 and *teen* for ages 14–17 (Office of Refugee Resettlement 2015).

We are mindful of these distinctions throughout this volume. However, we are also mindful that this terminology is imbued with values and beliefs.

The idea of *child* is often granted an innocence, vulnerability, and deservingness that *teen* and *adolescent* are not (Malkki 2010). Further, the word *youth* can be used by scholars to encompass not just an age category (typically 13–26) but a relational and social category that acknowledges the unequal power dynamics that are often at play between adults and young people (Wyn and White 1997). Finally, we intentionally avoid acronyms such as UC out of concern that they dehumanize and homogenize groups of people.

The Modern Evolution of Detention for Migrant Children and Youth in the United States

The detention of nonwhite and noncitizen children has a long, storied history. While our intention here is not to provide a comprehensive review of this system, it is worth noting that there are a range of precursors to immigration detention today.[2] Children have been held in migrant detention as early as the late nineteenth century, when detention at Ellis Island and Angel Island was used while migrants' admissibility was processed. Both European and Asian children faced possible detention and family separation, as they were forced to defend their sexual morality, prove their family relationships, and undergo invasive health screenings (Padilla-Rodríguez 2020). At the southern border, Mexican children were also entering the United States, alone and with family, and although the region was largely unguarded at this time, some faced similar interrogation as a condition for their entry.

Throughout the twentieth century, the world faced multiple, global refugee crises involving children; the response by the United States varied and was often mediated by political pressure and xenophobia. For example, during World War II, Congress debated a bill that sought to receive German Jewish children. Legislators ultimately failed to enact the bill due to antisemitic beliefs that Jewish children would become undesirable adults. Yet, not long after, private advocates successfully organized for the entry of British (and presumably Christian) children to the United States (Padilla-Rodríguez 2020). In a similarly political move two decades later, the United States engaged in Operation Pedro Pan, in which more than fourteen thousand unaccompanied Cuban children were airlifted to the United States from Cuba, ostensibly to avoid Communist indoctrination following the Cuban Revolution. These young people were originally placed in foster families, but as the numbers increased, military bases were converted to house the new arrivals.

While the rhetoric of the operation focused on the protection of children, historians have noted that the children themselves reported discrimination and abuse. Vietnamese refugees constituted another important and politically charged wave of child migrants. The United States began Operation Babylift in 1975, which airlifted more than two thousand children from Vietnam. Later legislation continued to allow for the entry of the Amerasian children of U.S. servicemen but barred entry of their mothers. Historian Ivón Padilla-Rodríguez (2020, 5) explains that these refugee programs were justified "on the basis of [the children's] status as victims of communist regimes and human rights principles . . . and efforts to recast US foreign policy during the Vietnam War."

The system of detention as we know it today took shape in just the past four decades. Although detention as a policy had been abandoned after the closure of Angel Island and Ellis Island, in the early 1980s the Reagan administration sought to revive detention in response to a wave of Haitian refugees. However, instead of being used as a holding space while a migrant's admissibility was processed, detention was enacted explicitly as a form of punitive deterrence. Within a year, the administration began to mandate detention for all migrants without authorization to enter the country, including a new wave of refugees fleeing political unrest in Central America.[3]

In the initial years of the new detention system, there was little difference in the treatment of adult and child migrants. Child advocates quickly discovered that young people were experiencing the horrors of detainment along with adults. One of the first cases included an eight-year-old Haitian girl who was incarcerated in a West Palm Beach city jail (Padilla-Rodríguez 2020). Perhaps the most well-known child who was incarcerated in the early years of the system—and the child whose name became immortalized in later policies dictating standards of care—was fifteen-year-old Jenny Lisette Flores. Jenny arrived in the United States alone from El Salvador in 1985. She was detained upon arrival at the border, having no visa, but had to wait for months before she could face an immigration judge who would determine her fate. While many children at the time were released to family or other "responsible parties" while they awaited their court hearing, Jenny's undocumented mother was afraid to report to the Immigration and Naturalization Services (INS) office as it was common knowledge that undocumented parents could be arrested and deported along with their newly arrived children should they come forward.

Jenny was detained by a for-profit government contractor, Behavioral Systems Southwest, which held Jenny along with adults in a converted Pasadena motel, surrounded by a chain-link fence and concertina wire (Schrag 2020). There were no visitors, no educational instruction, and no recreation. The treatment by guards was utterly dehumanizing, and several months into her detention, a doctor visit concluded that Jenny was suffering from severe stress, including anorexia, depression, and a "preoccupation with death" (affidavit quoted in Schrag 2020, 14). Reports from others of the more than five thousand children detained throughout the 1980s alleged that children were even subjected to daily strip searches, including vaginal and rectal exams.

Jenny was detained with another child, a young girl whose mother was a housekeeper for the well-known actor Ed Asner. Through his networks, Asner connected the immigrant families with a lawyer. Jenny Flores became the primary plaintiff in a federal, class-action lawsuit that would unfold over the following decades and resulted in the Flores Settlement Agreement, which would have wide-reaching implications for future children detained by the government. Among the agreements, the initial settlement contended that the government should implement standards for the care of children in detention and that the "least restrictive" setting should be used. However, attorneys were not able to eliminate detention altogether in order to return to the previous "catch and release" standard, as the government argued that detention was necessary for the protection of children (Schrag 2020).

As a response to the Flores Settlement Agreement and as a part of the Homeland Security Act in 2002, the government initiated the Office of Refugee Resettlement Unaccompanied Minors Division, which created a new system of shelters to care for all unaccompanied children in U.S. custody. This notably took the care and custody out of the hands of the newly created Department of Homeland Security (DHS, which housed both Immigration and Customs Enforcement and Customs and Border Protection) and in theory created a department whose sole purpose was the care of immigrant children who arrived alone.

Yet the program itself remains controversial. First, children are still detained in border intake facilities run by CBP, although by law, they should be transferred to an ORR shelter within seventy-two hours. Plus, critics have argued that the directives of DHS consistently supersede the protections of ORR. Although the Flores Settlement guides the standards of care for facilities that detain children, the actual quality of care varies tremendously.

On the one hand, some nonprofit organizations run homelike facilities with only a handful of youth. Yet other young people are sent to facilities that are accused of warehousing hundreds—sometimes thousands—of youth. Still other young people are sent to juvenile detention centers. The current infrastructure often fails to meet demand, so when there are periods of high migration, young people are sent to makeshift tent camps, referred to as "emergency intake facilities." These facilities are often on military bases and may be run through private contractors. Regardless of the type of facility, there are a few commonalities: the detainment is compulsory, the length of detainment is variable but can span for a year or longer, and contact between the detained young person and the outside world is strictly controlled.

The detention of immigrant children and youth is not solely for minors who are apprehended without legal guardians. In fact, in 2005, President George W. Bush ended the so-called catch-and-release policy for migrant families, resulting in the need for new ICE facilities. At the time, the new influx of undocumented migrants included an increase in family units, so ICE contracted with the former Corrections Corporation of America (CCA, now rebranded as CoreCivic), one of the nation's most profitable private-prison corporations, to open the T. Don Hutto Family Detention Center in Taylor, Texas. With the new contract in hand, CCA claimed to be proud of the innovation of "keeping families together" (Schrag 2020).

Not long after the facility opened, Hutto detained Kevin Yourdkhani, a nine-year-old Canadian citizen with Iranian parents (Goodman 2007; Talbot 2008; Lyda and Lyda 2009). A decade prior, Kevin's parents had fled Iran to pursue political asylum in Canada, after being harassed by government officials for providing a copy of a book considered blasphemous to local authorities. Kevin was born only two years after the couple's arrival in Canada, while their asylum application was processed, making him the first Canadian citizen in the family. However, the family's case was denied and they were deported to Iran. Immediately upon arrival, Kevin's father reports that both parents were detained by officials; the father was held and tortured for six months. As soon as he was released, the family sought ways to return to Canada, knowing that they were not safe in Iran. Family and friends helped collect $40,000 to help the family hire smugglers. The smuggler eventually got the family to South America and then on a flight from Guyana to Toronto, using fake passports. However, while en route a woman had a heart attack on the plane, and it made an unplanned landing in Puerto Rico, where the family was forced to pass through immigration. As the family had no visa for the United States, they were quickly detained. They were held for five days in a Puerto Rican jail, the father separated from Kevin and his mother, before being transferred to Hutto.

Kevin suffered both physically and emotionally in the facility. The family reported that he quickly lost weight due to the substandard food, and in an interview with a journalist with *Democracy Now!*, Kevin reported that he was sitting in a cell all day, sleeping next to a stinking toilet. His asthma was flaring with the air quality in the stuffy rooms, and his back was hurting from the beds. His mother reported that he often asked why he was being locked in a prison. Indeed, all detainees wore prison scrubs, required headcounts kept detainees stuck in their cells for up to twelve hours a day, and guards would often wake sleeping children at night when they would shine lights into their cells. Kevin pleaded with the journalist on the phone, "I want to be free. I want to go outside. I want to go to school. I want be in my homeland, Canada" (Goodman 2007). His parents also worried about the impact of imprisonment on the family. His mother explained to a reporter: "[My husband] and I cannot be good parents. We cannot provide Kevin with the basic things that he needs.... We cannot give him a pen to write with or any books to read. We cannot teach him about the outside world or let him run around, the way young boys should. We are totally helpless as parents and depend on the guards for everything." Her family, she said, "is falling apart in here" (Talbot 2008).

Indeed, when activists toured the facility, they noted an array of prisonlike conditions, including razor wire, cells with exposed toilets and thin mattresses, headcounts, and prison clothing. Psychologists warned that such incarceration was equivalent to child abuse. Once again, attorneys brought forth various lawsuits regarding this incarceration, referring specifically to stipulations from the Flores Settlement. Kevin was represented by the American Civil Liberties Union (ACLU), which argued that his detention violated the settlement. In Kevin's case, the Canadian government eventually granted reentry to the family, allowing for their release. Regarding Hutto more broadly, activists were able to encourage minor reforms to the prisonlike conditions, but ultimately, the lawsuits failed to end the project of family detainment altogether. Indeed, ICE drafted standards for family detention facilities, and while Hutto eventually closed as a family center in 2009, other facilities opened, including a converted law enforcement training center in

Artesia, New Mexico, the Karnes County Residential Center in Karnes, Texas (operated by the GEO Group); the South Texas Family Residential Center in Dilley, Texas (run by CoreCivic); and the Berks County Residential Center, operated by Berks County in Pennsylvania. Many of these facilities still operate today, and although previous settlements have "softened" some of the notably prisonlike conditions, activists still argue that the detainment of children in any detention facility, alone or with parents, exerts irreparable psychological harm.

The system of detention continued to operate steadily until 2014, when the country faced an increase of unaccompanied children at the U.S.-Mexico border. The Barack Obama administration was seemingly caught off-guard by these sky-rocketing numbers, and the relatively small system run by ORR was not prepared. The system had been built for several thousand children a year, not tens of thousands. As a result, many young people were held in the CBP detention centers longer than the seventy-two hours stipulated previously, and ORR scrambled to contract with more long-term shelter options, including, for a short period, the Lackland Airforce Base.

By 2016, the numbers of unaccompanied youth and family units crossing the border had remained consistently high, but a new factor was thrown into the equation: the election of Donald Trump. The immigration policies implemented by the Trump administration were swift, chaotic, and wide-reaching. They were also implemented explicitly for the deterrence of future immigrants (Dickerson 2022). For example, the Migrant Protection Protocols, beginning in January 2019, forced migrants to stay in Mexican border towns while awaiting their immigration hearings, essentially detaining the families in limbo. Although the policy did not apply to unaccompanied children and youth, it did impact children traveling with their families. These families remained in squalid and often dangerous conditions, prompting some parents to send their child across the border alone, in an attempt to provide a safer option.

One of the most heinous of the policies to catch the public's attention was the so-called zero-tolerance policy, which began quietly as a pilot program in mid-2017 in the El Paso region and then expanded to all regions by mid-2018. Under the policy, the United States separated close to three thousand children and youth from their parents, rendering them unaccompanied. The government claimed that the separation was due to the parents' criminal act of unauthorized crossing. Then attorney general Jeff Sessions (2018) explained: "If you cross the southwest border unlawfully, then we will prosecute you. It's that simple. If you smuggle illegal aliens across our border, then we will prosecute you. If you are smuggling a child, then we will prosecute you and that child will be separated from you as required by law."

Reports of this policy in practice reveal the depth of the cruelty. CNN profiled a mother whose child was ripped from her while she breastfed. ProPublica released a recording from a border patrol facility in which listeners hear the anguished wails of ten children (Lavandera, Morris, and Simon 2018; Thompson 2018). At one point, a CBP agent jokes about the orchestra of sound coming from the desperate children. Amid the sounds on the recording, a girl's voice is heard pleading for someone to call her aunt; she is reciting a number. This girl was six-year-old Alison Jimena Valencia Madrid. She and her mother had fled El Salvador to request asylum after a local gang had threatened to kill her and she had experienced an attempted kidnapping. The mother and daughter were being held together in a border facility when an agent called out Alison's name. The mother and Alison walked to the agent, thinking they were being taken elsewhere together, but instead officers led them each in opposite directions and never again reunited them. In a cruel twist of fate, it was the U.S. Border Patrol that succeeded in kidnapping Alison from her mother. Not long after, an unidentified informant recorded the audio of Alison and the other children begging for help. The widely published recording, and the child's clear-headed tenacity in the midst of horrific trauma, helped garner public outrage for the policy, and, in the Madrid family case, the assistance of attorneys to work for family reunification and asylum.

With the public's attention focused squarely on the Trump administration's migration policies, there was increased awareness of the imprisonment of children in CBP facilities and ORR shelters. The deaths of several children while in CBP custody, including a two-year-old boy from Guatemala, prompted particular outrage at a detention system that did not prioritize the health and safety of children. Several images became etched in the public's imagination. One was a series of aerial views of an encampment of white tents in a barren landscape with a line of children walking single-file through the center, flanked by staff members in khaki pants and neon-green shirts. These images, taken by Mike Blake with Reuters in 2018, were of the Tornillo Tent Camp, a makeshift shelter that housed thousands of migrant children in southern Texas. Another was a photo by Ross D. Franklin with the Associated Press, of the backs of two girls sitting on a bench looking onto the sleeping bodies of dozens of other children, covered in foil blankets. The girls are framed by a chain-link fence in the foreground of the photo. Although the photo had actually been taken in 2014, in the middle of the Obama era, it remained widely circulated as an indictment of Trumpian policies. Indeed, this photo represents not just the cruelty of cages but also the ahistoric nature of the public's understanding of child migrant detention.

Although the sights and sounds that prompted public outcry were often of the temporary facilities run by CBP, Trump's anti-immigrant policies brought the public's attention to ORR's permanent facilities as well. Although ORR remained adamant that its job was to shelter—not detain—youth, activists often felt otherwise, noting that the facilities were blinded on maps, that young people were not free to leave (nor were their parents free to visit), and there were increasing concerns about the hiring practices of shelters. Activists staged protests outside facilities, decrying the high-profile cases of sexual abuse and the haphazard hiring practices justified as emergency measures, along with the involuntary natures of young people's detainment (Gonzales 2019). In addition, some organizations came under fire for suspicious dealings, in addition to concerns about youth safety. A supposed nonprofit, Southwest Key, run by activist Juan Sanchez, received $1.7 billion in grants over the course of the decade and paid the CEO $1.5 million in 2017 alone. The organization ran twenty-four shelters, including an infamous converted Walmart with a 1,410-child capacity, which has been accused of warehousing children. Further, the *New York Times* revealed that the nonprofit possibly engaged in egregious self-dealings and profiteering (Barker, Kulish, and Ruiz 2018).

Unfortunately, the public's uproar over the inhumanity of the immigration system has decreased since Trump left office, even though the Biden administration has been relatively ineffective in overturning the policies impacting immigrant child detention. First, while the administration temporarily halted the Migrant Protection Protocol in June 2021, a battle over both the legality and the termination of the policy ensued over the following year. In addition, in response to the pandemic in 2020, the Trump administration invoked the Title 42 policy, which expelled migrants, including unaccompanied youth, under the guise of public health and extended the length of time for migrants waiting in Mexico for their court dates. When Biden took office in January 2021, he kept Title 42 in place. Although he loosened the policy to allow entry for unaccompanied children and some exceptional humanitarian cases, he continued to expel most children who arrived with families (Carranza, Villagran, and Migoya 2021).

With these changes to Title 42, 2021 saw a sharp increase of migrant children at the border, and very quickly the capacity of the border holding facilities was surpassed, leading to an increase in the number of children held beyond the three-day limit in severely crowded conditions (Montoya-Galvez and Verdugo 2021). In response, many of these unaccompanied children entering in 2021 were held in one of more than a dozen "emergency intake sites." One such makeshift shelter was Fort Bliss, a tent camp with a capacity for ten thousand young people, which opened in March 2021. Attorneys working with the children and youth detained at Fort Bliss raised the alarm at the level of despair experienced by the young people. In fact, CBS News reported that young people were under such distress at the site that they needed to be constantly monitored for self-harm, panic attacks, or escape attempts. One federal official explained: "They've gone from a small cage at Border Patrol to a larger cage at Fort Bliss.... It's a juvenile detention facility" (Montoya-Galvez 2021). Indeed, these emergency facilities do not have state licenses certifying that they can care for minors and have lower standards of care and case management. The contractor for the facility was identified as Rapid Deployment Inc., which had received $3.36 billion in contracts to maintain the facility through June 2023 (Ramirez 2022).

The numbers of migrant youth entering government custody remained at a historic high, with ORR receiving 128,904 referrals of migrant children in FY 2022. ORR worked to increase capacity in licensed facilities and was thus able to close many of the emergency intake sites in 2022 and early 2023. By September 2023, ORR reported that only three influx care facilities (Fort Bliss, Pecos ICF, and Greensboro Piedmont Academy) remained open but were placed in "warm status," meaning that they were operating in a limited capacity (ACF Press Office 2023).

Detention Today

What this history demonstrates is that the detention of child migrants today is not an anomaly but rather the status quo. A child migrant who enters the country today may be detained in a wide spectrum of facilities. The various facilities have different names; are run through different governmental, for-profit, and nonprofit entities; and express different explicit purposes. And, in many cases, a young person will experience multiple forms of detention in quick succession. The first space of detention is often the temporary border facilities, run by Customs and Border Protection, called "intake facilities," "emergency intake sites," and "stations." After CBP detention, young people who are alone will be transferred to ORR facilities, which are branded as "shelters" and include both permanent shelters that contract with nonprofit organizations across the country and temporary influx shelters. The temporary influx shelters are not licensed, and they include camps such as the "Tornillo Influx Facility," run by the nonprofit BCFS Health and Human Services, and "Homestead Temporary Shelter," which was run by a private subsidiary of Caliburn International. When there is limited space in shelters, young people may also be housed in local juvenile detention centers. Finally, when a young person turns eighteen while being held by the Office of Refugee Resettlement, they have historically been transferred to adult detention facilities, although this practice was ended in 2021, with no appropriate policy to replace it. Children in family units may be transferred to ICE custody and enter family detention facilities, which ICE brands as "residential centers." Over the past two decades, these centers have included those run by private-prison corporations in addition to facilities run by local county governments.

Our decision to label ORR shelters (both permanent and influx shelters) as detention and include these in the volume is perhaps the most controversial, although we are certainly not alone in this view, as activists and scholars alike have brandished heavy critiques against these facilities (Heidbrink 2014; Terrio 2015; Ruehs-Navarro 2022). Although these facilities are obligated to maintain higher standards of treatment or care, in this volume we still place them on the spectrum of detention due to the fact that the detainment in these shelters is involuntary, movement in the facilities is restricted, and release is subject to the government's, not the individual's, discretion.

It is also notable that just like ORR, CBP and ICE also explicitly state a paternalistic mission in their dealing with migrants, alongside more overt claims that criminalize migrants. So, while CBP's website focuses on the border patrol's work at preventing terrorism, drug smuggling, and illegal entry, it also includes language around human trafficking and the need to protect victims, including women and children (U.S. Customs and Border Protection n.d.-a). Similarly, ICE emphasizes its work in keeping migrants safe, noting that its "family staging centers" are "clean, well-organized, and efficiently run." It purports to address "the inherent challenges of providing medical care and language services and ensuring the safety of families in detention" (U.S. Immigration and Customs Enforcement n.d.). In fact, in an analysis of CoreCivic and GEO Group press releases, sociologists Miara L. Bailey-Hall and Emily P. Estrada (2022, 16, 15) found that the detention providers emphasized their playing a "vital role in times of 'crisis'" and produced a "paternalistic, infantilizing framing" that "uplift[ed] their image as kind guardians." So, while the standards of ORR facilities may be higher and more aligned with child-friendly policy, they are not unique in their claims to care for the needs of migrants.

Abolition or Harm Reduction?

For advocates of children's rights, there is little debate: detention is harmful for children. Many chapters in this volume will explicitly or implicitly explore these harms. The debate before us is not about the harm of detention but what our response to detention should be. In her oft-cited work, theorist and activist Audre Lorde (2007) declares: "The master's tools will never dismantle the master's house." Lorde's premise is that structures that exist to subordinate a group cannot also be used to protect that group. This abolitionist standpoint has driven many radical interventions into violent structures. And, in this volume, many contributors agree that the system of detention itself is so fundamentally violent, so fundamentally racist, and so fundamentally dehumanizing that work cannot be done within the system. Detention was built explicitly to deter migrants and thus can never be used to protect those same migrants. Instead, our focus should be on dismantling and abolishing immigration detention altogether.

Yet others, particularly many practitioners who work on the ground with youth in detention, will argue that while abolition might be a worthy goal, the need in the present moment is for targeted harm reduction. Philosopher and activist Ashley Bohrer (2022, 79) explains that the strength of a harm-reduction approach to social justice problems is its "actionable immediacy." Bohrer posits that harm reduction has significant benefits; it provides pathways for reforms that can have substantial, short-term effects: "the selective engagement with institutions of power can also lend an extraordinary concreteness to social justice demands" (79). Yet Bohrer explains that harm reduction also has many challenges: harm reduction approaches are "more easily co-opted by powerful institutions for their own ends. . . . Activists may face immense pressure to dampen their rhetoric or accept compromises" (80). The question asked of practitioners engaging in harm reduction is, "Does this course of action lead to better or worse effects on the status quote?" (79).

Abolition and harm reduction are not necessarily mutually exclusive. Indeed, activist and writer Ijeoma Oluo (2023) reminds us:

> Harm reduction is not the enemy of abolition and liberation—at least not on its own. Harm reduction is vital to our survival. It is regularly practiced by abolitionists every day. Therapy is often harm reduction. Mutual aid is harm reduction. Self-care and community care is harm reduction. Harm reduction reminds us that we are not to be sacrificed to the battle against white supremacist capitalist patriarchy, that we deserve to live now and not just in a revolutionary future. Harm reduction is also strategic. It creates the space and relative safety that we need to heal from wounds, to build and plan.
>
> But harm reduction that isn't self-aware can be very harmful itself. And harm reduction that pretends to be revolution can be our downfall.

Bohrer (2022) refers to this balance as a "both-and" approach, noting that although the middle ground may allow for the benefits of both worlds, it is also replete with its own dilemmas. Indeed, when responding to problems that are as violent and deeply entrenched as child migrant detention, perhaps the only certainty is the complexity of our actions and activism.

It is in this complexity that we center this volume. The chapters in this book provide a range of insights and responses into this system. Although some authors explicitly engage with ideas of harm reduction or abolition, most do so implicitly. Readers may note that some chapters indirectly highlight the importance of engaging in harm reduction, given the immediacy of the needs before us. The voices of practitioners, activists, and indeed youth themselves call attention to the harms of this very moment that need direct intervention. Yet, in other chapters, readers will note what is at stake when we focus solely on harm reduction: a historical, legal, and theoretical lens demonstrates that working within the system has inadvertently allowed for the maintenance of the same cruelty for decades. In sum, we believe that there is space and need for the entire spectrum of responses to detention.

Organization of the Book

This book is divided into three parts. The first part helps contextualize young migrants' experiences with detention by exploring the ways in which modern child migrant detention has been built, justified, and maintained. Collectively, we see detention as a form of state-sanctioned and institutionalized violence against young immigrants. Indeed, the immigration system as a whole is a "complex, dysfunctional system with extraordinary stakes and few protections specially tailored to the rights and needs of children" (Diaz and Vargas 2023, 1). The first chapter in this part works to provide a historical context and to chronicle the harms of detention. The authors, law scholars and practitioners from the Center for the Human Rights of Children, walk through the historical "othering" of children of color, which they argue has legitimized state-sanctioned violence against these children. The experience of migrant children today is the modern manifestation of this historical precedent. The authors then chronicle various ways in which violence is enacted in and through these facilities, a range of practices that include the separation of families, the mental anguish of incarceration, and the use of coercive medical practices.

In the following chapter, geographer Aireen Grace Andal uses an innovative methodological approach, taking a deep dive into the paperwork that guides ORR's daily practices. Paperwork might seem like a trivial matter, but it is the essential element that guides the decision-making around young migrants. Migrant children are trapped not only by the walls of the detention facility but also by the "iron cage" of bureaucracy. Furthermore, paperwork carries in it implicit ideas about migrant youth, creating knowledge that the bureaucrats themselves subconsciously absorb. In her analysis, Andal argues that detention is a type of "bureaucratic purgatory," and like the authors of the first chapter, she argues that the othering of migrant youth through this paperwork is one of the ways in which the practice of detention is justified.

The final chapter in this part is written by Marisa Chumil and Jennifer Nagda, practitioners with the Young Center for Immigrant Children's Rights. Here, the authors explore the lessons learned in an organization that has advocated for detained immigrant children and their families for nearly two decades. As practitioners with years of experience on the ground, they provide an invaluable lens by which to understand the traumas faced by detained children. They chronicle several areas in which the system of detention harms young people, and then follow with their recommendations for reducing harm.

In the second part of the volume, we place the focus squarely on the experiences and voices of young people themselves. The chapters in this part are written primarily by social scientists, but all use narratives, *testimonios*, and case studies of youth as they traverse the landscape of detention. The pieces are organized by the chronology of spaces that a young person enters, starting with detention that happens during migration itself, to detention by border agents with the CBP, detention in ORR facilities, and finally detention in adult facilities, when a minor ages out of ORR care. While the first part of the book focuses on violence, this part looks at survival. Readers will note that each chapter highlights forms of survival, whether through temporary relationships, building new forms of kinship, or subtle forms of everyday resistance.

Anthropologist Corinne Kentor opens this part of the book by expanding our understanding of detention. In the case studies she presents on two young men, she notes that their experiences of cages began before they reached the U.S.-Mexico border, as both young people were first kidnapped by criminal actors in Mexico; this experience thus parallels the experiences they have in the state-sanctioned cages of immigration detention. Yet Kentor notes throughout the narrative the importance of temporary relationships. In each space of detention, she finds that young people create bonds that help them survive; however, the bonds themselves are continually ruptured—a form of continued family separation.

It would be easy to understand the practice of detention as an all-consuming violence, which creates nearly insurmountable vulnerabilities for migrant youth. Yet, in the next chapter, social work scholar Jenn M. Lilly unveils the ways in which young people resist the oppression of the immigration system. Although the level of power detained youth maintain in detention is minute compared to institutionalized power, Lilly posits that there are small ways in which migrant youth exert control and resist exploitation. This chapter uses the testimonios of two migrant girls, specifically as they resist the violence of CBP detention. Lilly notes that resistance can come in the form of refusal and is often enacted in solidarity, once again emphasizing the importance of relationships to young people's survival.

Next, the focus turns to the space of ORR detention, where young people may remain for weeks, months, and even years. Sociologist Luis Edward Tenorio looks at two stories of LGBTQ-identified youth in ORR custody and explores the survival strategy of homemaking, which helps these young people cope with the liminality of detention itself and navigate the precarity of being a sexual or gender minority in the space of detention. As in the previous chapter, Tenorio finds that relationships are a primary tool for survival; indeed, youth's homemaking helps them contend with the limbo of detention, Yet Tenorio notes that among queer youth, these relationships are also met with further surveillance by shelter staff.

Finally, attorney Jajah Wu writes with former unaccompanied youth migrant Vida Opoku about her experience aging out of ORR custody and into ICE custody for adults. In this chapter, Opoku recounts her terrifying journey in the U.S.-Mexico borderlands, CBP detention, ORR custody, and then, when she was inaccurately determined to be eighteen years old, an adult jail. In Opoku's own words, we learn about the gaps, inconsistencies, and inadequacies of a system, particularly as youth migrants deal with the liminality of turning eighteen in detention. Once again, the authors note the importance of relationships; for Opoku, survival is achieved through daily interactions with kind strangers, whether they are fellow detained migrants or the attorneys and social workers who fight for migrants' freedom.

The final part of this volume turns from violence and survival to a focus on resistance, which is the work that is being done by a range of practitioners to alleviate suffering, care for the traumas, and work to dismantle detention altogether. We highlight a range of responses, which run the gamut from providing services and legal assistance to detained youth, to dealing with community pain after detention, to acting upon one's spiritual imperative to provide hospitality to the stranger.

Opening the part, psychologists and family scientists Sandra Espinoza, Iman Dadras, Jacqueline Florian, and Herlin Soto-Matute provide a deep dive into psychological practices used to respond to the traumas experienced by detained youth. Given the importance of relationships, they begin by exploring attachment theory and then offer a critique into how it is employed from a Western paradigm, particularly in its use in treating detained young people. They engage in a variety of theoretical critiques to argue that mental health professionals must understand that an individual's internal world is mediated by their political experience.

An important group of practitioners that work with immigrants comes from the faith-based community. Scholars have noted that while nationalism is often interwoven into many religious communities, there is simultaneously a strong tradition in an array of faith-based traditions to welcome the stranger (De La Torre 2014; Baker, Perry, and Whitehead 2020). Indeed, a quick survey of national organizations that assist in immigrant hospitality and refugee resettlement demonstrates that religious groups from an array of faiths have been essential in building everything from national and international organizations for migrants, to community-based programing, to interventions in times of crisis. Given this context, the next chapter focuses on a faith-based community that has developed an alternative to detention for young people. The chapter opens with commentary by Reverend Dr. Samuel Arroyo, who explores the Christian tradition of welcoming the stranger and simultaneously challenges religious doctrine that has been used to support nationalism. Then Father Corey Brost and Brother Michael Gosch, cofounders of Viator House of Hospitality, discuss the work being done to divert young migrant men from adult detention facilities or homeless shelters upon turning eighteen. To end the chapter, we hear from a cohort of women who run Bethany House of Hospitality, a sister organization to Viator House, that serves young women. Their contribution explores both the ways in which these alternative models can respond to the needs of migrant youth and the importance of approaching this work with flexibility.

We finish this part of the book with a chapter by artist and scholar Silvia Rodriguez Vega that explores a community arts program in which young people use art to grapple with xenophobia and state-sanctioned violence, including detention. Rodriguez Vega argues that the arts are a medium for community members to engage in collective grief, solidarity, and hope, and spaces such as the one she explores are essential in responding to the traumas experienced by individuals, families, and communities after detention.

The book concludes with a chapter by attorney and legal scholar Sarah J. Diaz, who explores the concept of abolition and envisions the potential of a decarceral future. We choose to end the volume on this note as we believe the best way forward is to imagine and fight for new possibilities for migrant youth in the United States.

Together, these chapters consider the violence of detention while centering on resilience and resistance. Collectively, the authors document, witness, resist, and survive the violence of detention. Their work and efforts forge spaces for healing and imagining new possibilities. It is our hope that this book helps provide a deeper context to current events, with the ultimate goal of fundamentally overturning this system of violence.

Notes

1. The exception here is that the official policy of separating children from their parents has ended; however, as many scholars have noted, children have been separated from family members at the border for decades and continue to be separated in more covert ways (Ruehs-Navarro 2022; Diaz and Vargas 2023).

2. Further discussion of these precursors can be found in chapter 1 of this volume.

3. There are several excellent books that provide a more complete history, including Lindskoog (2018), Loyd and Mountz (2018), and García Hérnandez (2019).

References

Abrego, Leisy 2014. *Sacrificing Families: Navigating Laws, Labor, and Love Across Borders.* Stanford, Calif.: Stanford University Press.

ACF Press Office. n.d. "ORR Influx Care Facilities for Unaccompanied Children Fact Sheet." Administration for Children & Families Office of Refugee Resettlement. Accessed October 31, 2023. https://www.acf.hhs.gov/sites/default/files/documents/orr/icf-uc-fact-sheet.pdf.

Bailey-Hall, Miara L., and Emily P. Estrada. 2022. "Private Immigration Detention Without the Immigrants: The Subtle Use of Controlling Images in the Contemporary Era." *American Behavior Scientists* 66 (12): 1645–68.

Baker, Joseph O., Samuel L. Perry, and Andrew L. Whitehead. 2020. "Keep America Christian (and White): Christian Nationalism, Fear of Ethnoracial Outsiders, and Intention to Vote for Donald Trump in the 2020 Presidential Election." *Sociology of Religion* 81 (3): 272–93.

Barker, Kim, Nicholas Kulish, and Rebecca R. Ruiz. 2018. "He's Built an Empire, with Detained Migrant Children as the Bricks." *New York Times*, December 2.

Bekiempis, Victoria. 2019. "Activists Call for End to Family Separations with Cage Installations." *The Guardian*, June 12.

Bohrer, Ashley J. 2022. "How Is It to Be Done? Dilemmas of Prefigurative and Harm-Reduction Approaches to Social Movement Work." In *Wicked Problems: The Ethics of Action for Peace, Rights, and Justice*, edited by Austin Choi-Fitzpatrick, Douglas Irvin-Erickson, and Ernesto Verdeja, 73–83. New York: Oxford University Press.

Carranza, Rafael, Lauren Villagran, and Clara Migoya. 2021. "Supreme Court Said Biden Could Not Stop 'Remain in Mexico' at the Border. Here's What That Means." *Arizona Republic*, August 27.

De La Torre, Miguel. 2014. *Doing Christian Ethics from the Margins.* 2nd ed. New York: Orbis Books.

Diaz, Sarah, and Oneida Molina Vargas. 2023. "Denormalizing Harm to Migrant Children in the U.S. Immigration System: A Comparative Perspective." *Children's Legal Rights Journal* 43 (2): 1–20.

Dickerson, Caitlin. 2022. "The Secret History of the U.S. Government's Family-Separation Policy." *The Atlantic*, August 7.

Dreby, Joanna. 2010. *Divided by Borders: Mexican Migrants and Their Children*. Berkeley: University of California Press.

García Hernández, César Cuauhtémoc. 2019. *Migrating to Prison: America's Obsession with Locking Up Immigrants*. New York: New Press.

Gonzales, Richard. 2019. "Sexual Assault of Detained Migrant Children Reported in the Thousands Since 2015." National Public Radio, February 26. https://www.npr.org/2019/02/26/698397631/sexual-assault-of-detained-migrant-children-reported-in-the-thousands-since-2015.

Gonzalez, Juan. 2011. *Harvest of Empire: A History of Latinos in America*. New York: Penguin Group.

Goodman, Amy. 2007. "'I Want to Be Free': A 9-Year-Old Canadian Citizen Pleads from Texas Immigration Jail." *Democracy Now!*, February 23. https://www.democracynow.org/2007/2/23/i_want_to_be_free_9.

Heidbrink, Lauren. 2014. *Migrant Youth, Transnational Families, and the State: Care and Contested Interests*. Philadelphia: University of Pennsylvania Press.

Heidbrink, Lauren. 2020. *Migranthood: Youth in a New Era of Deportation*. Stanford, Calif.: Stanford University Press.

Hernández Hernández, Oscar Misael. 2012. "Migración, masculinidad y menores repatriados por la frontera Matamoros-Brownsville." *Trayectorias* 33/34:76–94.

Kids in Need of Defense. n.d. "'Everyday Life Is Fear': Violence Against Children and Youth in Honduras." Accessed June 20, 2022. https://www.supportkind.org.

King, Jean. 2021. "Terminology." Office of the Director of the Department of Justice, July 23. https://www.justice.gov/eoir/book/file/1415216/download.

Lavandera, Ed, Jason Morris, and Darran Simon. 2018. "She Says Federal Officials Took Her Daughter While She Breastfed the Child in a Detention Center." CNN, June 12. https://www.cnn.com/2018/06/12/us/immigration-separated-children-southern-border/index.html.

Leónova, Olga G. 2019. "Crisis migratoria en Latinoamérica." *Iberoamérica* 3:104–24.

Lindskoog, Carl. 2018. *Detain and Punish: Haitian Refugees and the Rise of the World's Largest Immigration Detention System*. Gainesville: University of Florida Press.

Lorde, Audre. 2007. "The Master's Tools Will Never Dismantle the Master's House." In *Sister Outsider: Essays and Speeches*, 110–14. Berkeley, Calif.: Crossing Press.

Loyd, Jenna M., and Alison Mountz. 2018. *Boats, Borders, and Bases: Race, the Cold War, and the Rising of Immigration Detention in the United States*. Oakland: University of California Press.

Luibhéid, Eithne, and Karma R. Chávez, eds. 2020. *Queer and Trans Migrations: Dynamics of Illegalization, Detention, and Deportation*. Urbana: University of Illinois Press.

Lyda, Clark, and Jesse Lyda, dirs. 2009. *The Least of These: Family Detention in America*. Documentary film. Indiepix.

Mahr, Joe, Tony Briscoe, and Ese Olumhense. 2018. "Demonstrators Rally in the Loop Against Separation of Immigrant Families." *Chicago Tribune*, June 30.

Malkki, Liisa. 2010. "Children, Humanity, and the Infantilization of Peace." In *In the Name of Humanity*, edited by Ilana Feldman and Miriam Ticktin, 58–85. Durham, N.C.: Duke University Press.

Menjívar, Cecilia, and Néstor Rodríguez, eds. 2005. *When States Kill: Latin America, the U.S., and Technologies of Terror*. Chicago: University of Chicago Press.

Montoya-Galvez, Camilo. 2021. "Migrant Children Endure 'Despair and Isolation' Inside Tent City in the Texas Desert." CBS News, June 22. https://www.cbsnews.com/news/immigration-migrant-children-fort-bliss-tent-city-texas/.

Montoya-Galvez, Camilo, and Adam Verdugo. 2021. "Record 3,200 Migrant Children Stuck in Border Patrol Custody, with Nearly Half Held Past Legal Limit." CBS News, March 9. https://www.cbsnews.com/news/migrant-children-border-patrol-custody-past-legal-limit/.

Office of Refugee Resettlement. 2015. "Children Entering the United States Unaccompanied." January 30. https://www.ohchr.org/sites/default/files/Documents/Issues/Migration/CallEndingImmigrationDetentionChildren/CSOs/RAICES_Annex1.pdf.

Oluo, Ijeoma. 2023. "Harm Reduction or Abolition? Beyond the Book: Can We Have Both?" *Ijeoma Oluo: Behind the Book* (blog), March 23. https://ijeomaoluo.substack.com/p/harm-reduction-or-abolition.

Padilla-Rodríguez, Ivón. 2020. "Child Migrants in 20th-Century America." *Oxford Research Encyclopedia of American History*. https://oxfordre.com/americanhistory/display/10.1093/acrefore/9780199329175.001.0001/acrefore-9780199329175-e-855.

Ramirez, Cindy. 2022. "Migrant Children at Fort Bliss Shelter Faced Distress, Long Release Waits." *Government Executive*, October 11. https://www.govexec.com/oversight/2022/10/migrant-children-fort-bliss-shelter-faced-distress-long-release-waits/378246/.

Ruehs, Emily. 2016. "Adventures in *El Norte*: The Identities and Immigration of Unaccompanied Youth." *Men and Masculinities* 20 (3): 364–84.

Ruehs-Navarro, Emily. 2022. *Unaccompanied: The Plight of Immigrant Youth at the Border*. New York: New York University Press.

Schrag, Philip G. 2020. *Baby Jails: The Fight to End Incarceration for Refugee Children in America*. Oakland: University of California Press.

Sessions, Jeff. 2018. "Attorney General Sessions Delivers Remarks Discussing the Immigration Enforcement Actions of the Trump Administration." United States Department of Justice, May 7. https://www.justice.gov/opa/speech/attorney-general-sessions-delivers-remarks-discussing-immigration-enforcement-actions.

Talbot, Margaret. 2008. "The Lost Children." *New Yorker*, March 3. https://www.newyorker.com/magazine/2008/03/03/the-lost-children.

Terrio, Susan J. 2015. *Whose Child Am I? Unaccompanied, Undocumented Children in U.S. Immigration Custody*. Oakland: University of California Press.

Thompson, Ginger. 2018. "Listen to Children Who've Just Been Separated from Their Parents at the Border." ProPublica, June 18. https://www.propublica.org/article/children-separated-from-parents-border-patrol-cbp-trump-immigration-policy.

Tucker, Christine M., Pilar Torres-Pereda, Alexandra M. Minnis, and Sergio A. Bautista-Arredondo. 2012. "Migration Decision-Making Among Mexican Youth: Individual, Family, and Community Influences." *Hispanic Journal of Behavioral Sciences* 35 (1): 61–84.

United Nations Development Programme. 2013. "Citizen Security with a Human Face: Evidence and Proposals for Latin America." http://www.latinamerica.undp.org.

U.S. Customs and Border Protection. n.d.-a. "Human Trafficking." Accessed June 20, 2022. https://www.cbp.gov/border-security/human-trafficking.

U.S. Customs and Border Protection. n.d.-b. "Nationwide Encounters." Accessed June 20, 2022. https://www.cbp.gov/newsroom/stats/nationwide-encounters.

U.S. Customs and Border Protection. n.d.-c. "U.S. Border Patrol Southwest Border Apprehensions by Sector." Accessed June 20, 2022. https://www.cbp.gov/newsroom/stats/southwest-land-border-encounters/usbp-sw-border-apprehensions?language_content_entity=en.

U.S. Immigration and Customs Enforcement. n.d. "Detention Management." Accessed June 20, 2022. https://www.ice.gov/detain/detention-management.

World Food Programme. 2017. "Food Security and Emigration: Why People Flee and the Impact on Family Members Left Behind in El Salvador, Guatemala, and Honduras." September. https://docs.wfp.org/api/documents/WFP-0000019629/download/?_ga=2.211110359.35261770.1655480845-1468171411.1655480845.

Wyn, Johanna, and Rob White. 1997. *Rethinking Youth*. Thousand Oaks, Calif.: SAGE.

Zilberg, Elana. 2007. "Refugee Gang Youth: Zero Tolerance and the Security State in Contemporary US-Salvadoran Relations." In *Youth, Globalization, and the Law*, edited by S. Venkatesh and R. Kassimir, 61–89. Stanford, Calif.: Stanford University Press.

CAGES
Contextualizing the Violence of Child Migrant Detention

CHAPTER ONE

"Not 'Our' Children"

The Othering of Migrant Children and Youth and the Concomitant Use of State-Sanctioned Violence Through Immigration Law and Policy

SARAH J. DIAZ, KATHERINE
KAUFKA WALTS, AND LISA JACOBS

In the United States, the "othering" of migrant children and youth has culminated in the creation and perpetuation of massive governmental systems (laws, policies, and practices) that inflict systemic and widespread violence through the use of detention. The use of ubiquitous migrant child detention has resulted in the normalization of harmful practices inflicted on migrant youth that are tolerated as the natural consequence of the migrant state. Examining the historical and contemporary othering of Black and Brown children and youth in the United States can place the use of state-sanctioned violence against migrant children in context and begin to illuminate a path to dismantling the machinery of harm.

Othering and the Concomitant Use of State-Sanctioned Violence

At its most basic level, "othering" has been described as a process that serves to distinguish a group of human beings as different or "other" from ourselves in a fundamental way, which results in creating different or "other" standards of respect, treatment, and care (Canales 2000). The purpose of othering is to "reinforce notions of our own 'normality,' and to set up the difference of others as a point of deviance. The person or group being 'othered' experiences this as a process of marginalization, disempowerment, and social exclusion. This effectively creates a separation between 'us' and 'them'" (Grove and Zwi 2006, 1933).

The process of othering necessarily involves the creation of stories or narratives that emphasize real or perceived differences among groups of people and trigger anxiety and fear or loathing of "the other." Othering can be based on race, ethnicity, language, gender identity, LGBTQ status, religion, culture, immigration status, economic factors, or virtually any other aspect of human identity. The practice of othering fosters dehumanization and demonization of groups of people, gives rise to segregation and exclusion, and encourages and excuses mistreatment, subjugation, and oppression.[1]

At the systemic level, othering by governments and policymakers leads to the development and application of law or policy that harms human beings, including acts that rise to the level of state-sanctioned violence. State-sanctioned violence has been "deconstructed along two dimensions" requiring the components of (1) violence and (2) state-sanctioned acts (Delgado 2020, 15). To ascertain whether a person or group of people is experiencing state-sanctioned violence, the definition of violence is thus integral.

> The World Health Organization's definition of violence illustrates how it is viewed and manifested, with intended and unintended consequences (Krug et al. 2002, 5): "The intentional use of physical force or power, threatened or actual, against oneself, another person, or against a group or community, that either results in or has a high likelihood of resulting in injury, death, psychological harm, maldevelopment or deprivation." This definition is all encompassing. However, it places an emphasis on structural violence, which is commonly referred to as the most lethal form (Lee 2019). (Delgado 2020, 15)[2]

Structural violence has been defined as an ongoing form of violence in which "social structures or institutions harm people by preventing them from meeting their basic needs" (Galtung 1969). Structural violence, as a form of state-sanctioned violence, is insidious; it is embedded in the political and economic organization of our social world (Galtung 1969). For purposes of this chapter, we evaluate the immigration systems' state-sanctioned structural violence through the lens of "legal violence": "legal violence is . . . structural in that it is exerted without identifiable perpetrators, . . . [and] is so thoroughly imposed by the social order that it becomes normalized as part of the cognitive repertoire of those exposed" (Menjívar and Abrego 2012, 1413).[3] In this way, the normalized consequences of being a migrant (being detained, being separated from one's family, etc.) give rise to the notion that this is an appropriate social order—the consequences are unbiased in their application and befall only those who fail to follow the law.

> The concept of legal violence incorporates the various, mutually reinforcing forms of violence that the law makes possible and amplifies. This lens allows us to capture the aggravation of otherwise "normal" or "regular" effects of the law, such as the immigrants' predicament that results from indefinite family separations as a result of increased deportations; the intensification in the exploitation of immigrant workers and new violations of their rights; and the exclusion and further barring of immigrants from education and other forms of socioeconomic resources necessary for mobility and incorporation. All of these instances constitute forms of structural and symbolic violence that are codified in the law and produce immediate social *suffering* but also potentially long-term harm with direct repercussions for key aspects of immigrant incorporation. (Menjívar and Abrego 2012, 1384–85)

Over the course of U.S. history, it has been demonstrated time and again that othering has led to state-sanctioned violence, in the form of structural and legal violence, against Black, Brown, and Native children and youth. The contemporary othering of migrant children and youth and the concomitant use of state violence that permeates the U.S. immigration system must be situated in the long U.S. history of violence against "othered" children and recognized for the harm it causes.

The Chronic History of Othering and Dehumanization as a Facilitator of State-Sanctioned Violence Against Black, Brown, and Native Children and Youth in the United States

The historical and contemporary othering of children and youth in the United States has created a system of subjugation that has been and continues to be achieved via cultural and normative practices as well as laws and policies authorizing state-sanctioned violence. Some tactics have changed, yet others remain constant throughout history and the present-day United States. The purpose of this subjugation was not just establishing boundaries around citizenship and "belonging"; it also served to further blatant dispossession of land, resources, and rights, including human rights.

The attributes of these othering practices are not only steeped in racial and cultural subjugation but also undermine the concept of childhood itself. The notion of childhood or youth as developmentally distinct and vulnerable from adults, and thus requiring distinct legal protections, is still an evolving and relatively new historical concept.[4] What is clear, however, is that "other" children—migrant, Black, Brown, Native—have been consistently subjected to state violence at any given time in U.S. history.

Othered Black, Brown, and Native children and youth were subjected to servitude by the U.S. government. Dependency and subordination were common features of life for many children and youth traveling alone to the early American colonies. Colonial Calvinists, applying the doctrine of original sin, treated children as inherently sinful and unable to control their impulses as adults (Bernstein 2011). Poor children and youth from Europe, along with some Africans, were primarily recruited as servants under a system of indentured servitude to support the demands for cheap labor. By the eighteenth century, however, servitude and slavery were inextricably racialized by American laws and policies to apply nearly exclusively to Black Africans and people of African descent, Native Americans, and certain classes of immigrants. African slaves, as well as their children, were subjected to a lifetime of servitude.

Othered Black, Brown, and Native children and youth were dehumanized, stripped of their innocence, and subjected to abduction and forced assimilation by the U.S. government. Beginning in the mid-nineteenth century, childhood became synonymous with innocence. As the idea of childhood innocence took hold, it became racialized. Popular culture constructed white children as innocent and vulnerable while othering Black, Brown, Native, and migrant children from these qualities.[5] The dehumanized pickaninny figure was frequently contrasted with an angelic white child (Bernstein 2011). While white children and youth began enjoying protections in newly formed courts of juvenile justice, Native children were coerced, abducted, and removed from their homes to attend government-run schools with a goal of assimilating them to the dominant white Christian culture (Noriega 1992).

Native children were brutalized for their "own good." The official U.S. policy, "Save the man; kill the Indian," was blatantly dehumanizing (Adams 1995). In 1879, army officer Richard Pratt proposed a system where

Native children would be taken far from their homes at an early age and not returned to their reservation homes until they were young adults. By 1909, there were more than 25 off-reservation boarding schools, 157 on-reservation boarding schools, and 307 day schools in operation. The long history of taking Black, Brown, and Native children offers a glimpse into U.S. systems that sanctioned and systemized forced family separation of the racialized "other" typically legitimated under the guise of "helping" these same children (Briggs 2020).

Othered children, youth, and families have been explicitly excluded from civic participation by the U.S. government. In 1860, the California state legislature passed a law prohibiting Chinese children from attending public school with white children. The state superintendent, Andrew J. Moulder, argued that such a step was required to protect innocent white children and youth from the "moral and physical ruin" that could result from "contamination and pollution by a race reeking with the vices of the Orient" (quoted in Rouse 2019, 275).[6] Common parlance at the time also described the Chinese culture as "primitive" and "backward" (Zhongyun 1987). This nativist language and othering characterizations were not only part of the cultural norm but also drove U.S. policies. Twenty years later, the Chinese Exclusion Act was passed; it prohibited the entry of Chinese laborers to the United States and restricted permanency for those Chinese laborers and their families who had already entered.

Othered Black, Brown, and Native children and youth's bodies were subjected to eugenics and forced sterilization by the U.S. government. At the turn of the century, the United States was experiencing large-scale immigration from Southern and Eastern Europe, and the North was experiencing internal migration of Black Americans from the (Jim Crow) South. Othering practices evolved from adverse racial and cultural observations to purported scientific support for divisive human categories. The principle of "biological determinism" and the study of eugenics drove policies and laws that defined specific national and ethnic groups as inherently superior or inferior to others. Othering due to race was thus justified by "science." The result yielded unthinkable acts of state violence, including forced sterilization of individuals, many of whom were children and adolescents.[7]

Othered migrant Mexican children and their families were subjected to disproportional state violence. The increased presence of Mexican migrants in the United States during the early part of the twentieth century drew out the same xenophobia and nativistic othering that had been directed toward Black, Brown, and Native Americans. In 1924, the U.S. Border Patrol was created specifically to control entry of Mexican nationals (many who have been crossing the southern border for generations): "opponents to Mexican migration argued that 'the Mexican's Indian blood would pollute the nation's genetic purity, and his biologically determined degenerate character traits would sap the country's moral fiber and corrupt its institutions" (Young 2017, 224, quoting Reisler 1976, 38). The situation in California, one of the states with the most robust eugenics program at the time, shows that Latina and Black women and girls were disproportionately sterilized under eugenics laws and policies versus other populations (Kaelber 2012). Institutional authorities described Mexicans and their descendants as "immigrants of an undesirable type" and speculated that they were at a "lower racial level than is found among American Whites" (State Joint Commission 1918, 10).

Migrant children and youth continue to be "othered" in contemporary immigration politics. Racist sentiments and othering tactics continue to animate U.S. immigration systems and policies at the highest levels of governance. When describing the situation at the southern border, President Donald Trump disparaged Mexican migrants as "drug dealers, criminals, and rapists" (BBC News 2016).[8] He referred to the purported immigration problem as a "violent . . . invasion" (Scott 2019), as an "infestation" (Simon 2018) of people whom he (along with others in government) have described as subhuman: "These aren't people, these are animals" (Hirschfeld Davis 2018). The dehumanizing effects of this rhetoric have played out through violent immigration policies that have analogues in other American child-serving systems.

Othering of Black, Brown, and Native Children and Youth in the Context of Other Contemporary Child-Serving Systems

The legacy of othering Black, Brown, Native, and migrant children and youth has seeped into all systems designed to serve children, including child welfare, juvenile justice, and immigration. Black, Brown, Native, and migrant children and youth continue to experience state violence, often in the form of forced separation, in the context of child welfare. While the concept of the child welfare system was to center around general health, well-being, and safety of children, the implementation has been largely reactive versus proactive, including removing children from their (allegedly) abusive or neglectful parents and community, with the intention of protecting children from abuse and neglect. This includes not only removing the child or youth from a family member but also placing them with another family member, a nonfamilial home (stranger), a congregate care/residential facility, and even terminating parental rights. These reactive policies, while well intentioned, induce trauma for children and youth; have significant, lifelong negative consequences; and impact children's and adolescents' health and well-being. These measures are intended to be measures of last resort, yet they are, quite disparately, practiced against Black and Brown children and families.

Both historical and current data show that the United States' child welfare system is highly racialized, meaning that race determines levels of involvement with the child welfare system (Edwards et al. 2021). Black families are disproportionately overrepresented in the child welfare system: "While Black children and youth in American make up 14 percent of the United States' population, they make up 23 percent of children in foster care . . . The disparity becomes even more extreme in some urban areas, based on the intensity of structural racism. In New York, while Black children made up only 15 percent of the city's population in 2017, they comprised 57 percent of the foster care population" (Peprah 2021, 37). Compare this to the experience of abused or neglected white children, who are twice as likely as Black children to receive services in their own home. This avoids the emotional damage and physical risks associated with a child's placement in foster care (Peprah 2021).

Black, Brown, and Native children and youth experience disproportionate state violence in the context of the juvenile justice system. Within this system, children of color continue to be stripped of their innocence, criminalized, and subjected to disproportionate separation and incarceration. The criminalization of children of color manifests at the earliest stages of contact with the juvenile legal system and produces profound racial inequities at every stage of contact between these legal systems and the children and youth they purportedly serve (Hockenberry and Puzzanchera 2021). Once arrested, Black and Brown children are disproportionately removed from their families, securely detained, prosecuted in adult courts, and incarcerated (McCoy and Pearson 2019; Sentencing Project 2021).

Researchers have identified the adultification of children and youth of color as one driver of these profound disparities. The keystone of U.S. juvenile justice systems is the premise that children and adolescents are different from adults. Social science research and neuroscience demonstrate conclusively that children and adolescents are not adults in miniature. Indeed, the U.S. Supreme Court has ruled repeatedly and explicitly that young people are fundamentally different from adults, are "categorically less culpable" for their behaviors than adults, and must not be subjected to the harsh punishments (capital punishment and life without the possibility of parole) imposed on adult offenders.

Research demonstrates, however, that Black children and youth are othered, deprived of the presumption of innocence, and not seen as deserving of protection and care as their white peers.[9] At age ten, Black boys are more likely to be perceived as older than their white peers, more likely to be seen as guilty of a crime, and more likely to be deemed deserving of punishment. The "adultification" of Black boys is, in turn, associated with lower rates of supportive care and services and higher rates of arrest and referral to justice systems (Goff et al. 2014).

Black girls are similarly othered. Compared to their white peers, Black girls were perceived to be "more independent" and to need less protection, support, and comfort in one study. The report authors posit direct ties between the othering of Black girls and the stark racial disparities in punitive education system responses and juvenile justice system referrals (Epstein, Blake, and Gonzalez 2017).

While most states have significantly downsized their juvenile legal systems over the past two decades and now arrest, detain, and incarcerate far fewer youth, the impact of the juvenile legal system is still disproportionately born by othered children and youth. As with children and youth of color in contact with criminal and child welfare legal systems, migrant children have long been excluded from the protections of childhood. Today, othering is clearly evident in the narratives advanced by American politicians and the media, giving rise to egregious acts of state-sanctioned violence and endemic structural and legal violence that irreparably harm migrant children and youth.

Othering and the Contemporary Experience of State-Sanctioned Violence Against Migrant Children and Youth

The othering of migrant children and youth over the course of U.S. history—intensifying under recent discourse—has led to the creation and perpetuation of entire governmental systems (laws, policies, and practices) that engage in systemic and widespread violence against migrant children. This othering has given a sense of permission that leads to the toleration of violence: "casting of people of color as 'not human,' 'breeders,' 'takers,' 'killers,' 'other' or 'less than,' or 'illegal,' to list several labels, makes acts of government-sponsored violence, and even their deaths, more easily carried out against them, almost as a natural occurrence of daily life" (Delgado 2020, 5). The othering of migrant children and youth has been so effective that the state violence perpetrated against them has simply come to be understood as normalized practice.

Identifying the U.S. government's treatment of migrant children and youth as "state-sponsored violence" offers an opportunity to understand violence that is generated or supported by the state. This, in turn, allows us to connect laws, policies, norms, and actors, whether willing or unsuspecting (Delgado 2020, 5). The goal of this label is to give rise to deeper reflection on what has become normalized structural practice—to engage a critical dialogue on the prevention of violence against children and youth as an ordinary standard of practice, to understand immigration policies for the acts of violence that they are (Delgado 2020, 13).

As legal practitioners, having served migrant children and youth since the early 2000s, we have witnessed state violence that can only be described as ubiquitous—practices harmful to children permeate the immigration system from apprehension to adjudication. To capture the violence succinctly, the acts are categorized along three types: (1) systemic detention of all migrant children and youth and the violence that flows from these policies, (2) family separation in all forms and the violence that flows from these policies, and (3) legal violence associated with the failure to create a child-centered system that addresses the unique needs of migrant children and youth, opting to instead treat them as adults in miniature. Researchers and practitioners capture much of these data from years of practice within the child detention system, through our direct service working with migrant children, through our research on children in immigration custody, or through known litigation efforts by our colleagues.

Systemic Detention of All Migrant Children and Youth as a Form of State-Sanctioned Violence

Detention is defined as "the state of being kept in a place, especially a prison, and prevented from leaving" (Oxford Learners Dictionary n.d.). Scientific research overwhelmingly shows that detention, regardless of setting (shelter or jail) or for any length of time, is harmful to children and youth.

U.S. Detention of All "Unaccompanied" Migrant | Children and Youth in the United States

The Trafficking Victims Protection Reauthorization Act of 2008 (TVPRA) sets out processing procedures for "unaccompanied children" who are apprehended by border authorities. Customs and Border Protection (CBP), the apprehending authority, is required to determine if a child meets the legal definition of an "unaccompanied alien child."[10] Once this determination is made, the child or youth will be detained by the U.S. government with the goal of family reunification. While case management goals strive for prompt reunification, by the estimates of the Office of Refugee Resettlement (ORR), the "average length of time an unaccompanied child remained in ORR care in FY2020 was 102 days" (Office of Refugee Resettlement n.d.).

The standardized use of detention for all unaccompanied children encountering the immigration system is a form of legal violence against migrant children and youth: "Legal violence . . . is embedded in the body of law that, while it purports to have the positive objective of protecting rights or controlling behavior for the general good, simultaneously gives rise to practices that harm a particular social group. In these cases, the law enables various forms of violence against the targeted group" (Menjívar and Abrego 2012, 1387). While the purported purpose of pro forma detention is to protect migrant children and youth, the reality is that it is deeply harmful (Young Center for Immigrant Children's Rights 2020b; UNICEF 2021). Interdisciplinary research has repeatedly demonstrated that all children and youth, regardless of the form of detention, are harmed by being detained.

Even where children and youth are detained for only brief amounts of time, experts found that detention has negative implications for long-term mental health outcomes (Burrell 2013; Linton et al. 2017). Detention may cause post-traumatic stress disorder, substance abuse, and comorbidity in children and adolescents (Dmitrieva et al. 2012). This suggests that the psychological impact of detention lasts long after the child or youth has been released.

Detention is particularly harmful to young children who are more susceptible to environmental stressors (Galvan 2020). For children between the ages of four and eight, environmental stressors associated with detention lead to emotional stress, negative behavioral responses, and hyperactivity (MacLean et al. 2019). Migrant children and youth with preexisting trauma are also at significant risk from the deleterious effects of detention. In one study of migrant children and youth held in detention, all individuals who were examined showed symptoms of at least one psychiatric disorder; depression, anxiety, and PTSD were among the most prevalent (Werthern et al. 2018). Of those studied, 65 to 100 percent of children and youth reported having trouble sleeping and 100 percent of detained children and youth reported suffering from eating-related problems. Fifty percent of detained migrant children and youth reported having suicidal ideations and 25 to 80 percent reported inflicting self-harm.

The pro forma detention of migrant children and youth is not necessary; it is a choice. Because of the widely understood harms associated with detention, international guidance forbids the use of detention except as a measure of last resort.[11] The United Nations Children's Fund (UNICEF) (2019, 5) calls on states to take special measures to prevent the detention of unaccompanied children and youth and instead to refer them to "national child protection authorities" with "provision of a guardian." Advocates have called for the development of a mechanism in which child protection experts (outside of the federal immigration agencies) evaluate children and youth for safety or trafficking concerns, to expedite reunification in an appropriate placement (Young Center for Immigrant Children's Rights 2020b).

Nonetheless, the U.S. government chooses to use detention for all unaccompanied children who arrive at our borders without a parent or legal guardian. This includes children and youth arriving with adult family members or other nonlegal guardian caregivers, from whom they are separated, in order to be detained in facilities licensed for minors. The harm of this practice is compounded by the family separation that is discussed later in this chapter. Moreover, various additional state violence can befall children and youth as a consequence of detention, as detailed in the next section.

Detention of All Migrant Children and Youth in Customs and Border Patrol Processing Centers

Under the TVPRA, "unaccompanied children" can be held in CBP custody—custodial placements designed for adult migrants—for up to seventy-two hours. Under the Donald Trump administration, this timeline was routinely broken. The worst of these breaches occurred in a CBP detention facility in Clint, Texas. Starting in June 2019, reports emerged that children and youth were being detained in Clint, Texas, for weeks on end. Those same children, ranging in age from infants to teenagers, were detained with adults, lacked access to basic hygiene, reported being hungry, reported being afraid of the guards, were observed to be traumatized—"they consistently cried and some wept during our interviews"—and were observed to be sick (Mukherjee 2019, 8). At this same facility, guards "required children to take care of babies, toddlers, and other young children unrelated to them" (Mukherjee 2019, 9). At another CBP processing facility, an outside pediatrician acting as a monitor "identified five babies . . . who needed immediate hospitalization and who were admitted to the neonatal intensive care unit of a local hospital" (9). Even under the current administration, the seventy-two-hour timeline for CBP detention is routinely violated (Ordoñez and Ferrington 2021).

The detention conditions in CBP are so anathema to child and adolescent development and well-being that it is no surprise that children have died in or due to their detention in government custody. From 2018 to 2019, the following children died in immigration detention or immediately after their release:

> Jakeline Caal Maquin, 7, from Guatemala [Maya Q'eqchi Nation]; Felipe Gomez Alonzo, 8, from Guatemala [Maya Chuj Nation]; Wilmer Josue Ramirez Vasquez, 2, from Guatemala [Maya Ch'orti' Nation]; Carlos Gregorio Hernandez Vasquez, 16, from Guatemala [Maya Achi Nation]; Darlyn Critabel Cordova-Valle, 10, from El Salvador; Juan de Leon Gutierrez, 16, from Guatemala [Maya Ch'orti' Nation]; and Mariee Juarez, 1, from Guatemala. (Briggs 2020)

Migrant children face othering across intersections that exacerbate the harmful experience of detention, especially for Indigenous children. The intersection of Indigeneity and migration "means grappling with not only the politics and policies of genocide and erasure in sending countries, but also the hybridization of these with US racial hierarchies that are premised on Native dispossession" (Blackwell, Lopez, and Urrieta 2017). Of the seven children who died in custody between 2018 and 2019, five were Maya Indigenous. The detention of migrant children and youth in CBP custody, in conditions known to be deadly to children, is a form of state violence, an operation known to be harmful, and yet the chosen practice to enforce immigration law and policy, nonetheless.

Prolonged and Indefinite Secure Detention of Migrant Children and Youth

Some migrant children and youth, once detained, face protracted stays in custody in secure facilities designed for domestic juveniles who have been adjudicated delinquent and committed to confinement. Only in the most serious juvenile cases will a judge in the domestic setting order that minor to be confined (Kraut n.d.). As a result, these facilities are equipped for and used to house the most serious juvenile offenders in the United States. Migrant children and youth can be "stepped up" to secure custody—jail for all intents and purposes—for reasons ranging from "suspected gang affiliation" to "flight risk" to "behavioral issues."[12] No unaccompanied child in ORR care is serving time for a domestic juvenile offense.[13] Nonetheless, they have been placed in a secure detention setting. The average length of detention for a child or youth in a secure setting is unclear, but there are reports of protracted detention lasting for months and even years in secure settings.[14] By the time an unaccompanied child has reached the secure setting, they have generally already spent significant time in the ORR detention system.

In secure custody, migrant children and youth experience some of the most egregious forms of state-sanctioned violence—living through conditions such as indefinite detention, solitary confinement, coerced behavior modification, acts of law enforcement-related physical violence. Consider the most recent secure detention facility for ORR's unaccompanied children, the Shenandoah Valley Juvenile Center:

> [In 2018] Virginia's governor ordered state officials . . . to investigate abuse claims by children at an immigration detention facility who said they were beaten while handcuffed and locked up for long periods in solitary confinement, left nude and shivering in concrete cells. . . . They were included in a federal civil rights lawsuit with a half-dozen sworn statements from Latino youths held for months or years at the Shenandoah Valley Juvenile Center. The AP report also cited an adult who saw bruises and broken bones the children said were caused by guards. . . . Children as young as 14 said the guards there stripped them of their clothes and strapped them to chairs with bags placed over their heads. (Biesecker, Pearson, and Burke 2018)

Children and youth are placed in these settings absent due process of law, sometimes for admitting to past delinquent behavior in a confidential therapeutic setting (Dreier 2020). Migrant children and youth subject to state violence in secure settings often opt for the most expeditious exit to the situation: deportation to unsafe, sometimes deadly, conditions in their country of origin.

When secure facilities are brought to the fore for their abuses of migrant children, they are shut down, only to pop up in another remote location. The abuses at Shenandoah Valley mirror the treatment of unaccompanied children detained in secure settings since the inception of the Health and Human Services (HHS) detention system—such as those experienced at the Southwest Indiana Regional Youth Village (located in and colloquially referred to as "Vincennes"). Vincennes was the original secure contractor for the HHS system, detaining migrant children in that facility from 2005 to 2010. At Vincennes, children were subjected to systemic abuse, which eventually led to the termination of the HHS contract. In 2007, the facility called the local Knox County SWAT team to respond to a peaceful protest by migrant youth requesting the same treatment as their U.S. citizen counterparts—youth who were confined for committing very serious offenses.

> The facility issued a "code blue" and called the Sheriff's Office Emergency Response. The police arrived in full riot gear including nightsticks, shields, helmets and handcuffs and accompanied by at least one dog. Children were hit with nightsticks and their hands and feet

were bound. They were dragged to their cells, where they remained physically bound for hours, and were then left in isolation for days. (Women's Refugee Commission and Orrick Herrington & Sutcliffe LLP 2009)

The unaccompanied children involved in this incident reported being attacked by a police dog, being injured and denied medical treatment, and being injured and thrown into solitary confinement. ORR contract with Vincennes was ultimately shut down due to allegations of abuse. Shenandoah Valley Juvenile Center's ORR contract has now also been revoked amid litigation over the abuses discussed here.

Historically, secure facilities for migrant children have been located in rural areas with no access to attorneys or supervision. The remote locations are problematic for multiple reasons, the most important of which relates to othering. Due to the remote location of these settings, racist violence permeates the setting. One lawsuit alleges "multiple . . . violent incidents between Latino children and staff at the Shenandoah center. . . . It describes the guards as mostly white, non-Spanish speakers . . . [and] staff members routinely taunt the Latino youths with racially charged epithets, including 'wetback,' 'onion head' and 'pendejo,' which roughly translates to dumbass in Spanish" (Biesecker, Pearson, and Burke 2018). In the absence of a secure facility at the time of this writing, ORR contracts with "out-of-network" placements. These placements are not only out-of-network but out of the public eye, unable to be observed by lawyers or advocates. These may be the most dangerous placements yet for children.

Forced Psychotropic Behavior Modification and Coercive Medical Practices on Migrant Children and Youth

Apprehension, separation, and prolonged or indefinite detention all contribute to the psychological toll taken on migrant children and youth in custody. Children and youth who present in distress, caused perhaps by separation from family, or who present with perceived mental health or behavioral issues are then saddled with additional levels of state violence, ranging from coerced psychotropic behavior modification to additional time in detention to treat the perceived mental health or behavioral issue.

HHS shelters "lack sufficient counselors and too often turn to powerful psychotropic drugs when kids act out" (Chen and Ramirez 2018). While various shelters administer medication to unaccompanied children, there does not appear to be a "standard policy for determining who is responsible for making medical decisions on behalf of detained children" (Malina 2019). Facilities are reported to "use a variety of pressures" to coerce minors into taking medications (Malina 2019). One method of coercion involves telling the child that they will be subject to longer detention periods if they do not "consent" to the medication.

In 2018, advocates for migrant children filed a complaint alleging that the Shiloh Residential Treatment Center in Manvel, Texas, administered powerful psychotropic drugs without any explanation to children and youth and/or without informed consent (Malina 2019). Various examples show that drugs were administered through coercive methods or over the objection of the child. The drugs were administered in the face of reports that they caused suicidal ideation or lacked FDA approval for treatment in adolescents or children.

Reports of overmedication extend beyond the lawsuit. At least one other facility identified at least 70 percent of the residents as being prescribed antidepressants, anti-anxiety medications, and sleep aids, typically multiple at the same time (Malina 2019).

Family Separation as a Form of State-Sanctioned Violence Against Migrant Children and Youth

In addition to the violence associated with detention, migrant children and youth experience state violence in the form of family separation. The term *family separation* entered the social lexicon when the Trump administration began systematically separating all minors (including infants and toddlers) from their parents at the U.S.-Mexico border pursuant to the zero tolerance policy. For most migrants, however, the reality of family separation has been a form of state violence since the inception of the deportation system.

Parent-child separation, clinically referred to as "traumatic separation," is a form of childhood trauma and has lasting developmental effects (National Child Traumatic Stress Network 2016). The harmful effects of separating children from primary caregivers have been researched for decades.[15] Over the years, research has fortified the understanding that separation of a child from a caregiver is extremely harmful.

Separation from [primary caregivers] is linked with higher rates of PTSD and chronic mental health conditions like depression among children. The negative impact on the cognitive and emotional functioning of children can continue into adulthood, and contribute to lower academic achievement, attachment difficulties, and poor mental health. Extreme and repetitive stress is also correlated with increased risk of physical health conditions such as cancer, stroke, diabetes, and heart disease. (Physicians for Human Rights 2019)

Notwithstanding the research and known harms associated with traumatic separation, the United States has historically supported and continues to advance laws and policies that result in family separation, including the policies delineated in the following four sections.

The Historical Separation of Mixed-Status Families

Undocumented parents have routinely been removed and deported without their U.S.-born children, resulting in de facto family separation.[16] Approximately 5.1 million U.S. citizen children in the United States have at least one undocumented parent (Capps, Fix, and Zong 2016). Mixed-status families live under the constant threat of deportation. Studies have shown that children of undocumented parents exhibit startling adverse health outcomes attributed to the stress of potential separation, including negative education outcomes, increased risk of economic instability, and increased risk of ending up in the child welfare system (America Immigration Council 2021).

Family Separation Under Zero Tolerance

In April 2018, the Trump administration began systematically separating parents from their children (including nursing infants, toddlers, children, and adolescents) at the southwest border. The policy, known as "zero tolerance," employed a prosecutorial measure—the stated purpose at the time was to enforce criminal laws (Office of the Attorney General 2018). The actual purpose of zero tolerance became clear in the aftermath of the operation: "we have to take away children . . . no matter how young" (Shear, Benner, and Schmidt 2020). The result was that thousands of migrant children and youth were separated from their parents and scattered across the country into HHS detention facilities (Ainsley 2019). Today, thousands of these separated children have not been reunited with parents who were deported before they could reunify with their children. The medical community decried the policy as a form of child abuse and the torture of migrant children by the U.S. government (Peeler 2020).

Family Separation Under the "Migrant Protection Protocols" and "Title 42"

In January 2019, the United States began to implement a policy known as the "Migrant Protection Protocols" (MPP)—a program that forced asylum seekers to remain in Mexico for the duration of their immigration process.[17] Tens of thousands of children and families were forced to wait in "MPP camps" composed of crude makeshift tents and plagued by crime, abuse, and poverty. As a result, children and youth were subjected to unthinkable violence, including reported cases of murder, rape, torture, kidnapping, and assault (Young Center for Immigrant Children's Rights 2019; Kids in Need of Defense 2020).

In March 2020, under the guise of preventing the spread of the COVID-19 virus, the U.S. government began "expelling" all undocumented noncitizens appearing at the border (Centers for Disease Control and Prevention 2020). This policy, known as Title 42, has effectively denied access to the asylum process—a protected human right under domestic and international law.[18] Migrant children and youth were forced back to their countries of origin or simply forced back across the Mexico border into situations of extreme danger (including exposure to trafficking) and without a caregiver. The Joe Biden administration declined to apply Title 42 directly to unaccompanied children upon taking office. However, the policy is still applied to migrant families.

Pursuant to the intolerable living conditions upon expulsion under Title 42 or placement in an MPP camp, parents have been forced to send their children to seek asylum alone in the relative safety of the United States—again demonstrating the government's use of laws and policies to forcibly separate families (Young Center for Immigrant Children's Rights 2020a). While Title 42 has been lifted, the legacy of family separation remains.

Normalized Ongoing Family Separation from Nonlegal Primary Caregivers

Migrant children and youth who arrive at the border with nonlegal primary caregivers are routinely separated by border authorities. This applies even to children who are encountered in the custody of adult family members or other trusted caregivers if that family member or caregiver is not the legal guardian (e.g., a child arrives with the grandparent who raised them but the grandparent does not have legal guardianship documents or the child arrives with an adult sibling in whose care they desire to remain). The United States has interpreted the TVPRA to require physical separation and transfer of these children to detention facilities. These children and adolescents, like all children forced into the immigration detention system via family separation, suffer the compounded effects of state violence from separation and the subsequent detention.

Legal Violence and the Failure to Create a Child-Centered System

The outcomes of state violence detailed in this chapter can all be traced to the legal violence associated with the failure to create a child-centered system that treats migrant children as children first.

> Legal violence captures the suffering that results from and is made possible through the implementation of the body of laws that delimit and shape individuals' lives on a routine basis. Under certain circumstances, policy makers and political leaders enact laws that are violent in their effects and broader consequences.... [Violence] is embedded in legal practices, sanctioned, actively implemented through formal procedures, and legitimated—and consequently seen as "normal" and natural because it "is the law." (Menjívar and Abrego 2012, 1387)

Under the current immigration system, children are treated merely as adults in miniature—navigating an unforgiving system designed with no regard for the vulnerability associated with childhood. There is no other child-serving system in the United States that fails to contemplate, for example, the best interests of the child where the child is the subject of the litigation. This practice has been normalized by immigration adjudicators and practitioners alike who view the absence of a child-centered legal framework or the absence of a best-interests standard as "normal" because "it is the law."

The immigration system—even as it exists for adults—is rife with allegations of due process violations and other pitfalls resulting in unjust deportations to often dangerous, if not lethal, conditions. Report after report details the inequity in immigration court proceedings from lack of access to counsel (Eagly and Shafer 2016) to the weaponization of court processes by the executive branch (Innovation Lab and the Southern Poverty Law Center 2019). Unaccompanied children, seeking asylum or other remedies alone, are subject to this same system without regard for the age, developmental ability, safety, best interests, etcetera. Simply put, subjecting children and youth to the adult immigration system grievously harms them by keeping them from meeting even their most basic needs: safety, health and well-being, family integrity, an opportunity to develop.

The lack of a system designed to address childhood and adolescence leads to legal violence in many forms: the failure to create a just process related to child placement (Nagda and Woltjen 2015), the failure to timely release children from custody (Prandini and Kamhi 2017), the failure to appoint legal counsel to all children in an adversarial setting, and the failure to appoint a guardian ad litem to all children in order to represent the best interests of the child.[19]

The U.S. government could ameliorate some of the harsh effects of the immigration system by simply incorporating a best-interests standard "in all decisions affecting the child."[20] However, the government chooses not to employ even this normative approach to working with migrant children and youth. The result is that migrant children and youth in the United States experience unencumbered legal violence and the unavoidable acts of state-sanctioned violence via detention and family separation that flow from the system. The labeling of these children and youth as "other" or "not our children" renders the violent experience a normal or natural consequence of the migrant state rather than an avoidable act of state violence perpetrated against a child.

Dismantling State-Sanctioned Violence and Reducing Harm to Migrant Children and Youth

As the history of othering demonstrates, the distinctions made between groups of people need not be significant—or even accurate—to serve as the basis for oppression and subjugation. In other words, othering is not inevitable; it is not fixed. Othering is a social construct, and it can be deconstructed. Doing so requires all of us (social scientists, policymakers, lawyers, journalists, and the public) to recognize the ways in which our narratives, dialogue, media, and politics have othered migrant children and youth—recognizing, especially, the violence that results from doing so. We must confront those narratives and reshape them to recognize migrant children and their families for their humanity and to ensure the creation of humane policies to address child migration.

In exploring the impact of othering in our era of rapid social change and anxiety, john a. powell (2017), director of the Othering and Belonging Institute, says we have a choice: "Either we 'bridge,' reaching across to other groups and towards our inherent, shared humanity and connection, while recognising that we have differences; or we 'break,' pulling away from other groups and making it easier to tell and believe false stories of 'us vs them,' then supporting practices that dehumanise the 'them.'"

Recognizing the humanity of migrant children and youth—that all children are "our children," thus recognizing the migrant child's inherent vulnerability and promise—is essential in reducing the harms of our current immigration system and replacing it with a child-centered system that attends to their safety and creates pathways to their well-being.

Notes

1. See, for example, Shohat and Stam (2014) and the work of the Othering and Belonging Institute, https://belonging.berkeley.edu/.

2. See also Rutherford et al. (2007).

3. See also Kivilcim (2016) and Menjívar (2013).

4. The first international treaty focusing on child protection addressed the prohibition of child labor pursuant to the creation of the International Labor Organization. In 1924, the League of Nations passed a Declaration on the Rights of the Child, followed by a similar United Nations Declaration in 1959. In 1961, the Convention Concerning the Powers of Authorities and the Law Applicable in Respect of the Protection of Infants was passed. In 1989, the most universally adopted human rights document, the Convention on the Rights of the Child, was adopted by the UN General Assembly.

5. For example, Bernstein (2011) references the character of Eva, a blonde, blue-eyed white child, in Harriet Beecher's Stowe's *Uncle Tom's Cabin*.

6. In *Tape v. Hurley*, the California State Supreme Court ruled in favor of the Tape family, arguing that Mamie Tape, a Chinese national, had the right to attend the school since no law specifically prohibited the Chinese from going to school with whites. In response, the California legislature passed a new state segregation law and

the San Francisco Board of Education opened a segregated public school specifically for Chinese children in San Francisco's Chinatown in 1885.

7. With horror, these practices have been repeated in modern history. For example, *Madrigal v. Quilligan* was a civil rights class action lawsuit filed by ten Mexican American women against the Los Angeles County+USC Medical Center for involuntary or forced sterilization—not unlike practices under the Trump administration (Theobald 2020).

8. "When Mexico sends its people, they're not sending their best. . . . They're sending people that have lots of problems, and they're bringing those problems with us. They're bringing drugs. They're bringing crime. They're rapists. And some, I assume, are good people."

9. See generally the Illinois Juvenile Justice Commission (2021).

10. According to 6 U.S.C. § 279(g)(2), the term "unaccompanied alien child" means a child who—(A) has no lawful immigration status in the United States; (B) has not attained 18 years of age; and (C) with respect to whom—(i) there is no parent or legal guardian in the United States; or (ii) no parent or legal guardian in the United States is available to provide care and physical custody. Homeland Security Act, U.S. Code 6 (2002), § 279.

11. UN Commission on Human Rights, Convention on the Rights of the Child, March 7, 1990, E/CN.4/RES/1990/74, article 6, https://www.refworld.org/docid/3b00f03d30.html.

12. On gangs, see *Saravia v. Barr*, No. 18–60532 (5th Cir. 2020). ORR used unsubstantiated gang allegations to place children in severely restrictive conditions in distant detention facilities without notice to their parents or lawyers and did not afford the accused children a chance to challenge the charges against them. On behavior, see ACF policy manual 1.2.4. ORR guidelines call for placement in a secure setting when the child "poses a danger to self or others; or has been charged with or convicted of a criminal offense, or is chargeable with such an offense." This has been loosely constructed. In the authors' experience, there is no training or detailed guidance provided to facilities. Instead, it is observed that "chargeable with such an offense" has been interpreted to mean any time a child admits criminal conduct, and "danger to self or others" has been loosely interpreted to children whose behavior cannot be managed in a staff-secure setting whether they pose a flight risk or perceived danger to self or others.

13. In isolated cases, where children act out against guards, advocates have pushed for delinquency hearings to obtain predicate orders for special immigrant juvenile visas. However, no child is initially placed in an ORR secure setting pursuant to a juvenile justice hearing.

14. ORR does not publish this information, but the authors have worked with children subjected to significant periods of secure detention—tantamount to indefinite detention.

15. Decades of psychological research show that children separated from their parents can suffer severe psychological distress, resulting in anxiety, loss of appetite, sleep disturbances, withdrawal, aggressive behavior, and decline in educational

achievement. The longer the parent and child are separated, the greater the child's symptoms of anxiety and depression become (American Psychological Association 2020).

16. *Texas et al. v. United States et al.*, 14-cv-00254 (S.D. Tex. 2015).

17. See "Policy Guidance for Implementation of the Migrant Protection Protocols," U.S. Department of Homeland Security, January 25, 2019, https://www.dhs.gov/sites/default/files/publications/19_0129_OPA_migrant-protection-protocols-policy-guidance.pdf; see also *Innovation Law Lab v. Nielsen*, 19-cv-00807, Doc. 73 (N.D. Cal. 2019).

18. UN High Commissioner for Refugees (UNHCR), "The 1951 Convention Relating to the Status of Refugees and Its 1967 Protocol," September 2011, https://www.refworld.org/docid/4ec4a7f02.html.

19. While a best-interests standard is theoretically applied in placement decisions during the time that unaccompanied children are in federal custody, there is no policy or regulation defining the relevant factors for a best-interests consideration or requiring documentation of the placement decision. Of even greater concern, there is no policy designating how government officials are to make best-interests determinations generally.

20. See, generally, UN Committee on the Rights of the Child (2013) on the right of the child to have his or her best interests taken as a primary consideration.

References

Adams, David Wallace. 1995. *Education for Extinction: American Indians and the Boarding School Experience, 1875–1928*. Topeka: University Press of Kansas.

Ainsley, Julia. 2019. "Trump Admin Weighed Targeting Migrant Families, Speeding up Deportation of Children." NBC News, January 17. https://www.nbcnews.com/politics/immigration/trump-admin-weighed-targeting-migrant-families-speeding-deportation-children-n958811.

American Immigration Council. 2021. "U.S. Citizen Children Impacted by Immigration Enforcement." June. https://www.americanimmigrationcouncil.org/sites/default/files/research/us_citizen_children_impacted_by_immigration_enforcement_0.pdf.

American Psychological Association. 2020. "APA Urges ICE to Comply with Court Order to Release Immigrant Children from Family Detention Centers." July 23. https://www.apa.org/news/press/releases/2020/07/ice-immigrant-children.

BBC News. 2016. "'Drug Dealers, Criminals, Rapists': What Trump Thinks of Mexicans." August 31. https://www.bbc.com/news/av/world-us-canada-37230916.

Bernstein, Robin. 2011. *Racial Innocence: Performing American Childhood from Slavery to Civil Rights*. New York: New York University Press.

Biesecker, Michael, Jake Pearson, and Garance Burke. 2018. "Governor Orders Probe of Abuse Claims by Immigrant Children." AP News, June 21. https://apnews.com/article/north-america-lawsuits-us-news-ap-top-news-immigration-afc80e51b562462c89907b49ae624e79.

Blackwell, Maylei, Floridalma Boj Lopez, and Luis Urrieta Jr. 2017. "Introduction." In "Critical Latinx Indigeneities," special issue, *Latino Studies* 15:126–37.

Briggs, Laura. 2020. *Taking Children: A History of American Terror*. Oakland: University of California Press.

Burrell, Sue. 2013. "Trauma and the Environment of Care in Juvenile Institutions." National Child Traumatic Stress Network, September. https://njjn.org/uploads/digital-library/NCTSN_trauma-and-environment-of-juvenile-care-institutions_Sue-Burrell_September-2013.pdf.

Canales Mary K. 2000. "Othering: Toward an Understanding of Difference." *ANS: Advances in Nursing Science* 22 (4): 16–31.

Capps, Randy, Michael Fix, and Jie Zong. 2016. "A Profile of U.S Children with Unauthorized Immigrant Parents." Migration Policy Institute, January. https://www.migrationpolicy.org/sites/default/files/publications/ChildrenofUnauthorized-FactSheet-FINAL.pdf.

Centers for Disease Control and Prevention. 2020. "Order Suspending Introduction of Certain Persons from Countries Where a Communicable Disease Exists." March 20. https://www.govinfo.gov/content/pkg/FR-2020-03-26/pdf/2020-06327.pdf.

Chen, Caroline, and Jess Ramirez. 2018. "Immigrant Shelters Drug Traumatized Teenagers Without Consent." ProPublica, July 20. https://www.propublica.org/article/immigrant-shelters-drug-traumatized-teenagers-without-consent.

Delgado, Melvin. 2020. *State-Sanctioned Violence: Advancing a Social Work Social Justice Agenda*. New York: Oxford University Press.

Dmitrieva, Julia, Kathryn C. Monahan, Elizabeth Cauffman, and Laurence Steinberg. 2012. "Arrested Development: The Effects of Incarceration on the Development of Psychosocial Maturity." *Development and Psychopathology* 24 (3): 1073–90.

Dreier, Hannah. 2020. "Trust and Consequences." *Washington Post*, February 15.

Eagly, Ingrid, and Steven Shafter. 2016. "Access to Counsel in Immigration Court." American Immigration Council, September 28. https://www.americanimmigrationcouncil.org/research/access-counsel-immigration-court.

Edwards, Frank, Sara Wakefield, Kieran Healy, and Christopher Wildeman. 2021. "Contact with Child Protective Services Is Pervasive but Unequally Distributed by Race and Ethnicity in Large US Counties." *Proceedings of the National Academy of Sciences of the United States* 118 (30): e2106272118.

Epstein, Rebecca, Jamilia J. Blake, and Thalia Gonzalez. 2017. "Girlhood Interrupted: The Erasure of Black Girls' Childhood." Georgetown Law Center on Poverty and Inequality June 27.

Galtung, Johan. 1969. "Violence, Peace, and Peace Research." *Journal of Peace Research* 6 (3): 167–91.

Galvan, Cecilia. 2020. "Mental Health Inside Detention Centers: The Unknown Toll on Latinx Child Immigrants." University of Michigan School of Public Health, August 18. https://sph.umich.edu/pursuit/2020posts/mental-health-inside-detention-centers-the-unknown-toll-on-latinx-child-immigrants.html.

Goff, Phillip Atiba, Matthew Christian Jackson, Brooke Allison Lewis De Leone, Carmen Marie Culotta, and Natalie Ann DiTomasso. 2014. "The Essence of Innocence: Consequences of Dehumanizing Black Children." *Journal of Personality and Social Psychology* 106 (4): 526–45.

Grove, Natalie J., and Anthony B. Zwi. 2006. "Our Health and Theirs: Forced Migration, Othering, and Public Health." *Social Science & Medicine* 62 (8): 1931–42.

Hirschfeld Davis, Julie. 2018. "Trump Calls Some Unauthorized Immigrants 'Animals' in Rant." *New York Times*, May 16.

Hockenberry, Sarah, and Charles Puzzanchera. 2021. "Juvenile Court Statistics, 2019." Office of Juvenile Justice and Delinquency Prevention, June. https://www.ojjdp.gov/ojstatbb/njcda/pdf/jcs2019.pdf.

Illinois Juvenile Justice Commission. 2021. "Detention of Children 10–12 Years Old in Illinois: A Call to Action." February. https://ijjc.illinois.gov/wp-content/uploads/2021/08/Detention-of-Children-10-12-Years-Old-In-Illinois-A-Call-to-Action-.pdf.

Innovation Law Lab and the Southern Poverty Law Center. 2019. "The Attorney General's Judges: How the U.S. Immigration Courts Became a Deportation Tool." June. https://www.splcenter.org/sites/default/files/com_policyreport_the_attorney_generals_judges_final.pdf.

Innovation Law Lab v. Nielsen, 19-cv-00807, Doc. 73 (N.D. Cal. 2019).

Kaelber, Lutz. 2012. "Eugenic: Compulsory Sterilization in 50 American States." Presentation for the Social Science History Association, November 1–4. https://www.uvm.edu/%7Elkaelber/eugenics/.

Kids in Need of Defense. 2020. "Forced Apart: How the 'Remain in Mexico' Policy Places Children in Danger and Separates Families." February 24. https://supportkind.org/wp-content/uploads/2020/02/MPP-KIND-2.24updated-003.pdf.

Kivilcim, Zeynep. 2016. "Legal Violence Against Syrian Female Refugees in Turkey." *Feminist Legal Studies* 24 (2): 193–214.

Kraut, Michael E. n.d. "Juveniles and Confinement." Child Crime Prevention and Safety Center. Accessed October 31, 2023. https://childsafety.losangelescriminallawyer.pro/juveniles-and-confinement.html.

Krug, Etienne G., et al., eds. *World Report on Violence and Health*. Geneva: World Health Organization.

Lee, Bandy X. 2019. *Violence: An Interdisciplinary Approach to Causes, Consequences, and Cures*. Hoboken, N.J.: John Wiley & Sons.

Linton, Julie M., et al. 2017. "Detention of Immigrant Children." *Pediatrics* 139 (5): e20170483.

MacLean, Sarah A., Priscilla O. Agyeman, Joshua Walther, Elizabeth K. Singer, Kim A. Baranowski, and Craig L. Katz. 2019. "Mental Health of Children Held at a United States Immigration Detention Center." *Social Science & Medicine* 230 (June): 303–8.

Madrigal v. Quilligan, 639 F.2d 789 (9th Cir. 1981).

Malina, Giselle. 2019. "How Should Unaccompanied Minors in Immigration Detention Be Protected from Coercive Medical Practices." *AMA Journal of Ethics* 21 (7): 603–10.
McCoy, Henrika, and Emalee Pearson. 2019. "Racial Disparities in the Juvenile Justice System." *Encyclopedia of Social Work*. In partnership with National Association of Social Workers Press. New York: Oxford University Press. https://oxfordre.com/socialwork.
Menjívar, Cecilia. 2013. "Central American Immigrant Workers and Legal Violence in Phoenix, Arizona." *Latino Studies* 11 (2): 228–52.
Menjívar, Cecilia, and Leisy Abrego. 2012. "Legal Violence: Immigration Law and the Lives of Central American Immigrants." *American Journal of Sociology* 117 (5): 1380–1421.
Muhkherjee, Elora. 2019. Testimony Before the U.S. House of Representatives Committee on Oversight and Reform. Washington, D.C., July 12. https://images.law.com/contrib/content/uploads/documents/292/49517/Elora-Mukherjee-House-Oversight-Committee-Testimony-7-10-19.pdf.
Nagda, Jennifer, and Maria Woltjen. 2015. "Best Interests of the Child Standard: Bringing Common Sense to Immigration Decisions." First Focus on Children, March 11. https://firstfocus.org/resources/report/best-interests-of-the-child-standard-bringing-common-sense-to-immigration-decisions.
National Child Traumatic Stress Network. 2016. "Children with Traumatic Stress: Information for Professionals." https://www.nctsn.org/resources/children-traumatic-separation-information-professionals.
Noriega, Jorge. 1992. "American Indian Education in the United States: Indoctrination for Subordination." In *The State of Native America: Genocide, Colonization, and Resistance*, edited by Annette Jaimes, 371–402. Boston: South End Press.
Office of Refugee Resettlement. n.d. "Fact Sheets and Data." Accessed July 25, 2022. https://www.acf.hhs.gov/orr/about/ucs/facts-and-data.
Office of the Attorney General. 2018. "Memorandum for Federal Prosecutors Along the Southwest Border." April 6. https://www.justice.gov/opa/press-release/file/1049751/download.
Ordoñez, Franco, and Dana Ferrington. 2021. "Young Migrants Held by Border Patrol Far Longer than Allowed, Document Shows." NPR, March 16. https://www.npr.org/2021/03/16/977853878/young-migrants-held-by-border-patrol-far-longer-than-allowed-document-shows.
Oxford Learners Dictionary. n.d. "Detention." Accessed July 25, 2022. https://www.oxfordlearnersdictionaries.com/us/definition/english/detention.
Peeler, Katie. 2020. "Forced Family Separation Isn't Just Traumatic. It's Torture." Physicians for Human Rights blog, March 10. https://phr.org/our-work/resources/forced-family-separation-isnt-just-traumatic-its-torture/.
Peprah, Tierney Sheree. 2021. *Fostering False Identity: The Child Welfare System's Design of a Social Control of the Black Family*. n.p.: n.p.

Physicians for Human Rights. 2019. "U.S. Government Confirms Migrant Children Experienced Severe Mental Health Issues Following 'Family Separation.'" September 4. https://phr.org/news/u-s-government-confirms-migrant-children-experienced-severe-mental-health-issues-following-family-separation/.

powell, john a. 2017. "Us vs Them: The Sinister Techniques of 'Othering'—and How to Avoid Them." *The Guardian*, November 8.

Prandini, Rachel, and Alison Kamhi. 2017. "Practice Alert on *Flores v. Sessions*." Immigrant Legal Resources Center, July. https://www.ilrc.org/sites/default/files/resources/flores_v._sessions_practice_alert_final.pdf.

Reisler, Mark. 1976. *By the Sweat of Their Brow: Mexican Immigrant Labor in the United States*. Westport, Conn.: Greenwood Press.

Rouse, Wendy L. 2019. "Between Two Worlds: Chinese Immigrant Children and the Production of Knowledge in the Era of Chinese Exclusion." *KNOW: A Journal on the Formation of Knowledge* 3 (2): 263–82.

Rutherford, Alison, Anthony B. Zwi, Natalie J. Grove, and Alexander Butchart. 2007. "Violence: A Glossary." *Journal of Epidemiology and Community Health* 61 (8): 676–80.

Saravia v. Barr, No. 18–60532 (5th Cir. 2020).

Scott, Eugene. 2019. "Trump's Most Insulting—and Violent—Language Is Often Reserved for Immigrants." *Washington Post*, October 2.

Sentencing Project. 2021. "Black Disparities in Youth Incarceration: Racial Disparities Persist but Fall from All-Time High." https://www.jstor.org/stable/resrep36083.

Shear, Michael D., Katie Benner, and Michael S. Schmidt. 2020. "'We Need to Take Away Children,' No Matter How Young, Justice Dept. Officials Said." *New York Times*, October 6.

Shohat, Ella, and Robert Stam. 2014. *Unthinking Eurocentrism: Multiculturalism and the Media*. 2nd ed. London: Routledge.

Simon, Abigail. 2018. "People Are Angry President Trump Used This Word to Describe Undocumented Immigrants." *Time*, June 19.

State Joint Commission. 1918. *Surveys in Mental Deviation in Prisons, Public Schools, and Orphanages in California*. Sacramento: California State Printing Office.

Tape v. Hurley, 66 Cal. 473 (Cal. 1885).

Texas et al. v. United States et al., 14-cv-00254 (S.D. Tex. 2015).

Theobald, Brianna. 2020. "The History of Eugenics in the U.S. Has Made Migrant Women Vulnerable." *Washington Post*, September 20.

UN Committee on the Rights of the Child. 2013. "General Comment No. 14 (2013) on the Right of the Child to Have His or Her Best Interests Taken as a Primary Consideration (art. 3, para. 1)." May 29. https://www.refworld.org/docid/51a84b5e4.html.

UNICEF. 2019. "UNICEF Working Paper: Alternatives to Immigration Detention of Children." September. https://www.unicef.org/media/58351/file/Alternatives%20to%20Immigration%20Detention%20of%20Children%20(ENG).pdf.

UNICEF. 2021. "Building Bridges for Every Child: Reception, Care and Services to Support Unaccompanied Children in the United States." February. https://www.unicef.org/media/94341/file/Building%20Bridges%20for%20Every%20Child.pdf.

Werthern, M. von, et al. 2018. "The Impact of Immigration Detention on Mental Health: A Systemic Review." *BMC Psychiatry* 18:382.

Women's Refugee Commission and Orrick Herrington & Sutcliffe LLP. 2009. "Halfway Home: Unaccompanied Children in Immigration Custody." February. https://www.womensrefugeecommission.org/wp-content/uploads/2020/04/halfway_home.pdf.

Young, Julia G. 2017. "Making America 1920 Again? Nativism and US Immigration, Past and Present." *Journal on Migration and Human Security* 5 (1): 217–35.

Young Center for Immigrant Children's Rights. 2019. "The 'Migrant Protection Protocols' Are Harming Children and Must End." November. https://static1.squarespace.com/static/597ab5f3bebafb0a625aaf45/t/5df25d16b8b4c6785fa1d4f9/1576164630725/Young+Center+MPP+One+Pager.pdf.

Young Center for Immigrant Children's Rights. 2020a. "Family Separation Is Not Over: How the Trump Administration Continues to Separate Children from Their Parents to Serve Its Political Ends." https://static1.squarespace.com/static/597ab5f3bebafb0a625aaf45/t/5f032e87ff32c80f99c7fee5/1594044048699/Young+Center-Family+Separation+Report-Final+PDF.pdf.

Young Center for Immigrant Children's Rights. 2020b. "Reimagining Children's Immigration Proceedings: A Roadmap for an Entirely New System Centered Around Children." October. https://www.theyoungcenter.org/reimagining-childrens-immigration-proceedings.

Zhongyun, Zi. 1987. "The Relationship of Chinese Traditional Culture to the Modernization of China: An Introduction to the Current Discussion." *Asian Survey* 27 (4): 442–58.

CHAPTER TWO

Kids, Paperwork, and Cages

An Analysis of the Unseen Representations of Immigrant Minors in the Key Documents and Legal Resources of the Unaccompanied Children Program

AIREEN GRACE ANDAL

In recent years, the United States has witnessed an upsurge of apprehensions of minors crossing the U.S. borders without any legal guardian, which raises concerns on employing child-appropriate approaches on the entry of these minors to the United States (Cheatham 2021). The literature that focuses on child immigration has explored multiple frameworks for situating immigrant children, such as demographics, geographies, legal and historical accounts, and psychological perspectives (Boyden and Hart 2007; White et al. 2011; Kennedy 2014; UN High Commissioner for Refugees 2014; NeMoyer, Rodriguez, and Alvarez 2019; Coulter et al. 2020). Other studies on unaccompanied immigrant children and refugee children have also focused on the motives, experiences, and overall well-being of these minors (Sotomayor-Peterson and Montiel-Carbajal 2014; Terrio 2015; Lorenzen 2017; Ataiants et al. 2018; Diaz-Strong 2021). However, little is known about the representation of unaccompanied immigrant children in the procedural aspects of accommodation and release. This chapter employs a different approach in understanding child immigration—not in terms of statistics, location, or history of child immigration but with regard to the trivial practices imbued in unaccompanied immigrant children's detention. As a supplement to the popular media's visible spectacle to show children immigrants' experiences through news coverage, documentaries, films, or social media (Flores Morales and Farago 2021), this work pays attention to the often overlooked administrative documents to examine the framings and depictions of border-crossing unaccompanied immigrant children. This critical perspective on trivial bureaucracy—administrative or bureaucratic obstacles that, while seemingly minor or insignificant on their own, can collectively have a significant impact on unaccompanied minors and their experiences—is relevant to have a holistic view of the narratives imposed on the unaccompanied immigrant children and its implications in understanding the disposition and plight of unaccompanied immigrant children in the United States. By examining and questioning these seemingly trivial bureaucratic processes, one can gain perspective on the narratives imposed on unaccompanied minors and how these narratives influence their situation.

This chapter acknowledges that the term *unaccompanied alien children* (UAC) (Congressional Research Service 2021) is loaded with controversy with regard to the alleged discriminatory implications of its semantics. For the purposes of discussion, the term *unaccompanied immigrant children* is used throughout the chapter. Building upon prior research that has explored the representation of unaccompanied immigrant children and their families in institutional documents, this investigation scrutinizes the rigorous processes involved in verifying identities, including age, which determines eligibility for custody under the Unaccompanied Refugee Minors Program (Terrio 2015). Furthermore, it delves into the statutory standards that establish qualified adults as guardians for unaccompanied immigrant children when parents are considered unfit to fulfill this role (Heidbrink 2017). The overarching concern is that the impersonal approach of the U.S. immigration system may contribute to the stigmatization and potential criminalization of these children, merely because they lack documented status (Grace and Roth 2021). These examples illustrate how bureaucratic systems, often governed by strict regulations, may not necessarily serve the best interests of unaccompanied immigrant children and their families. Using content analysis, this chapter engages in a discourse analysis of bureaucratic constructs and narratives concerning unaccompanied immigrant children. It aims to answer three key questions: (1) How are unaccompanied immigrant children portrayed and defined within the information systems related to their accommodation and release?; (2) What underlying assumptions govern the dynamics between unaccompanied immigrant children and service providers, including authorities, lawyers, and social workers?; and (3) What rhetorical devices are employed in the descriptions of unaccompanied immigrant children?

Whereas paperwork seems docile, objective, and full of disembodied artifacts, it embeds ideologies and reproduces constitutive and sustaining narratives of the unaccompanied immigrant children. It reflects certain measures on how immigrant minors are represented and framed (Smith 1974). Not to be confused with a policy analysis, this chapter's focus is on the meanings and discourses imbued in the forms and legal documents related to detaining unaccompanied immigrant children. The aim is to offer a discursive analysis of the image of the unaccompanied immigrant children from a procedural perspective. Ultimately, bearing in mind that the law is to favor the best interests of children (UN High Commissioner for Refugees 2008, 2012), it is important to understand what version of the unaccompanied immigrant children's image is reproduced in prosaic documents. The implications of findings are subject for discussions on children immigration and juvenile justice policy, management, and theory.

Methodology

Paperwork as data sources plays an integral role in showing shared knowledge and assumptions about undocumented children, thereby revealing how unaccompanied immigrant children are framed within the legal institution. Bureaucratic policies reflect institutional dominant values, giving a sense of how unaccompanied immigrant children are understood and placed in the broader legal system. Specifically, this work examines the institutional resources and policies related to detention and release (e.g., required forms, agreements, program models). In the age of professionalization, an analysis of the bureaucratic process becomes increasingly relevant in terms of the circulation and production of knowledge about subjects involved in the process. In this regard, bureaucratic documents, such as forms and notices, are more than mere tools of administrative management. Rather, this paperwork cements the narratives of certain subjects to everyday practices (Hull 2012), which are subtly entrenched in policy and implementation (Jacob 2007). Paperwork is thus inextricably linked to knowledge generation about unaccompanied immigrant children (see Diaz, Walts, and Jacobs in this volume for more information on this historical othering). Through a discursive analysis (see Dryzek 2005) of the procedures and key documents required for detaining unaccompanied immigrant children in the United States, this chapter shows how narratives of these minors are formed within the bureaucratic material culture of paperwork, which produces and reproduces a discourse that reflects the enactments of its inclusion. In other words, these documents aid in understanding how belongingness of unaccompanied immigrant children is facilitated or curtailed in institutional settings (Riles 2006; Kafka 2009).

The Office of Refugee Resettlement (ORR) has operated the shelter, care, and other essential services to unaccompanied immigrant children under the Unaccompanied Children Program since 2003. After transferring custody from the U.S. Customs and Border Protection (CBP), ORR facilitates and coordinates a network of housing facilities across the United States to temporarily accommodate and address the needs of children within the program, during which ORR also processes paperwork to reunite the unaccompanied immigrant children with their family or approved sponsors (U.S. Immigration and Customs Enforcement et al. 2019). In ORR, children are assessed for placement in a shelter facility, group home, staff-secure or secure-care facility, residential treatment center, or other special-needs-care facility. The conditions of placement are determined after bond hearings. Table 2.1 provides information on the types of placements within ORR.

Table 2.2 shows the documents used in this analysis.[1] The selection of documents for analysis in this study was guided by a purposeful sampling approach, focusing on bureaucratic materials specifically related to the detention and release of unaccompanied immigrant children within the Unaccompanied Alien Children Program. The chosen documents encompassed a range of required forms, agreements, and program models used within the bureaucratic framework of the Unaccompanied Alien Children Program. This selection aimed to provide a comprehensive view of the institutional resources and policies governing the detention and release process. Furthermore, the number of documents selected was determined by the need to capture the diversity of bureaucratic constructs and narratives shaping the image of unaccompanied immigrant children within this legal institution. By analyzing a representative sample of these documents, the study seeks to reveal the shared knowledge, assumptions, and discourses about undocumented children, shedding light on how they are framed within the legal context. These selected documents serve as key entry points into understanding the bureaucratic processes that influence the inclusion or exclusion of unaccompanied immigrant children, and how their sense of belongingness is facilitated or curtailed within institutional settings. The analysis of this paperwork provides valuable insights into the production

TABLE 2.1 Placements of Unaccompanied Immigrant Children with ORR

Placement	Description
Shelter Care	A shelter is a residential care provider facility in which all the programmatic components are administered on-site, in the least restrictive environment.
Group Home	A group home is a care provider facility that offers a group home setting and that specializes in caring for specific populations (e.g., teen mothers). A group home, which is run by twenty-four-hour staff or house parents, typically houses four to twelve unaccompanied children.
Special-Needs Care	Whenever possible, ORR places a child with special needs in a facility that serves the general population but is able to provide services and treatment for special needs. In all instances, ORR strives for a least restrictive setting in the best interests of the child.
Residential Treatment Center (RTC)	A residential treatment center is a subacute, time-limited, interdisciplinary, psycho-educational, and therapeutic twenty-four-hour-a-day structured program with community linkages, provided through noncoercive, coordinated, individualized care; specialized services; and interventions. Residential treatment centers provide highly customized care and services to individuals following either a community-based placement or more intensive intervention, with the aim of moving individuals toward a stable, less-intensive level of care or independence. ORR uses an RTC at the recommendation of a psychiatrist or psychologist or with ORR Treatment Authorization Request (TAR) approval for an unaccompanied child who poses a danger to self or others and does not require inpatient hospitalization.
Secure Care	A secure care provider is a facility with a physically secure structure and staff able to control violent behavior. ORR uses a secure facility as the most restrictive placement option for an unaccompanied child who poses a danger to self or others or has been charged with having committed a criminal offense. A secure facility may be a licensed juvenile detention center or a highly structured therapeutic facility.

TABLE 2.2 Office of Refugee Resettlement Documents Examined in the Analysis

Requirements/Procedures	Key Documents/Standards
For Unaccompanied Immigrant Children	"An Introduction to What You Need to Know About Your Rights and Responsibilities Under the Law" "Notice of Rights and Provision of Services" "Know Your Rights Handout" "Notice to Juvenile Aliens in Federal Facilities Funded by DHS or HHS by Reason of Their Immigration Status" "Legal Service Provider List for UC in ORR Care" "Legal Resource Guide" "Request for a Flores Bond Hearing" "Motion Requesting Bond Hearing for Unaccompanied Children in Secure or Staff Secure Custody" "Policy Memorandum: Medical Services Requiring Heightened ORR Involvement"
For Providers, Sponsors, and Healthcare Providers	"Request for UC Case File Information (Instructions)" "Authorization for Release of Records" "Request for Specific Consent to Juvenile Court Jurisdiction" "Special Immigrant Juvenile Status—Specific Consent Program Instructions" "*Saravia v. Wilkinson*—Notice of Rights" "Requesting Vaccination Records" "Authorization for Release of Records"

Children Entering the United States Unaccompanied: Section 1	Includes procedures on placement in ORR care provider facilities such as: "Policies for Placement and Transfer of Unaccompanied Alien Children in ORR Care Provider Facilities" "ORR Standards for Placement and Transfer Decisions" "Referrals to ORR and Initial Placement" "Transfers Within the ORR Care Provider Network" "Placement Inquiries" "Determining the Age of an Individual Without Lawful Immigration Status"
ORR Guide to Eligibility, Placement, and Services for Unaccompanied Refugee Minors (URM): Section 2	"Standards" "Establishing Legal Responsibility" "Placements" "Interstate Movement" "Capacity Development" "State Planning" "Reporting"
ORR Unaccompanied Refugee Minor (URM) Policy Guide: Record of Posting and Revision Dates	Section 1, "Eligibility for the URM Program and the Application Process" Section 2. "Placement and Capacity" Section 3. "Services"

and circulation of knowledge about unaccompanied immigrant children involved in the Unaccompanied Alien Children Program.

There are different types of documents, such as memoranda, requests, notices, guidelines, and legal resource guides, specifically for the readership of unaccompanied immigrant children and for their families and sponsors. To ensure that the analysis represented the contemporary context, only documents published after 2003 were considered, coinciding with the establishment of the program. Given the potential variations in immigration policies under different administrations, documents from the presidencies of George W. Bush, Barack Obama, Donald Trump, and the early part of Joe Biden's tenure were incorporated. Initial codes were generated through a preliminary scanning of the documents, creating loose codes (Crabtree and Miller 1999). Thereafter, themes from first coding were regrouped, merged, separated, or excluded according to similarities, patterns, or links that emerged in relation to the theoretical framework of "community belonging." In addition, analysis includes the procedures outlined in the ORR policy and guidance and policy letters.

Detention as Bureaucratic Purgatory: Minors Under the Politics of Belonging Toward Entering a Foreign Imagined Community

This chapter argues that the bureaucracy of custody of the unaccompanied immigrant children reveals the function of detention as "boundary maintenance" (Crowley 1999). This means that the bureaucratic processes involved in the custody of these children serve to uphold the boundaries or divisions between different categories of individuals, particularly distinguishing between those who are detained and those who are not. Specifically, the custody procedures carried out by the Office of Refugee Resettlement are instrumental in defining who is included and who is excluded from U.S. society. Detention can be viewed as an interim phase, a form of "purgatory," that must be traversed en route to community acceptance, with paperwork acting as the gateway to determine the qualifications necessary to progress through this process. These bureaucratic procedures, as analyzed through textual government documents, maintain the system of detention. In this chapter, I seek to unveil how this process functions within the broader context of immigration.

The bureaucracy of paperwork touches on the broader politics of belonging (Yuval-Davis 2006), which is about understanding how the bureaucratic system shapes the concept of belonging for unaccompanied immigrant children. The choice of this frame helps reveal how these children are positioned within the legal and bureaucratic framework, including their experiences during border detention. Bureaucratic procedures are a way of highlighting how detained children's sense of belonging, or lack thereof, can be influenced by the bureaucracy. It is important to clarify that the analysis is not exploring the children's subjective feelings of belonging (see, for example, Tenorio, this volume) but rather the bureaucratic constructions and narratives surrounding this concept.

It is also important to understand the unaccompanied immigrant children's relationship with the land they enter as immigrants. Building on and extending scholarship of child immigration—from migration studies, to settler colonial analysis, to childhood studies—this chapter suggests that these children's identity as immigrants is not simply a label of being a minor foreigner coming to the United States. Rather, such identity can be read as an extended narrative of Benedict Anderson's (1983) notion of an imagined community, which describes how people develop self-identity and communities by having a shared imagination as fellow members of a group. Through imagination, people bond and create a mutual sense of community, "conceived as a deep, horizontal comradeship" (Anderson 1983, 16). Likewise, beyond having a legal immigrant status in the United States, unaccompanied immigrant children need a sense of belonging upon transitioning to U.S. society. However, it is of no surprise that these minors face numerous barriers to being integrated and having a sense of belonging in a foreign land. Less talked about on this matter is how the bureaucratic process of admitting unaccompanied immigrant children is inflected with depictions that highlight differences between unaccompanied immigrant children and U.S. society. The process of accommodating foreign minors to U.S. society raises critical questions concerning the kind of membership these minors are granted within their first encounter of the U.S. bureaucratic procedures.

At the core of the unaccompanied immigrant children's integration is having dignity and "becoming visible and gaining recognition" (Ferguson 2000, 97), which can be formed through a dignified transition toward becoming a member of a certain community (Pugh 2009). Being a stranger in another country takes up the mental and emotional space of wanting not only to survive and cope but also to belong (Carlson, Cacciatore, and Klimek 2012; see also Rodriguez Vega, this volume). Acquiring a legal status in the United States is beyond merely having an official label; it also entails transitions to belongingness. However, the process toward belongingness is in itself a complex subject that needs unpacking. The rhetorical choices in the paperwork suggest setting boundaries between who does and does not belong to the U.S. community. Seemingly trivial matters such as choice of words in the documents reflect how ideas and labels "take a life of their own" (Berman 1998, 21), which eventually solidifies the socially constructed boundaries to exclude the undocumented minors. In what follows, I discuss how the state of being undocumented minors articulates certain images and portrayals as a social and political identity.

Framings of Unaccompanied Immigrant Children Within the Trivialities of Paperwork

Double-Standard Narratives? Vulnerability and Noninnocence
Two diverging but clashing narratives transpire as constructions of unaccompanied immigrant children in the examined documents for detention under ORR: vulnerable but not (entirely) innocent (a theme reflective of the othering of children of color in American history, as depicted in chapter 1 of this volume). The discourse of vulnerability upon being involuntary victims emanates in the extensive state intervention plans for unaccompanied immigrant children, which primarily aim to meet any urgent needs of these children. For instance, the application for placement in the Unaccompanied Refugee Minor (URM) Program stipulates questions like "Does this child have physical or mental health issues that will need to be addressed by the URM program?," suggesting prioritization of immediate concerns of vulnerable children beyond legal matters. Vulnerability is also salient in policy letters specifically created for special conditions such as medical, disaster crisis, and war or armed conflict situations—"ORR Populations Displaced or Affected by Hurricanes Harvey and Irma" (2017), "Privately-Administered Refugee Medical Assistance Through a Medical Replacement Designee" (2019), "Extended Assistance for ORR Populations Affected by COVID-19" (2021), "Afghan Humanitarian Parolees and Unaccompanied Afghan Minors Eligible for ORR Benefits and Services" (2021), and "Ukrainian Humanitarian Parolees Eligible for ORR Benefits and Service" (2022). However, such

observations also reflect traditional humanitarian narratives of cultural disadvantage and deficit among unaccompanied immigrant children, a narrative often used to frame marginalized populations.

That the unaccompanied immigrant children are vulnerable is not new, but equally important is the image of noninnocence that comes with it. Noninnocence in this discussion refers to any exposure to criminal, sexual, or armed conflict, and/or other forms of violence, whether by firsthand experience or witnessing, which constitute "difficult knowledge" to encounter and process (Britzman 1998). The paperwork frames unaccompanied immigrant children within a struggle-induced existence, stripped of moral purity. Beyond the general media framings of immigrants as victims struggling for citizenship (Orgad 2012; Hoewe 2018), the combination of vulnerability and noninnocence is a more complicated and unique "immigration problem" (Becker Herbst et al. 2018; Ruehs 2018). Whereas the media depict unaccompanied immigrant children as "'proper' objects of humanitarian interventions" (Rosen and Crafter 2018, 67), these minors also carry the image of being threats from a bureaucratic perspective based on certain aspects of the process that unaccompanied minors go through during detention in the United States. For instance, when unaccompanied minors are processed by immigration authorities, detailed records are kept, including their full names and aliases. Such processes of documentation may be seen as a precautionary measure by the bureaucracy, but it also mirrors narratives of vigilance against potential "criminal" elements. This resonates with accounts whereby forced-migrant children are "criminalized as undeserving of those rights belonging to citizens" (Doná and Veale 2011, 1277), as evidenced in the documentation of minors' information, which includes not only full names but also their aliases.[2]

Additionally, during the initial phases of assessment, especially when apprehended at the U.S. border, unaccompanied minors may encounter border officials, and this interaction can frame them within a security or legal context, potentially casting them as threats or individuals who may not be entirely innocent. While the transfer to ORR can be characterized by a shift from "threat-focused assessment to child-focused assessment" (Hasson et al. 2019, 278), unaccompanied immigrant children are nevertheless seen as not guilt-free, which can produce and reproduce totalizing narratives about these minors. This view of noninnocence resonates with previous studies reporting the compromised treatment and proper care of unaccompanied immigrant children at the initial phase of assessment conducted by U.S. Customs and Border Protection (CBP) during apprehension at the border (U.S. Government Accountability Office 2015). Furthermore, the narrative of being "threats" is reinforced by a history of issues related to the treatment of unaccompanied minors, spanning more than two decades, in which "many of these [undocumented] children have witnessed atrocities that adults cannot even imagine—death by the masses, violence, and separation [from their families]" (Gates 1999, 300). This history highlights the bureaucratic perspective that some of these minors may have been exposed to or involved in experiences that could be perceived as threatening or linked to criminal activities. While many professionals involved in this process prioritize the well-being and rights of these minors, specific bureaucratic practices and assessments can contribute to a perception of potential threats from a security or legal standpoint.

The narrative of noninnocence also appears in the selectivity of the version of vulnerability attached to unaccompanied immigrant children. For instance, the document "*Saravia v. Wilkinson*—Notice of Rights" describes the case of an immigrant minor who was rearrested by immigration authorities "under suspicion of gang membership."[3] Likewise, labels such as "high risk" (Jani 2017) suggest a segregation of unaccompanied immigrant children's unique and potentially mature experiences at young ages. The label "high-risk" places the immigrant minor in a difficult position to access community belonging because they do not fit in the mold of an innocent child—an "unimpeachable moral status" (Duschinsky 2013, 764). Moreover, the bureaucratic procedures already expect the involvement of unaccompanied immigrant children in human trafficking activities, thus assuming them to have knowledge of criminal acts. While it is important to record criminal experiences for future treatments of unaccompanied immigrant children, it becomes a filter of who is worthy of certain eligibility in the system. This manifests in legal relief liabilities that require certain dispositions, such as having been victims of human trafficking or experienced threatening, beating, or being harmed. For example, to be a Special Immigrant Juvenile visa (SIJ visa) holder, a minor "must have been abandoned, abused, or mistreated by one or both of [their] parents."[4] Likewise, one "must have been forced or coerced to come to the United States, under threats or harm, to work against [their] will or [they] are a victim of sex trafficking" to obtain a T visa (ORR 2014).[5] In contrast, when a minor is married, this child is not eligible for the URM Program unless ORR secures that a court will be able to establish legal responsibility for the child. Being stripped away from some eligibility status because of some labels implies an early selection of who is included and excluded in obtaining a certain immigrant status. These documents imply noninnocence as a justification for securitization measures applied to unaccompanied immigrant children and a means for reproducing a culture of mistrust against immigrants and refugees (see Kyriakides 2017). To some degree, a "guilty" (see Roberts 1997) narrative applies to the noninnocence of unaccompanied immigrant children, who are typically young people of color. Overall, the discourses of guilt and risk create separation between a "normal" childhood and the unaccompanied immigrant children, which potentially hampers their sense of belonging to community.

The juxtaposition of noninnocence with vulnerability gives a picture of a liberal democratic attempt to balance protecting children as a matter of duty and to guard citizens against potential threats from outsiders, regardless of age (Humphris and Sigona 2019). This noninnocence-vulnerability discussion loops back to the complexities of state custodianship and intertwines with the broader discourse on state violence and othering. The categorization of these children as both noninnocent and vulnerable reflects the broader tendency to otherize some groups, drawing parallels with discussions on state power, exclusion, and the perpetuation of systemic violence. This context is what Jacqueline Bhabha (2014, 13) describes as a context "where perceptions of vulnerability (poor and innocent children) and otherness (not really like our children) coalesce." Such characteristics of unaccompanied immigrant children in the eyes of paperwork raise questions on the double-standard kind of state custodianship of the unaccompanied immigrant children and the role of state institutions and authorities in the interim between apprehension and release of unaccompanied immigrant children.

Assumed Relationship Dynamics Between Unaccompanied Immigrant Children and Service Providers

The paperwork reflects a paternal and professional relationship between the unaccompanied immigrant children and authorities managing their case such as law enforcement authorities, lawyers, and social workers. Upon the arrival of the immigrant minor to ORR's URM Program, section 2, "Placement and Capacity," designates a legal authority to "act in place of the minor's unavailable parent(s)." On a rather discernible note, a paternal protectionist treatment of unaccompanied immigrant children manifests through the extensive representations of lawyers and/or workers of unaccompanied immigrant children programs to answer questions on behalf of children. This paternal relationship is easily embodied between the unaccompanied immigrant children and ORR itself, as this office conducts background check processes for potential sponsors. ORR can also provide the unaccompanied immigrant children with ORR-funded legal services, pro bono lawyers, or volunteer attorneys or staff. Another paternal relationship is having the unaccompanied immigrant children be represented by an organization/agency/law firm with its duly authorized representatives. In such cases, the representative becomes a requesting party for the authorization for release of records. This kind of paternalism relates back to the discussion of paternalist-but-professional tendencies of the immigration system. While unaccompanied immigrant children are seen without agency at least in documents, they are *adultified* compared to non-unaccompanied immigrant children or children of legal migrants (see also Diaz, Kaufka Walts, and Jacobs, this volume). This is evident in having to pass the eligibility requirements to be "Special Immigrant Juveniles," which allows minors to "seek lawful permanent residence in the United States" (U.S. Citizenship and Immigration Services n.d). In contrast, the process of gaining lawful permanent residence (LPR) status for children whose parents are legal migrants is through petition, whereby the responsibility is devolved to the parent(s). But because the minors in ORR are "unaccompanied," the state takes over the parental responsibility, legitimizing power over children.

The paternalist treatment of the unaccompanied immigrant children also exhibits, albeit more subtly, an impersonalized and professionalized depiction of unaccompanied immigrant children in the bureaucratic procedures. For instance, in the "Notice for Special Immigrant Juveniles," children are addressed in a rather professional tone; phrases such as "If you have applied, or wish to apply, for lawful resident status in the United States as an SIJ, this Notice contains important information about your rights. Please read this carefully" assume the unaccompanied immigrant children are familiar with the legal semantics.[6] Moreover, the documents run the risk of exposing children to retraumatization, which may have short- or long-term consequences to children (Thomas and Byford 2003). For example, the phrase "If you have been abused, abandoned, or neglected, whether in the United States or abroad, you may be eligible to remain lawfully in the

United States as a Special Immigrant Juvenile" might trigger undesirable memories of the unaccompanied immigrant children (ORR n.d.-b). Moreover, the immigrant minor is expected to have come up with a signature to be able to decline a placement in the URM Program and to fill out the following information:

> My name is _____. I received approval for placement into the Unaccompanied Refugee Minor (URM) program on _____. I received an explanation of the program, its services and my rights and responsibilities from _____ on _____ in (insert language) and understand the information that was presented to me. I also understand that if I decline placement in the URM program at this time, I may not be able to enter the program at a later date.

Having a document signed by a child can be interpreted as reinforcing agency in the hands of the immigrant minor because the child gives consent. However, this should not be conflated with "pseudo-maturity" in children or "appearing to be more mature than is developmentally appropriate ... when children learn that they need to take care of themselves and when adults are not considered a source of support and protection" (Delaney 2012, 9). The sentence stipulating that the immigrant minor "may not be able to enter the program at a later date" denies the child the chance to change their mind. Furthermore, professionalism is indicated in the sponsor handbook's Notice to Appear (NTA), which requires the child to attend court procedures as part of the immigration proceedings. The document "Special Immigrant Juvenile Application for Placement," for example, asks for full name, alias, alien number, date of birth, country of birth, and gender.[7] Such forms have numerical representations that encode the unaccompanied immigrant children's identities, refining the quantification of their identity in the records while making invisible their personal identity. The gender section has checkboxes for male and female, which leaves no room for unaccompanied immigrant children who might identify as nonbinary or any gender. These rigid checkboxes reflect a hidden bureaucratic discrimination; such quantified and limited gender identity choices function as codes of exclusion entrenched within the bureaucratic system but remain unnoticed because documents are trivial. This resonates with the broader exclusions against sexual minority youth of color (see Harper, Jernewall, and Zea 2004; Rosario, Schrimshaw, and

Hunter 2011), foregrounding exclusive undertones within the community they are entering. Gender turning into narrow checkboxes implies a denial of minority identities in favor of easy compliance to documentation and recordkeeping. However, "even though it's a small checkbox, it's a big deal" (Rubin and McClelland 2015) because denial runs the risk of mistrust to the community for young people due to anxiety (Frost, Lehavot, and Meyer 2013) or fear of being outed (Rosario, Schrimshaw, and Hunter 2004).

The combined discourse of paternal protectionism and professionalized treatment of children suggests a relationship that is unstable at best, and contradictory at worst, between unaccompanied immigrant children and the legal entities managing their cases. While the children are seen as persons to be protected, such protectionism is imbued by a "separation of the rights-holder and the moral agent, who is empowered to act by the institutionalization of children's rights. Although the child is treated as a rights-holder . . . the child is not regarded as the moral agent who determines those rights" (Pupavac 2001, 99). While these children are protected, they are also depicted as docile subjects who only succumb in the paperwork to apply for release. This runs the risk of a compromised understanding of unaccompanied immigrant children since "it is not only children who are affected by these paternalist conventions [but also] the maturity, responsibility and autonomy associated with the classes, families, countries and even regions those children are associated with" (Burman 2008, 10). Such observations resonate with studies suggesting we give more voice to unaccompanied immigrant children through participation (see Schmidt 2017), not just mere representation.

Rhetorical Devices Used in Describing Unaccompanied Immigrant Children

The rhetorical devices that frame the depiction of unaccompanied immigrant children hinge upon the classic humanitarian visions of children's rights. Placing children's rights as a banner principle frames being an immigrant child as a hindrance to children's development and well-being, reinforcing program interventions toward productive citizenship to serve domestic benefits (Castles 1995; Stacey 1998). For instance, under section 1 of "Children Entering the United States Unaccompanied," the term *victim* appears four times in the subsections "Placement Considerations," "Safety Issues," "Referrals to ORR and Initial Placement," and "Determining the Age of an Individual Without

Lawful Immigration Status." The use of the term *victims* reverberates the image of powerlessness among children who have suffered from human trafficking or other crimes (Delaney 2012). Likewise, the introduction of the "Legal Resource Guide" presents the legal package that describes the rights of the unaccompanied immigrant children under ORR custody as well as their legal responsibilities, and how to access legal services to help these children with their immigration cases.

The descriptions include the rights as an immigrant minor in ORR custodianship and a formal notice describing rights for an immigrant status. These documents strongly emphasize unaccompanied immigrant children's need for pre- and postrelease representation by lawyers. While these documents are in goodwill and grounded upon the principles of best interests of the child, such documents also keep the traditional assumption of zero-sum conception of representation of an adult on behalf of a child rather than a shared representation (Leubsdorf 1992). Even if in practice there is back-and-forth consultation with the child, the documents still impose that lawyers be the surrogate decision-makers for children. While institutions only wish to provide thick layers of protection to the unaccompanied immigrant children, this treats the child as a passive legal actor and an apolitical subject (Crawley 2011). The zero-sum treatment of representation may create a limited sense of a child's participation, which is mostly referenced as attending court trials.

In resonance with the previous chapter, on othering Black, Brown, and Native children, the rhetorical devices employed in describing unaccompanied immigrant children show how the U.S. government engages in the process of filtering immigrant children as "others." In particular, by consistently framing them as "victims," the narrative reinforces a perception of others, depicted as powerless, thereby distinguishing these children as fundamentally different. This establishes a distinction from the perceived "normal children" of the host country. Additionally, the emphasis on legal representation in a zero-sum framework further underscores the state's approach to viewing these children as passive legal actors and apolitical subjects. This reinforces the notion that unaccompanied immigrant children require surrogate decision-makers, positioning them as others who are unable to actively participate in decisions affecting their lives, and casting them as individuals whose agency is secondary to the decisions made on their behalf.

The lack of shared representation in the legal documents resonates with previous literature that highlights depictions of children as persons who are nonetheless "incapable of citizenship" (Cohen 2005, 221). This aligns in David Archard's (2006, 6) argument that there is a "particularly modern and arguably Western view of the child as a vulnerable, weak, and dependent creature, bereft of those capacities that entitle adults to be regarded as full members of our society." The rhetoric of the paperwork also reflects Western constructions of unaccompanied immigrant children as having "vulnerabilized migrant childhoods" (Lind 2019, 337; see also Eastmond and Ascher 2011). This digs into Kyle Vella's (2016, 3) questions: "whose rights? Are we advocating for a right to protect (therefore of an authority to act and intervene in the life of a child) or the right for protection (the child as an autonomous being)?" and "Is this an opportunity for children to seek protection or for other actors to intervene and protect children?" These questions encourage a deep and retroactive review of whose interest the documents prioritize and forward. For instance, during detention, the unaccompanied immigrant children await "release." The term *release*, although harmless, highlights the moral ascendancy of the authorities responsible for the procedures related to these children. This suggests power over children and henceforth exclusion as it insinuates "captivity," in contrast to other children in the United States.

By carrying labels marked by the process of immigration, unaccompanied immigrant children are framed as separated from the community they wish to enter. In such rhetoric, these children are barely regarded as members of the community and instead remain "Others" who are "at once interior and foreign, therefore to be excluded" (Foucault 1970, xxiv). Ultimately, this conveys colonialist ideals of saviorism in responding to the cases of unaccompanied immigrant children, which runs the risk of not only essentializing these young people but also legitimizing the reproduction of the Orientalist discourse of northern supremacy, albeit unintentionally (Anderson 2013; see also Fassin 2012). Note that the colonialist ideals of saviorism are not exclusive to immigration but also echo within the everyday practices of care, education, and aid, whereby children are entangled with the adultist infantilizing tendencies. For instance, this manifests in the education system that champions helping marginalized youths of color (Baldridge 2014; Sondel, Kretchmar, and Dunn 2019) as they are "incapable of helping themselves" (Cammarota 2011, 244). Likewise, sympathetic feelings toward children of color such as pity and care need interrogation as these can be hidden disgust for the "Other" (Matias and Zembylas 2014). This narrative of "other" follows a long history of infantilizing the native "others" from the slavery period to post–Civil War context, wherein freedmen and freedwomen continued to be excluded from rights such as suffrage, land ownership, labor contracts, and other acts of political participation (Rodrigue 2001; Fields 2014). This mixed characterization of the undocumented minor is part of the broader discussions found within the history of hierarchies within immigration. As children from the Global South, they are given sets of identities—sometimes almost contrasting—such as vulnerable but not innocent.

Toward a Dignified Immigration for Unaccompanied Immigrant Children

This chapter acknowledges that significant change and reform in immigration systems, including alternatives to detention or outright abolition, are necessary in the long run. This can best be seen in the chapters of this book arguing that the current detention system often fails to provide unaccompanied immigrant children with the dignity and fairness they deserve. However, in the interim of reforming the ways to have alternatives or even abolition of juvenile detention, it is essential to recognize and address the immediate challenges that unaccompanied immigrant minors face within the current system. While long-term reform is necessary, it can be a time-consuming process. Addressing the short term acknowledges the immediate challenges they face and ensures a more humane and compassionate approach to their transitional phase. This dual approach reflects a commitment to both justice and humanity in immigration policy and practice. Failing to address the short-term concerns can lead to continued suffering and harm for these children.

The observations in this chapter touch upon the question of how the unaccompanied immigrant children can have a dignified transition in belonging to a community (Bloemraad, Korteweg, and Yurdakul 2008; Hughey 2012). But addressing the issue of having a more humane and equitable immigration system is not a quick fix. It involves policy changes, legal reforms, and shifts in societal attitudes. These transformations take time, effort, and collaboration among various stakeholders, including policymakers, legal experts, and advocacy groups. While the long-term goal is essential, it is crucial not to lose sight of the immediate needs of unaccompanied immigrant minors. This chapter argues that focusing solely on long-term reform without addressing the short-term challenges can leave these children in a vulnerable and uncertain position. Immigration procedures and bureaucratic processes can be daunting and intimidating for children who may already be traumatized by their experiences. It is important to provide a sense of belonging in the wider communities throughout their transition process (Glenn 2011). Although unaccompanied immigrant children may be provided with basic needs and eventually settle in U.S. communities, their sense of belonging depends on maintaining dignity in the process of transition, including the paperwork. There is no easy way to navigate securing dignity among unaccompanied immigrant children in the bureaucratic process, but perhaps the following modest steps can be taken as a way forward, at least in the short term.

First, a child-friendly version of the documents, especially those that require signatures of the unaccompanied immigrant children, needs to be considered. While the documents have Spanish versions and multilingual professionals in ORR can explain to children the documents involved in entering ORR custody, respect to children can be further embodied by generating documents written not only in their native language but also in a way they can understand. This has already been initiated in the "Know Your Rights Handout," whereby the vocabulary does not reflect legal jargon. In contrast to the vulnerability-laden narratives in ORR paperwork, a child-sensitive vocabulary suggests recognition of children's level of needs without undermining their agency as capable beings to participate in meaningful discussions.

Second, to challenge the condescending protectionism imbued in the bureaucrats of detention means to shift toward children's engagement. For example, the paperwork can diversify some terms by consulting children on their choices of terms they want to use. For instance, instead of using the word *victim*, which carries its own stigma, the documents can use more empowering terms, such as *survivor* (United Nations Office on Drugs and Crime 2018), among others. Also, expanding the categories on gender will provide insights into the sensitivities of the child. While these suggestions seem to be only small semantic play, they reflect whose interest is really advanced in the bureaucratic procedures.

Third, to ensure that children's participation is not only lip service and is beyond tokenism, it is important to have shared representation (Leubsdorf

1992). Acts of nontokenistic representations of children fight exclusions imbued in the paternal depictions of children in the paperwork examined in this chapter. As Susan Schmidt (2017, 76) puts it, "Adults working with migrant youth, in the United States, in transit, and in home countries, should proactively seek out means for youth to contribute their views and suggestions." Also important is providing the choice of returning, in case the minor changes their mind about applying to the URM Program.

Change is slow and necessary, but it should not come at the cost of the dignity and well-being of unaccompanied immigrant minors in the interim. There is a need for a balanced approach that simultaneously works toward a better long-term system while ensuring that the short-term experience is more humane and just. This fosters an imagined community that accommodates unaccompanied immigrant children as dignified members of the community. Otherwise, such paperwork reflects society that is unwilling to "imagine" these children as legitimate would-be members of the existing U.S. society.

Conclusion

The observations in this chapter bring the discussion on framing the immigrant minor as a loaded identity—a background that carries a weight that shapes who they are in the eyes of paperwork within the broader politics of immigration. This chapter, therefore, is not just an examination of the paperwork concerning the unaccompanied immigrant children in the United States. Rather, this work sets the stage to argue that the case of the unaccompanied immigrant children reinforces children as political subjects (Ansell 2009). Scholars of child migration have made repeated claims for understanding the politics of controlling undocumented minors as intersectional (Fiddian-Qasmiyeh 2016), and this could further demonstrate how child immigration has always been, and remains, deeply political. Discussions ranging from immigration to human rights to legal implications of how the unaccompanied immigrant children are depicted in paperwork demonstrate the complex politics informed by their identity. The bureaucratic procedures refracted three major framings of the unaccompanied immigrant children's subjectivity: vulnerable but noninnocent, paternalist but impersonal, and classic humanitarian vision. This calls for further examinations of the case of unaccompanied immigrant children not only in the broad policy discourses and public debates but also in the very small-scale trivialities of bureaucratic procedures.

The prosaic paperwork reveals the tensions in belonging to a community, with which human dignity constantly grapples. In the era of professionalized humanitarian work and heavy dependence on bureaucracies, there is a pressing call for a critical view of how administrative procedures uphold human dignity and a sense of belongingness. Thus, the question of how bureaucracy can be trusted to design a dignified process for integrating unaccompanied immigrant children will need further advocacy and intricate examination of each procedure of the paperwork to act in good faith for the interest of children. By considering the spaces and scales where the identity of unaccompanied immigrant children takes shape, this work encourages future research to devote attention to what discourses transpire through the documents related to the unaccompanied immigrant children. These concerns present an opportunity for further thought and research on child immigration. Crucially, this chapter hopes for a dignified process of integration and encourages investment in critical research to contextualize unaccompanied immigrant children on a global scale.

Acknowledgment

To the children who braved all storms of the cross-border journey and paperwork, this is for you.

Notes

1. Last updated on May 19, 2021.
2. See "Section 5: Program Management," in "ORR Unaccompanied Children Program Policy Guide," which contains information about record-keeping, staffing and training, monitoring, and other policies to ensure programs are compliant with ORR requirements and standards: https://www.acf.hhs.gov/orr/policy-guidance/unaccompanied-children-program-policy-guide.
3. A "Notice of Rights" includes statements such as "you may be eligible for lawful immigration status if you have been abused, abandoned, or neglected" (ORR n.d.-a).
4. Quoted in "Know Your Rights Handout."
5. A T visa is available for human trafficking victims.
6. See also ORR (n.d.-b).
7. It requests a copy of the birth certificate, if available.

References

Anderson, Benedict. 1983. *Imagined Communities*. London: Verso.

Ansell, Nicola. 2009. "Childhood and the Politics of Scale: Descaling Children's Geographies?" *Progress in Human Geography* 33 (2): 190–209.

Anderson, Bridget. 2013. *Us and Them? The Dangerous Politics of Immigration Control*. New York: Oxford University Press.

Archard, David. 2006. "The Moral and Political Status of Children." *Public Policy Research* 13 (1): 6–12.

Ataiants, Janna, Chari Cohen, Amy Henderson Riley, Jamile Tellez Lieberman, Mary Clare Reidy, and Mariana Chilton. 2018. "Unaccompanied Children at the United States Border, a Human Rights Crisis That Can Be Addressed with Policy Change." *Journal of Immigrant and Minority Health* 20 (4): 1000–1010.

Baldridge, Bianca. 2014. "Relocating the Deficit: Reimagining Black Youth in Neoliberal Times." *American Educational Research Journal* 51 (3): 440–72.

Becker Herbst, Rachel, Raha Forooz Sabet, Amelia Swanson, Lauren G. Suarez, Denise S. Marques, Edward J. Ameen, and Etiony Aldarondo. 2018. "'They Were Going to Kill Me': Resilience in Unaccompanied Immigrant Minors." *Counseling Psychologist* 46 (2): 241–68.

Berman, Sheri. 1998. *The Social Democratic Moment: Ideas and Politics in the Making of Interwar Europe*. Cambridge, Mass.: Harvard University Press.

Bhabha, Jacqueline. 2014. *Child Migration and Human Rights in a Global Age*. Princeton, N.J.: Princeton University Press.

Bloemraad, Irene, Anna Korteweg, and Gökçe Yurdakul. 2008. "Citizenship and Immigration: Multiculturalism, Assimilation, and Challenges to the Nation-State." *Annual Review of Sociology* 34 (1): 153–79.

Boyden, Jo, and Jason Hart. 2007. "The Statelessness of the World's Children: Statelessness of the World's Children." *Children & Society* 21 (4): 237–48.

Britzman, Deborah. 1998. *Lost Subjects, Contested Objects: Toward a Psychoanalytic Inquiry of Learning*. Albany: State University of New York Press.

Burman, Erica. 2008. *Developments: Child, Image, Nation*. London: Routledge.

Cammarota, Julio. 2011. "Blindsided by the Avatar: White Saviors and Allies Out of Hollywood and in Education." *Review of Education, Pedagogy, and Cultural Studies* 33 (3): 242–59.

Carlson, Bonnie E., Joanne Cacciatore, and Barbara Klimek. 2012. "A Risk and Resilience Perspective on Unaccompanied Refugee Minors." *Social Work* 57 (3): 259–69.

Castles, Stephen. 1995. "How Nation-States Respond to Immigration and Ethnic Diversity." *Journal of Ethnic and Migration Studies* 21 (3): 293–308.

Cheatham, Amelia. 2021. "U.S. Detention of Child Migrants." Council on Foreign Relations, May 4. https://www.cfr.org/backgrounder/us-detention-child-migrants.

Cohen, Elizabeth. 2005. "Neither Seen nor Heard: Children's Citizenship in Contemporary Democracies." *Citizenship Study* 9 (2): 221–40.

Congressional Research Service. 2021. "Unaccompanied Alien Children: An Overview." R43599. https://sgp.fas.org/crs/homesec/R43599.pdf.

Coulter, Kiera, Samantha Sabo, Daniel Martínez, Katelyn Chisholm, Kelsey Gonzalez, Sonia Bass Zavala, Edrick Villalobos, Diego Garcia, Taylor Levy, and Jeremy Slack. 2020. "A Study and Analysis of the Treatment of Mexican Unaccompanied Minors by Customs and Border Protection." *Journal on Migration and Human Security* 8 (2): 96–110.

Crabtree, Benjamin, and William Miller, eds. 1999. *Doing Qualitative Research.* Newbury Park, Calif.: SAGE.

Crawley, Heaven. 2011. "'Asexual, Apolitical Beings': The Interpretation of Children's Identities and Experiences in the UK Asylum System." *Journal of Ethnic and Migration Studies* 37 (8): 1171–84.

Crowley, John. 1999. "The Politics of Belonging: Some Theoretical Considerations." In *The Politics of Belonging: Migrants and Minorities in Contemporary Europe,* edited by Andrew Geddes and Adrian Favell, 15–41. Lanhan, Md.: Lexington Books.

Delaney, Stephanie. 2012. *(Re)building the Future.* Geneva: Terre Des Hommes International Federation.

Diaz-Strong, Daysi Ximena. 2021. "'When Did I Stop Being a Child?' The Subjective Feeling of Adulthood of Mexican and Central American Unaccompanied 1.25 Generation Immigrants." Emerging Adulthood, August.

Doná, Giorgia, and Angela Veale. 2011. "Divergent Discourses, Children and Forced Migration." *Journal of Ethnic and Migration Studies* 37 (8): 1273–89.

Dryzek, John S. 2005. *The Politics of the Earth: Environmental Discourses.* 2nd ed. New York: Oxford University Press.

Duschinsky, Robbie. 2013. "Childhood Innocence: Essence, Education, and Performativity." *Textual Practice* 27 (5): 763–81.

Eastmond, Marita, and Henry Ascher. 2011. "In the Best Interest of the Child? The Politics of Vulnerability and Negotiations for Asylum in Sweden." *Journal of Ethnic and Migration Studies* 37 (8): 1185–1200.

Fassin, Didier. 2012. *Humanitarian Reason: A Moral History of the Present Times.* Berkeley: University of California Press.

Ferguson, Ann. 2000. *Bad Boys: Public Schools in the Making of Black Masculinity.* Ann Arbor: University of Michigan Press.

Fiddian-Qasmiyeh, Elena. 2016. "The Faith-Gender-Asylum Nexus: An Intersectionalist Analysis of Representations of the 'Refugee Crisis.'" In *The Refugee Crisis and Religion,* edited by Luca Mavelli and Erin K. Wilson, 207–22. London: Rowman and Littlefield.

Field, Corinne. 2014. *The Struggle for Equal Adulthood: Gender, Race, Age, and the Fight for Citizenship in Antebellum America.* Chapel Hill: University of North Carolina Press.

Flores Morales, Josefina, and Fanni Farago. 2021. "'Of Course We Need to Help the Undocumented Immigrants!': Twitter Discourse on the (Un)Deservingness of Undocumented Immigrants in the United States During the COVID-19 Pandemic." *Sociological Perspectives* 64 (5): 765–85.

Foucault, Michel. 1970. *The Order of Things*. New York: Vintage Books.

Frost, David, Keren Lehavot, and Ilan Meyer. 2013. "Minority Stress and Physical Health among Sexual Minority Individuals." *Journal of Behavioural Medicine* 38 (1): 1–8.

Gates, Crystal J. 1999. "Working Toward a Global Discourse on Children's Rights: The Problem of Unaccompanied Children and the International Response to Their Plight." *Indiana Journal of Global Legal Studies* 7 (1): 299–334.

Glenn, Evelyn Nakano. 2011. "Constructing Citizenship: Exclusion, Subordination, and Resistance." *American Sociological Review* 76 (1): 1–24.

Grace, Breanne Leigh, and Benjamin J. Roth. 2021. "Bureaucratic Neglect: The Paradoxical Mistreatment of Unaccompanied Migrant Children in the US Immigration System." *Journal of Ethnic and Migration Studies* 47 (15): 3455–72.

Harper, Gary, Nadine Jernewall, and Maria Cecilia Zea. 2004. "Giving Voice to Emerging Science and Theory for Lesbian, Gay, and Bisexual People of Color." *Cultural Diversity and Ethnic Minority Psychology* 10 (3): 187–99.

Hasson, Robert G., Thomas M. Crea, Ruth G. McRoy, and Ân H. Lê. 2019. "Patchwork of Promises: A Critical Analysis of Immigration Policies for Unaccompanied Undocumented Children in the United States." *Child & Family Social Work* 24 (2): 275–82.

Heidbrink, Lauren. 2017. "Assessing Parental Fitness and Care for Unaccompanied Children." *RSF: Russell Sage Foundation Journal of the Social Sciences* 3 (4): 37–52.

Hoewe, Jennifer. 2018. "Coverage of a Crisis: The Effects of International News Portrayals of Refugees and Misuse of the Term 'Immigrant.'" *American Behavioral Scientist* 62 (4): 478–92.

Hughey, Matthew W. 2012. "Show Me Your Papers! Obama's Birth and the Whiteness of Belonging." *Qualitative Sociology* 35 (2): 163–81.

Hull, Matthew S. 2012. "Documents and Bureaucracy." *Annual Review of Anthropology* 41 (1): 251–67.

Humphris, Rachel, and Nando Sigona. 2019. "The Bureaucratic Capture of Child Migrants: Effects of In/Visibility on Children on the Move." *Antipode* 51 (5): 1495–1514.

Jacob, Marie-Andrée. 2007. "Form-Made Persons: Consent Forms as Consent's Blind Spot." *PoLaR: Political and Legal Anthropology Review* 30 (2): 249–68.

Jani, Jayshree S. 2017. "Reunification Is Not Enough: Assessing the Needs of Unaccompanied Migrant Youth." *Families in Society: The Journal of Contemporary Social Services* 98 (2): 127–36.

Kafka, Ben. 2009. "Paperwork: The State of the Discipline." *Book History* 12 (1): 340–53.

Kennedy, Elizabeth. 2014. *No Childhood Here: Why Central American Children Are Fleeing Their Homes*. Washington, D.C.: American Immigration Council.

Kyriakides, Christopher. 2017. "Words Don't Come Easy: Al Jazeera's Migrant–Refugee Distinction and the European Culture of (Mis)Trust." *Current Sociology* 65 (7): 933–52.

Leubsdorf, John. 1992. "Pluralizing the Client-Lawyer Relationship." *Cornell Law Review* 77 (3): 825–26.

Lind, Jacob. 2019. "Governing Vulnerabilised Migrant Childhoods Through Children's Rights." *Childhood* 26 (3): 337–51.

Lorenzen, Matthew. 2017. "The Mixed Motives of Unaccompanied Child Migrants from Central America's Northern Triangle." *Journal on Migration and Human Security* 5 (4): 744–67.

Matias, Cheryl, and Michalinos Zembylas. 2014. "'When Saying You Care Is Not Really Caring': Emotions of Disgust, Whiteness Ideology, and Teacher Education." *Critical Studies in Education* 55 (3): 319–37.

NeMoyer, Amanda, Trinidad Rodriguez, and Kiara Alvarez. 2019. "Psychological Practice with Unaccompanied Immigrant Minors: Clinical and Legal Considerations." *Translational Issues in Psychological Science* 5 (1): 4–16.

Office of Refugee Resettlement (ORR). 2014. "Know your Rights Handout." July 8. https://www.acf.hhs.gov/sites/default/files/documents/orr/lrg_3_kyr_handout_e07_08_14.pdf.

Office of Refugee Resettlement (ORR). n.d. "Notice for Special Immigrant Juveniles." Accessed April 1, 2024. https://www.acf.hhs.gov/sites/default/files/documents/orr/notice_for_special_immigrant_juveniles.pdf.

Office of Refugee Resettlement (ORR). n.d. "Notice of Proposed Settlement and Hearing in Class for Special Immigrant Juveniles." Accessed April 1, 2024. https://www.acf.hhs.gov/sites/default/files/documents/orr/notice_of_proposed_settlement_and_hearing_in_class_action_for_special.pdf.

Office of Refugee Resettlement (ORR). n.d. "Notice to Juvenile Aliens in Federal Facilities Funded by DHS or HHS by Reason of Their Immigration Status." Accessed April 1, 2024. https://www.acf.hhs.gov/sites/default/files/documents/orr/notice_to_juvenile_aliens_c_4_english.pdf.

Orgad, Shani. 2012. *Media Representation and the Global Imagination*. Global Media and Communication. Cambridge, UK: Polity.

Pugh, Allison J. 2009. *Longing and Belonging Parents, Children, and Consumer Culture*. Berkeley: University of California Press.

Pupavac, Vanessa. 2001. "Misanthropy Without Borders: The International Children's Rights Regime." *Disasters* 25 (2): 95–112.

Riles, Annelise. 2006. *Documents: Artifacts of Modern Knowledge*. Ann Arbor: University of Michigan Press.

Roberts, Dorothy. 1997. *Killing the Black Body: Race, Reproduction, and the Meaning of Liberty*. New York: Vintage.

Rodrigue, John C. 2001. *Reconstruction in the Cane Fields: From Slavery to Free Labor in Louisiana's Sugar Parishes, 1862–1880*. Baton Rouge: Louisiana State University Press.

Rosario, Margaret, Eric W. Schrimshaw, and Joyce Hunter. 2004. "Ethnic/Racial Differences in the Coming-Out Process of Lesbian, Gay, and Bisexual Youths: A

Comparison of Sexual Identity Development over Time." *Cultural Diversity and Ethnic Minority Psychology* 10 (3): 215–28.

Rosario, Margaret, Eric W. Schrimshaw, and Joyce Hunter. 2011. "Different Patterns of Sexual Identity Development over Time: Implications for the Psychological Adjustment of Lesbian, Gay, and Bisexual Youths." *Journal of Sex Research* 48 (1): 3–15.

Rosen, Rachel, and Sarah Crafter. 2018. "Media Representations of Separated Child Migrants." *Migration and Society* 1 (1): 66–81.

Rubin, Jennifer, and Sara McClelland. 2015. "'Even Though It's a Small Checkbox, It's a Big Deal': Stresses and Strains of Managing Sexual Identity(s) on Facebook." *Culture, Health & Sexuality* 17 (4): 512–26.

Ruehs, Emily M. 2018. *Front Door, Backdoor, No Door? An Exploration of Formal and Informal Means for Recruiting Unaccompanied Immigrant Youth for Research.* London: SAGE.

Schmidt, Susan. 2017. "'They Need to Give Us a Voice': Lessons from Listening to Unaccompanied Central American and Mexican Children on Helping Children like Themselves." *Journal on Migration and Human Security* 5 (1): 57–81.

Smith, Dorothy E. 1974. "The Social Construction of Documentary Reality." *Sociological Inquiry* 44 (4): 257–68.

Sondel, Beth, Kerry Kretchmar, and Alyssa Hadley Dunn. 2019. "'Who Do These People Want Teaching Their Children?' White Saviorism, Colorblind Racism, and Anti-Blackness in 'No Excuses' Charter Schools." *Urban Education* 57 (9): 1621–50.

Sotomayor-Peterson, Marcela, and Martha Montiel-Carbajal. 2014. "Psychological and Family Well-Being of Unaccompanied Mexican Child Migrants *Sent Back* from the U.S. Border Region of Sonora-Arizona." *Hispanic Journal of Behavioral Sciences* 36 (2): 111–23.

Stacey, Judith. 1998. *In the Name of the Family: Rethinking Family Values in the Postmodern Age.* Boston: Beacon Press.

Terrio, Susan J. 2015. *Whose Child Am I? Unaccompanied, Undocumented Children in U.S. Immigration Custody.* Oakland: University of California Press.

Thomas, Samantha, and Sarah Byford. 2003. "Research with Unaccompanied Children Seeking Asylum." *BMJ* 327 (7428): 1400–1402.

UN High Commissioner for Refugees. 2008. "Best Interests Determination Children—Protection and Care Information Sheet." https://www.refworld.org/docid/49103ece2.html.

UN High Commissioner for Refugees. 2012. "Guidelines on the Applicable Criteria and Standards Relating to the Detention of Asylum-Seekers and Alternatives to Detention." https://www.refworld.org/docid/503489533b8.html.

UN High Commissioner for Refugees. 2014. "Children on the Run: Unaccompanied Children Leaving Central America and Mexico and the Need for International Protection." https://www.refworld.org/docid/532180c24.html.

United Nations Office on Drugs and Crime. 2018. "From Victim to Survivor: A Second Chance at Life." https://www.unodc.org/documents/human-trafficking/Publication/UNVTF_Brochure_Achievements_Web.pdf.

U.S. Citizenship and Immigration Services. n.d. "Bringing Children, Sons and Daughters to Live in the United States as Permanent Residents." Accessed March 5, 2024. https://www.uscis.gov/family/bring-children-to-live-in-the-US.

U.S. Immigration and Customs Enforcement et al. 2019. "Apprehension, Processing, Care, and Custody of Alien Minors and Unaccompanied Alien Children." Federal Register 84 FR 44392. https://www.federalregister.gov/documents/2019/08/23/2019-17927/apprehension-processing-care-and-custody-of-alien-minors-and-unaccompanied-alien-children.

U.S. Government Accountability Office. 2015. "Unaccompanied Alien Children: Actions Needed to Ensure Children Receive Required Care in DHS Custody." Report to Congressional Committees, July. https://www.gao.gov/assets/gao-15-521.pdf.

Vella, Kyle. 2016. "Power, Paternalism and Children on the Move." *Journal of International Humanitarian Action* 1 (3): 1–12.

White, Allen, Caitríona Ní Laoire, Naomi Tyrrell, and Fina Carpena-Méndez. 2011. "Children's Roles in Transnational Migration." *Journal of Ethnic and Migration Studies* 37 (8): 1159–70.

Yuval-Davis, Nira. 2006. "Belonging and the Politics of Belonging." *Patterns of Prejudice* 40 (3): 197–214.

CHAPTER THREE

Centering Children's Experiences

Lessons for Advocates

MARISA CHUMIL AND JENNIFER NAGDA

We have written before, as have many others, about the absurd system that exists to evaluate the protection needs and immigration eligibility of migrant children in the United States (Bhabha and Schmidt 2006; Thronson 2010; Frankel 2011; Nagda and Woltjen 2015). Under the Homeland Security Act of 2002, children who are under the age of eighteen, lack lawful presence in the United States, and are not with a parent or legal guardian at the time immigration authorities apprehend them are designated as "unaccompanied" and afforded certain procedures not available to other children. Notably, unaccompanied children from Mexico are generally denied this protection.[1] The "unaccompanied" designation applies to both children arriving at our borders and children living within the United States who immigration authorities apprehend. Within seventy-two hours of apprehending an unaccompanied child, the government must transfer them from the Department of Homeland Security (DHS) to the Department of Health and Human Services (HHS) Office of Refugee Resettlement (ORR) (Homeland Security Act § 1232). After a child is transferred to ORR, that agency makes decisions about the child's placement, including release to a parent or caregiver, that are in the child's best interests (Homeland Security Act § 1232). This is the single statutory requirement: that federal officials with authority over immigrant children make decisions that are in each child's best interests.[2]

However, the DHS officials who initially apprehend and designate the child as unaccompanied *also* have the ability to charge the child with being "inadmissible to" or "removable from" the United States (terms set forth in the Immigration and Nationality Act). Those charges trigger what are known as "removal proceedings"—adversarial proceedings in an immigration court in which a judge determines whether the child may remain in the United States, may return to their home country without penalty, or will be ordered removed, which results in a prohibition against returning to the United States for years. Perhaps not surprisingly, DHS officials charge and place in removal proceedings nearly every unaccompanied child, which requires the child's appearance in immigration court.

Beginning in 2004, staff and volunteers at the Young Center for Immigrant Children's Rights have accompanied and advocated for unaccompanied children who must navigate the dual challenges of federal custody and immigration removal cases where their futures are determined.[3] Child Advocates serve as trusted allies for children while they are in removal proceedings. They advocate for children's best interests and fight for the creation of a dedicated children's immigrant justice system that ensures the safety and well-being of every child.[4]

Young Center Child Advocates are appointed to the most vulnerable unaccompanied children in federal custody. These include children and youth whom the government forcibly separates from their parents at the border, as well as children who have suspected or diagnosed mental or physical disabilities, are pregnant or parenting, survived human trafficking or other crimes, are under the age of twelve, face involuntary return to their country of origin, are unable to make independent decisions, or have witnessed or experienced violence and other forms of trauma. In addition to best interests advocacy grounded in a child's rights paradigm, Young Center Child Advocates accompany children through the immigration process, including their time in custody and their legal cases.

The Young Center has grown from a single Child Advocate program in Chicago to ten locations across the country, with more than 120 staff in three different programs. A significant milestone for our work occurred in 2008 when Congress passed the Trafficking Victims Protection Reauthorization Act (TVPRA), authorizing HHS to appoint independent Child Advocates (§1232). The TVPRA codified the independence of the Child Advocate role. As we advocate for the children's best interests, we remain independent from those agencies responsible for decisions about children's custody and legal cases as well as from other organizations and agencies that work with unaccompanied children. Although most federal agencies have no statutory obligation to act in the best interests of unaccompanied children and youth in their decision-making, the TVPRA demonstrates Congress's intention for federal agencies to consider children's best interests before making decisions that impact their lives.

We recognize that the term *best interests* carries increasingly negative connotations from its use in family courts, where "best interests" has been a reason to move children, primarily Black children and other children of color, from their families, with disastrous consequences (Roberts 2022). As Child Advocates for unaccompanied immigrant children thrown into government custody and legal proceedings where the children must fend for themselves, the Young Center has grounded its best interests advocacy in children's rights as set forth in the Convention on the Rights of the Child. Young Center Child Advocates identify each child's best interests by considering the child's wishes and the child's safety as well as the child's rights to be with family, to be free from detention, to develop, and to express their full identity. In a system that is grounded in an idea of "othering" child immigrants and their families, as set forth so clearly in "Not 'Our' Children" (Diaz, Walts, and Jacobs, this volume), rights-based best interests advocacy can be a mechanism to both center the individuality and humanity of each child and interrupt state action that would put the child directly in harm's way.

Children and youth face a complex process to leave government custody and seek permanent protection. They may experience multiple transfers, linguistic and cultural isolation, limited contact with family, and repeat court appearances in both state and federal systems without guarantee of an attorney or Child Advocate. In this chapter, we highlight children's experiences migrating not just across borders but across agencies, through government custody, and into families, communities, or foster placements and group homes while they await news of whether they will be able to remain permanently in the United States, as observed by the Child Advocates who accompany and advocate alongside them. We conclude by offering proposals for meaningful change grounded in children's lived experiences rather than political expediency.

Children Pursuing Safety and Seeking Family

Children have taught us powerful lessons as they navigate government custody and immigration court, and later integrate into families and communities. They take these journeys without any guarantee of permanency. In this section, we reflect on four key lessons and incorporate the reflections of Child Advocates who have accompanied children in their journeys, listened to their stories, kept their confidences, and fought for their safety.[5]

Family Matters
Family and community are critical for children's safety and well-being. A defining feature of current laws protecting unaccompanied children is their focus on children who are not in the custody of a parent or legal guardian when they encounter immigration officials. This definition reflected a concern for children—primarily children from Central America—traveling alone, with other groups of children and youth, or with smugglers to reach the United States in the late 1990s and early 2000s (UNHCR 2014). It also reflects the constitutionally protected rights of parents to the care and custody of their children (*Troxel v. Granville* 2000). However, the definition fails to account for the relationships that children foster with other family members, including in communities where it is not necessary or possible to secure formal declarations of legal guardianship. As a result, when children migrate with these adults—older siblings, grandparents, godparents, aunts, or uncles—immigration authorities separate them at the border. DHS designates the children as unaccompanied—supposedly for their protection—and transfers them to ORR while processing the adult family members in cases that are entirely separate from the children and where the result is often the adult family member's swift deportation.

Over the years, Child Advocates have been appointed to countless children who immigration officials unexpectedly and traumatically separated from the grown-ups they love and trust. We have been appointed to younger children raised by older siblings after the death of a parent, who came to the border together fleeing gang violence only to be torn apart. In those cases, siblings who were just toddlers or of middle school age were designated "unaccompanied" and transferred to ORR custody while their nineteen- and twenty-year-old siblings, who acted as the younger children's parental figures, were sent to immigration jails to face months of detention and a daily risk of deportation. We have been appointed to elementary-aged children taken from grandparents who migrated together from communities where seeking formal, legal guardianship is neither common practice nor accessible. Immigration officials also tear apart these families arriving together at the U.S. border despite the harm this will cause both children and adults. In some cases, we are able to facilitate the reunification of children with grandparents or older siblings, but in many other cases, our government deports the adult relatives to their home country before Child Advocates are even appointed to the children's cases.

Through years of being appointed to separated children, our Child Advocates have observed the effects of separation trauma—before, during, and after the Donald Trump administration's family separation policy. During "zero tolerance," immigration authorities did not provide parents or caregivers with an opportunity to say goodbye to their children—officials separated them without warning or placed them in separate rooms. One Child Advocate recalled how a father kept telling his child to "be strong" as immigration officials pulled the father away from his child. Child Advocates observed how children manifested separation trauma after they arrived in ORR custody. Some children experienced emotional dysregulation or regressed in eating, sleeping, or toileting habits. Other children reacted in unexpected ways or demonstrated alarming behaviors, such as trauma ticks or trembles (Young Center Roundtables 2023).

Unaccompanied children—whether traveling truly alone or separated from trusted relatives at the border—receive certain legal protections available only to children who are officially designated as unaccompanied. These protections include the chance to seek asylum first before an asylum officer in an interview, before having to present that claim in adversarial immigration court. However, for children separated from trusted relatives, the circumstances of the separation cause a new trauma that can prevent effective collaboration with an attorney in seeking asylum, and potential loss of facts and information necessary to make a successful legal claim. In other words, the separation that renders a child unaccompanied can undermine the child's ability to benefit from the protections afforded by their unaccompanied status. This routine separation of children from trusted adults does not just undermine the purpose of a law intended to protect children, but as Sarah J. Diaz, Katherine Kaufka Walts, and Lisa Jacobs suggest in this volume, it reflects state-sanctioned violence against migrant children and their families. We believe—as outlined later in this chapter—that for many children, these traumatizing separations from trusted family members can be avoided while ensuring children do not lose access to the benefits that attach to their legal status as "unaccompanied."

Government Custody Is Not Benign

For children who do not arrive with, or cannot remain with, family when they reach our border, government custody should be exceptionally brief—just long enough to ensure safe release to family while the children's legal cases wind their way through the immigration system. For those children who do not have family with whom they can live, government custody should be equally brief, needed only to ensure their safe transfer to a family- or home-based setting where they can live in a community while their cases wind their way through the immigration system. However, this is not the system most children encounter. We routinely work with children who have spent weeks, months, or even years in government custody while the government scrutinizes their family or other sponsors, or where children who have no family or community in the United States wait indefinitely to be accepted into one of a small number of foster placements or group homes.

Government custody—detention, in most cases—is not benign. If children do not feel safe in their environment, they can experience it as traumatic. How children experience their environment and interpret events may be linked to cultural beliefs and the availability of protective factors, such as social supports. Many trauma survivors perceive a neutral environment as threatening or psychologically distressing.

For example, some children have a plan when they travel to the United States to reunify with family. Detention interrupts that child's journey. Children may not land where they thought they would. Although detention facilities may aim to be child-friendly, children are acutely aware that the buildings are on lockdown and their movement is restricted. As one Child Advocate noted, no amount of artwork or decorations can address the trauma that detained children experience (Young Center Roundtables 2023). Moreover, when children do not have options to make even simple choices in their daily lives, they may feel disempowered. Child Advocates center weekly visits on children's wishes and encourage the child's agency and choice to the extent possible.

Detained children also experience a loss of identity or role within a family system, especially those who may have taken on responsibilities to care for younger siblings or worked to support family members. Some children experience ambiguous grief due to the separation from their cultural traditions. Children also lose their connection to language, especially Indigenous-language speakers who are placed in a detention facility where staff only speak English and Spanish. Child Advocates must frequently advocate for children's consistent access to culturally specific services and services in the language they prefer to speak.

Children who came here with a plan to live with a family member or trusted adult have taught us that the process to reunify with family is fraught with anxiety and uncertainty. In the previous chapter, "Kids, Paperwork, and Cages," Aireen Grace Andal explores the extent to which bureaucratic paperwork can render these processes unnavigable. Parents and other family members submit detailed applications to sponsor a child's release to their care, yet only recently did the government authorize the staff hired to oversee this process to actually support family members—including those whose location, access to the internet, or literacy level create barriers—in the process of completing and submitting the forms (U.S. Department of Health and Human Services 2023). In many cases, Child Advocates have observed that when government-contracted workers misunderstand a family's cultural practices and traditions, the child's reunification is delayed (Young Center Roundtables 2023). In other cases, Child Advocates have seen family members prove a close, trusted relationship with a child only to be told the reunification should be delayed because the government does not believe the family member sufficiently understands or is sufficiently prepared to address the child's mental health, physical disability, or other unique needs (Young Center Roundtables 2023). In other words, government officials assume that they, and not the child's family, are better suited to care for and make decisions about the child. Child Advocates consistently advocate for timely and safe reunification as each day in custody is another day separated from the child's family or loved ones. Children and families never recover that lost time, and limited contact with a child's family or caregiver causes undue distress.

Children are more than their trauma stories. They are individuals with hopes and dreams. Yet rather than allowing children to explore their strengths, interests, and unique coping mechanisms, services in custody often focus on the perceived deficits or misinterpreted behaviors of a child. Moreover, the need to "keep order" in congregate care facilities often results in a system that overmedicates children as a band-aid for detention fatigue or penalizes children's trauma-based responses to that environment rather than teaching children coping skills or conflict resolution (Young Center Roundtables 2023). A 2022 report by the Young Center and the National Immigrant Justice Center, "Punishing Trauma: Incident Reporting and Immigrant Children in Government Custody," analyzed in detail the government's system to track children's behavior and report on so-called infractions while they are in custody. As one author noted in a statement announcing the report,

> The federal government's incident reporting system . . . police[s] children's words and actions, including trivial rule infractions, developmentally appropriate behavior, and manifestations of their trauma, grief, or frustration. Some children—particularly those who endure the longest periods in government custody—are caught in a vicious cycle, where they may experience behavioral challenges due to detention fatigue only to receive an [incident report] that is later used to prolong their stay in ORR custody. (Jane Liu, quoted in Young Center for Immigrant Children's Rights 2022b)

The report concluded that the incident reporting system for children in custody results in transfers to more restrictive settings, prolonged stays in custody, and delayed family reunification or delayed transfer to federally funded foster care (Young Center for Immigrant Children's Rights and National Immigrant Justice Center 2022).

Detention fatigue is real and visceral. It may set in after weeks in government custody and certainly takes over after months in detention. Although the average length of federal custody for unaccompanied children has decreased significantly over the past fifteen years, the Young Center is often appointed to cases where children spend many months and even years in custody. Child Advocates recognize that detention fatigue may present as hopelessness, guarded emotions, sleep disruption, desperation, self-isolation, or incessant crying (Young Center Roundtables 2023). In addition, children may demonstrate symptoms of detention fatigue through observable behaviors such as outbursts, expressions of anger, or self-harm. Detention fatigue also impacts a child's sense of agency and their ability to navigate their daily environment. As a result, we witness children who feel they have no choice but to return to unsafe conditions in their home country—the very same conditions from which they fled when they migrated. The government should be responsible for identifying the cause of behavior and addressing, as appropriate, the underlying cause. Yet in congregate care settings with large numbers of children, staff may misinterpret behaviors or penalize children rather than provide appropriate support.

Transfers across placements in the detention system also negatively impact children. Transfers force children to start all over again in their relationships with staff, other children, and even attorneys. Transfers push children into yet another unfamiliar environment where they must build new relationships, learn unknown terms of engagement, and attempt to establish a sense of safety and comfort—and in many cases, they may not be informed of the reasons for their transfer in the first place. Child Advocates may remain the only professional consistent in a child's lengthy placement in custody.

Careful transition planning for reunification with family alleviates potential pressure points as children transition into the community. But in our experience, transition planning rarely occurs and even less rarely includes children in the process. Child Advocates fight for children to have a seat at the table and to participate in developing a transition plan. For example, we ask children: What would they like to see as part of a successful transition to reunify with family in the community? What activities can they do, or seek assistance to do, to feel supported during the reunification process? This simple step facilitates children's agency during what can feel like an uncontrollable experience as they anticipate reconnecting with caregivers they may not have seen in years.

Bigger Is Not Better

By federal law, ORR must place children in the least restrictive setting in their best interests (Trafficking Victims Protection Reauthorization Act §1232). ORR operates a wide variety of placements for children, including federally funded foster homes, group homes, shelters, residential treatment centers, and so-called staff-secure and secure facilities. Foster homes are the least restrictive setting, whereas staff-secure and secure facilities are the most restrictive settings, with significantly greater limitations on children's movement and contact with others. For secure settings, the federal government has historically contracted for beds in state juvenile jails, yet no judge makes or reviews the decision to place immigrant children in these jails, where children have spent weeks, often months, and sometimes years.

For the vast majority of children, ORR has relied on large, congregate care settings. Child Advocates, who visit children in a variety of both licensed and unlicensed facilities, struggle with the disconcerting environment of congregate care facilities where dozens or even hundreds of children reside. A Child

Advocate described how rooms in one large facility did not have ceilings or walls—the facility never turned off the lights and therefore prevented children's ability to sleep in complete darkness—and how noise inside and outside the facility was audible, rendering "private" meeting rooms futile (Young Center Roundtables 2023). While some large facilities are intolerably loud, others are too quiet. One of the facilities Child Advocates visited was a center for nearly one hundred youth—mostly teenagers. Despite these numbers, a Child Advocate observed that "you could hear a pin drop" as you entered the facility. Despite a caring staff, "keeping order" in a building of nearly one hundred children required significant and restrictive rules. Although the facility included classrooms and a cafeteria, it offered little outdoor space and required constant order and discipline, applied in the same way to all children. As another Child Advocate recalled, a child's release from government custody meant they could spend more than six minutes in a shower, a simple yet meaningful choice point in a child's daily life that signifies they are safe (Young Center Roundtables 2023).

In recent years, the U.S. government's reliance on massive, congregate care settings has become even more pronounced. ORR has used a provision in the law that allows it to operate unlicensed facilities when the number of unaccompanied children reaches "emergency" levels (*Flores v. Reno* 1997). The government typically opens these emergency facilities on federal land, such as military bases near the border (Burnett 2019; Villagran 2022). Because they are on federal land, state child welfare agencies do not issue licenses to ensure the facilities' compliance with standards for children removed from families and placed into government custody (U.S. Department of Health and Human Services 2022). Often, the government holds more than one thousand children in these unlicensed, emergency facilities—many in tents or modified trailers. With each iteration of these facilities, the government emphasizes how much better these locations are than the holding cells operated by immigration enforcement officers along the border. But those conditions—which are inappropriate for both children *and* adults—should not be the baseline for comparison.

Release and Reunification Should Activate, Not End, Services
Children have taught us that reunification is just the beginning of the next phase of their journey. Once released, children face prolonged exposure to stress, such as fears of deportation; a lack of community and social sup-

ports; disrupted attachments with family or caregivers; and barriers to accessing educational and medical services. Children must also navigate complex family dynamics. Children often reunite with parents or other caregivers they have not seen in years. They have to reconnect with familiar faces in unfamiliar terrain and rebuild relationships strained over years of separation. In some cases, the challenges they face are overwhelming and potentially paralyzing. Children have taught us that postmigration trauma exacerbates the trauma they experienced before entering into custody. Meanwhile, they are constantly admonished of the importance of attending immigration court, even though many if not most do not have an attorney to represent them.

Children have taught us that navigating their environment after release from government custody can feel like pushing a boulder up a mountain or taking one small step forward, only to have great weights push them back down. Children feel they cannot make meaningful progress when they face insurmountable hurdles to receive services, including public education, preventative health care, and appropriate mental health care.

For example, children with complex needs, either for medical or mental health reasons, encounter significant barriers to accessing medication or prescription renewals. Without health insurance or a primary care physician, children may not be able to take necessary medication or may not be able to appropriately wean off medications prescribed while they were in custody. Child Advocates consistently advocate for continuity of medical care that respects the child's wishes and supports the family's access to resources. One Child Advocate recounted how months of sustained best-interests advocacy ensured a child would have access to medical equipment immediately upon release (Young Center Roundtables 2023). Yet these services should not require such intensive advocacy, particularly when most children do not yet have access to Child Advocates or immigration counsel.

Child Advocates zealously advocate for children to enroll in and attend free public schools, a right that all children, regardless of immigration status, have and deserve. Yet enrolling children in school after a child's release is not always that simple. Caregivers who have not yet obtained legal guardianship may not be able to produce identity documents requested for enrollment. Children may not have a copy of the vaccinations and medical exam they received while in government custody to enroll in school. Moreover, as Andal suggests in her chapter in this volume, the dehumanizing structure and language of these forms may adversely impact children and families when they rely on these forms to access critical services. Children may face similar challenges accessing school records from their home countries, where documentation systems operate under different, and culturally nuanced, standards.

Children's need for family or community is paramount. Providing critical services to children *only* while they are in custody and not upon release undermines the safety that family or communities should be able to provide. As we argue in the rest of this chapter, children's release from custody should signal the beginning of a period of intensive services designed to facilitate their integration into families, long-term foster placements, schools, and communities.

Child-Centered Proposals for Change

The work of Child Advocates incorporates both advocacy and accompaniment. We hold weekly visits with children to build relationships of trust, engage in child-centered activities based on their interests, and learn their wishes over time. We gather information from stakeholders working with the children and the children's families or caregivers, whether they reside in the United States or their home country. We analyze this information as it relates to the child's rights to self-determination, safety, freedom from detention, family integrity, healthy development, and identity expression. We uplift children's voices, wishes, and safety as we advocate for decision-makers to consider the best interests in all decisions impacting children's custody and legal cases. This focus on children's best interests is one strategy to mitigate against what Diaz, Walts, and Jacobs describe in this volume as forms of state-sanctioned violence that permeate U.S. immigration law. In addition, Child Advocates accompany children and youth as they receive and make sense of information, contemplate upcoming decisions, attend court hearings, and reconnect with family and community members. We work in collaboration with, but also advocate with, other service providers and stakeholders, all of whom have a collective responsibility to respond to arriving migrant children. Grounded in this experience, we set forth the following child-centered proposals for change.

Keep Families Together

To ensure children's rights to health, safety, and family unity are protected, we recommend expediting the release of children who arrive with nonparent family members directly from the border, using the expertise of ORR staff to evaluate family relationships in real time. This would avoid a traumatic separation of the child from their trusted caregiver and reduce the number of children waiting for reunification in traditional ORR placements.

Right now, ORR staff only see these children after their separation from family members—and by that time, the U.S. government might already have removed the adult family member from the country. This puts ORR in the position of having to evaluate other adults who were not recent caregivers for the child, or, alternatively, to attempt to evaluate a relationship with a trusted caregiver who brought the child to the border but who is now in immigration detention. In a child-centered system, ORR would evaluate the child and adult together. If the agency—which has a child welfare rather than law enforcement mandate—determines that the relationship is legitimate and that the trusted caregiver does not pose a risk to the child, the government would release the child into the family member's custody directly from the border. Upon release, the child would retain the legal designation of "unaccompanied," which preserves the legal protections for children who arrive without a legal guardian. This would avert some family separations, minimize health risks to both children and adults, preserve ORR's resources, and ensure children remain with their adult caregivers, avoiding the weeks or months needed to reunify them under the current process.

This can be done. Outside of the immigration context, child welfare experts evaluate the suitability of "kinship" care providers in similarly brief timeframes (Beltran and Redlich Epstein 2013). Across the country, child protection agencies have developed a number of strategies to find safe placements for children quickly, to minimize children's time in government custody. Many states have a process for placing children with relatives or even fictive kin in forty-eight hours (Casey Family Programs 2018). Federal law and other HHS policies increasingly prioritize keeping children with trusted family members as research shows that "removing children from their families is disruptive and traumatic and can have long-lasting, negative effects" (Casey Family Programs 2018). In cases where children arrive with a family caregiver and where the government can quickly verify their relationship, the government can prevent the additional trauma of an unexpected family separation. Over time, adapting larger border facilities into reception centers for evaluating the most vulnerable migrants—including unaccompanied children—would create an organized setting for border authorities to complete their required tasks while qualified ORR experts provide child-appropriate and trauma-informed care for immigrant children, consistent with international standards. In cases where children arrive with a family caregiver and the government can quickly verify their relationship, the government can prevent the additional trauma of separating immigrant children from family members. Instituting a new system in which ORR staff trained in child welfare best practices are able to evaluate family relationships at the point of arrival would kickstart the reunification process at the earliest stage.

But right now, before making these modifications, the federal government can adapt border facilities to provide space for ORR staff to work with families—allowing conversations with children and family members apart from border officials and using HHS systems to review and store information. Ultimately, this model will work best in integrated, welcoming reception centers staffed not just with federal agencies but with service providers that have a mandate to both welcome and support arriving children, families, and adults.

Prioritize Family Contact and Expedite Reunification
Separation from family creates additional trauma for children in congregate care settings. A child's parent, caregiver, or other trusted adult is the person who can provide unconditional love and a sense of emotional and physical security. Children often do not understand why they were separated, where their parents are during the separation, or that their parents or caregivers often had no choice in this separation. Children may wrongfully blame themselves or accuse the parent of abandoning them. Children have told us that they did not know where their mother was, despite arriving at the border together, or why their father "left" them, though we knew that immigration authorities chose to separate the family. Child Advocates work—often through unnecessary barriers created by government agencies that either do not track or do not share information—to identify the adult family member's location, and then advocate for regular and meaningful contact. Often,

immigration officials are unwilling to provide video contact or place arbitrary and unnecessary limits on the number of minutes children and family members can speak.

Children who wish to communicate with family members living within the United States or in their home country face similar barriers to regular communication. As our colleagues noted in a 2022 report addressing policies that limited children's contact with family:

> ORR requires its providers to afford children the opportunity to make a minimum of two telephone calls per week, 10 minutes each, to family members and/or sponsors, in a private setting. Although ORR policy states that this limit is a "minimum," many ORR providers use this guidance as a ceiling, and limit children to no more than two 10-minute telephone calls per week. Some providers allow children to make as many calls as they wish but still limit children to a total of twenty minutes of telephone calls per week. In the Young Center's experience, only a small number of providers serving a small number of children will allow more than two calls or over 20 minutes of calls each week. Still, the amounts vary, and in some instances, children in the same facility are permitted different amounts of phone contact. (Young Center for Immigrant Children's Rights 2022a)

Child Advocates routinely observe how limits on a child's ability to reach out to a trusted adult causes incredible frustration and loneliness. Our recommendations for change in this area are clear: to provide children with unlimited telephone and video calls to any adult the agency has approved as a contact for the child, at the times the children choose, and with the privacy they need. Of course, establishing a broader network of brief respite shelters around the country where children could meet in person with family while awaiting reunification would be the most child-centered way to facilitate meaningful, regular family contact for children.

When children initiate and maintain contact with their families and caregivers, we recommend that children's wishes guide that engagement. Our staff have advocated against a harmful practice whereby children are forced to communicate certain aspects of their story as a condition of potential reunification, including abuse, illness, pregnancy, sexual orientation, and gender identity. When children are not ready or do not consent to disclose such personal details, Child Advocates have observed how children felt shame and abandonment, avoided what used to be welcomed communication with their family, experienced a diminished ability to trust, and encountered fabricated and unnecessary tension in their relationships with their caregivers (Young Center Roundtables 2023).

Furthermore, we recommend that the government implement culturally responsive processes and use strength-based approaches throughout the reunification process, which at the very least would mean careful review and restructuring of the way in which the government requests and captures information about children, as discussed in Andal's chapter. Many prospective caregivers work to provide for their family and may not have a flexible work environment to answer calls during typical business hours. One Child Advocate observed how government-contracted workers viewed a working parent's limited availability as a negative factor that stalled reunification rather than a strength reflecting their commitment to supporting the family financially (Young Center Roundtables 2023). In addition, a lack of cultural understanding of family norms may result in negative sponsorship assessments or erase aspects of a child's identity, especially when they do not have access to an interpreter.

Establishing meaningful therapeutic services for children in custody is another necessary change, particularly when the government insufficiently restricts how immigration officials use the information children disclose to counselors and therapists while in custody. Children need and deserve regular access to therapeutic services that are culturally and linguistically appropriate and trauma informed. This includes providing increased and consistent language access through in-person interpreters trained in ethical interpretation practices and establishing a network of preapproved community-based professionals trained in child development and qualified to provide mental health services.

Finally, no child should be placed in juvenile jails. We do not think any child belongs in a jail and recognize that progressive advocates for children have found ways to safely incorporate children who pose a risk to themselves or others into settings that are far less restrictive. Cities and counties across the United States are moving to "deinstitutionalize" children thrown into juvenile jails in an effort to limit harm (Office of Juvenile Justice and Delinquency Prevention 2014; McCarthy, Schiraldi, and Shark 2016). Despite this progress, through early 2023, ORR continued to rely on these jails as placements for immigrant children. In our experience, immigrant children sent to these facilities fall into two groups. The first are children with unaddressed trauma who were inappropriately "stepped up" to jails because staff in less restrictive settings did not have the training to support and redirect behavior—in some cases, behavior arising from the child's prolonged time in custody. The other group is composed of children whose alleged history before arriving in custody—allegations of gang affiliation or perceived bad acts—lead agency officials to place them in jails based on a fear of what might happen in the future. But these children do not have any access to a judicial process prior to losing their liberty. ORR must follow best practices for finding less restrictive placements for children, including those who do pose a risk to their own safety or that of others. At the same time, ORR must support children whose behavior is developmentally appropriate or reflects unaddressed trauma rather than designate them as dangerous.

Ensure Small Placements Are the New Norm

In addition to advocating for family reunification, Child Advocates work to minimize the impact detention has on children's safety, agency, and loss of freedom, development, and identity. As one Child Advocate recounted, "children are not allowed to touch doorknobs" in a certain facility (Young Center Roundtables 2023). Through a trauma-informed lens, Child Advocates recognize that powerlessness is a trauma trigger. When children are not afforded the option to make choices in their daily lives or about the future of their custody and legal cases, they face retraumatization. Child Advocates consistently center advocacy on children's wishes. They also advocate for children to have access to interpreters for their best language, or the language they prefer to speak for all interactions—not just in court but with the facility staff with whom they interact every day. This can be particularly difficult in facilities staffed with workers who speak Spanish but not Indigenous or less common languages. Children's experiences in large, emergency facilities—as recently as 2021 and 2022—confirm that children who do not speak Spanish are at even greater risk of isolation, vulnerability, and a lack of individualized service. This system requires fundamental reform, given that children spend prolonged time in congregate care and the government records their every action in a file that can be used against them in the separate legal proceeding addressing their right to remain permanently in the United States.

Children belong with families—but when they cannot be, they belong in family-like settings. The domestic U.S. child welfare system has moved away from placing children in large, congregate care facilities. In a 2015 survey of states' use of congregate care, the number of children in group homes or childcare institutions decreased by 37 percent from 2004 to 2013 (U.S. Department of Health and Human Services 2015). The Family First Prevention Services Act, passed in 2018, affirmed that family is the best setting for children. The statute incentivizes programs that provide services to keep children, including those at risk of abuse or neglect, with their families, and does not allow states to use federal funds for facilities that house more than twenty-five children. The law reflects years of social science research showing that children's health deteriorates in large facilities, while children in families thrive (Dozier et al. 2014).

Large facilities are inherently harmful to children. When facilities have large numbers of children, they restrict and closely regulate children's activities and movements to maintain order (Dozier et al. 2014). These strict rules deny children meaningful contact with an individual, loving caregiver who can adapt to the autonomy and boundaries that each child needs (Williamson and Greenberg 2010).[6] Large facilities also affect children physically and mentally, stunting physical growth, causing developmental delays, and increasing the risk of clinical attachment disorders (van IJzendoorn et al. 2011; Dozier et al. 2012).

In contrast, children have greater opportunities to flourish in family- and community-based settings. They can form a long-term, familiar relationship with an adult who will respond to their particular needs, allowing them to build trust (Annie E. Casey Foundation 2013). For children with past trauma, family- and community-based settings are healing and allow children to better adjust to their environment (Dozier et al. 2014).

In policy, if not yet in practice, the domestic child welfare system is taking steps to ensure that children remain with their families or, when they are removed, are placed with extended family members before they are placed with strangers. Unaccompanied children should have the same access to family-based or small community-based placements as children in state courts. While in ORR custody and before release to their family, the government should place unaccompanied children in settings that best support their health, safety, and development—foster families, group homes, and small facilities.

Make Communities—Not Government Custody— the Locus of Services for Children and Families

As children reunify with their families, they start a new stage of their migration journey. We believe that local communities should be the center of services advancing their best interests and supporting their safety and well-being. This approach should include services designed to welcome and support children as they arrive and to provide long-term access to immigration counsel, health services, financial support, and work authorization.

Welcoming networks and coalitions can include leaders and members of local immigrant communities, even older youth previously released from government custody. As partnerships form, coalitions strengthen connections and facilitate efficient and timely referrals and communication across disciplines and fields. Coalitions can include not only nonprofit organizations such as refugee resettlement agencies, community-based organizations, adult education or ESL programs, and trafficking victims' assistance programs but also government agencies, such as offices of new Americans; city, county, and state health departments; state boards of education; and local officials from public schools. Welcoming coalitions can include local hospitals and universities that create greater access to additional resources or have capacity to implement unique services, such as medical-legal partnerships and forensic evaluation clinics. Networks that regularly meet can develop and share comprehensive resource guides and toolkits, respond to local shifts in welcoming arriving migrants, and more effectively consider how to meet the unique needs of children. In addition, local coalitions can seek alternative funds from philanthropic sources or county and state departments with positions focused on building partnerships and facilitating referrals.

Government and philanthropy must invest in *expanding the collaborative capacity of community service providers* to support children released from government custody. Professionals who offer community services should have ongoing access to interdisciplinary training about trauma-informed care as well as cultural responsiveness, child development, and strength-based approaches. Training recipients should include public school teachers and staff as well as Federally Qualified Health Centers (FQHCs). National entities with existing networks, such as the American Academy of Pediatrics (AAP), National Association of Social Workers (NASW), American Psychological Association (APA), or National Child Traumatic Stress Network (NCTSN), may have members who can build capacity to specifically serve unaccompanied children. National networks as well as local coalitions can train mental health and medical professionals at community-based organizations, universities, and hospitals to conduct assessments on a pro bono basis. In addition, we have discovered organizations that offer services and resources not specifically targeted for unaccompanied children may have the capacity and skills to serve this population. Expanding the capacity and increasing the amount of trained service providers reduces the wait time for children to receive critical services.

Because the possibility of deportation is a constant threat to children's safety and stability, all children should have *access to immigration attorneys* the moment they are directed to appear in court. Children who remain particularly vulnerable after release should be appointed independent Child Advocates. Children eligible to work under state child welfare laws should have immediate access to work authorization so that they can engage in safe and age-appropriate work and, if needed, support themselves and assist their families.

Children who obtain immigration counsel are more likely to prevail in their legal claims to remain safely in the United States (Snider and DiBernardo 2022). The alternative is fundamentally unfair: children are left to navigate their legal case on their own. When we speak of immigration counsel, we have in mind attorneys required to engage in zealous representation that is client-centered, where they are partners with their clients as much as the child's age and maturity will allow. Children rely heavily on their immigration counsel to guide them through the U.S. immigration system, help them monitor the procedural aspects of their immigration case, keep track of court dates, inform the court of changes of address to ensure they receive notifications of upcoming hearings, and present evidence that bolsters their claims for protection under our immigration laws. Immigration counsel also help unaccompanied children navigate available services while fighting their legal case and understand the impact of accessing services on their case. If unaccompanied children prevail in their immigration cases, counsel educate children on the new options of services for which they are eligible. These social services may serve as a lifeline when a child needs access to medical care, mental health services, or basic necessities for survival, such as food, clothing, and shelter.

In addition to universal legal representation, we propose that all immigrant children, including unaccompanied children released from ORR custody, have *equitable access to physical and mental health care* (Beier and Fredericks 2023). This access includes established medical homes and universal medical insurance regardless of immigration status and without prejudice for immigration claim or public charge (Beier and Fredericks 2023).[7] In our experience as Child Advocates, children in legal proceedings may have unmet psychosocial or health needs. Child Advocates have observed how the daily routines of life after a child's release and reunification—which require families to direct immediate attention to basic needs, including housing, food stability, school, and health care—can impact their ability to focus on immigration proceedings (Young Center Roundtables 2023). Without equitable access to resources, the children's mental health and medical needs may remain unmet. Furthermore, lack of access to mental health services prevents children from participating in school or their legal case in a meaningful way, thereby impacting their ability to live safely in their communities. When providers can address children's comprehensive needs in a trauma-informed manner, it often results in better outcomes for children's immigration proceedings and overall well-being.

To provide equitable access to health services, local access points should increase through colocated and coordinated services. For example, local nonprofit organizations can house medical, legal, and mental health service providers. Schools can include medical clinics or legal service providers on-site, or newcomer initiatives at schools can include services for parent education and caregiver support for their child's social-emotional development. Public school officials can establish school enrollment services at immigration courts. Community fairs can include providers to enroll children in educational, medical, mental health, or legal services. Community colleges or adult education centers can provide legal screenings (Beier and Fredericks 2023). Colocated services increase the accessibility and effectiveness of community organizations and agencies. Regardless of which types of services are colocated, providers must establish and maintain clear rules that community service providers, including schools, are safe zones for children and family members who do not have legal status (meaning that schools do not actively engage in federal efforts to detain or deport undocumented immigrants). Furthermore, coalitions can ensure that comprehensive, colocated services for youth extend through twenty-one years of age, a critical period as they transition into young adulthood and continue to grow and mature, including identity formation and brain development.

Children and families should have *opportunities to access comprehensive in-person case management services* that extend beyond their immigration proceedings. An effective case manager can provide referrals with warm handoffs to intentionally introduce a child to additional service providers. A case manager also can share resources that support the child's holistic needs, such as tutoring, counseling, cultural liaison, peer support groups, economic support to make calls to family in their home country, as well as support groups for their caregivers. Furthermore, a case manager can coordinate communication and meetings across providers in various fields.

Even with comprehensive case management services, we recognize that children and families may face logistical barriers to accessing necessary services. Providers should work to reduce challenges and mitigate barriers. During the COVID-19 global pandemic, we experienced a renewed focus on telehealth services. Increased telehealth services with licensed professionals will benefit immigrant children and their families. While lack of access to computers or other devices, reliable internet, and digital literacy may present barriers, telehealth services may increase some children's connections to services not available in their local community. Cities and counties can invest in providing mobile hot spots available to families in underresourced communities and free workshops to increase digital literacy. In addition, while in-person interpretation is best, networks of trained interpreters can expand to national levels and through telephonic or remote means. For children or their families to attend appointments, service providers can offer reimbursements for childcare or provide qualified on-site childcare. In addition, service providers can offer transportation assistance or transportation vouchers to use public methods or rideshares. Furthermore, the federal government should provide all unaccompanied children released from detention with an acceptable form of identification since many community services are contingent on proof of identity.

Finally, children should have access to procedures for requesting protection that reflect their status as children. As recommended in the Young Center's 2020 report "Reimagining Children's Immigration Proceedings," this would include processes focused on conferences rather than courtrooms, applications rather than interrogations, and reasonable timelines rather than unduly rushed or prolonged cases. That report also set forth a proposal for children who wish to remain but who fail to win protection under standards created for adults (namely, in asylum cases), whereby the government would take on the burden of demonstrating that a child or youth could be safely repatriated. The government's failure to meet that burden in a timely manner would allow the child to remain in the United States until the age of twenty-five, with the opportunity to then seek permanent residence in the United States (Young Center for Immigrant Children's Rights 2020). In this way, we could—through changes to existing law and policy—ensure that no children were returned to danger against their will.

Conclusion

For nearly twenty years, Young Center Child Advocates have accompanied and advocated for immigrant children who are separated from family and community and who face adversarial court cases that will determine whether they remain in the United States or return to their country. As they navigate this system, they are subjected to laws, policies, and practices grounded in law enforcement or purported child protection priorities. Our proposals for change are grounded in children's rights and, more concretely, in the experiences of children who have spent months or years in custody and many more years in legal limbo. Because family and community are critical for their safety, we propose that the government recognize and respond to children's concept of "family" and extend protections offered currently just to unaccompanied children to *all* children. Because government custody is not benign, we propose changes to dramatically expedite children's release to family or to long-term community-based foster placements. Because size matters, we insist that small, family-like settings be the standard for all children. And finally, because limiting services to government custody increases the risk of prolonged detention, we recommend that communities—not government custody—become the locus for federally funded service delivery. Of course, a truly child-centered system would welcome children and families and support them to adulthood. Until then, we hope these recommendations will inspire many more ideas for change.

Notes

The authors express abiding gratitude for the work of many current and former Young Center colleagues in developing the ideas in this chapter, including but by no means limited to: Maria Woltjen, founding executive director; Elizabeth Frankel, founding associate director; Gladis Molina Alt, executive director; Olivia Peña, Child Advocate Program director; Mary Miller Flowers, director of policy and legislative advocacy; and Jane Liu, director of policy and litigation.

1. The Trafficking Victims Protection Reauthorization Act of 2008 distinguishes between unaccompanied children from contiguous countries (Mexico and Canada) and unaccompanied children from all other countries. Children from contiguous countries are denied the protections afforded to all other unaccompanied children unless they persuade border officials that they fall into one of three very difficult-to-meet categories. This different treatment has proven profoundly harmful to children from Mexico (Young Center for Immigrant Children's Rights 2019; Amnesty International 2021).

2. As a point of comparison, the Immigration and Nationality Act (INA) permits a grant of Special Immigrant Juvenile (SIJ) status for children who have received an order from a state court finding (among other things) that it is not in the child's best interests to return to their country of origin (Immigration and Nationality Act, §§ 1101 et seq.). But by the time a child submits a request to obtain this status to federal officials, the issue of a child's best interests has already been determined by the relevant state court.

3. We use the word *children* to refer to individuals under the age of eighteen. In addition, we sometimes use the word *youth* to refer to adolescents and individuals up to the age of twenty-one, especially as adolescents continue to undergo identity formation and present different developmental strengths and needs.

4. Young Center attorneys and social workers, as well as bilingual and bicultural volunteers supervised by Young Center staff, are appointed as independent Child Advocates.

5. Young Center for Immigrant Children's Rights Child Advocate staff who informed this chapter through two roundtable conversations (Young Center Roundtables) with the authors in 2023 include Mariana Alvarez, Estrellita Alvarado, Jessica Beecher Bell, Tami Benchoam-Rogers, Isobel Conroy, Sondra Furcajg, Leigh Gorman, Althea Klein, Dane Olsen, José Ortiz-Rosales, Rebecca Rittenhouse, and Amairani Rucoba; former Child Advocate staff includes Mari Dorn-Lopez.

6. The harm of institutionalizing children is further documented in a 2019 United Nations report by independent expert Manfred Nowak, which concludes that institutionalization is characterized by separation and isolation from family and community, depersonalization, lack of individualized care and love, instability of caregiver relationships, lack of caregiver responsiveness, lack of self-determination, and strict routines not tailored to children's individual needs.

7. According to the American Academy of Pediatrics, a medical home is "an approach to providing comprehensive primary care that facilitates partnerships between patients, clinicians, medical staff, and families. A medical home extends beyond the four walls of a clinical practice. It includes specialty care, educational services, family support and more." American Academy of Pediatrics, "Medical Home," accessed May 17, 2023, https://www.aap.org/en/practice-management/medical-home/.

References

Amnesty International. 2021. "Pushed into Harm's Way: Forced Returns of Unaccompanied Migrant Children to Danger by the USA and Mexico." June 11. https://www.amnesty.org/en/documents/amr51/4200/2021/en/.

Annie E. Casey Foundation. 2013. "Reconnecting Child Development and Child Welfare: Evolving Perspectives on Residential Placement." March. https://assets.aecf.org/m/resourcedoc/aecf-ReconnectingChildDevelopmentandChildWelfare-2013.pdf.

Beier, Jonathan, and Karla Fredericks. 2023. "A Path to Meeting the Medical and Mental Health Needs of Unaccompanied Children in U.S. Communities." American Academy of Pediatrics and Migration Policy Institute, April. https://www.migrationpolicy.org/research/medical-mental-health-needs-unaccompanied-children.

Beltran, Ana, and Heidi Redlich Epstein. 2013. "Improving Foster Care Licensing Standards Around the United States: Using Research Findings to Effect Change." February. https://www.grandfamilies.org/Portals/0/Documents/Foster%20Care%20Licensing/Improving%20Foster%20Care%20Licensing%20Standards.pdf.

Bhabha, Jaqueline, and Susan Schmidt. 2006. "Seeking Asylum Alone: Unaccompanied and Separated Children and Refugee Protection in the U.S." Harvard University Committee on Human Rights Studies, June. https://idcoalition.org/wp-content/uploads/2008/12/seeking-asylum-alone-us.pdf.

Burnett, John. 2019. "Inside the Largest and Most Controversial Shelter for Migrant Children in the U.S.," NPR, February 13. https://www.npr.org/2019/02/13/694138106/inside-the-largest-and-most-controversial-shelter-for-migrant-children-in-the-u-.

Casey Family Programs. 2018. "How Can We Ensure a Child's First Placement Is with a Family?" December 20. https://www.casey.org/first-placement-family-placement/.

Dozier, Mary, et al. 2012. "Institutional Care for Young Children: Review of Literature and Policy Implications." *Social Issues Policy Review* 6 (1): 1–25.

Dozier, Mary, et al. 2014. "Consensus Statement on Group Care for Children and Adolescents: A Statement of Policy of the American Orthopsychiatric Association." *American Journal of Orthopsychiatry* 84 (3): 219–25.

Family First Prevention Services Act, U.S. Code 42 (2018), § 622.

Flores v. Reno, No. CV 85–4544-RFK (Px) (C.D. Cal. Jan. 17, 1997).

Frankel, Elizabeth. 2011. "Detention and Deportation with Inadequate Due Process: The Devastating Consequences of Juvenile Involvement with Law Enforcement for Immigrant Youth." *Duke Law Journal* 3:63–107.

Homeland Security Act, U.S. Code 6 (2002), § 279.

Homeland Security Act, U.S. Code 8 (2002), § 1232.

Immigration and Nationality Act, U.S. Code 8 (1990), §§ 1101 et seq.

McCarthy, Patrick, Vincent Schiraldi, and Miriam Shark. 2016. "The Future of Youth Justice: A Community-Based Alterative to the Youth Prison Model." National Institute of Justice and Harvard Kennedy School, October. https://assets.aecf.org/m/resourcedoc/NIJ-The_Future_of_Youth_Justice-10.21.16.pdf.

Nagda, Jennifer, and Maria Woltjen. 2015. "Best Interests of the Child Standard: Bringing Common Sense to Immigration Decisions." In *Big Ideas—Pioneering Change: Innovative Ideas for Children and Families*, 105–16. Washington, D.C.: First Focus.

Nowak, Manfred. 2019. "The United Nations Global Study on Children Deprived of Liberty." July 11. United Nations Document A/74/136.

Office of Juvenile Justice and Delinquency Prevention. 2014. "Alternatives to Detention and Confinement." August. https://ojjdp.ojp.gov/model-programs-guide/literature-reviews/alternatives_to_detection_and_confinement.pdf.

Roberts, Dorothy. 2022. *Torn Apart: How the Child Welfare System Destroys Black Families—and How Abolition Can Build a Safer World*. New York: Basic Books.

Snider, Alyssa, and Rebecca DiBernardo. 2022. "Representation Matters: No Child Should Appear in Immigration Court Proceedings Alone." Vera Institute of Justice, December. https://www.vera.org/downloads/publications/representation-matters.pdf.

Thronson, David. 2010. "Thinking Small: The Need for Big Changes in Immigration Law's Treatment of Children." *University of California at Davis Journal of Juvenile Law and Policy* 14 (2): 239–62.

Trafficking Victims Protection Reauthorization Act, U.S. Code 8 (2008), § 1232.

Troxel v. Granville, 530 U.S. 57, 66 (2000).

United Nations High Commissioner for Refugees (UNHCR). 2014. "Children on the Run: Unaccompanied Children Leaving Central America and the Need for International Protection." https://www.refworld.org/docid/532180c24.html.

U.S. Department of Health and Human Services. 2015. "A National Look at the Use of Congregate Care in Child Welfare." Administration for Children & Families, Children's Bureau, March 30. https://www.acf.hhs.gov/cb/report/national-look-use-congregate-care-child-welfare.

U.S. Department of Health and Human Services. 2022. "Office of Refugee Resettlement's Influx Care Facility and Emergency Intake Sites Did Not Adequately Safeguard Unaccompanied Children from COVID-19." Office of Inspector General, June 22. https://oig.hhs.gov/oas/reports/region6/62107002.pdf.

U.S. Department of Health and Human Services. 2023. "ORR Unaccompanied Children Program Policy Guide: Section 2.3.2: Case Managers." Administration for Children and Families, Office of Refugee Resettlement, October. https://www.acf.hhs.gov/orr/policy-guidance/unaccompanied-children-program-policy-guide-section-2#2.3.2.

van IJzendoorn, Marinus H., et al. 2011. "Children in Institutional Care: Delayed Development and Resilience." *Monographs for the Society for Research in Child Development* 76 (4): 8–30.

Villagran, Lauren. 2022. "Two West Texas Shelters for Unaccompanied Minors Remain Open as Number of Migrant Children Declines." *El Paso Times*, January 1.

Williamson, John, and Aaron Greenberg. 2010. "Families, Not Orphanages." Better Care Network, August 31. https://bettercarenetwork.org/sites/default/files/Families%20Not%20Orphanages_0.pdf.

Young Center for Immigrant Children's Rights. 2019. "Border Screening for Children Has Failed." August 5. https://www.theyoungcenter.org/stories/2019/8/5/current-border-screening-of-unaccompanied-children-from-mexico-has-failed-and-should-not-be-a-model-for-reform.

Young Center for Immigrant Children's Rights. 2020. "Reimagining Children's Immigration Proceedings: A Roadmap for an Entirely New System Centered Around Children." October. https://www.theyoungcenter.org/reimagining-childrens-immigration-proceedings.

Young Center for Immigrant Children's Rights. 2022a. "Preserving Family Ties: Ensuring Children's Contact with Family While in Government Custody." August. https://static1.squarespace.com/static/597ab5f3bebafb0a625aaf45/t/639d0488ec01c36f79d75f1c/1671234696414/Phone_Calls_Final_Report.pdf.

Young Center for Immigrant Children's Rights. 2022b. "Protecting Immigrant Children in Government Custody: New Report Calls for an Overhaul of Incident Reporting System." Press release, September 27. https://www.theyoungcenter.org/media-press-releases/2022/9/27/protecting-immigrant-children-in-government-custody-new-report-calls-for-an-overhaul-of-incident-reporting-system?rq=punishing%20trauma.

Young Center for Immigrant Children's Rights. 2023. "Roundtable Discussions of Children's Experiences Navigating Federal Custody and Courts." May 18, 19. Chicago (virtual).

Young Center for Immigrant Children's Rights and National Immigrant Justice Center. 2022. "Punishing Trauma: Incident Reporting and Immigrant Children in Government Custody." September. https://static1.squarespace.com/static/597ab5f3bebafb0a625aaf45/t/632b4a5e7128a06d3855eb73/1663781479727/2022+09+21+FINAL+SIR+REPORT-HYPERLINKED.pdf.

SURVIVAL
Voices of Resilience

CHAPTER FOUR

"She Took Care of Me, and I Don't Even Remember Her Name"

Relational Ruptures in Detention Settings

CORINNE KENTOR

When Donald Trump first announced his plan to separate migrant children from their families, he was met with supreme outrage. Activists, academics, media outlets, and members of the immigrant community expressed their dismay at the policy, lambasting the cruelty of this latest invocation of a "zero tolerance" approach to immigration enforcement (Southern Poverty Law Center 2020). Nearly three thousand children were separated from their caregivers (Davis 2020), and to date many have yet to be reunited (Rose 2021). While Joe Biden's administration promised to end policies like child detention and family separation, young migrants continued to be detained under a host of provisions after his ascension to office. Many of those provisions were initially presented as attempts to combat the COVID-19 pandemic, but they soon expanded as a means of justifying the continued containment of migrants at the U.S.-Mexico border (Anthropologist Action Network for Immigrants and Refugees 2021).

The full emotional and psychological toll of child-family separation remains to be seen. However, much can be learned from the experiences of individuals who underwent different forms of separation and detention in earlier political eras. This chapter adds to a growing body of literature on child-family separation by exploring how unaccompanied minors who arrived in the United States before Trump was elected in 2016 experienced separation, detention, and reunification as they journeyed northward. The chapter draws on data collected as part of a larger, multiyear ethnographic study focused on the educational experiences of mixed-status immigrant families in Southern California. Using both retrospective and longitudinal data, I articulate how detention and separation experiences reverberate across time and space, providing insights for practitioners looking to cultivate healing spaces for children and youth in the years following their detention experiences.

Over the course of the chapter, I outline the relational formations and ruptures that take place as unaccompanied youth make their way toward the United States. I zero in on the migration trajectories of two adolescents from Guatemala who were thrice "detained" on their journeys to the United States: first, when they were arrested while passing through Mexico and placed in the custody of an organized crime group who demanded ransom money for their release; second, when they were temporarily detained by U.S. Customs and Border Protection (CBP) after crossing the Sonoran desert; and third, when they were transferred into long-term detention facilities managed by the Office of Refugee Resettlement (ORR) before reuniting with family members in Southern California.

This chapter contributes a narrative account of relationship building in detention and illuminates relational angles to the traumatic impact of detention on young people. By tracing these parallel journeys and placing them in the broader context established by ethnographic research with families with comparable experiences, I show how young migrants forge connections detention and unpack how they handle the traumas that ensue when these connections are inevitably broken in the transition from one carceral context to another. Simultaneously, I draw attention to the deep inhumanity of contemporary detention settings, showing how children's experiences in government facilities come to resemble the other traumas they endure.

The chapter offers two primary interventions. First, I expand the concept of "detention" to reflect its multiple valences in the lives of migrants, as well as the role uncertainty plays in experiences of detention. Second, I draw on the notion of "fictive kin" to explore the development of temporary relationships and the role they play in youth's experiences during and after detention. This shifts attention to another kind of "separation" migrants experience when in detention: separation from the people they bond with over a relatively short but deeply impactful time in their lives (Vogt 2016, 2018). While different from child-family separation as traditionally conceived, this experience also has lasting effects on young migrants and is critical to consider when working to craft healing spaces for children and youth who experience multiple forms of detention prior to arriving in the United States.

Youth Migration in Brief

Drivers of Youth Migration

As described in the introduction to this volume, in 2014, approximately sixty-nine thousand Central American minors were detained by U.S. Immigration and Customs Enforcement (ICE) while attempting to cross the U.S.-Mexico border, a 77 percent increase over the prior year (Chishti and Hipsman 2015). Later dubbed the "child migration crisis," their arrival instigated conversation about what might be driving higher numbers of youth to undertake perilous journeys northward. At the time, the trend was widely attributed to rising gang violence in Guatemala and neighboring countries (Chishti and Hipsman 2015; Swanson and Torres 2016). As Lauren Heidbrink (2020) points out, though, these narratives fail to capture the complex factors that alternatively motivate youth to pursue or resist migration (Nichols 2021).

For youth in my research, gang violence was rarely the sole factor that motivated their migration. Often, this formed one aspect of an intersecting set of concerns and desires, such as educational opportunity, family pressures, and economic interests—all of which were themselves the result of intersecting sociopolitical histories that complicated individuals' ability to pursue opportunities in their home countries. For Indigenous youth, like those profiled in this chapter, experiences of displacement and discrimination can exacerbate other factors that contribute to migration (Heidbrink 2020). This mirrors larger trends illuminated by recent migration scholarship, which shows how social and economic factors converge to complicate clean distinctions among migrant "types" (e.g., economic migrants vs. asylum seekers and refugees) (Oliveira and Becker 2019; Oliveira and Kentor 2020; Nichols 2021).

In some cases, youth migration forms part of a broader "elaboration of care," in which children and youth are both the providers and the recipients of acts of love involved in transnational movement (Heidbrink 2018). However, this is neither a conclusive nor a universal story. Youth may decide to migrate for a host of reasons, some of which may be at odds with the desires and expectations of family members (Belloni 2020). The reality is, instances of youth migration, like other forms of migration, are at once reflective of structural realities in one's country of origin, family contexts or considerations, and individual desires—none of which can necessarily be disentangled from one another.

Migrant Sociality and Fictive Kin

The same structural factors that motivate south-north migration in the Americas also imbue it with significant dangers. Journeys are long and arduous, entailing hardship posed by the duration of the travel, its financial cost, and the adverse effects of a warming climate (De León 2015). Transgender migrants and migrants identified as female face high levels of sexual assault (Schmidt and Buechler 2017; Brigden 2018), and all migrants risk being detained and physically abused by traffickers, regional gangs, and local police. While families typically hire smugglers to help their relatives complete the crossing safely (Triandafyllidou 2018), the risks persist, particularly given the increasing militarization of the U.S.-Mexico border since the early 1990s (Andreas 2009; Hernandez 2010; Nevins 2010) and the debt families take on to ensure their relatives' safe arrival (Triandafyllidou 2015; Heidbrink 2019; Bylander 2020). These realities not only shape experiences *during* migration but also in its lead-up and aftermath.

Migration is often (though not always) a collective endeavor. Migrants rarely make the journey on their own, and even when they do, they meet a variety of other people before entering detention facilities. Anthropologists have documented how migrants share information with one another throughout their journeys. For example, two of the main personages in Jason De León's *The Land of Open Graves* are repeat-crossers who, each time they are deported back to Mexico, bring with them new knowledge that they then employ to increase their chances of successfully making it to the United States on their next attempt. Abby C. Wheatley and Ruth Gomberg-Muñoz (2016, 397) characterize this kind of work as "collective agency," a process of "sharing and cooperation" migrants undertake in order to "keep moving." They argue that collective agency exemplifies "how strategies for survival become woven into social relations" that can eventually "be mobilized as part of organized political movements," demonstrating how migrant sociality relates to other efforts to counter and resist the structural violence of U.S. border policing (397). Wendy Vogt (2016, 2018) advances a similar argument, drawing attention to the intimacy forged among migrants, "smugglers," and shelter workers. The accounts featured in these and other ethnographies contrast with popular narratives that portray migrants as either non-agentive victims or sinister solo-invaders, offering a glimpse into the human connections that form even under unimaginably difficult circumstances.

Relationship building in detention facilities has proved more difficult to document, due in part to the fact that it is difficult for researchers and journalists to gain access to these spaces. However, there is evidence of similar assumptions among immigration officials and service providers. Heidbrink (2018) finds that institutional actors often frame migration as a negative experience foisted upon "vulnerable" children and youth. This perspective implicitly justifies a range of practices that undermine children and youth's autonomy, as well as the rights of their families. Critically, this understanding of child migration neglects the agency youth hold in undertaking transnational moves and vilifies the complex relational constellations they hold with the adults connected to their migration experiences.

While limited research has been conducted in detention facilities themselves, research on adult migrant sociality provides a potential framework for understanding the relationships built at different stages of a transborder journey. Wheatley, Gomberg-Muñoz, and De León show how these relationships are necessary for physical survival, but it is important to note their emotional significance as well. The trials of migration can speed up the process by which one forms a sense of connection with other travelers, with "violence or the threat of violence pushing . . . strangers to claim relatedness in attempts at self-protection and preservation of life of self and other" (Yarris and Castañeda 2016). The quest for physical survival under extreme duress can inspire forms of connection that may not have otherwise existed. To ignore these connections is to ignore the human realities of migration, which is itself full of both the messy and the meaningful intimacies intertwined with the act of surviving governmental brutality (Vogt 2016, 2018).

To analyze the relationships recounted by participants in my research, I employ the concept of "fictive kin." In my usage, "fictive kinship" refers to the deep relationships that resemble the kind of connection ordinarily associated with biological family but taking place among nonrelatives. These relationships can provide tangible benefits, such as access to jobs, housing, and resources, but their effects extend beyond the measurable resources they provide (Ebaugh and Curry 2000; Kim 2009; Lee 2013; Manohar 2013).

Fictive kinship can also reflect a desire for mental or emotional connection in circumstances that challenge one's sense of self and ability to communicate with family and community. Spaces of detention clearly fall within these parameters. How fictive kinship is built, challenged, and maintained as youth migrants move in and out of different contexts of detention provides insight into the affective dimensions of the instability incurred by detention as a punitive tactic. At the same time, this concept draws attention to the importance of the relationships, however short-lived, forged in the process of migration.

In the remaining pages, I focus on the following questions:

(1) What are the different contexts of detention youth experience on their journeys to the United States? How do these contexts compare to one another, per the testimony of youth who experience them?
(2) How do different contexts of detention facilitate, preclude, or disrupt the social connections youth form with other migrants? What effect does this have on their experiences of detention?
(3) What are the effects of the relational ruptures of detention on youth after migration?

Methods

This chapter draws on data collected as part of a multiyear ethnographic study. Research took place in the San Fernando Valley (SFV), a collection of suburbs north of Los Angeles, California. From April 2020 to May 2022, I partnered with three local high schools that serve large immigrant and English-language learner (ELL) populations. I spent time volunteering at each of the schools, supporting students and counselors with college and financial aid applications. I coordinated college and career workshops, provided tutoring and essay support for students, and assisted high school seniors with college registration and financial aid tasks. These activities allowed me to connect with students and gain a robust understanding of regional educational discourses. I kept detailed field notes of interactions with students and program staff (which took place virtually on Zoom for the first year and in person in the second year) and wrote biweekly thematic memos detailing emergent findings.

I invited students I met on-site and through counselor recommendations to participate in life history interviews focused on their childhoods, their relationships with their families, their early schooling experiences, their own or their families' journeys to the United States, their time in high school, and their experiences planning for the future. Throughout the year, I checked in with participating students intermittently via phone, Zoom, text, and FaceTime. These informal conversations gave me an opportunity to gain insight into students' daily lives, their feelings about school, and how they were managing the challenges of the COVID-19 pandemic. In total, I conducted multiple interviews with 73 students from 53 discrete families. The families involved mirrored the demographics of the research site, with members hailing from a range of countries but with the biggest representation from Mexico, Honduras, Guatemala, and El Salvador. I also conducted interviews with parents, educators, and counselors from the community. In total, I conducted more than 120 interviews as part of this project. In the second year of the research, I was also able to meet with interlocutors in person. While public health concerns and the restrictions of my institutional review board precluded me from conducting observations in participants' homes, I was able to meet them at cafés, in stores, outdoors in public parks, and at church or in other community settings. I also accompanied students on their college campuses, where we engaged in student-led walking tours that helped illuminate their experiences navigating the physical spaces of higher education.

Alongside original data generated through interviews and field notes, I collected artifacts that helped round out my understanding by replacing my research gaze with that of my interlocutors. These artifacts included photographs, writing samples, and narrative voice memos. I asked students to take photos in response to open-ended prompts focused on their learning space, the place they feel most at home, their feelings about family, and their hopes for the future. Photos were sent to me by text message, and respondents either recorded voice memos explaining their choices or called me by Zoom or FaceTime to talk about the experience. In some cases, multiple participants joined a focus group to discuss the process of taking the photos and engage in a dialogue with one another about their interpretation of the prompt. These conversations informed later instances of photo elicitation. I also collected writing samples from students as we worked together on their college applications and linked these documents to my field notes, producing two records of my research: one generated by students (in their own writing) and one I generated in response.

To analyze my data, I used a multistage coding technique. First, I created a topical index. I then compared content across my dataset and created thematic codes based on phrases drawn from students' writing. Finally, I recoded all interview transcripts and student essays using a closed codebook, paying particular attention to similarities and contradictions among and within participant groups. To analyze students' photo submissions, I relied on techniques outlined in Kate Wall et al.'s (2012) overview of visual methodologies. Finally, I wrote comprehensive portraits (Lawrence-Lightfoot 2005) of focal students and their families, which I shared with participants as a form of member checking (Carreta and Pérez 2019). This chapter is based off two such portraits, focusing on parallel journeys as a means of illuminating with depth and detail trends that were reflected in my larger dataset.

Positionality

Like the youth involved in this study, I grew up and graduated from high school in the San Fernando Valley. Our shared familiarity with the area, alongside the fact that participants and I shared social connections through work and family, helped me forge connections and facilitated the kind of trust that is critical to in-depth qualitative research. This was helped by the fact that I am a fluent Spanish speaker, meaning Spanish-speaking participants could flow among languages comfortably throughout an interview. However, I am also a native English speaker, a U.S. citizen, and an academic, all of which imbues me with an immense amount of privilege when compared to the families with whom I work. I am also a white Jewish woman and third-generation college attendee (meaning my parents and some of my grandparents attended college). Though I grew up in the same area as participants in the research, we occupied this space differently. For example, when participants hung out at the mall across the street from one of my field sites, where I also spent a lot of time as a high school student, they were often harassed by security staff or surveilled by retail employees who accused them of shoplifting, making their experience of the space very different from my own. While I conducted research in my "hometown," therefore, I was still involved with people who experienced a decidedly different version of that space than the one I knew firsthand.

These privileges were augmented by the fact that part of this study took place at the peak of the COVID-19 pandemic, which disproportionately affected participants and their families, many of whom continued to work in person in high-risk jobs, while I had the ability to isolate in order to ensure the health and well-being of my vulnerable relatives. I was keenly aware of these differences and took considerable care to ensure that participation in this study did not add to the burdens students and their families were already carrying in this time. To that end, I focused first and foremost on supporting students academically and emotionally, abandoning formal scheduled meetings in favor of spontaneous check-ins driven by student interest. I also planned interviews so they followed extensive collaborative work, which allowed me to learn about students through their writing before embarking on a formal interview. This is one way I established trust with students, engaged in reciprocity, and learned about them over time and in their own words, all of which deepened the research and front-loaded the human connection that grounds qualitative inquiry.

While it is impossible to avoid the privileges that shape my positionality in conducting this research, I did make every effort to engage in sustained, interpersonal fieldwork that allowed me to build connections over time. The data for this specific chapter draw on just over two years of concentrated fieldwork, but I have been connected with and committed to many of the participating families for far longer. The relationships that undergird this research are highly reciprocal, in that I have also been a mentor, a friend, and a colleague at various points in time. All of this has helped form the trust necessary for conducting research on sensitive topics like those discussed here.

In addition, I served from 2018 to 2020 as an interpreter and advocate for asylum seekers while living in New York. I did not recruit participants through this work, but I did gain hands-on experience in trauma-informed interviewing and service. I completed trainings and collaborated with social work colleagues to understand how to avoid retraumatizing asylum seekers while learning about their stories in order to support their cases. The knowledge and practice I gained through this experience also informed how I conducted this study, particularly when it came to conducting interviews around potentially traumatic detention experiences. I have remained involved with the families who participated in this project since the formal conclusion of fieldwork and am committed to ensuring that all research activities are participant-led and to avoid (to the extent possible) re-invoking traumatic experiences simply for the sake of research.

Accessing Stories in Hindsight

While this chapter focuses on the relational ruptures that attend youth migration, it is important to note that my methods did not include fieldwork in detention centers and thus cannot capture what interlocutors experienced in "real time." My study primarily investigated family caregiving practices and educational trajectories in the years following migration, meaning my fieldwork was simply situated elsewhere. Though I did not explicitly focus on youth experiences of migration and detention, I found these histories appeared again and again, in the stories shared in interviews, the narratives told in college application essays, and the way youth navigated daily life in the United States. I therefore became interested in how youth thought and talked about their detention experiences years after they had taken place. The data I draw on here all reflect how stories about the contexts of detention youth experience are communicated years after they first take place, as people reckon with the reverberations of past traumas. While the data that inform this chapter are limited in some respects, in that they cannot attest to the many and varied experiences of youth in detention, nor can they capture the stories of those who return (or are returned) to their countries of origin, they can attest to how youth remember and re-narrate salient experiences even after a significant period of time.

Featured Narratives: Axel and Sebastian

Though they are often painted with a broad brush, youth migrants who come to the United States each have individual stories. The two narratives featured in this chapter demonstrate the complex, personal experiences behind statistics about child migration and detention while illuminating common trends that shape the lives of immigrants who arrive in the country at a young age. While not dealt with in great detail here, it is important to clarify that the youth profiled in this chapter are members of Indigenous communities and spoke at length about political disinvestment in their regions and how this contributed to their decision to come to the United States. This is a topic that is worthy of further attention beyond the scope of this chapter.

Axel was born in Tzanixnam, Guatemala. In an essay he wrote as part of an application for a college scholarship, Axel described Tzanixnam as "a town far from the city, a town surrounded by mountains and trees, a place where people know each other and work hard to live, even the children." In the many conversations I shared with Axel in his first two years of college, he would often reminisce about the lushness of his hometown, describing the saturated colors that defined each season. In the fall, he told me about the deep greens that shaded houses and carpeted fields. When spring arrived, he talked about the auburn and crimson of things in bloom. As California dried out in yet another year without significant rainfall, Axel's memories of his walks through Tzanixnam seemed even more verdant.

Axel is the youngest of six siblings. His eldest brother, Elias, left Guatemala for the United States when Axel was young. While Axel spoke with him every so often on the phone, he told me that he does not have distinct memories of life before and after his brother's migration. However, he always held great admiration for Elias, who worked hard to provide money for the family. Axel and Elias's parents each worked in furniture construction. They managed every part of the process, from selecting and cutting down trees for lumber to building the final product. Axel helped his parents while attending school and, at age eighteen, he still remembered the feeling and rhythm of the work. "First, I think you need to have the right tools to do it. After that, you just need to find a good tree and start doing it," he explained. For Axel, a "good tree" was all about size: it had to be big enough so that a piece could be constructed entirely out of one wood sample but small enough that little would be wasted. This work allowed Axel's parents to care for their children, but they still depended heavily on remittances Elias sent back from California, which they used to make improvements on their home and pay for school supplies for Axel and his siblings.

As Axel grew up, he began talking with his brother about coming to the United States to continue his education. Axel's parents, siblings, and friends were not able to progress beyond the equivalent of middle school, as they needed to work and were unable to afford additional school fees. Axel loved school, loved learning, and wanted to continue expanding his knowledge. In addition, he dreamed of global travel and wanted to learn about different parts of the world. He explained, "In my country, we don't have a lot of opportunities to demonstrate what you can do. . . . I want to be someone. [My mother] never had the opportunity to have a good life because basically in my town, we just always work, work, work, and we never get opportunities to continue with your studies or go to college." Hoping to continue his education in the United States, Axel made plans to travel to California, where he arranged to live with Elias and enroll in high school, with the goal of establishing local residency and attending college.

I met Axel near the end of his senior year of high school. A few months later, he introduced me to Sebastian, a friend he made in his English as a second language (ESL) class. Sebastian was also from Guatemala, and the two bonded over their love of soccer and the insecurities of high school. For Sebastian, school in the United States was made more difficult by the fact that it had been several years since he had taken classes in a formal learning environment. In Guatemala, Sebastian's school was far away from the family home, and his parents could not afford the ever-increasing bus fare. To get to school, Sebastian and his siblings (an older sister and a younger brother) walked two to three miles each way, for a total of five to six miles every day. After school, Sebastian assisted his mother, Carmela, with her agricultural work, taking care of animals (such as cows and chickens) and helping her plant and harvest crops. He also helped out in his uncle's construction business when needed and received modest financial compensation, which he gave to his mother. Despite the physical challenges this kind of work presented, Sebastian remembered his town as a "peaceful" place where he was "happy" and "free."

When Sebastian was young, his parents migrated to the United States and found work in Atlanta, Georgia. After a few years, his mother returned to Guatemala to care for her children. During this time, she separated from Sebastian's father. She stayed about four years, then moved back to the United States. Sebastian and his siblings moved in with their neighbors, then with an aunt and uncle. Sebastian's parents each met new partners and had more children, ten in total. Throughout this time, Carmela called at least twice per week "to make sure that we have enough food, clothes, shelter, and of course to make sure we're doing really good in school and [tell us] that she cared for us and that she loved us." In spite of Carmela's check-ins, Sebastian was not able to attend school frequently, and his grades began to slip. Carmela had been planning to bring Sebastian's older sister to the United States, but she was excelling academically and hoped to go to nursing school in Guatemala. Sebastian missed his mother terribly and asked her if she might consider bringing him to California to live with her instead. Carmela consulted with

Sebastian's sister, her eldest child, and eventually agreed. A few weeks later, Sebastian prepared to leave for the United States.

By the time I met them, Axel and Sebastian were about to start college, and the pursuit of education was top of mind and influenced how they each thought about the decision they had made years earlier to leave their respective hometowns. While they framed these motivations differently, with Axel describing a long-standing ambition to attend college and Sebastian intimating that coming to the United States would give him a chance to course-correct, schooling, and the opportunity represented by a close relative already living in the United States became important parts of how they retroactively narrated the decision to migrate, reflecting the role education played in their memories of their migration decisions, as well as the broader structural patterns that made comparable opportunities unavailable to them in their hometowns.

Leaving Home

Before their departures, Axel and Sebastian exchanged numerous phone calls with the family members they would meet in California. Once they began their journeys, however, they were no longer able to contact their loved ones independently. As is common, each joined an organized group led by a known smuggler, who had successfully managed other groups' trips northward. The smugglers assured Axel and Sebastian's families that they would manage the entire journey, from departure to arrival and reunification. The families paid several thousand dollars up front, which was intended to cover the cost of travel, lodging (when available), and bribes (when needed). This is a routine practice (Sanchez 2017) but one that comes with many risks.

While both Axel and Sebastian admitted their families were nervous about the perils they might encounter on their trips and stressed by its cost, they also were not fazed by the requests they encountered before departing their hometowns. This demonstrates the role expectations played in their experiences of this first relational "rupture": because Axel and Sebastian (and their families) understood that they would not be able to contact one another for this first stage of the journey, the loss of communication was interpreted as temporary and reasonable, at least to start.

In the first few days, Axel and Sebastian began forging connections with other migrants. Sebastian's group was on the smaller side. He began the journey with two companions, one of whom was a trusted neighbor who had known him since he was a child. Axel, meanwhile, joined a group of around twenty. He did not know anyone at first, but he soon developed a rapport with his fellow travelers, describing them as "friends" who made the trip more fun. The unique circumstances in which they found themselves helped foster deep relationships within a relatively short period of time, transforming neighbors into caregivers and strangers into companions.

For both boys, the first few days of the journey were relatively unremarkable. Each dealt with some sadness about leaving home, but in general the trip progressed smoothly. Sebastian thought the entire journey would be like this. At thirteen, he did not really understand the distance separating California from his hometown in Guatemala. "I thought the U.S. was kind of like behind that mountain over there," he explained. "That's what I thought when I was a kid. I was like, 'The U.S. is not that far. It's just crossing that mountain and I'll be there.' I didn't expect it to be that long of a journey." This statement reinforces the notion that the stress posed by their initial separation from family members, and their inability to control their own movement or contact loved ones, was assuaged by its "known-ness."

Detention in Mexico

After several days of travel, the groups reached Mexico. They were initially told they would need to wait a few days to reach the ideal conditions for crossing. The reality, though, was different.

As they approached the Mexican border, Sebastian, along with his companions, was loaded into the back of a large truck with about fifty other migrants. Within minutes, he began to panic. "Honestly, I think it was kind of like suffocating for me because I couldn't breathe and since I was little, I was a little bit short, I couldn't breathe, and I was running out of breath. I saw people just dropping on the floor.... It was kind of like a box, so we couldn't breathe. I was about to collapse, but then we arrived at the mountains," he told me, his voice quickening as he recounted this stage of the journey. Sebastian was small for his age and was worried that if he fainted he would be crushed or otherwise injured by his companions.

Once they reached a mountainous area, the travelers were allowed to leave the truck and sleep outside for the next two days. Then, they got back in and were driven to another town closer to the U.S.-Mexico border. The group arrived in the middle of the night, and Sebastian was immediately placed in a small apartment with several other migrants. Once he was in the apartment, things took a turn. What was supposed to be a three- to five-day stay stretched out for two weeks. Carmela grew anxious when she did not hear from her son as expected. When they were finally able to talk on the phone, the conversation did not bring much relief. The stress of the journey had begun to wear on Sebastian, who was no longer sure he could withstand the remaining challenges of the trip. During his two-week stay in the apartment, he had a close view of the perils to come. "I saw a lot of people coming back after crossing the river," he recalled. "It was pretty sad because some of them were kind of like in shock and some of them had kind of like cut off their skin because they started crossing the wall. They started crossing the wall but they didn't make it so they came back and they got hurt in the process. I was freaking out during that time and I called my mom [and told her I didn't want to do it]." Sebastian's reaction to the images of other would-be border crossers shows how he began to build a new empathy and connection based on his developing identity as a fellow migrant, presaging the experiential connections that would arise as he continued his journey.

Carmela called the smuggler and told him her son would not be able to withstand this kind of crossing. She agreed to pay more money to facilitate an alternate route, in which Sebastian and his companions from their hometown in Guatemala would pose as tourists on a boat tour in order to get across the river. While this allowed them to avoid one physical challenge, it was by no means easy. Once they got to the other side, they resumed traveling on foot. "I recall crossing Mexico in the mountains in the night. . . . I was exhausted. I could see people just staying behind and I didn't want to leave the lady who was taking care of me behind too because she was getting exhausted." The bond Sebastian had formed with his neighbor had deepened in the time he had been unable to contact Carmela and, in this moment, his testimony indicates the mutual responsibility each felt toward the other. While Sebastian continued to describe her as "the lady who was taking care of me," his concerns about her ability to continue the journey shows how he, too, began to take care of her.

Sebastian and his companion both made it across the border to Texas, where they stopped at a safe house and were given fake IDs and placed on a bus to Houston. When they arrived at their destination, another smuggler met them and took them to yet a third apartment, where they were supposed to spend the night before completing the final leg of the journey.

At this point, Sebastian's sense of the story becomes hazy. He remembers meeting someone at the bus station, and he recalls feeling a sense of unease. Something did not sit right about the man. However, the group did not have a choice. While they had technically made it across the border, they were still in an area where they did not know anyone and that was heavily trafficked by CBP agents. They decided to go with the man but were then confined to another apartment. They were not allowed to leave or contact Carmela.

The smugglers demanded more money from Carmela for Sebastian's release. Having spent additional funds to reroute her son and neighbors by boat, Carmela's finances were stretched thin. Sebastian and his companions were kept in the apartment for about three weeks. All Sebastian knows is that his mother somehow scraped together the money to pay for their release. Throughout the entire process, she was in agony. Finally, Sebastian and his caretaker were released, but the smugglers refused to take them the rest of the way to California. They decided to stay with the neighbor's sister, who had a house in Texas. Now in the United States and out of danger, at least for the moment, Sebastian began to relax. "We stayed with the lady's sister there for like two weeks. And I was starting to make friends in there because there were a lot of people living in there, so I started making friends and I was starting to get used to it," he shared. Finally, his mother found a driver willing to take them to California, but they would need to stop in several states, including New Mexico, Colorado, and Arizona, on the way. Despite the protracted nature of this stay, the knowledge that they could leave once their next steps were determined (unlike before) allowed Sebastian to relax, make friends, and develop a sense of routine.

Like Sebastian, Axel was also detained while traveling through Mexico. He was also kept in a locked apartment in an unfamiliar country, in sight of the U.S. border but unable to cross it or even go outside into the nearby plaza. The apartment was extremely hot—it was the middle of summer and numerous migrants had been crammed into a few rooms. Axel later described the experience in the same scholarship essay referenced earlier, writing,

> One day, when I had almost reached the U.S., I was walking on the road and some people grabbed us and took us to a house, where I

was locked up for fifteen days. We could not do anything. They took all our belongings and told us they would tell us what was going on the next morning. No one knew what was happening until we were told that they belonged to a group of gang members and that we had been kidnapped. The only way out of that place was paying them the money they asked for and, if we did not pay, we could never go back to our families and they would kill us. I started crying, but I couldn't do anything to escape. Three days later, they allowed us to inform our families where we were. I remember when I talked to my mother, we both started crying when I told her I was not sure I could get out alive.

The smugglers who had been facilitating Axel's journey contacted Elias, asking him to pay a ransom fee to ensure Axel's release. Elias worked as a janitor in an office building in Los Angeles. The work was reliable but not highly compensated. Fortunately, he had been saving up in anticipation of Axel's arrival and was able to wire the funds over within two weeks, though this put a dent in the money he had been collecting to help pay for his brother's anticipated expenses. Until he was released, Axel was not sure what was going to happen. He was able to speak with his brother, but their calls were closely monitored and cut short. Up until this point in the journey, Axel had grown close with some of his fellow travelers, but he found himself withdrawing when it became clear that they were being held and their families extorted. When he was eventually released, he felt immense guilt knowing that others were still being held until their families could pay the fees.

After leaving the apartment, Axel realized he would have to find another group to help him cross the U.S.-Mexico border. Unlike Sebastian, he undertook the river crossing, then hid in bushes during the day, proceeding on foot overnight. One evening shortly after crossing, he was apprehended by a group of CBP agents and brought to a detention facility. It was in this moment that Axel realized for the first time that he had crossed the border and was in the United States.

For both Axel and Sebastian, four key features characterized their experiences of detention in Mexico. First, they were confined unexpectedly and for far longer than they initially anticipated. This was the moment for each of them where the general sketch of the journey diverted from what had been planned and discussed prior to their departure, introducing an uncertainty that exacerbated the fear instilled by their confinement and the threats levied by their captors. Second, their access to communication with loved ones was constricted, increasing the fear each already felt. Third, their release and continued movement were no longer contingent on factors like the climate or the potential presence of immigration enforcement. Instead, they depended on their families' ability to negotiate with their captors and marshal the funds to pay their ransom, which was no easy task and could easily lead to further extortion. All of this contributed to the fourth characteristic: a shift in their relationships with their companions. For Sebastian, the relationship with his neighbor became deeper, transforming to one of mutual caretaking. Meanwhile, for Axel, it became emotionally necessary to withdraw as it became clear that many of them would not be able to access the funds being demanded of them. These relational reformulations reflect the complex ways migrants (young and old) might respond with deep humanity to the circumstances they encounter (Vogt 2018).

Detention in the United States

The car carrying Sebastian and his companions broke down somewhere in Colorado, and "everyone started to get nervous because they thought that the police were going to arrest us." The entire group hid in the car while a group of officers (presumably CBP agents) questioned the driver. They were then made to exit the vehicle and taken to a detention center. As a juvenile, Sebastian could not be held at the Colorado facility, which was only sanctioned to detain adults, so he was transferred to a different center for unaccompanied minors. Of all the hardships he had experienced so far in his travels, this proved to be the most emotionally wrenching, as it involved separating from the neighbor who had watched over him since he first left Guatemala.

> The lady who was taking care of me, she was literally crying. I remember it was sad because she didn't want to let me go, because she had been taking care of me. I was let go and was put in a box, kind of like in a freezer. It was cold, but I only stayed there for a day, I think. And after that someone came for me and took me to the airport in Colorado. . . . We flew all the way to Arizona. I stayed there for three months, I believe.

Axel and Sebastian were each initially detained in an adult facility in southern Arizona. Because they were underage, though, the boys needed to be transferred to a facility for unaccompanied minors managed by ORR. In many ways, this secondary detention was a relief for Axel, as it allowed him a bit more freedom than he had had in the first center. He was able to begin taking classes and gained more exposure to both English and Spanish, a language he spoke in school but did not use colloquially. Ironically, while he had studied the latter at home in Guatemala, it was in an ORR facility in the United States that he really became proficient, as he needed the language in order to communicate with other youth. In this location, Axel was given more food and a legitimate bed on which to sleep.

For Sebastian, this transfer was bittersweet. Like Axel, he was excited to be a little closer to his family and to enjoy the freedoms that the ORR facility afforded. However, he was devastated to leave behind the woman on whom he had come to depend throughout his journey. He remembers the heaving sobs of his companion and caretaker as he bid her goodbye, a recollection tempered only by her assurances that she was relieved he would soon be free and reunited with his mother. Over time, though, this relief began to wane. Sebastian ended up spending more than three months in this center. He cried constantly, even though conditions were arguably better than the prior detention center, where he had spent less time.

Sebastian's memories of this period are complicated. On the one hand, he had access to more resources and creature comforts, such as movies and game centers. Like Axel, he also started taking classes and learning English. At the same time, his life was heavily monitored. "We had a specific set of times which we should take a shower, do our laundry, do our bed, time to wake up, time to go to sleep, time to watch movies," he told me. "We had our own schedule and we had time to play as well. It was okay but I wasn't feeling comfortable in there though. I wanted to get out of there."

Sebastian's main comfort came from the connections he developed. As he explained, "The only thing that I like about it is that I met friends . . . that was the only thing." Even though he was able to take comfort in the relationships he built with other youth, he became increasingly anxious as time went on and he lost autonomy over how to spend his day. This effect was compounded as the days stretched on, turning into weeks and eventually into months. As before, his communication with Carmela was restricted and monitored, and he had little sense of when, if ever, and under what conditions he would be able to leave. In these ways, the facility began to sharply resemble the other places he had been detained along his journey, in which his communication with loved ones was constrained and he faced the anxiety of uncertainty, as well as restrictions on his physical movement and day-to-day activities. In hindsight, Sebastian recognized the detention center as a "happy place," at least in comparison to challenges he would later encounter, but at the time, he thought it was "horrible" and could not wait to get out—whenever that might be. Moreover, the fact that a government-run detention center felt akin to other spaces of detention Sebastian experienced shows how such facilities can operate under the same logics as those run by criminal networks.

Reunification and Aftermath

After they were released from detention, Axel and Sebastian undertook one final journey, traveling to California to finally reunite with their families. After years of separation and the trauma they had experienced since leaving Guatemala, the transition into life at "home" was difficult. Sebastian had longed to be reunited with his mother, but he found that the reality of reunification did not live up to his expectations. When he first met Carmela at the Los Angeles airport, he was taken aback.

> She was looking all different. I didn't even recognize her. I was afraid to go with her because she looked way too different, I don't know, after I saw my mom, I was like, "Please just take me back to Arizona again." I don't know, after that, it took me a while to get used to my mom because like I said, I didn't know her that much. I still don't.

For Axel, even more time had passed since he had last seen Elias. "When my brother left me, or left us, I was too young that I didn't really know him," he explained. But, unlike Sebastian, seeing his brother flooded him with relief. "I knew that I was finally free, basically, from all of the suffering that I had to come [to the United States]." These two different recollections reflect the complexities of family reunification, as members learn to live together again after the trauma of extended separation and protracted detention.

In the ensuing months, life in California was complicated. Axel and Sebastian each struggled to adjust to new homes, schools, and languages. In addition, each carried closely the effects of their journeys to the United States, including the multiple detentions they had experienced and the knowledge that their family members had literally invested significant resources in getting them to the United States. For years, neither shared any details about what they had undergone. The boys each had to figure out how to integrate themselves into the lives their relatives had established. Axel, for example, was often lonely, as his brother worked long hours and was in a committed relationship, meaning he was often away from home. Sebastian, meanwhile, found himself at odds with Carmela. "I started seeing a lot of things about my mom that, I don't know, it didn't make me comfortable. So I didn't want to stay anymore." Being with his mom again instigated a new rupture in their relationship. When she was no longer an encouraging voice on the phone, Sebastian began to see her limitations, and friction ensured. When Carmela moved the family to Maryland, Sebastian decided he had had enough. He moved in with his uncle for about six months, then, after some tense negotiations with Carmela, her husband (Sebastian's stepfather), and his dad, who was still in Atlanta, he moved back to California with the promise that he would increase his work hours to be able to support himself while continuing school.

For his first few months in the United States, Sebastian kept in contact with the neighbor who had cared for him throughout his journey. She was still being held in the adult detention center in Colorado. Their calls formed an anchor for Sebastian as he navigated unexpectedly complex relationships with the adults who now surrounded him. After a while, though, she stopped answering his calls. To date, Sebastian does not know if she made it into the United States, was sent to Mexico, or was deported to Guatemala. "I don't know what happened to her." He paused. "She took care of me, and I don't even remember her name."

Discussion: Relational Implications of the Multiple Contexts of Migrant Detention

At first glance, Axel and Sebastian's stories might seem to reflect established patterns in youth migration experiences. Both traveled with groups. Both were held hostage by the professionals their families had hired until they could produce additional funds. Both endured physically arduous passages. Both were detained upon arrival in the United States, then transferred to youth facilities, precipitating a separation from the other migrants with whom they had formed attachments throughout their journeys. In the center for unaccompanied minors, both began adjusting, learning new languages, and forming attachments once again, even as they underwent new traumas and were subjected to intense surveillance. Both were eventually released and moved to California to their families. And then, both landed in the same place, South Valley High School, where they began taking classes, learning English, participating in extracurricular activities, making friends, and formulating plans for the future. Both met me.

What is important to note about their stories, though, is the way they complicate understanding of the effects of youth migration and detention and broaden the definition of the latter category. On their journeys to the United States, Axel and Sebastian formed relationships with the people who traveled with and cared for them. These relationships varied in intensity and duration, but in every case they represent the ways in which the two boys found community—a resource that was critical for their ability to survive the traumas they encountered as they made their way from Guatemala to California. At the same time, these relationships were, by definition, short-lived, ruptured by the realities of migration and the boys' multiple experiences of detention. In Axel's case, maintaining relationships was simply too painful, especially when threats to his physical safety and that of his companions increased.

Years have passed since Axel and Sebastian first arrived in the United States. In the interim, we have seen an explosion of concern over the experiences of unaccompanied minors and separated families in federal detention centers. The impact of this attention cannot be overstated. At the same time, it is important to recall that such stories are not new. As other chapters in this volume show, young people have been moving, and their movement has been constricted, for years prior to Trump's arrival in office. Axel's and Sebastian's experiences as migrants and in the aftermath of detention provide a possible window into the effects children and youth currently being detained might experience upon their release, particularly when it comes to reintegrating into schools and families and establishing in the United States. In addition, their experiences are not limited to migrants classified as children. The adults with whom they traveled faced their own versions of these multiple contexts of detention and resulting relational ruptures.

What Axel's and Sebastian's stories also show is that detention is a broad experience that crosses borders. Confinement is not something that only takes place at the institutional level. At the same time, legalized detention and its illegal counterpart (i.e., kidnapping and family extortion) are not so different experientially. In each case, movement is constricted, contact with family is limited, languages are unfamiliar, captors are intimidating, temperatures are extreme, and fear abounds. Relationships within each of these spaces are critical for surviving detention in the immediate term and for living through its aftereffects. At the same time, such connections are consistently interrupted, introducing a new kind of "family separation," even when the "family" is someone young migrants have only known for a matter of weeks. These experiences can layer onto one another, becoming part of tangled crossing stories whose effects reverberate even after release and reunification. Understanding the multiple contexts of detention—and the relationships that form and rupture as migrants move among them—can help inform how families and communities support children and youth adapting to new lives in the United States. Most importantly, mapping out the clear similarities among these spaces should incense and motivate all members of the global community dedicated to protecting children and defending human rights across borders. Drawing parallels among U.S. detention centers and the extortion, confinement, and fear migrants experience before they cross the border is much more than an interesting analytical exercise. It is a tactic for illuminating the brutality of detention as it manifests in both physical and emotional or relational dimensions.

While Axel and Sebastian each survived the experiences recounted in this chapter, these pages are not intended to be a reflection on resilience. Rather, what I have aimed to do in sharing their stories is to show how the circumstances of migration—themselves a result of decades of anti-immigrant legislation and antihuman patrol and enforcement tactics—create iterative experiences of disruption that continuously break the very bonds that are forged in wrenching circumstances of displacement. The relationships young migrants form as they move through multiple contexts of detention provide a truncated encapsulation of the extended impacts of an immigration system whereby both fictive and biological connections are continuously severed, reimagined, and re-formed as young people and their families work to care for one another.

References

Andreas, Peter. 2009. *Border Games: Policing the U.S.-Mexico Divide.* 2nd ed. Ithaca, N.Y.: Cornell University Press.

Anthropologist Action Network for Immigrants & Refugees. 2021. "AANIR Calls on Biden Administration to Cease the Separation of Im/migrant Families and the Detention of Children." May 14. http://www.anthropologistactionnetwork.org/statement-on-ceasing-separation-of-families-may-2021.html.

Belloni, Milena. 2020. "Family Project or Individual Choice? Exploring Agency in Young Eritreans' Migration." *Journal of Ethnic and Migration Studies* 46 (2): 336–53.

Brigden, Noelle K. 2018. "Gender Mobility: Survival Plays and Performing Central American Migration in Passage." *Mobilities* 13 (1): 111–25.

Bylander, Maryann. 2020. "Destination Debts: Local and Translocal Loans in the Migrant Experience." *Geoforum* 137 (December): 194–202.

Caretta, Martina Angela, and María Alejandra Pérez. 2019. "When Participants Do Not Agree: Member Checking and Challenges to Epistemic Authority in Participatory Research." *Field Methods* 31 (4): 359–74.

Chishti, Muzaffar, and Faye Hipsman. 2015. "The Child and Family Migration Surge of Summer 2014: A Short-Lived Crisis with a Lasting Impact." *Journal of International Affairs* 68 (2): 95–114.

Davis, Kristina. 2020. "U.S. Officials Say They Are Highly Confident to Have Reached Tally on Separated Children: 4,368." *Los Angeles Times*, January 18.

De León, Jason. 2015. *The Land of Open Graves*. Berkeley: University of California Press.

Ebaugh, Helen Rose, and Mary Curry. 2000. "Fictive Kin as Social Capital in New Immigrant Communities." *Sociological Perspectives* 43 (2): 189–209.

Heidbrink, Lauren. 2018. "Circulation of Care Among Unaccompanied Migrant Youth from Guatemala." *Children and Youth Services Review* 92 (September): 30–38.

Heidbrink, Lauren. 2019. "The Coercive Power of Debt: Migration and Deportation of Guatemalan Indigenous Youth." *Journal of Latin American and Caribbean Anthropology* 24 (1): 263–81.

Heidbrink, Lauren. 2020. *Migranthood: Youth in a New Era of Deportation*. Stanford, Calif.: Stanford University Press.

Hernández, Kelly Lytle. 2010. *Migra! A History of the U.S. Border Patrol*. American Crossroads 29. Berkeley: University of California Press.

Kim, Esther Chihye. 2009. "'Mama's Family': Fictive Kinship and Undocumented Immigrant Restaurant Workers." *Ethnography* 10 (4): 497–513.

Lawrence-Lightfoot, Sara. 2005. "Reflections on Portraiture: A Dialogue Between Art and Science." *Qualitative Inquiry* 11 (1): 3–15.

Lee, Catherine. 2013. *Fictive Kinship: Family Reunification and the Meaning of Race and Nation in American Immigration*. New York: Russell Sage Foundation.

Manohar, Namita. 2013. "Support Networks, Ethnic Spaces, and Fictive Kin: Indian Immigrant Women Constructing Community in the United States." *AAPI Nexus: Policy, Practice and Community* 11 (1–2): 25–55.

Nevins, Joseph. 2010. *Operation Gatekeeper and Beyond: The War on "Illegals" and the Remaking of the US–Mexico Boundary*. New York: Routledge.

Nichols, Briana. 2021. "Nothing Is Easy: Educational Striving and Migration Deferral in Guatemala." *Journal of Ethnic and Migration Studies* 49 (7): 1919–35.

Oliveira, Gabrielle, and Mariana Lima Becker. 2019. "Immigrant Latina Youth and Their Education Experiences in the United States." In *Comparative Perspectives* on *Refugee Youth Education*, edited by Alexander W. Wiseman, Lisa Damaschke-Deitrick, Ericka L. Galegher, and Maureen F. Park, 220–44. New York: Routledge.

Oliveira, Gabrielle, and Corinne Kentor. 2020. "Latin Americans in the United States: Considerations on immigrant and refugee access to higher education." In *Refugees and Higher Education*, edited by Lisa Unangst, Hakan Ergin, Araz Khajarian, Tessa DeLaquil, and Hans de Wit, 98–112. Leiden: Brill Sense.

Rose, Joel. 2021. "Biden's Task Force Has Reunited 36 Migrant Families—with Hundreds to Go." NPR, June 8. https://www.npr.org/2021/06/08/1004205868/bidens-task-force-has-reunited-36-migrant-families-with-hundreds-to-go.

Sanchez, Gabriella. 2017. "Critical Perspectives on Clandestine Migration Facilitation: An Overview of Migrant Smuggling Research." *Journal on Migration and Human Security* 5 (1): 9–27.

Schmidt, Leigh Anne, and Stephanie Buechler. 2017. "'I Risk Everything Because I Have Already Lost Everything': Central American Female Migrants Speak Out on the Migrant Trail in Oaxaca, Mexico." *Journal of Latin American Geography* 16 (1): 139–64.

Southern Poverty Law Center. 2020. "Family Separation Under the Trump Administration—a Timeline." June 17. https://www.splcenter.org/news/2020/06/17/family-separation-under-trump-administration-timeline#2020.

Swanson, Kate, and Rebecca Maria Torres. 2016. "Child Migration and Transnationalized Violence in Central and North America." *Journal of Latin American Geography* 15 (3): 23–48.

Triandafyllidou, Anna. 2015. "Migrant Smuggling." In *Routledge Handbook of Immigration and Refugee Studies*, edited by Anna Triandafyllidou, 346–53. New York: Routledge.

Triandafyllidou, Anna. 2018. "Migrant Smuggling: Novel Insights and Implications for Migration Control Policies." *ANNALS of the American Academy of Political and Social Science* 676 (1): 212–21.

Vogt, Wendy. 2016. "Stuck in the Middle with You: The Intimate Labours of Mobility and Smuggling Along Mexico's Migrant Route." *Geopolitics* 21 (2): 366–86.

Vogt, Wendy A. 2018. *Lives in Transit: Violence and Intimacy on the Migrant Journey*. California Series in Public Anthropology 42. Berkeley. University of California Press.

Wall, Kate, Steve Higgins, Elaine Hall, and Pam Woolner. 2013. "'That's Not Quite the Way We See It': The Epistemological Challenge of Visual Data." *International Journal of Research & Method in Education* 36 (1): 3–22.

Wheatley, Abby C., and Ruth Gomberg-Muñoz. 2016. "Keep Moving: Collective Agency Along the Migrant Trail." *Citizenship Studies* 20 (3–4): 396–410.

Yarris, Kristin, and Heidi Castañeda. 2016. "'The Stress Along the Way': Medicalization and Transit Migration." *Youth Circulations: Tracing the Teal and Imagined Circulations of Global Youth*, February 9. https://www.youthcirculations.com/blog?offset=1456866897049.

CHAPTER FIVE

"I'm Not an Animal. I'm a Girl."

Recognizing Resistance in Latinx Migrant Youths' Testimonios of Being Detained by Customs and Border Protection

JENN M. LILLY

In scholarly and journalistic discourse, migrant children are frequently conceptualized as a particularly "vulnerable group" in need of protection (Podkul 2015; Gilodi, Albert, and Nienaber 2022). Indeed, there are many risks and harms associated with being detained by Customs and Border Protection (CBP) from which migrant children should be protected (Chavez and Menjívar 2010; Podkul 2015). From the moment youth migrants arrive on U.S. soil, they interact with carceral and legal systems that expose them to inhumane and unsafe conditions, which can lead to irreparable damage (Chavez and Menjívar 2010; Podkul 2015; Claro Quintans 2018). This research has been essential in establishing that child detention practices in the United States inflict biopsychosocial harms on migrant youth by unequally exposing them to greater risks for chronic and toxic stress, threatened or damaged attachment relationships, chronic disease, organ damage, mental illness, and other adverse health conditions that negatively impact migrant children's health and development (Chavez and Menjívar 2010; Podkul 2015; Cohodes et al. 2021; Edyburn and Meek 2021), constituting state-sanctioned, structural violence as defined by Sarah J. Diaz, Katherine Kaufka Walts, and Lisa Jacobs in chapter 1. Calling attention to the need to protect migrant children from these risks, a great deal of scholarly research emphasizes migrant children's vulnerability to trauma, abuse, and other forms of violence as a means of advocating for institutional and policy change (Ensor 2010; Van de Glind, International Labour Office, and ILO International Programme on the Elimination of Child Labour 2010; Lind 2019).

"Vulnerability" is, however, a contested term within the migration arena, which some migration scholars and practitioners have critiqued as distracting from structural violence (Brown, Ecclestone, and Emmel 2017; McLean 2019; Gilodi, Albert, and Nienaber 2022). Many conceptualizations of vulnerability seem to locate this condition within the individual or group rather than examining the systems of oppression and social structures that produce vulnerability (Gilodi, Albert, and Nienaber 2022). As social theorist Judith Butler (2021, 46) argues, we are all vulnerable to the social structures on which societies rely, as it is these structures that shape "the conditions that make our lives possible or impossible." From this view, structural conditions are responsible for vulnerabilities, wherein violent structures expose individuals to risks, harms, and precarity (Cole 2018; Butler 2021). Because we live in an unequal society characterized by social hierarchies, our social structures render some groups and individuals, such as children and migrants, more vulnerable than others (Cole 2018; Butler 2021).

When we consider vulnerability not as an attribute of a group but as a condition with which groups must contend, we are able to see the ways they persist in and resist that condition of vulnerability (Butler 2021). This conceptual move offers us a strengths-based perspective of youth migrants who persist in a condition of vulnerability, as Butler (2021, 201) explains:

> To avow vulnerability not as an attribute of the subject, but as a feature of social relations, does not imply vulnerability as an identity, a category, or a ground for political action. Rather, persistence in a condition of vulnerability proves to be its own strength, distinguished from one that champions strength as the achievement of invulnerability.

Operating from this theoretical perspective, I use the term *vulnerability* throughout this chapter with the understanding that vulnerability is a condition produced by oppressive social structures with which migrant children must contend. Acknowledging migrant youth's vulnerability to structural violence in CBP custody, this chapter presents and analyzes Latinx migrant youth's *testimonios* to reveal how they persist in and resist their vulnerability to the state-sanctioned, structural violence inflicted by CBP. The aim of this chapter is to illuminate the nonviolent strategies of resistance that migrant youth employ to struggle against their vulnerability within violent legal and carceral structures, allowing us to comprehend the strength of migrant youth persisting in a vulnerable condition.

Recognizing Migrant Youth's Everyday Acts of Resistance

Conceptualizing resistance is a transdisciplinary, fluid, and ongoing project that has thus far resulted in a plurality of proposed definitions and concepts (Baaz et al. 2016; Johansson and Vinthagen 2019). Despite varying viewpoints on whether or not and by whom resistance needs to be recognized as such, scholars agree that resistance is an act that is always oppositional to power (Baaz et al. 2016). Butler (2021, 192) argues that the condition of vulnerability opens up new sites for resistance, which we can only appreciate by considering "how vulnerability and resistance can work together." The many ways in which migrant youth are both vulnerable to and resist structural violence in their interactions with the CBP and its agents attest to Butler's claim. To understand and interpret the acts of resistance migrant youth employ in immigrant detention, we must recognize that acts of resistance can take place even in conditions of vulnerability through interactions with power in everyday life (Johansson and Vinthagen 2019).

Most examinations of resistance have focused on confrontational, blatant, public acts organized through some formalized process with the intent of disrupting or undermining power relations (Johansson and Vinthagen 2019). Such overt acts of resistance are essential to social change in certain contexts, but an overfocus on these forms of resistance can overshadow and render invisible the many ways people challenge, negotiate, and redistribute power in their everyday lives (Butler 2021). In the context of CBP detention, migrant youth's acts of resistance are often informal, nonconfrontational, and sometimes purposefully hidden. These "everyday" forms of resistance are not necessarily politically motivated but are nevertheless performed by migrant youth out of a desire or need to subvert the authority of the immigration enforcement system's power (Johansson and Vinthagen 2019). This chapter aims to increase recognition of these forms of resistance in migrant youth's narratives of CBP detention.

Drawing heavily from leading resistance theorists (Hollander and Einwohner 2004; Baaz et al. 2016; Johansson and Vinthagen 2019), I define resistance, for the purposes of this chapter, as an act done by a person or group in a condition of vulnerability that has the potential to challenge, negotiate, or undermine violence or power. Using this definition recognizes that where there is vulnerability, there is resistance (Foucault 1980). It also calls attention to the political relevance of the seemingly ordinary, needs- or desire-oriented actions of youth migrants in detention by acknowledging the potential of these actions to struggle against the violence of immigration enforcement systems and their agents. Thus, this chapter examines the nonviolent ways youth migrants resist the structural violence inflicted by the CBP, inviting readers to consider the ways in which youth migrants are both vulnerable and struggling against that vulnerability.

Capturing Subaltern Narratives Through *Testimonio* Research

This chapter presents and analyzes migrant youth's migration narratives documented through a participatory digital *testimonio* research project. *Testimonio*, an oral history method that originated in Latin America, is a collaborative process of documenting a narrator's previously untold, first-person account of socially or culturally significant events (Delgado Bernal, Burciaga, and Flores Carmona 2012). Defining features of the *testimonio* approach include the following: (1) the narrator is an ordinary person who is able to offer a subaltern (i.e., underrepresented or marginalized) perspective based on their social location and identity; (2) the narrator's *testimonio* is connected to or meant to be representative of an oppressed group and that group's struggle for social justice; and (3) the narrator speaks out in response to the group's oppression, imbuing *testimonios* with a sense of political urgency and invoking a call to action (Delgado Bernal, Burciaga, and Flores Carmona 2012). Latin American *testimonio* is considered "the most authentic representation of subaltern lives" (Henderson 2001, 83), making it a methodology well suited to illuminating migrant youths' acts of everyday resistance in immigrant detention. *Testimonio* is also a meaning-making process, creating the opportunity for narrators and researchers to make sense of the narrator's experiences together through the dialogic and collaborative processes of oral storytelling, representation, and dissemination (Delgado Bernal, Burciaga, and Flores Carmona 2012).

For this project, narrators were Latinx youth (ages 18–21; eight female, four male) who immigrated to the United States from Central America or Mexico irregularly and were engaged together in a youth organizing initiative to protect and advance their rights and well-being. These narrators entrusted their *testimonios* to me, a doctoral researcher at the time, who had worked in solidarity with their youth organizing initiative for two years. Although I am not a part of the Latinx or immigrant population, I am an ally to the immigrant rights movement, and I sought to leverage my position of privilege within the academy to increase awareness, attention to, and action against the repression and struggles of Latinx immigrant youth in New Orleans.

New Orleans had a long history of a stable but small Latinx presence before experiencing a rapid growth in Latinx residents following Hurricane Katrina in 2005 (Drever 2008). In contrast to the existing Latinx population in the area, Latinx newcomers tended to be low-skilled workers with limited English proficiency and no legal immigration status, and therefore were perceived to have unique needs (Drever 2008). The city also saw a rise in unaccompanied minors in the 2010s, with the number of juvenile immigration cases in Louisiana jumping from 71 in 2011 to 450 in the first six months of 2014, all but 20 of which were referred to the New Orleans immigration court (Maldonado 2014). Many of these young people, including those who participated in this project, migrated to New Orleans to reunite with family members who came to the city to work on recovery efforts following the storm.

We (the youth co-researchers and I) sought to conduct research that would increase understanding of the barriers and bridges to well-being for Latinx young people in New Orleans and advocate for needed resources to support their well-being. Leveraging funding from a fellowship program focused on community-engaged scholarship, I was able to secure the resources needed to carry out a participatory digital research project with this group of young people. The digital *testimonio* research project was born of the group's desire to use media to organize around issues important to them and formed the subject of my dissertation research. Over approximately six months of data collection, we digitally documented (using audio and video recordings) the *testimonios* of twelve young people, asking them to share their life stories. Each narrator shaped their own narrative, with clarifying and probing questions from me. We collaboratively analyzed the twelve *testimonios* to identify key themes in relation to our research questions. A journal article critically analyzing the research process provides a more detailed account of our collaborative approach to this work, its methodological underpinnings, and further details on the data collection methods and analytic techniques employed (Lilly 2022).

The stories presented in this chapter are excerpts from the *testimonios* of two participants, Estrella and Cindy, who shared their life stories with me.[1] These two *testimonios* were selected as case studies of experiences in CBP custody because the narrators chose to describe this part of their migration story in greater detail than other participants. Each narrative is interpreted through the lens of Butler's (2021) theoretical perspective on vulnerability and resistance to highlight the ways in which Estrella and Cindy challenged, negotiated, or undermined violence or power while persisting in vulnerable conditions. While not intended to be representative of all participants' experiences, Estrella's and Cindy's stories offer a glimpse into two migrant youth's experiences of being detained and held in CBP custody and provide illustrative examples of their perceptions of themselves as protagonists with the capacity to persist in and resist structural violence and power intended to render them vulnerable.

Estrella's Story

I first met Estrella in 2018, during her junior year of high school in the United States. Estrella was seventeen and had been living in the New Orleans area with her mother and siblings for two years. She had an impressive command of English, which she learned in just six months. In addition to attending school, Estrella had held a few different part-time jobs and helped care for her younger siblings. She had a close relationship with her older sister, Evangeline, and her grandmother, who lived in Mexico but visited the family in the United States for a few months at a time. Estrella was actively involved in her church and several extracurricular activities at school. In my experiences with her in one-on-one conversations and in group settings with her peers, Estrella loved to crack jokes—she exuded a positive attitude, often making light of situations, laughing, and making others laugh. When she gave her *testimonio*, which was more than two and a half hours long, she told me her life story with great animation and detail, parts of which I summarize here to introduce Estrella and her life experiences prior to being detained.

Estrella was born in Oaxaca, Mexico, the second of two daughters born to her parents. Her father, who was gang involved, was never part of Estrella's life. Estrella's mother struggled to provide for her children as a single parent, so she made the difficult decision to migrate to the United States to support her family when Estrella was just three years old. Estrella and her sister, Evangeline, remained in Mexico, where they were raised by their maternal grandmother, with whom they shared a very strong bond. Estrella grew up as a devoted Christian who enjoyed spending time with her family, reading, and playing sports.

When Estrella was ten or eleven years old, her family began receiving death threats because of her father's gang-related activities. Because they were estranged, the details of her father's activities were unknown to Estrella, but her family became aware that a rival gang killed her father's brother in an act of vengeance. Soon afterward, the rival gang threatened the lives of Estrella and Evangeline, forcing them to flee Oaxaca with their grandmother. Estrella's grandmother was unable to endure a lengthy journey, so they made temporary arrangements to live with a family friend in El Salvador. After a few years, the threats subsided and Estrella's mother arranged for her daughters to reunite with her in the United States. First, the girls returned to Mexico with their grandmother, where Estrella was able to celebrate her fifteenth birthday with her family in Oaxaca. Then, Estrella and Evangeline bid farewell to their grandmother and made the arduous journey through Mexico together, eventually arriving at a great expanse of desert at the U.S.-Mexico border. This is Estrella's story of what followed, in her own words.

We made it across the border. We had to walk for like two hours and it was one in the morning. I was so tired from running and walking and being bitten by so many mosquitos. At one point, I was just like, "I can't, I need to stop." But my sister told me we were so close, we had to keep going. It was a hard moment, it was a really tough moment. And at like 3 a.m., we got to a place where we could see lights, you could actually see your own body. We found another group walking. They were Brazilians, and one woman was pregnant. And I was like, "If she can do this and she's pregnant, I can do it too. I'm not giving up right now. I'm so close to seeing my mom, and this is just one last step and I'm there."

I remember a truck coming. It was border control. And there was this super tall guy. I looked at his face and he was staring at us like he was mad. And he started yelling, "Take your shoes off! Throw it away, everything!" And I was like, "Why would I throw everything away?" They kept telling us to take off our shoes. And I remember that for that trip, I wore my favorite shoes. Oh, it hurt me so much to leave them lying there. I was like [in Spanish], "No, my shoes! My shoes! My feet are cold!" And this man was telling me to take them off. And I thought, I'm going to tell them that I don't understand and I'm not going to take them off.

And then this woman comes. It was a black lady who was in really good shape, and she was like, "Why are you looking at me?" And I was like [in Spanish], "I don't understand." And then she was like [in Spanish], "I do understand you." And I was like, "Ha! You speak Spanish?" And she said, "Yes, I speak Spanish." And she said, "He says you have to take off your shoes and remove your shoelaces." And I was like, "Oh, that's what he was saying?" And she says to me, "Yes, take them off," she says, "and also remove your ponytail, your earrings, your necklace, and everything else you're wearing." And I said, "They're going to undress us here?" And she said to me, "No, not here. But take off your shoes and your ponytail." They wanted to see if we were armed. She told me, "We want to see if you brought a gun or a knife or a phone or anything." And I told her, "But what if I didn't bring anything? Why do they have to search me?" And she told me, "You just do what they say," she says. "They can punish you."

Well, my sister, she has always been the kind of person who, when she feels like she's in danger, she obeys without thinking about what she's doing. But not me. I was like, "No and no." At that moment, I was like, "I'm not leaving my shoes. They're my favorite shoes." And this woman was like, "I don't care about your shoes. You have to take them off." And I remember that I took them off and took out my ponytail.

Then another woman came, she was fat and white, and she told us, "We're going to get into this van, and you're going to sit and put on your seatbelt because we need to bring you somewhere else." I remember that van smelled fucking terrible. And I was like, "Evangeline, do you smell that? I think someone vomited. Or else, who knows why it smells so bad?" And I was complaining the whole car ride. And the woman was like, "Cállense! Silencio! [Shut up! Be quiet!]" It was the only word she could say in Spanish. And I was like, "No te entiendo

[I don't understand you]." And she was like, "It's Spanish!" And I told Evangeline, "I think I'm going to throw up. And I'm thirsty. And it smells so bad. I can't take this anymore. My feet are cold." And they kept shouting at me to be quiet. They poked me in the ribs. And I was like, "Okay, I'm going to be quiet."

Then we got to this place where they had everything. They took away our last backpack that we had brought with us—it was a small one. And that's where they made us take off all of our clothes. They stripped us completely. No one had ever seen me nude before, except my mom. And I was like, "No, I'm not going to undress," I said to my sister. And then I looked at the other boys and girls naked and I was like, "Huh? Don't they feel bad?" Or like, "I don't want to let them see me." And the black lady who spoke Spanish came and she told me, "We need to see if you have any tattoos or marks, or if you have an infection or if you've gotten cut, or anything like that." And I was like, "No, I'm good." And actually, I wasn't. But I didn't want them to see me because I felt embarrassed. I didn't want anyone to see me because no one had ever done that.

And so, I said to my sister, "What are we going to do now?" And she says, "We have to undress." And so, I looked at the black lady and she said, "Hurry up, or they're going to come hit you." I said, "Hit me? Why? I mean, they can't force me to do anything." And she said to me, "You're in another country. The rules are different." And I said, "Okay," and I was like in shock. And then she was like, "Hey, quick, quick!" And I was like, "No." And she told me, "If you don't get undressed, we will undress you." And I said, "No, that's sexual assault." And she comes and says to me, "No, because no one is touching you. We're just going to remove your clothes." I said, "It's the same thing, just a different way of saying it." And she said, "Okay, undress yourself then." And I told her, "I'm not going to undress until you take me to a place where there are only girls and only policewomen." And I remember this other fat man came, and who knows what they said, but they took me and my sister and the other girls to another place. So, in that room, we got undressed.

Then all of the women started lowering their heads, and I was like, "Why are they doing that? Are they praying?" in my ignorance. And my sister told me, "Just do what you see them doing. Remember what Grandma told us—wherever you go, do what you see." So, I lowered my head and since I had taken my ponytail out, my hair was loose. And a woman came with like an extinguisher, and she started spraying our hair. And I screamed at her, "This hurts! It burns! It's burning my head!" And I started crying because my head hurt a lot. "It's burning me, I can't take it!" And the black woman came and said, "You're always complaining! Don't worry about it." And then she smacked me in the butt with the baton she was carrying. And I was going to push her when Evangeline pulled me and said, "No, don't do that." Later, I asked, "What was it that they sprayed on us?" And they told me, "It's for lice." And I said, "I don't have lice!" And she said, "The lice here are white. You can't see them. So, we don't know if you have them or not." I said to Evangeline, "Even the lice here are white?"—making a joke again. And the woman told me, "You be quiet. You complain about everything."

Then they brought us to this room, it was like a cooler. I had no shoes, no ponytail. And they make you put on this pajama thing. Kind of like a hospital gown or a jail thing. It was white and see-through. I was covering myself because I didn't want anyone to see me. And so was Evangeline—she wanted me to stand in front of her so nobody could see her. And they put us in this cooler. It was so cold. And they didn't give us anything. And I was without socks even because they take them off. So, I had this stupid stuff that they sprayed in our hair, and I was like, "Oh my god, this hurts so much." And then, there was only one bathroom and one sink. And it was like a bunch of girls and babies in the same spot. And all of us had to use the same bathroom with no doors, with no windows, and no paper either. And I was like, "Oh my god. It stinks. This place is disgusting." I was regretting so many things, that I was like, "I should've stayed at home. At this time, I should be sleeping." You lose track of the time. You don't even know if it's day or if it's night, or if it's hot outside. You don't even remember the sun.

We were there for maybe three to four days. I lost track. And I was like, "I can't do this. I'm still thirsty. And this stuff is hurting my head and my hair, and my eyes too," because I had a cut on my eye from a branch that scraped me, and all they did was give me a Band-Aid. So, I was bleeding, I was thirsty, and my hair and all this, and I was super cold. And I was just like, "Evangeline, you need to help me because I feel like I can't." And then she was like, "But I'm cold too." And she was so pale. I was like, "You don't look like you're brown, you look super white now." And I got scared. So, I just started hugging her and I just remember her falling asleep. I grabbed her into my arms, and then she started sleeping. Then at that moment, I needed to use the bathroom. But I had her in my arms, so, I was like, I can hold it.

A few hours later, they called us and said, "Do you have any papers? Do you have someone in the United States? Do you know someone? Why are you coming here? And what's the reason you're coming here?" Or, asking a bunch of questions that I didn't even remember the bunch that they did. So, I was like, "I don't want to answer questions until I get water, because I'm thirsty." So, I told them, "I need water. I'm super tired. And this stuff is hurting my head and I can't take it." And this young woman arrives who was a police officer too, and she was mad. I think she was like the boss; I don't know. And she had a packet of water for me.

I told my sister, "I don't understand what they're saying. I feel like I'm lost in the desert, but unlike a desert, it's freezing. And it's so bright." Because if it was night, it was fucking bright in there, and if it was day, the same. And always so cold. They kept the girls separate from the boys, and every time more kids arrived, they came to the same place—everyone. There wasn't even space, not even on the floor. There were pregnant girls and young kids, little girls and babies. And I was like, "I want to leave. I should have stayed home. I shouldn't have come." And Evangeline told me, "Remember our purpose, why we came. Just remember that and we're going to be okay." She said, "Remember the promise we made?" And I said yes, and I calmed down.

They brought us to another place, and I remember this young woman, she started to scream. And later she said in Spanish, "These sons of bitches! They don't know what they're doing. They're kids!" And she got mad. So, we got there, and they opened the door, and they started giving water to everyone, and a small little packet. And I was like, "What is this?" And they said, "Open it—it's to cover yourself." It was like a little thin, tiny foil. And we had to cover ourselves with that. I was like, "How am I supposed to cover myself with this?" But Evangeline was like, "Take it." And we took it and covered ourselves.

Every five or ten minutes, they would come and call more people—people that sometimes returned to the room afterward and people that never came back. And I asked Evangeline, "Where are they bringing these people? Look—you remember the girl that was pregnant? She didn't come back. What did they do with her?" And Evangeline said, "I don't know. Just relax or they're not going to call us."

There were people sleeping in there, but you couldn't sleep, because if you were asleep when they called you, they didn't call you again. And you couldn't even tell them who you were because they asked for identification and they had taken everything away from us, so it was illogical. I was almost sleeping; my eyes were super heavy and they were closing on themselves. But Evangeline was like, "No, don't sleep. Or let's take turns sleeping." So, I said, "Yeah, good idea." So, she fell asleep first, and then I went next, and then she went next. Until they called us.

It was this other white man. He was like, "Do you know anybody? Do you remember any phone numbers? Do you have someone here?" And I was like, "Yeah, my mom." And they called her, and I was so happy to hear her voice, it was like, "Okay, finally, I'm going home." I was crying when I heard her voice in there and Evangeline was too. And mom was like, "Oh, my babies." Then, I could only hear her say one thing: "I miss you." And then the man was like, "Okay, I need to talk to her. You need to move." And they kicked us out of the room and brought us back to the cooler. I wanted to talk to my mom. I wanted to say something. I wanted to get out of there. I was so tired, and I needed clothes, and I was cold. And I was just like, I can't. And then they called us again to answer more questions, which we did.

We spent three or four days in there, and then they brought us to another place. This place wasn't cold. It wasn't a cooler. And at least they gave us clothes. But it was some sort of jail. I was like, "They treat us like animals. They treat us like we're worthless." The only thing they gave us to eat was yogurt and a really acidic juice—it was so bitter; it burned your throat—and a piece of bread. That's all they gave us the whole day. Nothing else after that.

Then, they brought us to another place where they made us bathe, in bathrooms without doors, everyone there in a straight line. And they passed out clothes—underwear, an undershirt, a top, a long-sleeve shirt that was like a sweater, and some pants. And some awful blue shoes that were like slippers. But I was like, "At least we won't be so cold." And Evangeline was like, "Yeah, it's a little better." But this place was kinda like a prison, like a cage for animals. There were mattresses at least. And they gave us the same stupid aluminum foil again for blankets. But it was cleaner there. They didn't call us again, since the last time when we talked to our mom and she told us, "I miss you." After that, we didn't talk to her anymore. And we were in this other place for like two days. They didn't let us go outside. They didn't let us see anyone. They separated me from my sister. She was in another cell, and I was in this one. And there were walls, so we couldn't see each other. The only thing they gave us was a book to read in English. How are you going to read something in English if you don't know English? And they gave us some crayons to color. But I was like, "I don't want these. I want to see my sister." They didn't let me talk to my mom, and now I couldn't talk to my sister either.

I was super depressed. I just laid down on the mattress and cried. And I started thinking, "If God loves me and he's my Father, why is he making me go through all of this? I can't take it anymore." I was like, "I would rather have died than come here." I remember this old guy—he was in really nice clothes—and he came, and he was like, "Why are you crying?" I was surprised that he spoke Spanish. And I told him, "They separated me from my sister." I said, "I don't know where she is, or if they took her. I don't know if she left me here alone. I don't know," I said. And he told me, "Don't cry. We're going to find her." And I said, "But you don't even know who she is. You don't know her name." And he told me, "But you can give it to me." I said, "And what happens if you don't find her? I can't go without her. I can't leave her by herself. I made her a promise." And he was like, "Don't cry. Everything is going to be okay. Just relax. We're going to find her." And I was like, "No, we're not going to find her. Why did they separate me from her? I'm not an animal. I'm a girl. I'm a person. They don't let me talk to my mom or see my sister. So, what do I do?" And he told me, "No, we're going to find her." And he took me out of there.

He put his arm around me, and he brought me to a desk, and he said, "We're going to play something." "What?" I said. "You close your eyes," he told me, "and imagine that you're in a place, your favorite place. And imagine your family," he said. "Imagine that you're going to be with them." And I told him, "How can you ask me to do that if I don't have my sister? I'm not going to relax. Don't ask me to be calm because I'm not." Well, he got up and went and got a laptop or a tablet. And I was like, I felt lost. I didn't know where I was, I didn't know what he was doing, I didn't know what was going to happen. And he was like, "Okay, do you feel better?" And I was like, "No." And I remember that he went and got me a candy, a lollipop. And he gave it to me. And I was like annoyed and sad, and I took it and threw it. And I said, "I don't want that. I want my sister. I don't know what you did with her, if she's lost or what." And he said, "Don't be that way. I'm a good guy. I'm not one of those bad guys. I'm not the police. I'm just here to help you find your mom. That's who you're looking for, right? So, I'm going to help you. I have your paperwork and I'm going to help you."

So, he looked through all these binders. And he asked me, "What is your sister's name?" And I said, "Evangeline." And he said, "She's in this room. Want to go and see her?" And I said, "What if she's not there?" He said, "We'll find her." And I was crying, and I said, "Okay, but if she's not there, I'm going to be mad at you because you said you would find her." And he said, "Okay," and we went.

And we found her—she was coloring too. And I said, "Evangeline!" And we both ran towards each other and hugged. And I said, "What did they do to you? What happened? Why did they separate us?" And she said, "I don't know either. Why are you crying?" And I said, "Because they separated us, stupid!" And she said, "Don't cry. I'm here. I was worried too, but a woman told me that you were in the cell next to me and not to worry." And I said, "What made you believe them? After everything that they've done?" And she said, "Relax." I said, "Okay." And then the man specifically asked the guards not to separate us. And he said to me, "Now you're with your sister. Do you feel better?" I said yes. "Do you want a candy now?" he asked. I said no. And he asked why not. "Because I don't want a candy. I want to go to my house." And he said, "You're a difficult girl." And I said, "It's not that I'm difficult, it's that I don't want to be here."

Estrella's Resistance

Acts of resistance are the driving forces in Estrella's narrative, as she describes a series of mounting conflicts between the authorities' will and her own. As the protagonist of her story, Estrella is an agent of resistance against the system's attempts to dehumanize her—as clearly demonstrated by her insistence that she is not an animal, she's a girl. In her telling of events, Estrella was placed in situations designed to render her vulnerable and strip her of agency, yet she maintained and exercised her power as demonstrated through many acts of resistance that challenged her condition of vulnerability.

Estrella first engaged in purposefully hidden acts of resistance by struggling against CBP agents' demands to remove her shoes. Although her limited English proficiency created a vulnerability in interacting with English-speaking agents, this vulnerability opened up a site of resistance for Estrella (Butler 2021). Rather than obeying their orders and exposing her bare feet to the elements, Estrella feigned ignorance of what they were ordering her to do. By choosing to act as though she didn't understand their directives (a hidden form of resistance) and then outright refusing to comply with agents' orders, Estrella demonstrated her opposition to an order that would have increased her vulnerability to harm. In her narrative, Estrella indicated that this choice was motivated by her desire to keep her favorite pair of shoes (*Oh, it hurt me so much to leave them lying there*) and her need to protect her feet (*My feet are cold!*). Estrella's agentic decision to pretend that she could not understand any English was an act of resistance and self-protection, signaling her understanding that she did not need the CBP to protect her, but she needed to protect herself *from* them.

Estrella's account of the dehumanizing strip-search practices employed by CBP further demonstrates her desire to protect herself from the violent practices with which she was compelled to interact. It is hard to imagine a more vulnerable condition than that of a child being forced to remove all her clothing in front of militarized agents (or having it forcibly removed by them). Estrella actively struggled against this practice, refusing to enter a condition of heightened vulnerability by not removing her clothes. In response to Estrella's refusal to undress, a CBP agent threatened Estrella, a fifteen-year-old child, with physical force. When Estrella persisted in her refusal to comply, the agent threatened to remove her clothing from her—an act Estrella verbally identified as sexual assault, demonstrating her recognition that such practices constitute acts of violence from which she needed to protect herself. Estrella's statement (*That's sexual assault*) emphasized her vulnerability to violence, opening up a new site of resistance by naming the agents' threat as a prohibited violent act (Butler 2021). Doing so redistributed power in this situation, allowing Estrella to set conditions (she would only undress in the presence of other females) for her compliance. By resisting the condition of vulnerability foisted upon her and denouncing the acts of violence with which she was threatened, Estrella demonstrated *with* her own vulnerability to limit her exposure to potential harm.

Estrella's *testimonio* also reveals how as her resistance escalated, so too did the responses of the Spanish-speaking CBP agent who appears several times in her story. At first, the agent responded to Estrella's questioning, providing some explanation for why the children were asked to do certain things, such as removing their clothing. But in instances when Estrella refused to comply with the directives she was given, the agent was quick to remind her that she would be punished if she did not do as she was told. At the height of Estrella's resistance, when she outright refused to remove her clothing in front of others, the Spanish-speaking agent threatened Estrella with direct violence. This was not an empty threat, as the agent then struck fifteen-year-old Estrella with her baton when Estrella cried out about the lice spray hurting her head. Although Estrella struggled against the condition of vulnerability to protect herself from the violence that the CBP inflicted, the agent responded to that resistance with increasing violence, forcing Estrella into an increasingly vulnerable state.

Estrella's story culminates with her efforts to reunite with her sister, Evangeline. Estrella's solidarity with Evangeline is itself a form of resistance against vulnerability. We see their solidarity throughout Estrella's narrative: when Estrella felt like giving up in the desert, Evangeline refused to leave her behind; when Estrella wanted to fight back against the violent blow she sustained from a CPB agent, Evangeline restrained her from doing so; when Evangeline felt vulnerable in her see-through gown, Estrella shielded her with her own body; when Evangeline grew pale and fatigued, Estrella cradled her sleeping body in her arms. By cleaving together, the sisters were able to help protect themselves from harm, caring for one another so that they could persist in a vulnerable condition. Their separation not only distressed Estrella; it posed a threat to their solidarity, increasing Estrella's vulnerability and resistance.

Estrella's tears of anger at being separated from her sister attracted the attention of a so-called good guy—most likely a lawyer or Child Advocate meant to help her. However, placing oneself in a position of needing help from another individual is also a condition of vulnerability that Estrella resisted. Estrella was reluctant to accept the man's assistance, perhaps seeing him as part of the immigration enforcement system that she rightfully distrusted and felt the need to protect herself against. Although Estrella eventually, tentatively accepted his offer to help, she still guarded against her own vulnerability to the situation by refusing the candy and games he thought would assuage her, decrying the hypocrisy of being asked to remain calm in a distressing situation, and threatening to become angry with him if he didn't find her sister. Only after he stated that he was "not the police" was Estrella able to perceive him as someone capable of helping her find Evangeline.

The man did help Estrella find her sister and ensured that they would be able to stay together for the remainder of their time in detention. But when Estrella still refused his candy afterward, the man responded by labeling her a "difficult girl"—a label Estrella rejected as she pointed out the obvious: she didn't want candy; she wanted to free herself from a violent system of restriction and containment. For as long as Estrella remained in immigrant detention, her only choice was to persist in and resist the structural violence to which she was vulnerable.

What is perhaps most striking in Estrella's account of her interactions with the "good guy" is her active assertion of the value of her life in telling the man, "I am not an animal. I'm a girl. I'm a person." This statement resonates with Butler's theory of nonviolence as a way "of entering the force field of violence to stop its continuation," not by overcoming vulnerability but by demonstrating it and demonstrating with it (Butler 2021, 194). In claiming, "I'm a girl. I'm a person," Estrella was asserting what Butler (2021, 202) refers to as her grievability—the living value of her life that would make her loss worthy of grief. With this statement, Estrella demands to be recognized as a living, grievable life, demanding that she "ought to be able to persist in [her] living without being subject to violence, systemic abandonment, or military obliteration" (Butler 2021, 202). In a context in which the lives of migrants are not valued or considered worthy of grief, and migrant children are placed in "conditions that attack the very conditions of persistence" (Butler 2021, 201), Estrella asserted the value of her life and her right to live in a world that supports her ability to live free from violence.

Cindy's Story

I met Cindy in January 2018 when she was nineteen years old. Cindy had been living in the United States since age twelve and was an exceptional student while in school. She aspired to attend college but could not pursue this dream due to financial limitations associated with her undocumented immigration status. After she graduated from high school, she entered the work force full-time and was often exploited and treated unfairly as an undocumented worker, which forced her to change jobs frequently. When I met her, she was working in the office of a construction company. Outside of working hours, Cindy was actively involved in immigrant organizing efforts and enjoyed playing soccer. In my experience with Cindy, I knew her to be a passionate advocate for others who often took time to reflect and formulate her own opinions. Cindy didn't share much about her family life with me until giving her two-hour *testimonio* in 2019, during which she tearfully confided that she was living with her aunt in the suburbs of New Orleans because she had a falling-out with her mother after coming out as gay. She also shared many details of her life prior to migrating to the United States, which I summarize here to provide context for her detention story.

Cindy was the youngest child born to an Indigenous K'iche' Maya family in the Highlands region of Guatemala. When she was very young, her parents moved the family to Guatemala City (the nation's capital) in search of better economic opportunities. Her parents separated during her childhood, and Cindy rarely saw her father, though he remained in Guatemala City. Not long after the separation, Cindy's mother migrated to the United States in search of better economic opportunities to support her family. Cindy was five years old when her mother migrated, leaving Cindy and her two older siblings, a sister and a brother, in the care of their aunt. Cindy was very close with her aunt and her cousins (her aunt's biological children), who were like siblings to her. Cindy and her siblings received scholarships to attend a local, private Catholic school where Cindy became involved in oration contests and played soccer.

When Cindy was twelve, her mother made arrangements for Cindy and her brother to migrate to the United States. At first, Cindy wasn't interested in reuniting with her mother (a woman she barely knew), preferring to remain in Guatemala with her aunt. But later, she decided to migrate because she did not want to live apart from her brother. The two of them traveled to the United States together, facing many perils and setbacks before arriving at the border, where they were apprehended by the CBP. The following is Cindy's first-person account of this experience.

> We crossed the border around ten at night. We went into the river. We had to get into floats, and we crossed. Once we crossed, we were soak-

ing wet, and we had to wait until everybody else crossed. We were being guided by two men—an older man and a younger one. The younger one was around twenty or twenty-one and before we crossed, he was doing cocaine. And the other dude was drunk. I knew about drugs and all that because people do it back home like it's nothing. But I was worried because what if something happened and we got caught and they wouldn't have known what the hell they were doing, and we would have to pay for their irresponsibility?

But we crossed. I made sure my brother was with me. And right after we crossed, we walked like an hour and then we started hearing the helicopters on top of us, looking for us. The older man said, "Don't look up! Just take cover, stay down!" And after like twenty to thirty minutes, the helicopters left, and we kept walking. We walked the whole night. And then around six or seven in the morning, we were all tired because we walked a lot, and I don't know where these two dudes went. Everyone went their separate ways.

We were so tired, I told my brother, "Let's just stay here for a little while until we catch our breath." There was like a hiding spot by a bunch of trees. But what we didn't see was that there was a car parked on the road, and it was immigration. The dude in the car, the policeman, he was sleeping. But then he woke up and realized we were there. And everybody started running because we didn't want to get caught. My brother and I got separated because he ran faster than I did. And I got arrested. Then I was like, "Where's my brother?" I couldn't see him. I kept asking the officer to ask the other officers if they had found my brother. I told them his name. Later, my brother told me that he had gotten on top of a tree and was hiding there and nobody saw him. But then he realized that he didn't know where I was and he thought I was probably already arrested, so he turned himself in because he wanted to be with me. Whatever we had to go through, we wanted to go through it together, instead of I go by myself, and he goes by himself.

Around eight in the morning, we got to the jail. And they told us to take everything off—just keep one shirt, one pants, and no socks. They were mean—just because I don't want to curse. We thought they took our clothes because it was really hot out, so we thought "Oh, we don't want to be hot in there." And we had good sweaters and pants and socks and everything. They took the laces off my shoes, and we went in there, and it was so cold. They kept us in a little cell for like three to four days, something like that. And they would feed us like twice. I talked to one of the ladies in there, because they separated ladies from men, and she told me, "You gotta wake up in the morning, like five in the morning, four in the morning because that's when they bring the food. If you don't get food, then you will have to wait up until like twelve noon, and then that's the only thing you're going to eat. But I will make sure, if I wake up, I'm going to wake you up." And I said, "Okay, thank you." Because I didn't know anything.

I didn't talk to my mother the whole time. I didn't talk to my brother. And I remember I woke up one time and saw that my brother was out of the cell. They had him sitting down on a chair. I tried to ask him what he was doing, but of course, he couldn't talk to me because they were telling him not to. And they would just make fun of us and laugh and look at us like we didn't belong. It was obvious through their body language that they didn't want us there. They didn't want us at all. I remember seeing my brother get his fingerprints taken, and then they told me that they called my mom and asked if she had two kids and told her our names and ages. And she told them she was waiting for us and asked if she was able to get us out of there. And they were like, "We can't tell you anything, but we will call you back."

We didn't take showers during the whole time that we were there. I think like three or four days. We didn't shower, and we didn't have clothes. Like I told you, we were sweaty, because we had run all that way, and then we came in there, and it was so cold. They didn't give you water. Like they had a toilet—on top of the toilet they had a little drinking fountain. And nobody wanted to drink water from there because I thought, at least, I thought that it was water from the toilet. I was like, I'm not drinking that. And I remember one time they gave us a sandwich with cheese, but the cheese was rotten. And so, I didn't eat it. My brother did though, and he got sick to his stomach.

Then they were going to send us to a home in Arizona, I think, but they only had space for me. And then they were going to send my brother to another home. And then I told them in Spanish that I wasn't going to go anywhere without my brother. I didn't care if they were going to send us back [to Guatemala] or not, just send me with my brother. Then a woman came, and she told me that they weren't going to send us apart and they were going to send us to another place but that we had to wait a little longer until they got the flights or something like that, I don't know.

Then on the fifth day, I think it was, we were going to be allowed to take a shower. And right before we were going to go through to the showers, they called my brother and me and they told us that they were going to send us to Virginia, I think. And we took two flights there. And during this time, mind you, we hadn't eaten. It was around 6 or 7 a.m. They only gave us an apple, a banana, and some water in a little bag for the whole day—which we ate right away because we were hungry. And then we were sent off. And everybody at the airport was looking at us weird because we were all dirty and we stank. I remember we were traveling with two officers, and they went and got McDonald's and they ate it right in front of us. And we didn't eat anything during the whole night until we got to Virginia.

I think we got there at like five in the morning, something like that. It was raining. It was so cold. And we didn't have sweaters. We didn't have anything. And when we finally got there, at the home, they gave us new clothes, clean clothes, and told us to go take a shower. They showed us where we were going to be staying and they gave us food and they told us to go to sleep. The next morning, we woke up and they told us more about what the process was going to be like. And then, for the first time in a long time, we felt safe because we weren't with officers, guns, none of that. We were just with other kids at a home, and we were all going through the same thing, and it was kind of relieving. The good thing was that they were just opening it [the ORR facility], so there weren't many kids there. There weren't really a lot.

Cindy's Resistance

Cindy's narrative also demonstrates how she struggled against vulnerability through solidarity with others. Maintaining solidarity with her brother so that they could persist through the condition of vulnerability together was Cindy's chief priority from the moment of her apprehension. As she was being detained, Cindy repeatedly demanded information about her brother from the agents. Although the agents were not responsive to her queries,

Cindy's brother turned himself in to the authorities to be with her, attesting to their mutual support.

Once inside the detention center, Cindy was separated from her brother and placed into a cell with only women. But she remained vigilant to her brother's whereabouts, maintaining her solidarity with him despite their physical separation. At one point, Cindy described her brother being removed from his cell by CBP agents to a location where Cindy could see him. She immediately tried to communicate with him but understood that CBP agents were attempting to disrupt their solidarity by ordering him not to speak to her. In this part of Cindy's story, it is clear that she sees her brother and herself as a united "us" against "them"—the CBP agents.

Cindy's solidarity with her brother was so strong that she was even willing to be deported back to Guatemala rather than be separated from him in the United States. In staunchly demonstrating her solidarity with him, Cindy was able to prevent the agents from sending them to separate Office of Refugee Resettlement (ORR) facilities. Looking at Cindy's actions through the lens of Butler (2021) allows us to see how she used her solidarity with her brother as a nonviolent means of stepping into the force field of the violence to stop their separation from happening.

When away from her brother, Cindy sought out information by talking to another young woman in her cell. Her account of this experience reveals the ways in which migrants form relationships of solidarity while in detention based on their shared experiences of vulnerability to the system. Another young woman in the cell, previously unknown to Cindy, provided her with information about mealtimes, even offering to wake up Cindy to ensure she received food. By helping one another persist in a condition of vulnerability, migrant youth demonstrate their resistance to being rendered vulnerable, sharing information and resources across peer networks in a show of collective strength.

Cindy also used refusal as a means of resisting institutional violence, which, as Butler (2021, 202) argues, "is not the same thing as doing nothing." Refusal is a deliberate choice, as evidenced in Cindy's narrative. When Cindy received food that she perceived as rotten, she refused to eat it. Cindy also refused to drink from the water fountain that she believed to be contaminated. Cindy's refusal to consume what the facility provided was an act of resistance she saw as necessary to protect her health and signal her mistrust in the institution responsible for protecting her. Although it increased her vulnerability to hunger, Cindy's refusal of the food and water provided within the detention center can be seen as her refusal to consider spoiled, contaminated food as acceptable. In refusing to eat this food, Cindy demonstrated to others her judgment that CBP should provide decent provisions to the people in its custody.

At several points in her narrative, Cindy described how she believed the CBP agents perceived her—as someone who didn't belong in the United States, as someone whose life wasn't valued enough to provide adequate food or hygiene practices, as someone deserving of the violence she endured. In Cindy's experience, the agents with whom she interacted did not see or treat her as a vulnerable child in need of protection; like Estrella, she felt she needed to protect herself from them. The immigration system and its agents increased Cindy's vulnerability to illness, hunger, separation from her brother—structural violence that Cindy resisted through her solidarities and refusals. When Cindy and her brother finally arrived at the ORR facility, she expressed that "for the first time in a long time, we felt safe." Cindy connected this feeling of safety to being away from "officers, guns"—the constant threat of violence she had to persist in and resist while in CBP custody.

Conclusions and Implications

Together, Estrella's and Cindy's *testimonios* reveal that although migrant youth in CBP custody must persist in a state of vulnerability, they employ everyday acts of resistance to struggle against that condition. Their stories demonstrate how vulnerability and resistance operate simultaneously, underscoring Butler's (2021, 192) argument that "the situation of those deemed vulnerable is, in fact, a constellation of vulnerability, rage, persistence, and resistance that emerges under these same historical conditions." Both Estrella's and Cindy's accounts of immigrant detention are rife with examples of their rage, persistence, and resistance within a condition of vulnerability, demonstrating the need for analyses of the experiences of migrant youth and members of other vulnerable groups to consider resistance alongside vulnerability. If we document the violence migrant youth have endured without also considering how they maintain and exercise their own power even within carceral systems meant to constrain and restrict them, we run the risk of contributing to disempowering narratives about child migrants that emphasize their vulnerability and victimhood (Esposito and Kellezi 2020;

Butler 2021). Although it is important to acknowledge that such nonviolent acts of resistance alone cannot relieve migrant youth of their vulnerability, we can affirm the dignity of their struggle by recognizing their agency, solidarities, and power within contexts of structural violence while working to dismantle the oppressive social structures that produce their vulnerability (Butler 2021; Gilodi, Albert, and Nienaber 2022).

The forms of resistance that Estrella and Cindy described were nonviolent, informal, and sometimes covert acts that propelled their stories forward (Johansson and Vinthagen 2019). These acts of resistance were motivated by Estrella's and Cindy's need to protect themselves from state-sanctioned, structural violence and ultimately to survive the detention experience. In examining the ways that resistance and vulnerability show up in Estrella's and Cindy's narratives, two predominant parallels emerge that help us understand the forms of resistance available to migrant youth in CBP custody—refusal and solidarity.

Both Estrella and Cindy exercised their power to refuse to comply with or accept the inhumane circumstances with which they were forced to contend. Estrella refused to remove her shoes because she needed to protect her feet from the cold and refused to remove her clothing because she needed to protect her body from violation. Cindy refused to eat spoiled food because she needed to protect herself from illness. When young people engage in acts of refusal, they are often seen as being defiant, disobedient, or "difficult"—as Estrella was called. In many institutional settings, young people are expected and taught to exhibit deference to authority through compliance; there are typically negative consequences for young people who refuse to do what they are told. However, in a context of structural violence that poses numerous threats to migrant youth's well-being, refusal can be seen as an act of resistance that signals an unwillingness to surrender to vulnerability. These refusals were self-protective behaviors that helped Estrella and Cindy resist structural violence and safeguard themselves from harm.

Refusal in Estrella's and Cindy's narratives was also a means of demonstrating their mistrust in the institutions and agents responsible for protecting them. Estrella refused candy from the "good guy" within the detention center because she didn't trust that he wanted to help her. Cindy refused to drink water from the fountain on top of the toilet because she didn't trust that the CBP had provided a sanitary water source. These acts of refusal illustrate Estrella's and Cindy's mistrust of the CBP and its actors, based on their understanding that this institution does not operate to protect them but to inflict violence against them. In their narratives, Estrella and Cindy use carceral language to describe the conditions of the CBP facility—"I got arrested," "we got to the jail," "kinda like a prison, like a cage for animals," "they kept us in a little cell"—demonstrating their awareness that this was a carceral institution, not one designed for their protection and safety. Their experiences in the prisonlike conditions reaffirmed their mistrust in the CBP, and their acts of refusal were a way of expressing that mistrust.

Scholars and practitioners working with this population can learn from Estrella's and Cindy's use of refusal as a strategy of resistance to protect themselves from a violent institution they didn't trust. Rather than labeling migrant youth who refuse to comply or accept what is offered as "difficult" to engage, practitioners working with migrant youth might recognize their refusals as acts of resistance motivated by their need for safety. With this understanding, practitioners might focus their efforts on establishing trust with migrant youth or engaging them in conversations about what would help them feel safe. Perceiving and acknowledging migrant youth's acts of refusal as self-protective acts of resistance allows us to appreciate and emphasize their strengths and their vulnerability to the structural violence from which they have tried to protect themselves (Esposito and Kellezi 2020; Gilodi, Albert, and Nienaber 2022). In research and direct practice with migrant youth, a strengths-based perspective that highlights youth's agency rather than solely their vulnerability offers a more holistic analysis of the "constellation of vulnerability, rage, persistence, and resistance" that emerges in various immigration contexts (Butler 2021) and may help youth recognize and exercise their own power and strengths (Chappell Deckert 2016; Catallozzi et al. 2019).

Estrella's and Cindy's narratives also show how the solidarities youth enact and maintain within vulnerable conditions are forms of resistance, allowing them to better protect themselves from violence and its consequences by joining together in mutual support. By maintaining solidarity with others, Estrella and Cindy were able to provide and receive needed support. Estrella recounted how she and her sister took turns sleeping and kept one another warm while in the detention center. Cindy recalled the vital information about food distribution she received from another young woman in her cell.

These acts of solidarity helped Estrella and Cindy protect themselves from the perils of sleep deprivation, cold, and hunger, allowing them to resist the vulnerable conditions that would result from such perils.

Both Estrella and Cindy acted in solidarity with their siblings throughout their migration journeys, even when physical separation while in CBP custody threatened their ability to maintain solidarity. Many of Estrella's and Cindy's acts of resistance were motivated by a desire to remain with their siblings above all else. Estrella was willing to accept the assistance of a man she distrusted to locate her sister within the detention center. Cindy was willing to be deported back to her home country rather than be sent to an ORR facility without her brother. These acts of solidarity demonstrate Estrella's and Cindy's resistance against the violence of family separation and the risks they were willing to take to maintain their solidarities with their family members.

Solidarities among and with migrants are well recognized in the scholarly literature as essential sources of resource mobilization, information sharing, and movement building—all forms of collective resistance (Martinez 2008; Ataç, Rygiel, and Stierl 2016; Hughes 2019; Díaz de León 2020; Ordaz 2021). Estrella's and Cindy's narratives help us understand how migrant youth enact and maintain solidarities as a form of resistance within a context of structural violence, and the practical purposes these solidarities serve. These narratives showed that solidarity among youth migrants provided mutual support, as demonstrated by youth caring for one another and protecting each other from the harms to which they were vulnerable and functioned as a form of collective resistance against family separation.

Estrella's and Cindy's *testimonios* underscore the need for policies and procedures that keep migrant families, including siblings, together throughout the migration process, as separating migrant children from their siblings with whom they migrated can be traumatizing. Although a great deal of scholarship and advocacy focuses on the inhumane practice of separating migrant children from their families at the border (Suárez-Orozco and Hernández 2012; Lovato et al. 2018; Monico et al. 2019), less is known about sibling separation practices in CBP custody. Future research in this area is needed to empirically examine the impacts of sibling separation on migrant children. Practitioners working with this population can advocate for policies and procedures that keep siblings together in CBP custody, recognizing the importance and benefits of their bonds.

Although Estrella's and Cindy's narratives demonstrate their resistance to structural violence in CBP custody, they also attest to the vulnerable conditions in which migrant children are routinely placed upon arrival to the United States. Estrella's and Cindy's acts of resistance demonstrated their struggle to protect themselves from the vulnerability produced by an oppressive immigrant detention system with which they were forced to contend. To recognize Estrella's and Cindy's acts of resistance is to recognize the struggle of all youth migrants who endure the structural violence of immigration detention practices designed to dominate and render them vulnerable (Mayers and Freedman 2019). Their first-person accounts of CBP detention remind us that youth migrants are not passive victims of the violent structures with which they must interact—they are actively struggling against the cruelty and injustice of those structures, and we must join them in that struggle by fighting for an end to the practice of child detention and advocating for more humane, supportive, community-based responses to the migration of children and their families (García Hernández 2019). Abolishing immigrant detention practices is a first step toward ensuring that migrant children and their families can seek safety in the United States without being made vulnerable to structural violence (Butler 2021).

Note

1. Pseudonyms chosen by the narrators are used throughout this chapter to protect the identities of the youth migrants.

References

Ataç, Ilker, Kim Rygiel, and Maurice Stierl. 2016. "Introduction: The Contentious Politics of Refugee and Migrant Protest and Solidarity Movements: Remaking Citizenship from the Margins." *Citizenship Studies* 20 (5): 527–44.

Baaz, Mikael, Mona Lilja, Michael Schulz, and Stellan Vinthagen. 2016. "Defining and Analyzing 'Resistance': Possible Entrances to the Study of Subversive Practices." *Alternatives* 41 (3): 137–53.

Brown, Kate, Kathryn Ecclestone, and Nick Emmel. 2017. "The Many Faces of Vulnerability." *Social Policy and Society* 16 (3): 497–510.

Butler, Judith. 2021. *The Force of Nonviolence: An Ethico-Political Bind*. New York: Verso Books.

Catallozzi, Marina, Chelsea A. Kolff, Rachel A. Fowler, and Terry McGovern. 2019. "Adolescent Migrant Health." In *Migrant Health*, edited by Bernadette N. Kumar and Esperanza Diaz, 101–12. Boca Raton, Fla.: CRC Press.

Chappell Deckert, Jennifer. 2016. "Social Work, Human Rights, and the Migration of Central American Children." *Journal of Ethnic & Cultural Diversity in Social Work* 25 (1): 20–35.

Chavez, Lilian, and Cecilia Menjívar. 2010. "Children Without Borders: A Mapping of the Literature on Unaccompanied Migrant Children to the United States." *Migraciones Internacionales* 5 (3): 71–111.

Claro Quintans, Irene. 2018. "Detention of Migrant Children: If So, Under What Conditions?" Paper proposal, August. https://repositorio.comillas.edu/xmlui/handle/11531/29790.

Cohodes, Emily M., Sahana Kribakaran, Paola Odriozola, Sarah Bakirci, Sarah McCauley, H. R. Hodges, Lucinda M. Sisk, Sadie J. Zacharek, and Dylan G. Gee. 2021. "Migration-Related Trauma and Mental Health Among Migrant Children Emigrating from Mexico and Central America to the United States: Effects on Developmental Neurobiology and Implications for Policy." *Developmental Psychobiology* 63 (6): e22158.

Cole, Alyson. 2018. "All of Us Are Vulnerable, but Some Are More Vulnerable than Others: The Political Ambiguity of Vulnerability Studies, an Ambivalent Critique." In *The Politics of Vulnerability*, edited by Estelle Ferrarese, 260–67. New York: Routledge.

Delgado Bernal, Dolores, Rebeca Burciaga, and Judith Flores Carmona. 2012. "Chicana/Latina Testimonios: Mapping the Methodological, Pedagogical, and Political." *Equity & Excellence in Education* 45 (3): 363–72.

Díaz de León, Alejandra. 2020. "'Transient Communities': How Central American Transit Migrants Form Solidarity Without Trust." *Journal of Borderlands Studies* 37 (5): 897–914.

Drever, Anita I. 2008. "New Orleans: A Re-emerging Latino Destination City." *Journal of Cultural Geography* 25 (3): 287–303.

Edyburn, Kelly L., and Shantel Meek. 2021. "Seeking Safety and Humanity in the Harshest Immigration Climate in a Generation: A Review of the Literature on the Effects of Separation and Detention on Migrant and Asylum-Seeking Children and Families in the United States During the Trump Administration." *Social Policy Report* 34 (1): 1–46.

Ensor, Marisa O. 2010. *Children and Migration: At the Crossroads of Resiliency and Vulnerability*. New York: Springer.

Esposito, Francesca, and Blerina Kellezi. 2020. "Border Violence, Migrant Resistance, and Acts of Solidarity at Individual, Collective, and Community Levels: Critical Reflections from a Community Psychology Perspective." *Community Psychology in Global Perspective* 6 (1): 1–16.

Foucault, Michel. 1980. *History of Sexuality, Volume 1: An Introduction*. Translated by Robert Hurley. First Vintage Books Edition. New York: Vintage.

García Hernández, César Cuauhtémoc. 2019. *Migrating to Prison: America's Obsession with Locking Up Immigrants*. New York: New Press.

Gilodi, Amalia, Isabelle Albert, and Birte Nienaber. 2022. "Vulnerability in the Context of Migration: A Critical Overview and a New Conceptual Model." *Human Arenas*, April.

Henderson, Sandra. 2001. "Latin American Testimonio: Uncovering the Subaltern's Gender, Race, and Class." *History Journal Ex Post Facto* X (Spring): 83–94.

Hollander, Jocelyn A., and Rachel L. Einwohner. 2004. "Conceptualizing Resistance." *Sociological Forum* 19 (4): 533–54.

Hughes, Gillian. 2019. "From Individual Vulnerability to Collective Resistance: Responding to the Emotional Impact of Trauma on Unaccompanied Children Seeking Asylum." In *Unaccompanied Young Migrants: Identity, Care and Justice*, edited by Clayton Sue and Gupta Anna, 135–58. Bristol, UK: Policy Press.

Johansson, Anna, and Stellan Vinthagen. 2019. *Conceptualizing "Everyday Resistance": A Transdisciplinary Approach*. New York: Routledge.

Lilly, Jenn M. 2022. "The AltaVoces Project: A Digital Narrative Approach to Anti-Oppressive Social Work Research with Latino Youth." *Qualitative Social Work* 22 (3): 465–83.

Lind, Jacob. 2019. "Governing Vulnerabilised Migrant Childhoods Through Children's Rights." *Childhood* 26 (3): 337–51.

Lovato, Kristina, Corina Lopez, Leyla Karimli, and Laura S. Abrams. 2018. "The Impact of Deportation-Related Family Separations on the Well-Being of Latinx Children and Youth: A Review of the Literature." *Children and Youth Services Review* 95 (December): 109–16.

Maldonado, Charles. 2014. "New Orleans Immigration Court Handling More than 1,200 Cases of Unaccompanied Minors Fleeing Central America." *The Lens*, August 4, sec. Government and Politics. https://thelensnola.org/2014/08/04/new-orleans-immigration-court-handling-more-than-1200-cases-of-unaccompanied-minors-fleeing-central-america/.

Martinez, Lisa M. 2008. "'Flowers from the Same Soil': Latino Solidarity in the Wake of the 2006 Immigrant Mobilizations." *American Behavioral Scientist* 52 (4): 557–79.

Mayers, Steven, and Jonathan Freedman. 2019. *Solito, Solita: Crossing Borders with Youth Refugees from Central America*. Chicago: Haymarket Books.

McLean, Lisa. 2019. "Protesting Vulnerability and Vulnerability as Protest: Gender, Migration, and Strategies of Resistance." In *Routledge Companion to Peace and Conflict Studies*, edited by Sean Byrne, Thomas Matyók, Imani Michelle Scott, Jessica Senehi, 178–88. New York: Routledge.

Monico, Carmen, Karen Rotabi, Yvonne Vissing, and Justin Lee. 2019. "Forced Child-Family Separations in the Southwestern US Border Under the 'Zero-Tolerance' Policy: The Adverse Impact on Well-Being of Migrant Children (Part 2)." *Journal of Human Rights and Social Work* 4 (3): 180–91.

Ordaz, Jessica. 2021. *The Shadow of El Centro: A History of Migrant Incarceration and Solidarity*. Chapel Hill: University of North Carolina Press.

Podkul, Jennifer. 2015. "Detention and Treatment of Unaccompanied Migrant Children at the U.S.-Mexico Border." In *Childhood and Migration in Central and North America: Causes, Policies, Practices, and Challenges*, edited by Rebecca Katz and Joanne Kelsey, 357–82. San Francisco: Center for Gender and Refugee Studies at the University of California Hastings College of Law.

Suárez-Orozco, Carola, and María G. Hernández. 2012. "Immigrant Family Separations: The Experience of Separated, Unaccompanied, and Reunited Youth and Families." In *The Impact of Immigration on Children's Development*, edited by Cynthia T. García Coll, 122–48. Basel: Karger.

Van de Glind, Hans, International Labour Office, and ILO International Programme on the Elimination of Child Labour. 2010. *Migration and Child Labour: Exploring Child Migrant Vulnerabilities and Those of Children Left Behind*. Geneva: ILO.

CHAPTER SIX

Detained Homemaking

The Liminal Homemaking of Sexual and Gender Minority Central American Unaccompanied Youth

LUIS EDWARD TENORIO

As research on Central American unaccompanied youth has grown over recent years, two areas of study remain underexplored. First, while research has analyzed how unaccompanied youth interact with, and are even socialized by, state actors in detention (with Customs and Border Protection [CBP], Immigration and Customs Enforcement [ICE], or the Office of Refugee Resettlement [ORR]) (Heidbrink 2014; Terrio 2015; Galli 2020), we know less about how youth interact with one another in such settings. This is an important oversight. Peers may not only be an equally important source of socialization but also fulfill other unaccompanied youth's fundamental need to feel a sense of belonging, recognition, and care (Tenorio 2020). At the same time, detention may create a context in which peer interactions and relationships exacerbate unaccompanied youth's social vulnerabilities. For example, feeling the need to distinguish themselves from their peers to advance the likelihood of success in their pursuit of legal protections (Galli 2020), youth's interactions among themselves may be more hostile. Second, while studies have contributed to our understanding of how demographic factors like gender shape Central American unaccompanied youths' experiences upon arrival and in integrating into the United States (Diaz-Strong 2022), the experiences of sexual and gender minority youth remain significantly absent in the literature. This reinforces their social erasure, carrying critical legal repercussions as the validity of their identity and experiences is often called into question when used as the basis for immigration protections (Hazeldean 2011; Hedlund and Wimark 2019). Aimed at narrowing these gaps, this chapter explores the detained homemaking that sexual and gender minority Central American unaccompanied youth engage in among one another as a means of adapting to and resisting the violence of detention.

I offer detained homemaking as an extension of sexual and gender minority unaccompanied youth's liminal homemaking in the context of ICE and ORR detention. Liminal homemaking has been used by queer and migration scholars to reference "a search for belonging, comfort, and safety" (Wimark 2021, 649). Traditional notions of a home evoke depictions of a static and stable place. Liminal homemaking destabilizes these expectations. Instead, it recognizes homemaking as an ongoing and potentially ambiguous process that can occur even in the least expected of places, such as state-controlled spaces (Brun and Fábos 2015). For those at the margins of society—such as immigrants and sexual and gender minorities—liminal homemaking may be perpetual as physical and social displacement is not confined to a single environment or group (Wimark 2021). In this way, liminal homemaking cautions against the romanticization of a home or homemaking. It acknowledges that homemaking can be an expression of resistance as people create alternative "homes" where orthodox versions of home are inaccessible, allowing individuals to access fundamentally human experiences of love, desire, and care. However, it also recognizes how this process can exacerbate violence. For example, while family or queer community members have been noted as a support for some queer refugees, this may come at the expense of following painful prescriptions of identity and performance that do not always align with their comforts, desires, or identities. Thus, detained homemaking encourages us to examine inherent tensions between the profuse control and legal violence of the state's intrusion into migrant's lives and what limited agency unaccompanied youth have in navigating and coping with such structural circumstances.

Background on Sexual and Gender Minority Migrants

Prior to 1990, the United States actively discriminated against, if not outright barred, sexual and gender minorities from seeking asylum admission (Luibhéid 2002; Canaday 2009; Vogler 2016). Contemporary research, however, suggests that claims for humanitarian protection based on sexual and gender minority status are becoming more successful in the United States (Vogler 2021). This is separate from the symbolic violence that may still take place via the perversion and invalidation of sexual and gender minority experiences and narratives as migrants' legal cases are processed (Crawley 2011; Spijkerboer 2013; Terrio 2015; Akin 2017; Dhoest 2019; Hedlund and Wimark 2019). Further, it does not mean that legal violence is not experienced in interactions with the immigration regime prior to legal cases being adjudicated.

In fact, while research on sexual and gender minority migrants in U.S. detention are scant, extant research has noted the acute precarity faced by sexual and gender minorities. For example, reports suggest sexual and gender minority migrants are ninety-seven times more likely to experience sexual assault compared to their heterosexual or cisgender counterparts (Gruberg 2018). Scholars have also argued that being classified as transgender in immigration detention may exacerbate punishment and violence rather than provide necessary protections. To this effect, scholars outline how being classified as transgender still led to individuals being strip-searched by officers not of the requested gender, increased verbal harassment, destruction of property, and misgendering (Vogler and Rosales 2023). Thus, some scholars suggest that the withholding of information or performance of behavior related to sexual and/or gender minority status is a common approach migrants employ when navigating both state-controlled and non-state-controlled spaces (Bögner, Brewin, and Herlihy 2010; Gorman-Murray, Mckinnon, and Dominey-Howes 2014; Wimark 2021). This curation of sexual and gender minority performance—informed by the state's disciplinary role in detention as well as youths' internalized self-discipline—may have critical implications on the number, types, and depth of relationships formed by sexual and gender minority unaccompanied youth in detention.

In other country contexts, research has highlighted the liminality sexual and gender minorities face across different state-controlled spaces, and how this liminality endures into perpetual liminality even outside state-controlled spaces (Wimark 2021). Keeping this liminality in mind, in conjunction with the studies suggesting youth may engage in behavioral management and regulation, suggests that youths' relationships may not only serve as a form of resilience but also be a site of further state violence.

Data and Methods

This chapter draws on data from a larger qualitative research project on Central American unaccompanied youth pursuing legal relief in the New

York metropolitan area. The research project was centered out of a legal nonprofit organization I will refer to as Relief for Migrant Children (RMC). At the RMC, for a total of fifty months between May 2014 and May 2019, I served as a volunteer in order to gain access to the space and its clients as a participant observer. My involvement and tasks ranged from the work of an interpreter and translator to that of a paralegal with responsibilities ranging from conducting client screenings to drafting documents for court proceedings. Each case that I was a participant observer on was invited to be part of the research project. Apart from the observations conducted on each respondent's legal case, each respondent also participated in semistructured in-depth interviews that were conducted in Spanish and lasted anywhere from thirty minutes to three hours each. Interview topics ranged from migration decision-making to experiences integrating into the United States. All respondents were successfully interviewed an average of three times. Overall, the repeated discussion, revisitation, and processing of youths' narrative through the mixed qualitative approach allowed deeper aspects of that experience to be brought into youth's conscious awareness (Ochs and Capps 1996) and captured in research interactions, whether one-on-one interviews or observations.

The total sample for the project was sixty-three Central American unaccompanied youth, of which eleven respondents who disclosed identifying as a sexual or gender minority individual inform the focus of this chapter. Four respondents had marginalized gender identities and seven had marginalized sexual orientations (this includes men who have sex with men and men who were questioning their sexual orientation). Although these marginal statuses can in some cases overlap, the respondents I observed in my study did not indicate such an overlap. In order to assure protection of the legal interests of my respondents, the attorneys at the RMC assisted in supervising my data collection. In addition, the study was approved by my university's institutional review board, which limited potential respondents of the study to youth seven years of age or older. All names used in this chapter are pseudonyms selected by the respondents themselves.

In this chapter, I largely focus on the stories of two respondents—Stefano and Yaqueline—and the individuals with whom they reported to have developed meaningful relationships during detention. Their stories illustrate how migrants experience fractures in their social network as a function of migration and the lives that await (many) of them as undocumented or quasi-documented (Menjívar 2006), and as sexual and gender minority migrants aim to build relationships, the relationships they try to build in order to press forward are fractured as a means of state discipline and self-governance.

Stefano and Javier

Stefano arrived in the United States from El Salvador when he was fifteen years old. He recalled knowing he was gay "as early as seven years old." While he did not feel being gay was a "bad thing," it was evident to Stefano that being gay brought "trouble" and "problems" in El Salvador with members of his family, local gangs, and administrators at his Catholic school. Though his family in El Salvador was unsupportive of his migration, Stefano felt he "had no choice," and joined a group of young men from his town who were making the journey to the United States. Upon arrival at the U.S. southern border, Stefano was apprehended by the CBP and eventually placed into an ORR shelter in New York, where he stayed a total of five months before being transferred to another shelter for two months in Maryland; after seven months total in ORR custody, he was released to his sponsor.

During our first interview, when asked about what he envisioned for himself, and for his life, in the United States, Stefano referenced someone we had not talked about before—Javier. Stefano met Javier while he was in ORR custody. Javier's name alone brought a glow about Stefano as he blushed. "Javier was always smiling. Thinking of him makes me smile," Stefano reminisced. "I first talked to [Javier] when I was begging [an ORR staff member] to let me have more time on the phone with my family my first day there," Stefano shared.

> [The ORR shelter] would only let us be on the phone for five minutes. . . . Javier [who had arrived at the shelter before Stefano] told me it was going to be okay and to stop crying. He said, "The rules are there for a reason." . . . I was confused, "Why was he taking their side?" but then he asked the staff person if I could have his five minutes. . . . Javier was always like that, even when others were crying or felt sad, he was calm. . . . He always tried to be positive. . . . Everyone knew

> Javier and everyone liked Javier ... Because Javier always showed good behavior, [the ORR staff member] agreed to let me call with Javier's five minutes.

Javier's comments about the rules of the ORR shelter illustrate something that was observed across a number of my respondents, both sexual/gender minority youth and their cisgendered, heterosexual counterparts—their strategic reference to "the rules" of the shelters where they were detained as a way of attempting to gain favor with staff. In addition, my findings suggest youth who had been at the shelter for some time served to socialize newer arrivals into these rules and norms. This socialization pattern between unaccompanied youth reflects how the state's power in detention not only is enacted upon youth but encourages youth to enact this disciplinary power upon themselves and others—even as they seek to stay resilient—which also serves as grounds for initial interactions between youth. This pattern, as I will explain in detail later, also heightened the sense of constant surveillance felt by youth in the ORR shelters.

After their initial encounter, Javier and Stefano began to grow closer.

> We talked a bit during our breaks from class when we would play soccer.... We got close, like friends at first, just friends.... We didn't even know that we liked each other, which was fine.... It had been a long time since I felt what it was like to have a friend.... It was hard for me to make friends [at the shelter]; I didn't feel comfortable with a lot of them.... I didn't know how they'd treat me ... because I'm gay ... and I didn't want to cause any trouble.

Stefano's comments illustrate a challenge that many of the sexual and gender minority youth in my study noted. Many traveled in a group that was led by a guide or *coyote* and while the group at times included youth, they did not grow close or build relationships with those they migrated with. From leaving their home country to entering detention, many indicated feeling "alone," "anxious," or "sad"; further, many noted being "hesitant," "afraid," or "cautious" of befriending their peers in detention, like Stefano, due to the legacies of their treatment in their origin country. As a result, many recounted limited relationships—often only one or two that were substantive—formed during detention. These relationships often began through socializing relationships as referenced earlier, which while useful in learning to navigate spaces of detention also introduced their own form of uneasiness.

Stefano explained the tension in deciding to establish a peer relationship with Javier as follows: "At first, I wasn't really sure if I should be friends with [Javier].... I really liked him, but I wasn't sure [if] maybe he would report me if I said or did something he didn't like.... Since it seemed everyone knew and liked him, I also thought maybe being close to him would mean that everyone would be watching me even more." Most of the sexual and gender minority respondents in my study, like Stefano, noted being hyperaware of the surveillance they were under. Part of this surveillance came from ORR staff who were "always watching," "constantly taking notes," and "writing up [incident reports]." However, surveillance also took the form of other youth in detention being quick to "report bad behavior to look better" or "have less attention put on them"—one of the more covert impacts of self-discipline being internalized by youth and enacted upon their peers.

Other aspects of ORR detention also posed challenges to youth's sociality. Key informants who met through the RMC shared that the ORR shelter Stefano and Javier were at in New York had strict rules around "personal space," "individual boundaries," "inappropriate contact," and "intimate contact." Other studies have highlighted shelters located in different areas having similar or longer lists of behaviors deemed inappropriate and grounds for the writing of an incident report (Terrio 2015). As a result, the climate and environment of being in ORR shelters influenced how sociality was used to cope with the challenges of detention, its limits, and its drawbacks.

The friendship Stefano and Javier initially built became an important source of comfort for Stefano, serving as a critical coping mechanism. To this end, Stefano shared,

> Before [the ORR shelter], I didn't know how to feel anymore.... I realized everything that I had left behind.... I wasn't even sure if [the United States] was going to be what I imagined. I thought about telling the [CBP] and even the [ORR staff] to send me back to El Salvador, even though I knew it was too dangerous for me.... [Being detained] felt like waiting.... All I could do was wait, it made me so mad, and I had no idea when I would stop waiting or what would happen after the waiting was over.... Meeting Javier ... made me have hope.... I was willing to keep waiting.... "If Javier is positive, I have to be positive

too," I would tell myself. . . . I was afraid if he would actually be a good friend, but I really just needed someone, someone who I could be close to . . . to not feel like I had nothing, no one.

Stefano's comments illustrate how the feelings of helplessness spurred by the liminality of detention—the constant waiting, feeling stunted and stalled—exacerbate what is already a fundamental need: a need to belong, to have comfort, to have supportive social relationships, and to feel a sense of home. In Stefano's case, the prospect of building a relationship with Javier, though at the time potentially precarious, was the only form of coping to push past the temptation of contemplating voluntary departure even further.

After a month or so of knowing each other, Stefano recalled their connection deepening:

He told me about his family in Boston; he even asked if I would ever go to visit or stay with him in Boston if I stayed [in the United States]. I didn't know what to say, I just said, "What about my family?" And he just smiled and said, "What about *our* family?" and we laughed. . . . I asked him once if I was his friend and he told me, "much more than that" and he made eyes towards the people around us and that's how I knew he liked me . . . but he could never tell me just like that because someone could hear. . . . You could be gay, but you had to act appropriately . . . so you couldn't act romantically in any way.

As a result, Stefano recalled how he and Javier needed to be careful in how they allowed their relationship to develop and be displayed. This regulation of sexual minority performance then translated into how Stefano and Javier went about conveying intimacy.

We had a lot of little things we had to do to be careful. . . . We would wait until [the ORR staff] weren't looking, which was pretty rare, and I would touch his arm. That was one of the signals, and I would wait, wait for him to hold my hand for a little or give it a squeeze. . . . We would try to do the same chores at the shelter to spend more time together—things like wash dishes together or clean different areas together. . . . That was really all we could do since we were supposed to always be distanced from one another in [the shelter].

While these strategies worked for a while, concerns over surveillance and its potential consequences overshadowed them to the point of Stefano and Javier needing to develop a different approach. Stefano shared, "We were afraid.... What if someone said something or made a big deal about how close we were.... So for a bit we tried to be around each other less—we had to make sure it looked like we didn't care about each other too much, sometimes we just had to ignore each other on purpose." Stefano began to tear up as he explained, "I knew he really cared about me, loved me, so that was hard.... Sometimes I wasn't sure if he was doing it to be safe or if maybe he was really trying to avoid me or maybe he really didn't like me.... That was really hard for me."

While adapting to the contours of the disciplinary power of detention allowed Stefano and Javier to maintain a semblance of the intimate relationship they had, doing so also introduced yet another liminal quality into their relationship. Where before their feelings and intentions were known in their own way, even amid highly restricted interactions, the changes in performance—even if only for the purposes of temporary conformity—raised powerful doubts, as Stefano shared. Having limited comfort and relationships with others in the shelter meant these changes in performance also brought Stefano greater feelings of isolation and sadness.

Toward the five-month mark at the shelter, an ORR staff member started asking Stefano questions about Javier. "She asked if we were friends," Stefano recalled.

> We hadn't been caught or anything, Javier and I hadn't gotten in trouble, so I told her that we were dating. I thought, if she knew she could help us stay together and stay in the United States because it was dangerous for us to go back.... I would see a lot of kids leave to be moved to other shelters and I wanted to stay with Javier as long as possible....
> I even told her that even though we were dating, we were being respectful of one another and maintaining personal space.... I thought everything was good. She didn't react badly; she smiled when I told her. But then the next day, they told me I was going to go to another shelter.

In my interview results, separation of individuals who were in some way indicated to have some kind of romantic interest or connection was only noted by sexual and gender minority youth. In the cases of heterosexual, cisgendered youth, it was reported that staff members would write up incident reports, sit youth down to a "serious talk" about their behavior, or reprimand them either in the presence of their peers or in private, but never separate them by relocation to different sites. The difference in these responses to unaccompanied youth sociality illustrates not only the greater liminal quality of sexual and gender minority homemaking but also the state's intrusion and investment in disrupting this process.

Even in cases where the relationship that developed between same-sex unaccompanied youth was not romantic, the disciplinary tactics of ORR custody reframed behavior aimed at cultivating critical social relationships into reasons for suspicion and the sexualization of sexual minority youth. For example, Maria, who identified as lesbian, shared,

> [The ORR staff member] saw me hugging my friend because I was feeling sad and needed a hug. She was the only friend I had at [the shelter]. . . . [The staff member] called me in to meet with him later and told me that what I was doing was "inappropriate." . . . I told him that it was just a hug with my friend, and he said, "I'm not stupid, it looks like a hug but then it leads to other touching very quickly," and that if I kept talking back to him things would only get worse for me.

In the new ORR shelter Stefano was moved to, several states away, he described being placed under one-on-one observation for the time he was there. "It was horrible, but I didn't care then. I wasn't with Javier anymore. . . . Sometimes I would just talk to myself, pretending it was Javier . . . all the things I never got to talk about yet with him. I would make up conversations. . . . I missed him that much," he shared as tears streamed down his face. Stefano also noted how this behavior resulted in staff "forcing [him] to take medication [he] wasn't even sure about."

Not only did these experiences exacerbate the effects of detention for Stefano, but they also carried critical spillover effects into his sociality outside detention. Though Stefano "came out" to his sponsors and those in his immediate network in New York, Stefano noted spending "a lot of time alone," which was further corroborated by his family, who noted how "withdrawn" Stefano could be. Stefano also mentioned struggling to make friends at his school and completely resigned from "any kind of [romantic] relationship."

Stefano attributed much of this behavior to not being able to get over his separation from Javier.

Yaqueline and Antonio

I met Yaqueline when she was seventeen years old. Originally from El Salvador, Yaqueline left her hometown due to the violence she experienced as a result of being trans. Yaqueline continued to experience physical violence due to her gender identity even after leaving El Salvador. In our interviews, she reported being "molested" on a train she took in Mexico on her way to the United States as well as another instance while in CBP custody. In CBP custody, she was detained with male migrants, despite requesting to be moved to a space where she could be detained with female migrants. The nights she spent in CBP custody "scarred" her. She was "unable to sleep more than an hour at a time." In her words, "I would immediately wake up thinking someone was feeling up my leg or pulling at my underwear. . . . I'd wake up and there would be no one there that looked like they did it, but it felt so real to me. . . . I'd go through that again and again, unable to sleep." Given her experiences, Yaqueline was adamant about not forming any relationships with those she met in CBP detention—"I couldn't trust any of them," she added.

Yet, in our conversation, a ray of optimism shone through as she recalled Antonio. Antonio, as Yaqueline described, "always defended" her and "was always looking out" for her. Antonio entered CBP custody the day after Yaqueline. Their first interaction involved Antonio forcing a man off Yaqueline who was making advances toward her. From what Yaqueline indicated, the CBP officers did nothing about the incident. Antonio told Yaqueline that he would "keep an eye out" so that no one would do anything to her. "I didn't believe him at first," Yaqueline confessed, "but every time I woke up, I could see him looking around making sure I was okay."

The initial interactions between Yaqueline and Antonio, similar to that of Stefano and Javier, illustrate how even in contexts where unaccompanied youth may be wary of one another, under immense stress, and in a state of heightened uncertainty as they move through various forms of state custody, they continue to exhibit altruism, sociality, and compassion for one another. These exhibited behaviors, though small acts, carried considerable weight in the support they offered and the future interactions they facilitated.

Following CBP custody, both Antonio and Yaqueline were transferred to the same ORR shelter. Yaqueline, still having her guard up, did not make any close friends at the shelter. However, she continued to have difficult encounters with state actors, as ORR staff refused to give Yaqueline "girl clothes." Having taken notice of Yaqueline's interactions with the staff, Antonio offered in private, "You don't need certain clothes to be a girl." Recalling that moment, Yaqueline felt her "face burn red." "When he said that I felt, I felt normal. . . . He made me feel normal when none of the officers [or staff] were willing to accept who I was. . . . It reminded me of what my grandma used to tell me. . . . She would always say, 'The only thing that makes you a woman is the knowledge and feelings that you have that that is who you are.'"

Though hesitant at first, Yaqueline described gravitating toward Antonio. In her words, "I still couldn't trust him . . . but I wanted to be around him . . . because of how he made me feel. . . . Even if I couldn't trust him, you know, completely, I still felt safe around him. . . . I needed someone I could feel that with after feeling so alone." Yaqueline's comments illustrate the way in which building her relationship with Antonio spoke to a fundamental need to feel safe and seek comfort, while also speaking to a desire to be seen and validated in her trans identity. For many of the youth in my study who identified as trans or gender nonconforming, validation of their gender expression was pivotal in determining whom they built a social relationship with.

To Yaqueline's dismay, the invalidation of her trans identity only continued the longer she spent in ORR custody. The ORR shelter had youth attend classes, one of which was focused on having youth learn about etiquette and proper presentation. In discussing the etiquette of young men, staff singled out Yaqueline for demonstration. Her "long hair," which "sometimes was messy" without the proper grooming tools, was described as "inappropriate," suggesting she "was lazy" and "couldn't be taken seriously." After the series of berating comments, the staff cut Yaqueline's hair to "about the length of [her] fingernail." The loss of her long hair was incredibly painful as it had become "very important" to her, as the only thing she had left that really made her "feel like a girl." However, her short hair was not an issue for Antonio; she recalled him making the comment, "It lets people see more of your pretty face."

As far as her other peers' reactions to her new hair, Yaqueline noticed that others around her grew more comfortable interacting with her. In their engagement with Yaqueline, they offered comments that reaffirmed the norms set by ORR: "You look a lot better," "It makes you look cleaner, instead of all that hair everywhere that made you look dirty," or "You look like one of us now, the way you're supposed to!" The comments caused Yaqueline to contemplate her own gender identity, though more often than not the messaging Yaqueline was receiving about how she did not fit in as she was most comfortable caused her great distress as she recalled "often crying." Yaqueline found herself torn; she had the support of someone like Antonio, someone who "did not need [her] to change anything," but was also experiencing newfound tolerance by people she "never thought would talk to [her] like that." In response, she—herself—began to adapt her behavior to get to know her peers better. "I changed my voice a little and I tried to talk like them. . . . I thought at least that way they'd like me better," Yaqueline shared, "even though it made me feel worse about myself."

Yaqueline's case also illustrates a snare that was noted among the few youth who attempted broader sociality and homemaking—doing so at the expense of their own identity, sense of self, and/or other relationships. In the case of Yaqueline, apart from the internal troubles it caused her, regulating her behavior to present as less feminine created tension with Antonio. "He didn't know how to feel about me anymore when I behaved differently. . . . I felt like he wasn't as interested in me anymore." In an attempt to rectify the perceived damage done to their relationship, Yaqueline noted engaging in greater romantic performativity and "behaving more like a girl." She would "hug Antonio," "hold on to his arm," and "play with his hair." This quickly grabbed the attention of ORR staff, though Yaqueline was adamant in retaliating.

Yaqueline recalled, "I saw one of the staff members writing down her notes as I hugged Antonio one time, and [the staff member] called over someone else. . . . I knew they were going to do something to me. . . . I didn't care anymore, so I kissed Antonio. . . . That was worth it." Surely enough, the ORR staff members reprimanded Yaqueline and moved her to a different group, where she never saw Antonio again. The separation from Antonio was difficult for her, as she even confessed to contemplating hurting herself a few times the days after being separated. After a week, Yaqueline was transferred to a different shelter, where she stayed for a month before being released to her U.S. sponsor.

For Yaqueline, her experiences in detention caused her to reflect on her own identity as a trans girl. In turn, her sociality in the United States focused on cultivating a network of individuals that would allow her to "be the kind of woman [she] wanted to be." Over the two years that I interacted with her, she played with the expression of her trans identity and decided to undergo gender confirmation surgery. Yet developing romantic relationships was something Yaqueline was "not ready for." In my final interview with her, she described how one of her biggest takeaways from her experiences in detention was that relationships were not for her. She offered:

> I learned that being who I am—how I am—can be painful for people, it sometimes is still painful for me. . . . Someone, like Antonio, would really be happier with someone who was *really* "normal." I've learned that there are times I can *feel* normal, some people may even *treat* me sometimes like I'm normal, but I will never *be* normal. . . . A relationship, like the ones I would fantasize about, those don't work out for someone like me. . . . So, I've accepted what my life can look like, my surgeries, being safe, having the chance to go to school, all that stuff, and what just is not meant to be for me.

Conclusion

The cases of Yaqueline and Stefano reveal how even in an environment wrought with state disciplinary action and legal violence, youth engage in detained homemaking. For both Stefano and Yaqueline, the intimate relationships they developed during detention—with Javier and Antonio, respectively—provided relative forms of comfort, safety, and belonging. These affective results of homemaking—even if only temporary—allowed both Stefano and Yaqueline to remain resilient, whether in overcoming the contemplation of voluntary departure or simply providing reprieve from the loneliness brought by migration and the shuffle through different venues of state custody. In addition, both relationships served as means of affirming their sexual orientation or gender identity in ways that had been significantly denied of them previously; for some of the respondents in my study like Yaqueline and Stefano, these were the first romantic or intimate relationships they had ever developed in this regard. However, the structure and environment of state custody constrained the development of these relationships, led to the curation and management of behavior that inflicted greater pain on youth, and ultimately fractured relationships through direct intervention, a climate of surveillance, and/or internalized disciplinary norms. Moreover, these effects of state intrusion into the lives of sexual and gender minority unaccompanied youth not only impacted their homemaking within the confines of detention but saw its effects ripple into how they navigated relationships beyond and outside detention. In illustrating this connection, my findings corroborate the notion that sexual and gender minority youth migrants may experience a state of "perpetual liminality," particularly around homemaking (Wimark 2021), that follows them across both state- and non-state-controlled spaces. However, it is important to note that constraints on homemaking are not just a function of the receiving state; youths' legacies of abuse, mistreatment, and fractured relationships also constrain sociality in state-controlled spaces, which magnifies the impact of the state's disciplinary power and can exacerbate harm to youth.

References

Akin, Deniz. 2017. "Queer Asylum Seekers: Translating Sexuality in Norway." *Journal of Ethnic and Migration Studies* 43 (3): 458–74.

Bögner, Diana, Chris Brewin, and Jane Herlihy. 2010. "Refugees' Experiences of Home Office Interviews: A Qualitative Study on the Disclosure of Sensitive Personal Information." *Journal of Ethnic and Migration Studies* 36 (3): 519–35.

Brun, Catherine, and Anita Fábos. 2015. "Making Homes in Limbo? A Conceptual Framework." *Refuge: Canada's Journal on Refugees* 31 (1): 5–17.

Canaday, Margot. 2009. *The Straight State: Sexuality and Citizenship in Twentieth-Century America*. Princeton, N.J.: Princeton University Press.

Crawley, Heaven. 2011. "'Asexual, Apolitical Beings': The Interpretation of Children's Identities and Experiences in the UK Asylum System." *Journal of Ethnic and Migration Studies* 37 (8): 1171–84.

Dhoest, Alexander. 2019. "Learning to be Gay: LGBTQ Forced Migrant Identities and Narratives in Belgium." *Journal of Ethnic and Migration Studies* 45 (7): 1075–89.

Diaz-Strong, Daysi Ximena. 2022. "'Estaba Bien Chiquito' (I Was Very Young): The Transition to Adulthood and 'Illegality' of the Mexican and Central American 1.25 Generation." *Journal of Adolescent Research* 37 (3): 409–38.

Galli, Chiara. 2020. "The Ambivalent U.S. Context of Reception and the Dichotomous Legal Consciousness of Unaccompanied Minors." *Social Problems* 67 (4): 763–81.

Gorman-Murray, Andrew, Scott Mckinnon, and Dale Dominey-Howes. 2014. "Queer Domicide: LGBT Displacement and Home Loss in Natural Disaster Impact, Response, and Recovery." *Home Cultures* 11 (2): 237–61.

Gruberg, Shartita. 2018. "ICE's Rejection of Its Own Rules Is Placing LGBT Immigrants at Severe Risk of Sexual Abuse." Center for American Progress, May 30. https://www.americanprogress.org/article/ices-rejection-rules-placing-lgbt-immigrants-severe-risk-sexual-abuse/.

Hazeldean, Susan. 2011. "Confounding Identities: The Paradox of LGBT Children Under Asylum Law." *University of California Davis Law Review* 45 (December): 373–443.

Hedlund, Daniel, and Thomas Wimark. 2019. "Unaccompanied Children Claiming Asylum on the Basis of Sexual Orientation and Gender Identity." *Journal of Refugee Studies* 32 (2): 257–77.

Heidbrink, Lauren. 2014. *Migrant Youth, Transnational Families, and the State: Care and Contested Interests*. Philadelphia: University of Pennsylvania Press.

Luibhéid, Eithne. 2002. *Entry Denied: Controlling Sexuality at the Border*. Minneapolis: University of Minnesota Press.

Menjívar, Cecilia. 2006. "Liminal Legality: Salvadoran and Guatemalan Immigrants' Lives in the United States." *American Journal of Sociology* 111 (4): 999–1037.

Ochs, Elinor, and Lisa Capps. 1996. "Narrating the Self." *Annual Review of Anthropology* 25 (1): 19–43.

Spijkerboer, Thomas. 2013. *Fleeing Homophobia: Sexual Orientation, Gender Identity and Asylum*. New York: Routledge.

Tenorio, Luis Edward. 2020. "Special Immigrant Juvenile Status and the Integration of Central American Unaccompanied Minors." *RSF: The Russell Sage Foundation Journal of the Social Sciences* 6 (3): 172–89.

Terrio, Susan J. 2015. *Whose Child Am I? Unaccompanied, Undocumented Children in U.S. Immigration Custody*. Oakland: University of California Press.

Vogler, Stefan. 2016. "Legally Queer: The Construction of Sexuality in LGBQ Asylum Claims." *Law & Society Review* 50 (4): 856–89.

Vogler, Stefan. 2021. *Sorting Sexualities: Expertise and the Politics of Legal Classification*. Chicago: University of Chicago Press.

Vogler, Stefan, and Rocio Rosales. 2023. "Classification and Coercion: The Gendered Punishment of Transgender Women in Immigration Detention." *Social Problems* 70 (3): 698–716.

Wimark, Thomas. 2021. "Homemaking and Perpetual Liminality among Queer Refugees." *Social & Cultural Geography* 22 (5): 647–65.

CHAPTER SEVEN

Emerging into Darkness

Coming of Age in the American Immigration Detention System

JAJAH WU AND VIDA OPOKU

> I was thrown in jail and didn't know what was going on or who to seek help from. I had just come to the country, and I had no family or friends to support me. I became terrified and started crying because I have never been to prison or jail before.
>
> —VIDA OPOKU

Jajah: Introduction

I met Vida Opoku more than six years ago, on what was to be her last day in Office of Refugee Resettlement (ORR) custody. She had just been told that Immigration and Customs Enforcement (ICE) officials would be taking her to an adult detention center because she was over eighteen. Vida was not, at the time, over eighteen, but the Department of Homeland Security (DHS) had decided to redetermine her age on the basis of a flimsy dental radiograph.

A staff member at the ORR-funded children's facility reached out to the Young Center for Immigrant Children's Rights to request a Child Advocate for Vida a few days before the DHS planned to take her into custody. I was working as the supervising attorney of the Young Center's Chicago office. The Young Center was little more than a pilot project at the time; its mission was not only crucial but unprecedented in the immigration world. Through assigning Child Advocates, or best-interests guardians ad litem, to work one-on-one with immigrant children, the Young Center sought to implement a best-interests model within the immigration system based on domestic and international law, to push for children to be treated as children rather than be confronted with the same rules and standards set out for adults.

Once assigned to the case by ORR, I drove to Chicago on a cold January day to meet Vida for the first time. I knew next to nothing about her case. I had no promises to offer to her other than this: *I will find you in adult detention*. I did not know how I could help her, only that I would try.

This chapter serves as a history of Vida's journey through the immigration detention process, and our journey together in attempting to free her from it.

In the years following Vida's ordeal, the landscape for children who are aging out of ORR detention has changed for the better following a class action lawsuit mounted in 2018. In the suit, *Garcia Ramirez et al. v. U.S. Immigration and Customs Enforcement*, the plaintiffs, who aged out of ORR custody and were placed in adult detention, argued that the government "routinely and systematically fails to adhere to the statutory provisions that require them to consider placement in 'the least restrictive setting available,' and to provide meaningful alternatives to detention," such as community group housing, as required by the Trafficking Victims Protection Reauthorization Act of 2008 (TVPRA) (8 U.S.C. §1158(b); *Garcia Ramirez v. ICE* 2021). For years, ICE field offices varied in their treatment of whether to detain children aging out of ORR custody—with some field offices detaining more than 90 percent of children who aged out (NIJC 2022).[1]

In response, the court granted a five-year permanent injunction against ICE in 2021, requiring the agency to comply with the TVPRA and other measures to protect children from being turned to adult detention on their eighteenth birthday. Today, ICE has standardized its process for releasing youth on their own recognizance, which has allowed the majority of children to be released on their eighteenth birthday. However, even if children are released on their own recognizance, the housing and stability they need once released are often nonexistent. Without access to suitable alternatives to detention that offer case management and continuum of care support, they are much more likely to end up in short-term hospitality systems, and when their stay is complete, they are at risk of homelessness, exploitation, and mental and physical health crises.

Furthermore, the DHS and ORR are still placing a subpopulation of children into adult detention based on concerns that they are actually over eighteen. These so-called age redetermination cases are less common. However, age redeterminations appear to be carried out on racist and dubious legal grounds and have damning circumstances for children who are deemed to be older than they represent themselves to be. Age redeterminations are carried out predominantly on children from South Asian or African countries. The DHS appears to place heavy reliance on dental radiographs to determine age, despite these exams being inaccurate and unethical. Against agency policy and the TVPRA, age redetermined children are reclassified as adults, lose their unaccompanied alien children (UAC) status and the protections they have as children, and are detained with adults. This chapter delves further into age redeterminations and reflect on Vida's very personal experience with her own age redetermination.

In writing this retrospective on Vida's experience, we hope to shed light on the grave injustices suffered by the hundreds of children who were inappropriately age redetermined or simply aged out into adult detention, and how housing alternatives that serve youth from seventeen to twenty-one can serve as a bridge into a life of safety and independence.

Vida: The Borderlands

I reached the U.S. border on January 10, 2016. When I picture myself standing at the border, I see a young girl, just seventeen, looking a mess, confused, helpless, with no idea what to do. I desperately needed a place to sleep and a real meal. Ever since I had run away from Ghana, I had been homeless, with no idea where I would eventually be safe. I begged and fought my way through the jungles of Ecuador, and I did it alone.

Across the border, I saw a big sign that said: "Welcome to the United States." I had been through a lot by the time I reached that sign: the very first time I set my feet on the soil of the United States, I was in a completely different world. It felt like I had been resurrected from death. Everything looks different here—the buildings, the cars, the air that I breathe, the people and the way they look; everything is different.

I remember his name was Officer John. He was white and over six foot tall, wearing a uniform. He asked me: "Do you speak or understand English? What is your name? Where do you come from? Where are you going? Are you alone? How old are you? Do you have a passport, ID, or a birth certificate to prove your nationality?"

I said, "I am coming to the U.S."

"Do you have a passport?" he asked.

"I don't know."

Officer John had blue eyes, which were strange to me, and they stared right into mine as he talked. He told me he could repeat things or slow down if I needed him to. He said it was important to tell him the truth and that we would be recorded. He asked if I understood him, and that if I didn't, then he could get a translator.

I said, "Yes, sir, I understand." But I didn't really know what was happening. But at the time, I thought, I will tell him the honest truth so I don't need a translator. But I should have had one. I couldn't read or understand any of the documents that they asked me to sign at the end of my interview. The officer switched my last and middle name on the document, but I didn't know the difference on the form. I just agreed to it.

Then he asked me questions. He asked me my name, my birthday, my age, why I came to the United States, if I had a passport, if I wanted to go to another country, if I wanted to go back to Ghana, did I know anyone in the United States. I was just answering yes or no for the most part. I had no idea my answers would be important for my case later.

Then, Officer John said that they had processed my fingerprints and that I was already in the system but that my birthday was different in the system from what I had told him. I explained that when I arrived in Panama, I had given my birth date to the officer, but he told me that if I was under eighteen, he would keep me in the refugee camp in Panama until I was an adult. Conditions in the Panamanian camp were very bad: there was no food, no shelter, no medical supplies. People were sick. The Panamanian officer was worried about me because I was among the few kids in the group and the only female teenager. He took me aside and told me: "You need to get out of here, and this is the only way." And then he wrote down a false birth date for me, making me older, so I could leave.

I explained this to Officer John and said I was still under eighteen, just about a month from turning eighteen. Officer John said he understood, but he wasn't in a position to decide my age; he would process me as a child and let ICE decide what to do with me. At the time, I didn't know why my birth date was important.

I thought America was going to be crowded and open like Ghana, where you can ask for help easily. In Ghana, in the smaller villages, it is easy to ask for help, food and shelter, even if you don't know someone. We aren't afraid of each other. You can ask anyone for help. We welcome everyone into our home. So I didn't worry about finding a safe place to sleep once the border patrol let me go.

After the interview, I thought somebody would take me home. I didn't also know that there were rules to coming to the country without a visa. I had a very distant contact in the United States, who I called "uncle." On my journey, I had talked to him, and he said I should call him when I reached Texas and he would come get me. I don't think he understood the system anymore than I did, but I trusted him. I thought once the interview was over, I would get picked up and finally be safe. I would be home.

But the border patrol agents didn't let me leave. Instead, they put me in a van with no windows, with wire netting between the passenger area, where I was sitting, and the driver. They locked the door. I felt like a criminal.

I was scared and shaking. They drove me to a place, a warehouse. I was given a uniform and a foil blanket. I got one apple and a small snack. The building was so large and there were many children and adults crying, everyone in a fence made into a cage. Everyone was cold, and I noticed that they used foil to cover themselves, like a blanket. I thought, "Oh my god, is this really happening?"

They put me in a cage inside the building. I was with ten or fifteen kids. Some of them were sitting by themselves, others were crying, some were sleeping. It was so confusing, but I had no one to talk to or ask questions. Most of the kids only spoke Spanish, and I couldn't communicate with them.

The next morning, an officer came in and told me to take a shower, and I would be sent to Chicago. I might have heard people talk about Chicago while traveling to the United States, but I had no idea what "a Chicago" was, no idea if it was a city or a state. I was in a small group—it was just me and one child from Pakistan, accompanied by an officer. The officer asked me if I had ever seen snow.

"No," I said. I had never seen snow in my life.

"Well," she said, "it is snowing eleven inches in Chicago."

When I landed, I saw she was right. There was snow on the ground. When I saw it, I was so happy. It was beautiful.

Jajah: Eighteen-Year-Olds vs. the System

Under the Flores Settlement Agreement, unaccompanied children under eighteen have been afforded a limited set of protections. Most of these are procedural: the children are detained under the auspices of services-oriented ORR rather than enforcement-oriented DHS; children are eligible for release to family and other sponsors, so that they can wait for their day in court while living in the community.

Children under eighteen are also eligible for a few limited substantive protections as they are herded through the immigration process: they are eligible to be classified as a Special Immigrant Juvenile (SIJ), a special status afforded to children whose parent or parents abused, abandoned, or neglected them. Children in detention are eligible to apply for asylum affirmatively (8 U.S.C. §1158(b)(3)(C)).[2] Affirmative asylum allows applicants to be heard before a United States Citizenship and Immigration Services (USCIS) asylum officer in a less adversarial setting. The officer can grant them asylum or punt their case to the immigration court, affording the applicants two chances to be heard and avoid deportation.

However, the moment these children turn eighteen, these limited protections are abruptly terminated.[3] Children who would have been able to apply for asylum affirmatively as UACs lose this chance upon turning eighteen (*Matter of M-A-C-O-*, 2018).[4] Those who are released on their own recognizance by the DHS risk homelessness and instability. Any young person age redetermined is taken in handcuffs to adult detention, where they may languish for months or even years.

The American Bar Association (ABA) has recognized that this subset of children on the edge of adulthood deserves special recognition:

> Children who turn 18 years old while in Custody, although legally adults, are still considered from a child welfare perspective to be children transitioning to adulthood. Many of these Children have been subjected to harrowing experiences, such as flight from great danger, traveling to and through foreign countries alone, introduction to a novel environment and finally, Custody. The emotional effect of these circumstances alone militates in favor of continuing to treat them as children, even after they turn 18. As such, they should continue to possess certain residual rights even upon release from Custody. (ABA 2018, § VII.G.3)

The ABA's recommendation is backed by scientific research into how brains mature. Research has shown that adolescent brain development emerges around age ten but that individuals do not come into full cognitive

Emerging into Darkness　　　　　　　　　　　　　　　　　　　　**195**

maturation until age twenty-five (Arain et al. 2013; Ledford 2018). For youth turning eighteen, this means their psychosocial maturity (i.e., temperance, responsibility, perspective, and long-term planning skills) and prefrontal cortex are nearly seven years away from fully developing (Cauffman and Steinberg 2000; White 2019).

Youth who turn eighteen while in ORR care are thrust into a world where they are suddenly treated as fully formed adults. Shoehorning young people into an adult system has serious implications for their life and liberty. USCIS has recognized that "an applicant whose claim is based on events that occurred while under the age of eighteen may exhibit a minor's recollection of the past experiences and events," indicating an awareness that these young people in this position are entitled to additional procedural considerations (USCIS 2019, 22–24).[5] Yet this recognition is extremely limited—and given the discretionary nature of immigration hearings, judges are certainly not compelled to recognize youth who are over eighteen as anything other than adults. Even if an immigration judge wanted to apply a different standard to a young person, there is little, if any guidance, for her to do so.

Beyond losing the few rights afforded to UAC, these young people are also cut off from the fragile support system available to children in ORR custody. Aged-out children are cut off from communicating with the staff who have worked with them and who may hold crucial information that could make or break their immigration case. Legal services providers have similar rules. If a legal services provider has the ability to take on adult cases, a child's case may be transferred internally, though the vast majority of children who age out do not have this continuity of care.

The only service provider that regularly continues to work with children who have aged out is the Young Center for Immigrant Children's Rights. The independent nature of the organization, coupled with the volunteer-based services, means that children with Child Advocates through the Young Center may continue to rely on them in adult detention. Yet the Young Center is only able to serve a portion of the population, those deemed "most vulnerable" under the TVPRA.

Vida: ORR Custody

I didn't know it at the time, but I had been sent to a detention center for children, called the International Children's Center (ICC).

Life at the center was based on rules. We woke up around six, took a shower, had breakfast, and then class started at eight and ended at three. Sometimes there would be activities in the house, or we would go to the park or play basketball. At nine, we had to be in bed.

But even though we had a bed, school, and three meals a day, that place was still jail because we couldn't leave. We couldn't walk through the halls by ourselves, and staff members were always with us. I wanted to be outside, to walk around and look at the snow, but unless we were taken on a special outing, we were not allowed to leave the building. We didn't even know the address.

Kids could call their family, but only for fifteen to thirty minutes a week. I tried calling my uncle, but at some point, he realized I was in immigration detention, and he refused to take the calls. There would be no family to help me leave the center. I was completely stuck. I wondered if I would be there for the rest of my life. I was worried about my son in Ghana, and I wanted other family to know where I was, but I couldn't reach them. None of my numbers for my father or aunt worked. I had nightmares that someone was hurting me, and when I woke up, I wouldn't be able to sleep again. Instead, I would look outside and see the snow and realize I was in a different world. I cried a lot.

Jajah: How Detention Works for Children

ORR itself is a behemoth of a federal agency, founded in the 1980s as "an attempt to design a coherent and comprehensive refugee admission and resettlement policy" (Zucker 1983, 172). As part of its work with unaccompanied children, ORR contracts with many different nongovernmental organizations (NGOs) on the ground, which ultimately provide services to the children. As part of their contractual obligations with ORR, the NGOs must provide adequate food, clothing, shelter, and medical care, including mental health services. They must also allow legal services providers to present Know Your Rights presentations to the children and perform legal screenings. These NGOs are responsible for keeping the children safe but also for limiting and monitoring their access to the outside world, including phone calls with family, and sharing information they learn about the child and her family to ORR, and sometimes with the DHS.

When Vida was transferred to Chicago, she was placed in one of these NGO sites, the International Children's Center, run by Heartland Alliance,

Emerging into Darkness

one of the longest-running children's shelters in the city. As mentioned in the introduction of this volume, the actual quality of care at these facilities "varies tremendously." At the time Vida entered the ICC, it was managed by a warm and competent director, Sarah, who cared about the children and often found herself caught between policy dictates and what she felt was truly in the best interests of the children.

Vida's overall experience echoes many children's experiences in ORR custody: they feel cooped up and deprived of simple liberties, but they are fed and sheltered, receive some sort of schooling (though the education is not up to state curriculum standards), and receive some limited medical and mental health care. But the ORR shelters are set up to be temporary. Under the TVPRA, children must be placed in the least restrictive environment in their best interests. Therefore, ORR's goal is to release children to a sponsor—usually a parent, relative, or family friend—who has to pass a number of economic and bureaucratic hurdles before a child can be released into their care.

If a child has no viable sponsors, they can be eligible for long-term foster care through ORR, but only if a legal service provider finds that they can make a case for legal relief. However, long-term foster care programs come with long wait lists, and many children age out before they are placed. In Vida's case, she spent a little more than two weeks at the ORR shelter. There was no time for her case managers to go through the lengthy process of getting her into a foster care placement.

Concurrently, DHS officials were concentrating their efforts on removing her from the relative safety of the ORR shelter, based on concerns regarding her age. But, like most children in ORR custody, Vida had a very limited understanding of the age redetermination process and what it would mean for her. In the end, the age redetermination process happened suddenly and changed the course of her life, threatening her safety and well-being overnight.

Vida: My Age Redetermination

I met a woman named Sarah, the director of the center.[6] She felt like a safe person. She would always check on me to see how I was doing. I was confused about why Sarah was worried about my age. I did not understand that I was in danger of aging out. I didn't understand what that meant. Eventually, the other kids told me if I turned eighteen at the center, I would be taken to jail. I knew that back home, jail was not a place that good people go. In my country, no one comes back from jail healthy. They come home sick, and some even die while in jail.

After about two weeks at the center, Sarah told me that the Department of Homeland Security asked her to take me to a dentist so they could look at my teeth to review my real age. Sarah asked me if I was scared. I wasn't sure what was happening, so I said no. I didn't understand why my teeth would tell them anything about my age, especially because I was going to turn eighteen in a month or so anyway. I let them do the exam.

Sarah talked to me when she got the results. She would try to help me as much as possible, but it was out of her hands. Based on her voice, I could tell she was hurting, and she didn't want to tell me straight. Finally, she said that immigration could come anytime and take me to jail. That's when I started to cry. I thought Sarah was the boss, and if she wanted to, she could have done something to stop me from going to jail. The fact that she didn't, made me give up hope. My head was full of negative thoughts: that I should have stayed in Ghana and died, that I should jump off a bridge. I had lost hope.

That afternoon, Sarah told me she had asked someone to come to the center, called Jajah, from a group called the Young Center, and that she would help me. I asked if this person would help me stay out of jail. She said no, but it was important to ask her for help. I was so tired by then, and I didn't want to talk to anyone, especially another person who wasn't going to help me stay out of jail. Honestly, I thought, if this person can't help me get out, then how can they help me later?

But an hour later Jajah arrived. I didn't want to look at her. I just wanted to give up. Jajah told me we wouldn't know where immigration would take me, but she would find me in a few days. *If immigration takes you, I will find you.* These were the only words that gave me a bit of hope. After she left, I sat waiting for the worst to happen. I imagined I would stay in prison until I died. Later that night, two officers came into the center, a male and a female. They handcuffed me, and they told me to get in their car. I was sitting in the backseat crying and crying, but there was no one to cry to.

Jajah: Age Redetermination

Vida's age redetermination story is unique, but it is not singular—since 1998, thousands of children have been subjected to dental radiographs (X-ray) to determine their age (Mejia and Morrissey 2019). In 2018, 2.2 percent of unaccompanied children in ORR care, or about 1,080, were age redetermined and transferred to DHS custody (U.S. ICE 2019).[7] While the *Garcia Ramirez* litigation changed the landscape for children who chronologically turn eighteen in ORR, children who are age redetermined—found to be "lying" about their identity—are still routinely taken into adult custody and stripped of the protections they enjoyed as children (U.S. ICE 2019). Even those who are living in ORR's long-term foster care program can be taken into adult custody on the basis of an age redetermination.

Under the TVPRA, the procedures for determining a child's status as a minor "at a minimum . . . shall take into account multiple forms of evidence, including the *non-exclusive use* of radiographs" (8 U.S.C. § 1232 (b)(4), emphasis added). The DHS and ORR have developed a set of age redetermination policies when either agency believes an individual's age is in question (ORR 2022). The government may conduct an age inquiry if there is a "reasonable suspicion" that a child in ORR custody is over eighteen, by reviewing records; statements from interested parties, including the child themselves; and medical assessments, including dental radiographs, though radiographs must be used "in conjunction with other evidence" (ORR 2022).

In practice, when a child is flagged for age redetermination, they—like Vida—will be subject to a dental radiograph and/or a wrist X-ray (Mejia and Morrissey 2019). If the results of the exam show that there is more than a 75 percent chance that they are above eighteen, the DHS will almost certainly take that child into adult custody (Mejia and Morrissey 2019).

But the use of dental radiographs to help determine age in these cases is questionable, unscientific, and unethical (British Dental Association 2021). Dental radiographs are known to overestimate age (Jayaraman et al. 2014). Even the most precise of dental exams can only provide age ranges, not a specific age (Cohen, Woltjen, and Nagda 2011, 3–4). There is, to date, no medical test or group of tests that "lets us know the exact chronological age of a human being," particularly given the "wide variations in the chronological ages" across ethnic groups (Cohen, Woltjen, and Nagda 2011, 3–4). A 2020 American Dental Association (ADA) report noted that dental radiographs for age determinations must be compared to a reference population, a standard against which the results are analyzed. But given the significant variability in dental development based on "race/ethnicity, sex, socioeconomic status, systemic disease, nutritional health, and other environmental factors," it is impossible to fix on appropriate reference populations for the wide-ranging backgrounds of migrant children who come through the system (Laniado et al. 2021, 349).

The inconsistency and imprecision of dental age estimations indicates that practically, a dental radiograph would fail to be reliable enough to help assess whether a teen is over or under eighteen, particularly when the youth is, according to all other evidence, just months or weeks away from her eighteenth birthday.

Yet, for Vida, as for other children, the dental exam proved to be the *only* evidence that mattered to the DHS. This practice of effectively relying solely on dental radiographs has come under scrutiny in recent years. In *L.B. v. Charles Keeton, et al.*, No. CV-18–03435-PHX-JJT (MHB), at *2–3 (D. Ariz., Oct. 26, 2018), the court overturned an age determination as in violation of ORR/DHS policies as well as the TVPRA. In that case, the child, like Vida, had given officials outside the United States a different birth date, and, like Vida, spent months in adult custody based on the results of the radiograph.

Conspicuously, the government appears to rely heavily on one particular dentist to evaluate the radiographs, a Dr. David Senn at the University of Texas Health Science Center at San Antonio. Dr. Senn has reviewed more than two thousand cases since 2008 (Mejia and Morrissey 2019). In fact, Dr. Senn reviewed both Vida's dental radiograph as well as that of L.B., the claimant in the other case mentioned here. Dr. Senn's name was associated with nearly every child I worked with who had been age redetermined on the basis of a radiograph. An article in the *Los Angeles Times* notes that Dr. Senn is one of the "few dentists the government uses for [radiographic age] analyses," perhaps because he spearheaded the program that the government relies on to estimate an individual's mean age and the probability that they are over eighteen (Mejia and Morrissey 2019). The Innocence Project has issued a cease-and-desist letter to Dr. Senn on the grounds that he has "repeatedly generat[ed] misleading 'forensic reports' that, in boilerplate language and form, provide scientifically indefensible age 'estimates'" (Innocence Project et al. 2021).

The American Association of Public Health Dentistry (AAPHD) released an issue brief in 2021 condemning the practice of using dental radiographs to determine age because "misclassification can have a major impact on health and safety" since children mistakenly placed in adult detention are at risk of "physical harm, anxiety, depression, suicidal ideation, and post traumatic stress syndrome" (AAPHD 2021). The AAPHD stresses that it is unethical to give dental radiographs to children who (1) have not given their informed consent, as they are neither afforded the right to refuse nor a full explanation of the ramifications of the results, and (2) are exposed to radiation for nonmedical purposes (AAPHD 2021).[8]

Vida: Adult Detention

They took me to a large building. Inside, I was told to strip naked and a female officer came in to pat me down. I was given an orange uniform with a pair of rubber sandals to put on and thrown in a small cell alone.

The next morning, they called me into a different office. There was a white man there, and he introduced himself as an immigration officer. He told me he was going to interview me again, and it was important for me to tell him the truth. After hours of interviewing and pretty much asking the same questions as Officer John did at the border, he recommended getting a lawyer, even though I didn't know how to do that. On the way out, he said, "Good luck."[9]

After another day or so, they put me in handcuffs and chains on my legs and waist, together with seven or eight other people. They took us out to a van, locked us in, and we left Chicago for a jail in Juneau, Wisconsin.

When we eventually arrived at the new jail facility, the building looked very different from the other places I had been. This one was huge with all the security that you could think of. All the officers I saw had guns on them. They talked on a little radio and were watched on the camera before they could get access to every single door.

I cried the whole time. I was so sad that the police officer who was processing me felt bad. She kept saying: "Poor girl, poor girl, you don't belong here." I could tell she was worried about me, even though there was not much she could do.

They made us strip naked, and then they gave us another uniform and took us to yet another cell. There were about eight white women who were already there. I say women because they were over eighteen, but they were all so young. They seemed like girls to me. They could tell that I was different, and as soon as I settled in, they started asking me questions: "Who did you kill? You didn't kill anyone? Then what did you steal?"

"Nothing, nothing. I'm just here, waiting for them to take me to jail."

"You're in jail," they said. I had no idea that I was already in jail. All my knowledge of what jails were like came from ones that exist in African countries, with no amenities!

I told them why I had ended up in jail. When the girls heard that I was put in jail just for crossing the border, they were so mad for me. It was the first time I heard the f-word, but they used it again and again, F immigration, F the system, F the government. They didn't think I belonged there.

They were curious about my life, so I told them my story, from the very beginning. They thought my life was crazy and that it was amazing that I had survived what I did. Soon, they would come to me every night and ask me to tell them stories about what had happened to me in Ghana and during my long journey to the United States.

As they learned about me, I learned more about them too. One girl said she had wanted to be a doctor, but now she had a ten-year sentence. Another inmate told me that she wished she could take back what she did. I tried to comfort her. Sometimes she would feel better after we talked. This was when I started thinking that I could get an education. I thought if I could do something good outside, it would be to help girls like these.

I wasn't expecting anyone to call me or follow up. I was lost and frustrated, and waiting for the worst to happen. I had some suicidal thoughts. I wondered how I would die once they sent me back to Ghana. Some of the girls said the officers took people in the night. I was scared at night, thinking I would be taken and forced to go back to Ghana.

A few days later, I was in my room and the officer said I had a call from Chicago. My cellmate was so happy for me. "Someone is going to help you," she said, but I told her I didn't know who it was. When the call came in, I heard: "Hello, Vida? This is Jajah, do you remember me?"

From that moment, it clicked and I remembered her. Jajah introduced herself again. She said she was with a group called the Young Center, a group that was not with the government. Then, she clarified that she was not my immigration lawyer (I didn't have one, yet) but that she was something called a Child Advocate, a person who would help me as much as she could. Then, she asked me if I was okay, if I was being fed, how many meals I had a day, if I was warm enough, if I needed anything, if anyone was hurting me.

Then, Jajah asked me more about my story. She explained that understanding my story would allow her to help me better. It was the first time I had a chance to tell her what had happened. We were cut off before I could finish the full story, but Jajah said she would call again and to hang in there.

Jajah called twice a week after that. It was a long process to get the call through. She had to get approval three days in advance every time, and we had a limited time to talk. But during these conversations, I was able to share more about what had happened to me.

After a week or two in jail, I had a court hearing, by video. Some other inmates said I could ask the judge to set bond, though Jajah said she didn't think I was eligible for bond, only for parole by the DHS. Jajah was right. The judge said he couldn't grant me bail because DHS officers were reviewing my custody case. I felt so down. They gave me a sheet of numbers for free lawyers, but they all went to voicemail.

Honestly, I was so confused about what was happening in my case. None of the inmates knew about the immigration system, so I couldn't learn from them, and there was nowhere else to ask for help or explanations. Jajah tried to help me understand over the phone. She told me that in order to be eligible for parole, I would have to get documentation about my identity, about my age, that I would need to find a place to live, and it would be helpful to get an immigration attorney to represent me. I couldn't do any of these things by myself. Jajah said she was helping gather these proofs and talk to the DHS officer, but I really didn't understand how it would help.

Some of the immigrants had been at Juneau for more than a year. I was scared that this would be the case for me too. Some days we looked out the window to see the weather. Watching the cold snow in winter, the rain, or the beautiful sky in the spring, we wondered when we could leave.

Jajah: The Dangers of Adult Detention on Youth and Children

Like Vida, many unaccompanied children have fled abusive or neglectful relationships, targeted gang violence, or wartime environments in their home countries (LIRS 1998; Uehling 2008). Moreover, the dangers of the voyage to the United States are well documented, with many children experiencing "beatings, rape, robberies, extortion, hunger, accidents, and health problems" during the overland voyage through Central America and Mexico (Urrutia-Rojas and Rodriguez 1997). The destabilizing effects of being misidentified as an adult and placed in adult detention pose a real threat to their mental and physical health. They have limited ability to contact family or contact legal aid and other services, all barriers to achieving any hope of mounting a successful legal claim.

As with all detainees, youths who are age redetermined or age out are treated as criminals, regardless of their backgrounds. They may be housed in the same buildings and room with adult detainees, some of whom have criminal records. Studies indicate that juveniles housed with adults in prison experience far higher rates of sexual and physical violence (Schiraldi and Zeidenberg 1997). While strip searches that require removing one's clothing are not permitted as a matter of "routine" under ICE directives (U.S. ICE 2011), these invasive and abusive practices are still routine in ICE detention centers (Santus 2018; Miroff 2020), and immigrants who are housed in state detention centers, like Vida, can be strip-searched per state prison directives (Duran 2022).

Even beyond risks of violence and abusive practices by staff, adult detention facilities are ill-prepared to meet the varying cultural and linguistic backgrounds of detainees. Interpretation services are often lacking, even for medical services, with a 2003 Physicians for Human Rights study finding that 37 percent of immigrant detainees reported either no interpreter for health services or difficulty accessing one for health services. Mental health services in detention facilities are also lacking, with many issues related to access to medication, transfer of prescriptions, and shortages of providers (Physicians for Human Rights 2003).

Finally, as previously discussed, once a child is age redetermined, they are no longer considered a UAC and lose the slim legal protections afforded to them as a child. Due to the remote location of many detention facilities, often phone calls with their attorneys are the only means for detainees to prepare for immigration court hearings (NIJC 2011).

As Vida coped with life in jail, I worked toward getting her released from adult detention so she could live freely while she waited for her immigration case to be heard. Vida had been designated as an "arriving alien," defined as an "applicant for admission coming or attempting to come into the United States at a port-of-entry" (8 U.S.C. § 1101).[10] Admission in the context of immigration law means the "lawful entry" of a noncitizen after inspection and authorization by an immigration officer (8 U.S.C. § 1101(a)(13)(A)). Arriving noncitizens are generally those who are seeking admission but are not actually "admitted" into the United States. As an arriving noncitizen, Vida was not eligible for the bond process, which would have taken place before an immigration judge, who would have set her bond anywhere between $1,000 and $20,000. Instead, arriving noncitizens must parlay with the DHS, as DHS officers may parole noncitizens into the United States for urgent humanitarian reasons or where there is a significant public benefit to that person (8 U.S.C. § 1182(d)(5)(A)). Parole is not considered an "admission" into the United States, and conferred no permanent benefit to Vida (8 U.S.C. § 235.3(b)(4)(ii)), but it would allow her release from jail so she could live in the community and attend school while her immigration case wended its way slowly through the system.[11] If her parole were denied, she would have to wait in prison, possibly for years, to have her asylum case heard via videoconference while she sat in chains.

In order to be eligible for parole, Vida needed to pass a credible fear interview before the USCIS. After that, the DHS officer assigned to her case would consider her parole based on the following factors: (1) her identity, (2) whether she was a flight risk or (3) a danger to the community or U.S. security, and (4) any other factors DHS deemed appropriate, as parole is "inherently discretionary" (U.S. ICE 2009).

Luckily, Vida had passed her "credible fear" interview. (Her meeting with the USCIS official the day after she had been removed from ORR care had been to determine whether or not she had a credible fear of persecution or torture in Ghana.) The DHS officer was reluctant to parole Vida because the DHS believed she had lied about her identity, that is, her age, when she presented herself at the U.S. border. In short, he wanted proof that she was who she said she was, beyond her birth certificate, which he considered unreliable.

Under the TVPRA, we also needed to show that Vida would not be a flight risk—in other words, that she would appear for court and at DHS check-ins. Flight risk is mitigated by factors that anchor an individual to the community (family and employment ties, for example) or acceptance into an alternative-to-detention (ATD) program, which usually provides wraparound services along with long-term housing. Securing an immigration attorney would also support Vida's parole and be hugely beneficial to her ability to acquire legal status in the future.[12]

I had hoped that we could quickly find Vida an attorney through the legal services provider funded to take cases through the Midwest, but they told me they also needed proof of Vida's identity before they would be willing to sign her as a client.

Children often lack access to documents necessary for their immigration cases, sometimes because they were born into situations where their births were never registered. Vida, like more than a quarter of the children born in Ghana, never had her birth registered with the state (Dake and Fuseini 2018). Although she had a birth certificate, it had been issued shortly before she fled Ghana, and the DHS gave it no credence. Instead, we would have to rely on other evidence: a written affidavit from a family member willing to go on record.

But Vida had lost contact with her family. Together, we called every number she could remember to try to contact her family, but we were met with disconnected lines or phones that rang unanswered. After hours of attempts over a period of weeks, we finally reached a distant family friend who provided Vida with a new number for her father. We were able to talk to her father, who was not able to provide an affidavit; and then to Vida's aunt, who knew the details of why she fled Ghana and could corroborate her story but could not write; and finally to Vida's sister, whom she had not seen in years. Her sister was in nursing school in Accra and not only became a fierce advocate for Vida but also had access to a computer, email, and a printer.

Vida's sister worked with us to draft an affidavit, in which she stated that she knew Vida's true age and date of birth, both consistent with what Vida provided to Officer John at the U.S. border. She then brought the document to a judge in a Ghanaian high court to notarize. A week or two after that, we received that precious affidavit in the mail, along with documents proving Vida's sister's own identity. The legal services provider reviewed the affidavit, along with other information I had gathered from her family and Ghanaian country conditions experts, and they decided to take her case.

In the meantime, I had also been working to find Vida a stable housing situation in Chicago that would take her for the long term and supply the case management services that she needed, since she had no ties in the community. Without the help of community-based housing programs, Vida might have languished in jail for years. In an ideal world, Vida would have been placed in an alternative-to-detention program by the government. Instead, I scrambled to call the few places in Chicago with housing programs to advocate for Vida's acceptance.

Apna Ghar, a local NGO with a transitional housing program, accepted Vida into its program, as long as it had a week to prepare for her arrival. A week's notice was very reasonable but presented another issue for Vida. The DHS was never forthcoming about release dates and clients were often released with no warning to their attorneys or advocates. Luckily, another housing project, an alternative-to-detention program created specifically to support newly arrived immigrants, had recently started up in Hyde Park. At the time, Brother Michael Gosch, who now runs Viator House with Father Corey, directed it. He agreed to accept Vida into the Illinois Community for Displaced Immigrants (ICDI) program whenever she was released.

With these pieces in place, I resubmitted Vida's parole request to the DHS officer and waited.

Vida: Free

One of the worst days in jail happened in the early spring. That morning, a lawyer visited me to do an intake. Jajah had asked her to come and review my case, but she kept saying she didn't have enough information to take on my case. Later that day, I saw the judge by video again, who said again that he didn't have the power to release me. I went straight to my room and cried more.

But then that night, at 3 a.m., a knock came at my door. The officer said: "Vida, you're going to Chicago."

"No," I said. "You don't want me. That's Maria who's going." Maria was the girl who was my roommate who was going to be deported any day. We had been waiting for her to be called.

"Isn't your name Opoku?"

"That's me."

"Well, I don't know who is out there working hard for you, but they got you released. You are going to Chicago, and you might not be coming back here again."

I broke down. Deep inside my heart, I melted. I was crying and screaming. Some of the girls woke up and asked me what happened. When they found out that I was leaving, they were so happy.

One of my friends passed me a note: *Keep your head up. There are good people and bad people out there. Be positive. Write me.*

I was driven back to Chicago. I still wasn't sure what was happening or who was behind this. When the DHS officer processed me for release, he asked me to sign a document, and I was so excited I did it without reading, which was not good, because it could have been an agreement to be deported, but I was too excited to read it. Then, he opened the door and led me into a hallway.

I saw Jajah and Maggie, the student who had been helping Jajah on my case, standing there.

Jajah said, "Welcome to Chicago."

We got in the car and I looked at the beautiful city. I reached ICDI with Jajah and Maggie. They showed me my room for the night. I thought it was the best place I had ever seen. I had my own room. I loved it.

Rachel, who would later be my case manager, asked me if I had clothes. I said yes, but it was just the clothing I had from ICC. I had the clothes on my back and one more set. Rachel laughed and said we can get you some more clothes. I appreciated everything: the food, the shelter, the house. I was grateful to be in a safe position, that I didn't have to work like a slave for someone, and having freedom.

Jajah: Finding Safe Havens

The immigration detention system is one of the most egregious and racist forms of incarceration in the United States. Rooted in the anti-Chinese sentiment that led to the 1882 Chinese Exclusion Act, this procedural "othering" of migrants from East Asian countries formed the basis of how America has viewed and dealt with immigration since: through a combination of racist policies, dehumanizing treatment, and the criminalization of migrants.[13]

In the past century, immigration detention has continued to grow along these perverse and inhumane tracks: prison facilities were used to detain Haitian asylum seekers in the 1980s (Lindskoog 2018); radical politics criminalized migrants from Mexico and Central America "regardless of legal or immigration status" and has led to mass incarcerations of migrants from those states (Longazel et al. 2016); and post-9/11 fears spurred on a slew of restrictive immigration laws under the guise of national security, though many restrictions only served to harm refugees and asylum seekers and did little to prevent terrorist attacks (Kerwin 2005).

In truth, immigration detention confers no benefits to the country that could not otherwise be met through alternative-to-detention housing programs or a supervised/conditional release program.[14] The erstwhile purpose of the immigration detention system is to ensure that noncitizens comply with court hearings and that those individuals who have no means of legal relief, or are otherwise removable, leave the country. The DHS does not have the authority to punish or imprison real criminals—only the U.S. criminal justice system does. The DHS merely "processes" and "detains" noncitizens who were not admitted into the United States—including asylum seekers, migrants, and families, children, and youth who have no criminal record.

There is no rule that the DHS must use mass detention in prisons and prisonlike systems to carry out this role. In fact, U.S. immigration laws expressly permit release of noncitizens who pose no "danger to property or persons" and are "likely to appear" for proceedings (8 CFR Sec. 236.19(c)(8); 8 CFR Sec. 3.19(h)(3)). Under the TVPRA, children who are aging out are "eligible to participate in alternative to detention programs, utilizing a continuum of alternatives based on the alien's need for supervision, which may include placement of the alien with an individual or an organizational sponsor, or in a supervised group home" (8 USC 1232(c)(2)(B)). Immigrants who have access to community housing programs maintain higher compliance rates (some 80–90 percent), while the programs themselves are far less costly than detention (NIJC 2019; HRW 2021). Despite this, the DHS-ICE has comfortably contracted with private detention centers as well as state and local prison systems to confine tens of thousands of people daily. ICE spent $3 billion between October 2015 and June 2018 to contractors operating the 106 detention facilities to assure the detention of noncitizens who were waiting for their day in court (Franzblau 2021).

This enormous outlay must be redirected.

The U.S. government must apply funds toward housing programs and attorneys for those seeking relief. Specifically, we urge the creation of housing programs with wraparound services that would support young people from ages seventeen through twenty-one. A youth-centered alternative to detention that acts as a bridge during the late teen years would allow ORR and the DHS to coordinate on a smoother, humane transition for individuals who fall in this age range. When a young person's age is unclear or in question, such a placement could ensure their care while they work to establish their identity without fear of being taken to jail based on an age redetermination. Teens in this phase of life would not be at risk to "age out" and anyone turning twenty-one could be accepted into an adult housing program or be supported as they entered the community. In order to be successful, alternative-to-detention housing programs for young people must offer comprehensive social assistance: wraparound services like individualized case management that incorporates legal services, education, and physical and mental health support (Executive Committee of the High Commissioner's Programme 2016).

But even an alternative-to-detention program with robust services would still be cost effective and within reach of the government's budget. Housing programs are much cheaper to run than jails, averaging only $50 a day for housing and wraparound services for an entire family, compared to $319.37 for family detention and $161.27 for contract detention facilities (ALIA 2019; AIC 2020). Alternative-to-detention programs are "highly successful at ensuring high appearance rates" by helping young people understand their duty to appear and by providing essential transportation and moral support (USCCB 2018). ICE's own numbers show that alternatives-to-detention programs that provide case management can ensure that 95 percent of participants appear for their final hearing.[15] Coupled with strong legal services, these programs can prevent youth from being incarcerated, from abandoning their legal claims, from risk of exploitation and trafficking, and from mental and physical health crises.

This is not to say that alternative housing programs are a silver bullet for all that ails the immigration detention system. Housing programs should not be used to "expand detention capacity" or to enforce "intensive reporting and monitoring programs" that would "stigmatize and incapacitate" participants (USCCB 2018). Nor are they a good fit for young people who have family or friends with whom they can safely reside. Instead, these placements should provide a haven for youth who, like Vida, have no safety net in the United States and who emerged into young adulthood from a series of traumatic experiences, including being uprooted from their homeland.

Viator House of Hospitality in Chicago is an example of a thriving and successful alternative-to-detention program for young immigrant men. Viator House's lead architects, Father Corey and Brother Michael (who are contributors to this volume), crafted a program responsive to the advice and insights of attorneys, advocates, and young people themselves, based on interfaith principles, welcoming of all youth, and committed to creating long-term success and independence for their participants. To that end, Viator House implements individual care plans, with a trauma-informed approach, ensures their participants have useful knowledge regarding their rights and duties, works with young people to reach educational or career goals, sees that youth are treated with dignity and respect, and encourages their eventual independence and self-sufficiency in the community.

* * *

It would be another four years before Vida was finally granted asylum before an immigration judge. In those four years, Vida achieved success upon success. She graduated from Truman Alternative High School in two years while working in the restaurant and retail industry. She won scholarships that enabled her to continue her education. She gave a graduation speech to the cheers of her commencement class. She was enrolled in the prestigious Loyola University Chicago. She eventually moved into her own apartment, learned to drive, and began to do work for UNICEF.

But while these successes were real and hard-earned, the truth is a little more complicated. Vida struggled in her first years out of detention: with school, with housing, with depression. She was shunted back and forth between housing providers, often because those providers lacked space and/or lost funding. Throughout this time, Vida continued to be haunted by her immigration case, which dragged out for years.

Vida felt adrift, unmoored, and infinitely lonely. There were few young people she considered friends. School peers mocked and bullied her. Money was always tight, and Vida was also under pressure to save up enough to send back to her family. Some months, Vida pulled two shifts after school, trying to keep her head above water.

But Vida survived. She made a life for herself with the help of her attorney, Child Advocates, case workers, teachers, and mentors. She hopes to be reunified with her son someday soon. She continues to study and dream and make her life as big and vibrant as she can.

Vida: Afterward

The immigration system was so hard to navigate. It's stressful and something I wish could be changed. I was out of detention, but the struggle continued.

I needed to figure out how to get a job, go to school, get a scholarship, how to get food, how to get people to help you in court. It's tiring.

If you don't have people to help, you would give up. Because it's too hard. Even school was hard. You get bullied by the other kids for looking different. Some people would ask me if I spoke English. That hit me hard. Everywhere you go, you get it shoved in your face that you don't belong. Sometimes at school, I hear other students say: *how did she even get into this class?* Professors don't make you feel comfortable either. They don't understand and just expect you to know things. You just feel isolated.

As much as you try to stay in school, you might end up doing factory work, or something else you didn't want to do. It is so hard.

What helped was me getting to know Jajah and Rachel, my first case worker at ICDI. Some of the NGOs and organizations helping me were amazing. But other places would ignore you because you spoke with an accent, and you would have to reach someone who spoke English really well to get their attention. People who were supposed to help immigrants might make you feel like you didn't belong and didn't deserve help.

My journey and immigration experience as a teenager in the United States will forever be an unforgettable one. I have been homeless, helpless, and mistreated. I've also been helped by many total strangers, like Jajah, Rachel, and Maggie, and even received kindness from people like Officer John or the one woman officer in jail.

Dealing with the American immigration system has had a huge impact on my life from different perceptions. I have learned the importance of nonprofit and nongovernmental organization, and how cruel the system could be for most foreigners. Moreover, being an immigrant here in the United States also comes with a very challenging price: learning a new language, adapting to a new culture, and trying to fit in to the society are still difficult for me. Being an immigrant means constantly confronting challenges like discrimination, racism, and belittlement in the eyes of others.

Notes

1. A sample of ICE field offices' age-out detention rates between April 2016 and May 2019: Houston, 96 percent; Miami, 96 percent; New York, 90 percent; San Antonio, 4 percent; Chicago, 64 percent. This information came from a confidential source.

2. According to an anonymous informant: "An asylum officer . . . shall have initial jurisdiction over any asylum application filed by an unaccompanied alien child."

Emerging into Darkness   213

3. This gap in services and recognition is not solely an issue in the immigration context. Twenty percent of the children who age out of foster care at eighteen, or in some states, at twenty-one, are immediately left homeless (Fowler et al. 2017).

4. The Board of Immigration Appeals published *Matter of M-A-C-O-*, holding that immigration judges have the power to decide whether they or USCIS will have jurisdiction over a former UAC's asylum case, and that because M-A-C-O- was over eighteen at the time of his asylum filing, the immigration judge was correct in determining that she had jurisdiction over his case.

5. Note that while the Refugee, Asylum and International Operations (RAIO) Directorate is a step in the right direction, there has been no codification of these additional procedural protections for children.

6. Name has been changed.

7. While the government does not generally release numbers for how many children it has placed into DHS custody based on age redetermination, it did release the percentage of children placed in DHS custody based on age redetermination for fiscal year 2018, as part of a final rule amending regulations related to "Apprehension, Processing, Care, and Custody of Alien Minors and Unaccompanied Alien Children" (U.S. ICE 2019).

8. The British Dental Association is also strongly opposed to the use of dental X-rays to determine age in young asylees, citing the lack of accuracy of these exams and the unethical nature of subjecting young people to radiation for nonmedical purposes (BDA 2021).

9. This was likely Vida's credible fear interview. Children do not undergo credible fear interviews, but when Vida was reprocessed as an adult, they put her through the interview.

10. The term *arriving alien* is "offensive and demeaning" when applied to humans (*Flores v. USCIS*), and therefore, in this chapter, we replace this damaging term with the more neutral *arriving noncitizen*.

11. Parole is intended for the limited purpose of being released from custody.

12. According to court records, detained immigrants who had an attorney were four times more likely to be released from detention (44 percent vs. 11 percent), and immigrants who are not detained are five times more likely to pursue their immigration cases with an attorney by their side (AIC 2020).

13. The Chinese Exclusion Act banned immigration from China, the first Congressional move to place limits on immigration in America. Even prior to the Chinese Exclusion Act, immigrants to Angel Island, most of whom were Chinese, were likely to be detained for weeks or months—the longest for two years—while European immigrants who passed through Ellis Island were unlikely to be detained, and if they were, they were allowed to enter the country after a day or two (Aneja and Waxman 2021).

14. We set aside discussing the policy of holding children under eighteen in ORR custody—a more complicated discussion than we have space for here—and concentrate on DHS's custodial authority.

15. ICE currently employs the phrase *alternatives to detention* (ATD) to signify a number of methods it may employ instead of detaining individuals, including the use of ankle monitoring or checking in by phone without a housing component. However, in this chapter, we use the term *alterative to detention* more broadly to encompass community-based group housing, in line with the term's usage in the TVPRA. We condemn the use of ankle monitoring, which is a method of tracking that criminalizes and degrades migrants while literally hobbling them.

References

American Association of Public Health Dentistry (AAPHD). 2021. "AAPHD Issue Brief: The Use of Dental Radiographs for Age Estimation of Unaccompanied Migrant Minors." July. https://www.aaphd.org/issue-briefts.

American Bar Association (ABA). 2018. "Standards for the Custody, Placement and Care; Legal Representation; and Adjudication of Unaccompanied Alien Children in the United States." Commission on Immigration, August. https://www.americanbar.org/content/dam/aba/publications/commission_on_immigration/standards_for_children_2018.pdf.

American Dental Association (ADA). 2020. "Human Age Assessment by Dental Analysis." Technical Report No. 1077, July 23. https://www.nist.gov/system/files/documents/2021/02/23/ADA%20Technical%20Report%20No.%201077_July_2020.pdf.

American Immigration Council (AIC). 2020. "Immigration Detention in the United States by Agency." January 2. https://www.americanimmigrationcouncil.org/research/immigration-detention-united-states-agency.

American Immigration Lawyers Association (ALIA). 2019. "The Real Alternatives to Detention." https://www.aila.org/library/the-real-alternatives-to-detention.

Aneja, Arpita, and Olivia B. Waxman. 2021. "The Overlooked History of Angel Island, Where the U.S. Enforced Rules Designed to Keep Asian Immigrants Out." *Time*, May 3.

Arain, Mariam, et al. 2013. "Maturation of the Adolescent Brain." *Neuropsychiatric Disease and Treatment* 9:449–461.

British Dental Association (BDA). 2021. "Written Evidence Submitted for the Nationalities and Borders Bill." Parliament session, August 19. https://publications.parliament.uk/pa/cm5802/cmpublic/NationalityBorders/memo/NBB02.htm.

Cauffman, Elizabeth, and Laurence Steinberg. 2000. "(Im)maturity of Judgment in Adolescence: Why Adolescents May Be Less Culpable than Adults." *Behavioral Sciences & the Law* 18 (6): 741–60.

Cohen, T., Maria Woltjen, and Jennifer Nagda. 2011. "ICAP Recommendation to Re-evaluate the Policy Pertaining to Use of Dental Examinations to Determine the Age of a Child in ORR-DUCS Custody." Immigrant Child Advocacy Project.

Dake, Fidelia A. A., and Kamil Fuseini. 2018. "Registered or Unregistered? Levels and Differentials in Registration and Certification of Births in Ghana." *BMC International Health and Human Rights* 18.

Duran, Alelur. 2022. "Prisons Overuse Strip Searches to Dehumanize People like Me. End This Horrific Practice Now." *USA Today*, April 18.

Executive Committee of the High Commissioner's Programme. 2016. "Alternatives to Detention." *International Journal of Refugee Law* 28 (1): 148–55.

Flores v. USCIS, 718 F.3d 548, 551 (6th Cir 2013).

Fowler, Patrick J., et al. 2017. "Homelessness and Aging Out of Foster Care: A National Comparison of Child Welfare-Involved Adolescents." *Child Youth Services Review* 77 (June): 27–33.

Franzblau, Jesse. 2021. "Phase Out of Private Prisons Must Extend to Immigration Detention System." National Immigrant Justice Center, January 28. https://immigrantjustice.org/staff/blog/phase-out-private-prisons-must-extend-immigration-detention-system.

Garcia Ramirez v. ICE, No. CV 18-508 (RC), 2021 WL 4284530 (D.D.C. Sept. 21, 2021).

Human Rights Watch (HRW). 2021. "Dismantling Detention: International Alternatives to Detaining Immigrants." November 23. https://www.hrw.org/report/2021/11/03/dismantling-detention/international-alternatives-detaining-immigrants.

Immigration and Nationality Act of 1952, 8 U.S.C. §§ 1101, 1182, 1232, 1235, 1236 (2023).

Innocence Project, et al. 2021. "Re: Unlawful and Unethical Use of 'Dental Age Estimation' X-Rays on Asylum Applicants to Justify the Jailing and Deporting of Children." June 3. https://innocenceproject.org/wp-content/uploads/2021/06/2021.06.03-Dental-Age-Estimation-Cease-and-Desist-Letter_Final-2.pdf.

Jayaraman, Jayakumar, et al. 2014. "The French-Canadian Data Set of Demirjian for Dental Age Estimation: A Systematic Review and Meta-analysis." *Journal of Forensic and Legal Medicine* 20 (5): 373–81.

Kerwin, Donald. 2005. "The Use and Misuse of 'National Security' Rationale in Crafting U.S. Refugee and Immigration Policies." *International Journal of Refugee Law* 17 (4): 749–63.

Laniado, Nadia, et al. 2021. "The Use of Dental Radiographs for Age Estimation of Unaccompanied Migrant Minors: Scientific and Ethical Concerns." *Journal of Public Health Dentistry* 82 (3): 349–51.

L.B. v. Charles Keeton, et al., No. CV-18–03435-PHX-JJT (MHB), at *2–3 (D. Ariz., Oct. 26, 2018).

Ledford, Heidi. 2018. "Who Exactly Counts as an Adolescent?" *Nature*, February 21. https://www.nature.com/articles/d41586-018-02169-w.

Lindskoog, Carl. 2018. *Detain and Punish: Haitian Refugees and the Rise of the World's Largest Immigration Detention System*. Gainesville: University of Florida Press.

Longazel, Jamie, et al. 2016. "The Pains of Immigrant Imprisonment." *Sociology Compass* 10 (11): 989–98.

Lutheran Immigration and Refugee Service (LIRS). 1998. "Working with Refugees and Immigrant Children: Issues of Culture, Law & Development." https://www.legaltechdesign.com/2014/09/lirs-working-with-refugee-immigrant-children/.

Matter of M-A-C-O-, 27 I&N Dec. 477 (BIA 2018).

Mejia, Brittny, and Kate Morrissey. 2019. "U.S. Is Using Unreliable Dental Exams to Hold Teen Migrants in Adult Detention." *Los Angeles Times*, June 2.

Miroff, Nick. 2020. "Immigrants Held at Md. Jail Were Excessively Strip-Searched, According to the DHS Inspector General." *Washington Post*, October 30.

National Immigrant Justice Center (NIJC). 2011. "Isolated in Detention: Limited Access to Legal Counsel in Immigration Detention Facilities Jeopardizes a Fair Day in Court." September. https://immigrantjustice.org/sites/default/files/Detention%20Isolation%20Report%20FULL%20REPORT%202010%2009%2023_0.pdf.

National Immigrant Justice Center (NIJC). 2019. "A Better Way: Community Based Programming as an Alternative to Immigrant Incarceration." https://immigrantjustice.org/research-items/report-better-way-community-based-programming-alternative-immigrant-incarceration.

National Immigrant Justice Center (NIJC). 2022. Garcia Ramirez, et. al. v. ICE, et. al., Case Summary. September 7. https://immigrantjustice.org/court_cases/garcia-ramirez-et-al-v-ice-et-al.

Office of Refugee Resettlement (ORR). 2022. "ORR Unaccompanied Children Program Policy Guide." §1.6 Determining the Age of an Individual Without Lawful Immigration Status. https://www.acf.hhs.gov/orr/policy-guidance/unaccompanied-children-program-policy-guide-section-1.

Physicians for Human Rights and the Bellevue/NYU Program for Survivors of Torture. 2003. *From Persecution to Prison: The Health Consequences of Detention for Asylum Seekers*. Boston and New York: Physicians for Human Rights and the Bellevue/NYU Program for Survivors of Torture.

Santus, Rex. 2018. "Some ICE Facilities Strip-Search Everyone and Don't Report 'Proven Sexual Assaults, Watchdog Says." Vice News, July 29. https://www.vice.com/en/article/wjbvzb/some-ice-facilities-strip-search-everyone-and-dont-report-proven-sexual-assaults-dhs-inspector-general-report-says.

Schiraldi, Vincent, and Jason Zeidenberg. 1997. "The Risks Juveniles Face When They Are Incarcerated with Adults." Justice Policy Institute. https://justicepolicy.org/wp-content/uploads/2022/02/97-02_rep_riskjuvenilesface_jj.pdf.

Trafficking Victims Protection Reauthorization Act (TVPRA). 8 U.S.C. § 1158(b)(3)(C), INA § 208(b)(3)(C) (2008).

Uehling, Greta L. 2008. "The International Smuggling of Children: Coyotes, Snakeheads, and the Politics of Compassion." *Anthropological Quarterly* 18 (4): 833–71.

Urrutia-Rojas, Ximena, and Nestor Rodriguez. 1997. "Potentially Traumatic Events Among Unaccompanied Migrant Children from Central America." In *Health and Social Services Among International Labor Migrants: A Comparative Perspective*, edited by Antonio Ugalde and Gilberto Cárdenas, 151–66. Austin, Texas: CMAS Books.

U.S. Citizenship and Immigration Services (USCIS). 2019. "RAIO Combined Training Program: Children's Claims Training Module." RAIO Directorate. https://www.uscis.gov/sites/default/files/document/foia/Childrens_Claims_LP_RAIO.pdf.

U.S. Conference of Catholic Bishops (USCCB) and the Center for Migration Studies (CMS). 2018. "Unlocking Human Dignity: A Plan to Transform the US Immigrant Detention System." www.usccb.org/about/migration-and-refugee-services/upload/unlocking-human-dignity-report.pdf.

U.S. Immigration and Customs Enforcement (ICE). 2009. "Parole of Arriving Aliens Found to Have a Credible Fear of Persecution or Torture." https://www.ice.gov/doclib/dro/pdf/11002.1-hd-parole_of_arriving_aliens_found_credible_fear.pdf.

U.S. Immigration and Customs Enforcement (ICE). 2011. "Performance-Based National Detention Standards." § 2.10 Searches of Detainees. https://www.ice.gov/doclib/detention-standards/2011/2-10.pdf.

U.S. Immigration and Customs Enforcement (ICE). 2019. "Apprehension, Processing, Care, and Custody of Alien Minors and Unaccompanied Alien Children." 8 CFR 212, 8 CFR 236, 45 CFR 410, 84 FR 44392.

White, Holly N. S. 2019. "Why We're Letting Americans Vote, Marry and Drink Far Too Young." *Washington Post*, May 29.

Zucker, Norman. L. 1983. "Refugee Resettlement in the United States: Policy and Problems." *Annals of the American Academy of Political and Social Science* 467 (May): 172–86.

RESISTANCE

A People's Response

CHAPTER EIGHT

Reimagining Treatment for Children Caged at the Border

From Therapy to Liberation

SANDRA ESPINOZA, IMAN DADRAS, JACQUELINE FLORIAN, AND HERLIN SOTO-MATUTE

> I wish I could separate trauma from politics, but as long as we continue to live in denial and treat only trauma while ignoring its origins, we are bound to fail.
>
> —BESSEL VAN DER KOLK, *THE BODY KEEPS SCORE*

In April 2018, after the Department of Justice announced a zero tolerance policy, a new terrifying chapter of dehumanization began to be written in the United States' voluminous history of oppression. A lawsuit against Donald Trump's administration claimed that Customs and Border Protection (CBP) and Immigration and Customs Enforcement (ICE) had exhibited abusive behaviors against young women during detainment by denying their right to personal hygiene, sanitary products, and humane conditions. Another claim stated that children were fighting with each other to get food in the detainment camps they were held in while U.S. Border Patrol guards threw food into their cages.

In the midst of humanitarian outcry, critique, and objections by experts, including human rights activists, psychologists, and lawyers, came an observation from Philip Zimbardo, a social psychologist famous for his 1971 Stanford Prison Experiment. His commentary was a frightening reflection of what is happening in America. In an interview with Chancey Devega that was published in September 2019, Zimbardo claimed,

> You can very easily see—in the extreme of what we are seeing now in Trump's camps—exactly how guards in the Nazi concentration camps

behaved. Those Nazi guards believed whatever Hitler and Goering said about the Jews potentially as poison and invaders in the "Fatherland." Now, instead of Jews, for Trump and his supporters, it is people from Latin and South America. The last time we've seen such a thing at the national level was in Nazi Germany. This is exactly what happened. In Nazi Germany they began by labeling Jews as vermin, having images of Jews as rats. This is the same thing as Donald Trump saying these migrants are filthy, dirty, criminals, drug addicts, and drug dealers. Again, this is stereotyping a whole group of people in order to dehumanize them.

While Zimbardo's Stanford Prison Experiment is criticized for its many ethical problems, it has offered important insights into the darker side of human nature, such as an understanding of political and power structures and how they evolve into violence and domination. Although this is an excerpt from the era of Trump, improper and dehumanizing detainment has existed before Donald Trump's presidency and continues to exist under Joe Biden's.

The present book chapter hopes to propose a different way of thinking about the relationship between trauma inflicted by child detention and mental health. Psychology in many ways continues to reinforce the status quo. Through its focus on the individual as opposed to the broader societal context, traditional psychology has placed an excessive importance on individualistic principles, obstructing the achievement of mutual cooperation and community bonds, while strengthening inequitable establishments (Fox, Prilleltensky, and Austin 2009). As a result, there can be a common belief among clinicians who work with underserved clients to assume that trauma-informed psychology services automatically promote social justice just by virtue of their focus on addressing the effects of trauma (Goodman 2015).

Furthermore, we wish to explore the direct link between the psyche of the detained child and their sociopolitical context. Much of the literature on how to treat the mental health of immigrants is often written from a depoliticized Western paradigm. However, by ignoring the sociopolitical context of a person, psychological violence, and oppression, we tend to reduce the client's experience to symptomatology, which further depoliticizes the therapeutic treatment the person receives and perpetuates social injustice: "If we conceptualize society as a larger family and each family as an individual member, then symptom-bearer individuals and families are merely scapegoats of purposefully disguised structural dysfunctionality of the society (larger family)" (Dadras and Daneshpour 2018, 15).

Ultimately, this chapter advocates for an abolishment of the existing trauma treatment that is used to treat detained children as well as an intention to engage in an examination of the anti-immigrant sociopolitical climate, violence committed by the state, and its contribution to the relational ruptures in their lives.

Attachment Theory

Attachment theory at a glance provides a useful template to understand the relational experiences of migrant youth. This section covers how family practitioners have historically thought about relational ruptures in migrant families. Later, we also provide a critique of attachment theory and its birth from a Western paradigm (Keller 2013).

Carola Suárez-Orozco, Hee Jin Bang, and Ha Yeon Kim (2011) found that children who were separated from their mothers for four years or longer reported higher levels of depression and anxiety in the first year than children who did not experience such separation. The age of when the separation occurs also seems to play a role in how the child perceives the experience. Although it is rare for an infant child to cross unaccompanied, there has been documentation of unaccompanied minors crossing the border as young as infants. According to the American Civil Liberties Union (ACLU 2018), the average length of detention for children awaiting reunification for their parents is 154 days—more than five months. This temporary yet sometimes permanent change for immigrant families can leave emotional consequences for children, such as feelings of abandonment, symptoms of trauma, fear, isolation, and depression (Brabeck and Xu 2010). Attachment theorists believe that experiencing a separation does not necessarily put an individual at risk for pathology. However, attachment theory does believe that loss that is perceived as permanent will impose a risk on children (van Ecke 2005). Though several hypotheses exist behind how attachment transforms from secure to insecure, some believe that children have to experience loss, confusion, fear, or isolation in caretaker relationships in order for their attachment to be impacted (van Ecke 2006).

When children are being separated from a parent due to the child detention process, numerous attachment ruptures occur, which is likely to affect their ability to securely attach to others (Makariev and Shaver 2010). Children who are placed in foster care after being released from detention may experience two sets of disruptions to the attachment system. The first is the disrupted attachment to the parent and the second is to the changes within the attachment to the caregiver who has assumed the parent role (Suárez-Orozco, Bang, and Kim 2011). These disruptions in the attachment make it difficult to relate to the parent once reunited. Past studies report that children feel abandoned and may respond with despair and attachment. They may also feel withdrawn from their parents and exhibit depressive symptoms (Suárez-Orozco, Bang, and Kim 2011). This supports that although reunification is the best-case scenario, children will still feel the effects of the separation long after being reconnected with their parents.

Amanda Venta et al. (2021) found that "family separation due to migration appears to have significant relations to psychosocial functioning (i.e., attachment security) in young adulthood, suggesting long term effects for family separation even when it is likely to be planned and sought out by the parents." Venta et al.'s (2021) study also supports the idea that separation from a caregiver at an early age promotes attachment insecurity. We also argue that separation via migration is not much different from that of detention. Separation via child detention can be even more traumatizing due to the violent and forced nature of the experience, therefore exacerbating these effects.

Challenging Attachment Theory

One of the criticisms of attachment theory is that it has been developed through a Western paradigm lens. Most of the studies conducted using attachment theory have been conducted in Western countries such as the United States or in European cultures (Rothbaum, Weisz, et al. 2001; Rothbaum, Rosen, et al. 2004), with very few studies taking place in collectivistic cultures such as China, Japan, and Kenya, among others (Cowan and Cowan 2007). One of the ways in which attachment theory highlights its Westernized focus is through its use of labels to describe families or relationships between a parent and a child. A large majority of the time, there are labels assigned to collectivistic families that may carry a negative connotation, such as "unmeshed" or "undifferentiated" (Rothbaum, Rosen, et al. 2004). In Western or European societies, these labels are usually associated with negative factors that describe a family and are normally things that families stray away from. However, for collectivistic cultures, such as those pertaining to detained/incarcerated children, characteristics or labels such as enmeshed, overinvolved, or undifferentiated are characteristics of their family that may bring about a great sense of pride. These are values that are embodied by collectivistic immigrant families, and therefore the use of attachment theory can be somewhat pathologizing when applied to this group. Vivian J. Carlson and Robin L. Hardwood (2003) also highlight that attachment theory's Westernized view of caregiving may not be the same as that of a collectivistic culture's caregiving—and therefore does not account for that difference. They also highlight that attachment theory does not focus on situational factors that could affect the care of a child, such as migration and acculturation (Carlson and Hardwood 2003). Similarly, attachment theory highlights and focuses on "protection, care and felt security" (Rothbaum, Rosen, et al. 2004, 329). These can be considered important factors regardless of the culture; however, it may look different depending on the culture that is being analyzed. An individual may feel a sense of security with their parent in a completely different context than that of an individual in a Westernized culture, and mothers may express maternal sensitivity in a different way than that of Western mothers (Cowan and Cowan 2007).

Another limitation of attachment theory is its inability to consider different sociocultural aspects of a family aside from cultural aspects such as social class, ethnicity, and gender (Kagan 2011). These are important aspects to consider as they may help us understand its influence on a child's development despite the care that is provided by their caregiver. Jerome Kagan (2011) highlights that one of the things that has the ability to predict an individual experiencing depression or anxiety in the future is through identifying whether they were raised in a disadvantaged situation despite having a secure attachment throughout the first few years of their life. Being able to pay attention to the socio-environmental factors can help an individual obtain a better understanding of what is impacting a child's development. Despite this important factor, attachment theory lacks this important aspect and continues to view families through this Westernized view despite many families not being able to fit this specific mold.

Another critique of attachment theory includes that of the theory's focus on the dyad versus a communal family system. Fred Rothbaum and Karen Rosen et al. (2004) explore how attachment theory's main focus has been on the dyad, usually between a child and the mother; however, attachment theory does not focus on a child's ability to have an additional attachment with their father, caregiver, or partner at the same time as that of their attachment with their mother (Field 1996; Lee 2003). Rothbaum et al. (2004) also criticize the fact that a lot of the work occurring within the attachment theory takes place among individuals, referring to it as an internal working model, in contrast to other theories that may place an emphasis on the engagement and interaction occurring within groups of people. Tiffany Field (1996) examines how attachment theory can only be applied to specific stages of development, such as infancy, childhood, and puberty. However, she also explains that attachments with others can continue to occur past the puberty stage and can play an important influence in an individual's life (Field 1996).

Despite the theory's positive influence in understanding child development, there are significant aspects of the theory that make it difficult to apply it to collectivistic culture and families, such as that of detained children, who tend to be from collectivistic immigrant families. There are different factors that need to be addressed in order to use it with this population. We discourage clinicians and practitioners from engaging in a psychological form of reductionism. By reducing and labeling children as solely symptom bearers, we perpetuate the goal of sociopolitical traumatogenic structures, which is to pathologize and reduce human beings as abnormal and unhealthy.

Attachment Theory and Its Application to Detained Children

Although attachment theory has been widely researched and is one of the most common theoretical frameworks to conceptualize the psychological ruptures that are experienced by separated families, the previous critique offers a different perspective. There is no doubt that separations at the border and child detention cause long-term psychological and health implications for those affected. However, like many Western models of treatment, attachment theory further pathologizes the experiences of those who do not come from an individualistic culture. This can lead to family practitioners undermining and overlooking strengths associated with a person's cultural background and upbringing.

Another issue with its application to the conceptualization of treatment is that attachment theory is a depoliticized and decontextualized way of viewing an attachment rupture. There is little to no attention on how the rupture occurred; instead, the focus is placed on the caregiver and child bond.

The context as to what prompted the rupture is very important, as it can depathologize a person's experience and place blame on the sociopolitical structure instead of the individual.

Trauma and Child Detention

As children grow, learn, experience, and explore the world and environments around them, there are a variety of factors that influence their development and conceptualization of the world. Ernestine Briggs et al. (2021) state that trauma can affect any individual, regardless of life's developmental stage, but it can be especially damaging to children and their developing brain and has even been linked to an increase in health risks and early death. Trauma can be defined as a deeply distressing or disturbing experience or an event in which there is an actual or perceived threat. This includes physical, sexual, and emotional abuse; neglect; witnessing or experiencing violence or aggression (domestic, relationship, and/or community); witnessing or taking part in drug use; witnessing or experiencing death, abduction, or war; and experiencing natural disasters (Legg 2020). Generally, trauma encloses experiences in which an individual endures high amounts of stress; if they are unable to cope in healthy ways, trauma will leave long-term effects on the individual. Children being held in immigration detention centers demonstrate high rates of mental health outcomes such as depression, stress, fear, and anxiety (MacLean et al. 2019). Research findings also indicate that children held in immigration detention settings may experience social, emotional, and behavioral difficulties at higher rates than those seen in the community (MacLean et al. 2019).

The experience of being a child detainee, with limited ways of communicating or expressing their journey, shapes one of the many forms of expression of trauma as distress, depression, anxiety, post-traumatic stress disorder, and suicidal ideation (Newman and Steel 2008). Health and mental health clinicians need to see the distress and symptoms of mental disorder as emerging in the context of the dehumanizing detention environment rather than just within a traditional Western medical model. The use of traditional diagnosing without elaborating on the sociopolitical circumstances of the child's mental state does not provide culturally sensitive or culturally appropriate information about the migrant child's difficulties.

Post-Traumatic Stress Disorder Is a Western Concept
For some groups, there is no such thing as "post" trauma due to the ongoing violence they experience in their context. The conventional perspective on trauma often treats the self and its connections to others and the external environment as predetermined, while traumatic events are typically considered to affect this self and these relationships separately, without considering the broader social, political, and cultural backdrop (Bracken, Giller, and Summerfield 1995). Migrant children detained at the border have often experienced trauma multiple times by the time they have arrived at a detention center. One study found that 97.4 percent of children being held in migrant detention have already experienced at least one traumatic event during pre-migration (Sidamon-Eristoff et al. 2022). This trauma is then amplified by being kept in inhumane conditions during detention with very little oversight (Peeler et al. 2020). These settings can further traumatize the children, as they are subjected to emotional and physical distress, fear, and isolation, without proper oversight or support from the authorities.

The trauma does not conclude with their release or deportation, as the fate of these children remains uncertain. Whether they are sent back to the perilous conditions of their home country or placed with temporary families in a new environment, they continue to face ongoing challenges that can trigger or exacerbate their trauma. Therefore, it is crucial to shift our understanding of trauma away from a limited "post" perspective and consider the broader social, political, and cultural contexts in which these traumatic experiences occur. This broader perspective allows us to recognize the intricate and persistent nature of trauma for individuals like migrant children and, in turn, to develop more comprehensive and effective interventions to support their well-being and recovery.

Colonial Psychology, Trauma Industry Complex, and Detained Children
Traditional psychological theory was ontologized based on the political-ideological structure of the dominant ruling class and successfully mystified the objective social sufferings as psychological inadequacies of individuals and represented itself as a value-free naturally occurring epidemic phenomenon (Maiers 1991). The field of psychology and its academic research productions, which supposedly inform its clinical praxis in different forms of psychotherapy schools, have fulfilled their mission as an ideological tool

that maintains the hegemonic status quo. Many scholars have addressed the ideological role of psychology and psychotherapy for promoting the false consciousness of neoliberal capitalism, the separation of the psyche from society, and ultimately the depoliticization of the psyche. Karen D. Pyke (2010) argues that the Western psychological paradigm is infiltrated by neoliberal hyperindividualistic values such as meritocracy and self-responsibilization. Lillian Comas-Díaz (2007) discusses that colonial, ahistorical, depoliticized, and Eurocentric American psychology is merely strengthening the hegemonic dominant discourse of neoliberalism and systematically further mystifying both structural and psychological oppressive experiences of marginalized populations. From a feminist critical perspective, Sue Wilkinson (1997, 253) argues that "by locating 'causes and cures' within individuals (families), and by ignoring or minimizing the social context, psychology [psychotherapy] obscures the mechanisms of oppression." Lynn Layton (2005, 427), a psychoanalyst and researcher, laments the dissociation of clinical from larger sociopolitical context and claims "it is always at risk of creating subjects who do not question social inequities: not just the inequities that keep middle-class privilege unconscious, but even the inequities that keep us oppressed and powerless."

Additionally, Sunil Bhatia (2020) criticizes the colonial mentality of American psychology research as many empirical results are based on approximately 5 percent of the world population. However, these American findings of an individual's` functionality on emotional and cognitive characteristics claim universal applicability, relevance, and effectiveness to the remaining 95 percent of the world population. Joseph Henrich, Steven J. Heine, and Ara Norenzayan (2010) dispute American psychology for simply addressing the issue of a privileged minority of WEIRD (Western, Educated, Industrialized, Rich, Democratic). They go on to critique that American psychology methods and theories are shaped by sociocultural assumptions of neoliberal rugged individualism, compulsive consumerism, trauma, and stress and at the same time disregard the psycho-political experience of racially othered individuals, families, and communities.

Furthermore, Boaventura De Sousa Santos (2014) claims that WEIRD/American knowledge systems have committed a form of epistemic violence and epistemicide or "killing of knowledge." Bhatia (2020) describes such epistemic violence as the core of American psychology when someone like an immigrant child is dehistoricized and ripped out of the core social context they are living in. Also, dominated by the spirit of neoliberal capitalism, the Western academic discipline of psycho-traumatology fails to comprehend the wound of being a "racial other subhuman." The white-dominant field of traumatology lacks the historical epistemology and political grammar to analyze the pathogenic nature of neocolonial oppression as a form of social machinery that manifests itself through the representation of a psychological disorder by the oppressed. Stef Craps (2014, 50) discusses that "problems that are essentially political or economic are medicalized, and the people affected by them are pathologized as victims without agency, sufferers from an illness that can be cured through psychological counseling. The failure to situate these problems in their larger historical context can thus lead to psychological recovery being privileged over the transformation of a wounding political, social, or economic system."

From an emic perspective, Latin American psychoanalysts such as David Becker (1995) and Elizabeth Lira Kornfeld (1995) criticize the Westernized hegemonic trauma discourses and their healing promises as limited in both scope and effectiveness. Similarly, other scholars argue that the implication of the dominant biomedical and disease model of trauma has created further isolation for individuals since it awfully fails to recognize the core social structure that caused their pain and suffering as an unjustly targeted group of people. In order to address individuals whose suffering was in fact socially created and happened to them as part of a class or group of people, we often fail to bear witness to the cause of their pain, producing further isolation (Langer 1989; Puget 2002). The trauma industry is fixated by the medical model of treating symptoms of social suffering and reducing it to intrapsychic characteristics of individuals while ontologically and epistemically obscuring the core structure of the very social suffering that causes the symptomology and so-called mental disorder in individuals.

In his thought-provoking book *The Harmony of Illusions: Inventing Post-Traumatic Stress Disorder*, Allen Young (1995) deconstructs the ontological limitation of trauma conceptualization in the West by arguing that trauma discourse was invented during the late nineteenth century based on both medical and psychological models in order to address the Euro-American subject experiences of modernism, industrialization, gender relations, and contemporary warfare. He further claims that by ignoring the sociohistorical and geographical context of trauma discourse, it is a problematic position to think such discourse can be applied to other sociocultural contexts. Similarly, psychiatrists such as Derek Summerfield (2004) condemn the colonial approach of "psychiatric universalism" in humanitarian interventions and psychological services provided to the nonwhite subject in cases of international conflict. Summerfield (2004, 238) declares that such trauma intervention reproduces a form of cultural imperialism and "risks being imperialistic, reminding us of the colonial era when what was presented to indigenous peoples was that there were different types of knowledge, and theirs was second-rate."

More radically, Judith Butler (2005, 125) criticizes the colonial mentality of trauma discipline in the West by introducing the concept of ethical violence, "or the violence we perpetrate on others when we claim to know them or demand of them a knowledge that we have defined in the first instance." Also, Butler (1990) disputes some of the contemporary trauma-related identities such as "trauma survivor" by claiming that such reductionist psychological categorization overlooks the complexity of human experiences and subjectivities in the face of life tragedies.

The Western trauma model and its conformist and opportunist apparatuses, including both academic researchers and practitioners, commit an epistemic injustice and ethical violence by obfuscating the lack of consciousness of their limited epistemology and ontology of the Other's suffering. Indeed, similar to all colonial discourses, the field of trauma and its followers do not accept the fact that they do not know what is unknown to them in regard to their both unconscious and significantly limited knowledge about the nonwhite individual's psychosocial experiences of oppressive traumatic life events. The "unknown unknown" remains the epistemic Achilles of the Western trauma field. The case of children in cages reveals such a category of knowledge where the so-called Western trauma experts remain in denial about not knowing that they do not know. More precisely, the trauma field does not know that it does not know how to provide treatment for detained children. Indeed, the problem of children in this situation is what Sabelo J. Ndlovu-Gatsheni (2020, 5) identifies as a symptomatic representation of "epistemic crisis—a crisis of knowledge which is no longer able to predict challenges and problems, as they come and let alone being able to successfully protect people." The Western trauma field must rehabilitate and decolonize itself from its magnificently limited sociocultural knowledge of the racial other. Otherwise, it remains another pathologizing ideological tool that simply depoliticizes socially unjust experiences of detained children and mainly explains it via the description of symptomatology of trauma, which can furthermore maintain the status quo of traumatizing structure.

Biopolitics, Necropolitics, and the Destiny of Detained Children

The reductionist psychologism of the Western medical model fails to comprehend the everlasting traumatic experiences of refugee children; therefore, one must conceptualize such experiences in relation to the geopolitical context and zeitgeist that one is living under. After addressing the theoretical and methodological limitations of the Western psychological approach of trauma and attachment theories, in order to achieve a congruent theoretical analysis of children in cages, we aim to expand the theorization of those children's experiences through a politico-philosophical theory of the modern subject based on works by Michel Foucault, Hannah Arendt, Giorgio Agamben, and Achille Mbembe.

Through a series of lectures at the College de France in 1975–76 that later on were published as *"Society Must Be Defended,"* the French philosopher Michel Foucault expanded his concept of biopower and biopolitics. Throughout his genealogical endeavors and examination of subjectivity in the modern state, Foucault (1978) discovers the birth of a new form of governmentality and management of population that did not exist before the eighteenth century. Foucault (2003, 240) found that in the traditional sovereign monarchial authority, or juridico-legal order, the main exercise of sovereign power was "the right to take life or let live," whereas in the modern sovereign state a new regime of governmentality emerged that politicized life itself with a new doctrine: "the right to make live and to let die." The classical sovereign power was negative, destructive, deductive, subtractive, and enslaving, which was operating to seize, end, and impoverish life. Foucault (1978, 136) showed that the classical sovereign "exercised right of life only by exercising his right to kill, or by refraining from killing; he evidenced his power over life only through the death he was capable of requiring. The right which was formulated as the 'power of life and death' was in reality the right to take life or let live." On the other hand, the new regime of governmentality and regularization, which he calls "biopower," is the power "to foster life or disallow it to the point of death" (Foucault 1978, 138).

The new form of a regime of population regularization (biopower) and its mechanism of administration of life (biopolitics) function in order "to ensure, sustain, and multiply life, to put this life in order" (Foucault 1978, 136). For Foucault (1978, 137), biopolitics operates as "a power that exerts a positive influence on life, that endeavors to administer, optimize, and multiply it, subjecting it to precise controls and comprehensive regulations." Therefore, biopolitics governs citizens of the society by the creation of new social regulatory mechanisms and standardization (health, hygiene, life expectancy, social productivity, welfare policies, etc.). The modern sovereign state addresses those issues through the implication of so-called cutting-edge scientific rationality and a new regime of technical knowledge from statistics, demographics, economics, psychology, and psychotherapization of everyday life. Thus, the ultimate goal of biopolitics is about improvement, optimization, and reformation of social issues at the collective level. The biopolitics in modern states focuses on reforming, redressing, enhancing, or maximizing the life of the human by targeting individual bodies through disciplinary practices and power. Thus, the absolute power of the sovereign ruler to "make die and let live" transformed into the "let die and make live" of biopolitics (Foucault 1978, 136). In the current discourse of immigration, border, and refugee crisis, the disciplinary system (such as ICE) functions as a regulatory mechanism to maintain the biopolitical rationality of letting die of those whose life is not deemed to be worthy of protection, such as detained children, refugees, and other nonwhite migrants. ICE, Border Patrol, and the immigration system as a whole practice and reinforce a legalized form of biopolitics that results in the disposability of undocumented Brown bodies.

Several decades later, in his seminal 2003 article "Necropolitics," Achille Mbembe agrees upon Foucault's concept of "biopolitics" and its functionality within the modern industrial state yet argues it suffers from a theoretical limitation due to its lack of attention to the life of those neocolonial subjects and racial others whose existence does not equate to the expected protection of biopolitics. Mbembe develops his concepts of necropower and necropolitics upon the previous work of Hannah Arendt (1958) and Giorgio Agamben (1995), who analyzed the condition of stateless individuals and refugees, respectively.

Arendt (1998, 7) argues that "all aspects of the human condition are somehow related to politics." She describes the stateless persons as "the most symptomatic group in contemporary politics" (1958, 277). In her magnum opus *The Origins of Totalitarianism*, Arendt (1958, 293) asserts that when a subject is denied any legal protection by their own state, Rights of Man become unenforceable. According to Arendt, "the inability of nation-states to treat stateless people as legal persons" and the strengthening of "arbitrary rule by police decree" over stateless people finally will result in deprivation of "all citizens of legal status and rule them with an omnipotent police" (290). For Arendt, the stateless individual is the subject being abandoned by rule of law that does not consider them worthy of protection and is "forced to live outside the common world" (302).

Similar to Arendt's conceptualization, the Italian philosopher Giorgio Agamben (1995) defines the refugee as the symbolic representation of the current global imperial capitalist sociopolitical reality par excellence. He claims that the condition of the modern refugee is similar to the ancient figure of the *homo sacer*—a disposable subject in Roman law whose life was not worth protecting, so they could be killed by anyone without committing manslaughter in the eyes of the legal system. Therefore, killing *homo sacer* is not considered a punishable crime.

Agamben's assertion is that the central paradox within the Western sociopolitical order lies in the fact that sovereign power not only holds the ability to create laws and maintain order but also possesses the authority to suspend those laws, creating a "state of exception" that operates outside the normal framework. Agamben (2004, 12) argues that the "fundamental biopolitical fracture of the West" revolves around the separation of *bios* (the sociopolitical life of an individual) and *zoe* (bare life or biological existence). This division, by excluding individuals from the realm of *bios*, gives rise to the concept of the abandoned modern *homo sacer*. According to Agamben (1995), the camp serves as a physical manifestation of this "state of exception," where individuals are stripped of their *bios* (their sociopolitical existence and meaningful life) and ultimately face death through the deliberate actions of the state.

During the Holocaust, Jews were treated as a form of *"homo sacer*," and today, within the U.S. context, various marginalized groups, such as Black individuals, Latinas, Muslims, transgender people, and Indigenous communities, can be seen as contemporary equivalents of this modern *"homo sacer."*

The most distressing and existential condition experienced by children in detention facilities does not solely revolve around the emotional trauma of being separated from their families. Instead, it involves the denial of their political existence (*bios*) and their reduction to the status of mere living beings with no inherent rights—essentially, living in a state of "bare life." This profoundly degrading psychological experience of being treated as disposable others represents a deeply traumatic ordeal that can significantly shape the overall psychosocial development of detained children.

Finally, In the context of the current neoliberal capitalist world, Achille Mbembe's (2003, 39) necropolitics is the "subjugation of life to the power of death." Mbembe (2003, 27) claims that "sovereignty means the capacity to define who matters and who does not, who is disposable and who is not." Therefore, necropolitics and the idea of "who must live and who must die" is unlike biopower that optimizes life and "to make live"; the necropower functions toward "the creation of death-worlds, new and unique forms of social existence in which vast populations are subjected to conditions of life conferring upon them the status of living dead" (Mbembe 2003, 40). The children in cages are prime examples of the "living dead." Mbembe's idea of a "death world" and its status of living dead is theoretically an explanation of the core existence of camps and detention centers where the bare life prevails among those who are "kept alive but in a state of injury" (Mbembe 2003, 21). For Mbembe, necropolitics and biopolitics are dialectical forces of subjugation of life and death itself, where the state determines that one whose life is unworthy must die and one whose life is worthy must be protected. Necropolitics is the distinction of abandoning the individual who is illegal, illegitimate, alien, and othered and preserving those who are perceived as worthy, lawful, productive, and human. It is the link between a sovereign's right to kill and "the capacity to define who matters and who does not, who is disposable and who is not" (Mbembe 2003, 27). The question of who is disposable and who is not has become the core dynamics of modern life.

In the context of our contemporary world, marked by racism and global capitalism, the concept of necropolitics plays a significant role in determining whether individuals are protected or seen as disposable. Within this framework, asylum seekers, refugees, and children in ICE and deportation camps are categorized as disposable. For instance, during the early stages of the COVID-19 pandemic, older people were viewed as disposable in order to protect younger individuals who contribute to the productive-consuming machines of the capitalist system. Similarly, Black individuals are considered disposable in the face of the law enforcement apparatus. Additionally, Indigenous populations, LGBTQI+ individuals, disabled individuals, prisoners, and psychiatric patients are all seen as disposable subjects, their lives perceived as unworthy under the logic of the state's necropolitics.

In the case of children in cages, one must conceptualize their emotional experience within the framework of the structural violence of necropolitics, ethical violence, and epistemic injustice of the trauma field and its colonial gaze. Similar to Mbembe's questions of whose life must be protected and whose life is disposable, Butler (2006, 20) states, "The question that preoccupies me in the light of recent global violence is, who counts as human? Whose lives count as lives? And, finally, what makes for a grievable life?" Additionally, in another influential book, *Frames of War: When Is Life Grievable?*, Butler (2009, 25) argues that there are socially ascribed forms of grievability across different groups of people where "those whose lives are not 'regarded' as potentially grievable, and hence valuable, are made to bear the burden of starvation, underemployment, legal disenfranchisement, and differential exposure to violence and death."

Detained children in North America have become the contemporary embodiment of "*homo sacer*," individuals whose lives are deemed unworthy of protection and whose deaths go ungrieved. It is unsurprising that when at least six Latinx children died while in U.S. custody, there was a glaring absence of moral outrage within a society that prides itself on being democratic, civilized, and morally conscious. The tragic reality is that nearly everyone acknowledges that the same tragic events would be considered unimaginable if they had happened to children from privileged groups in the United States.

The current dominant trauma models and their therapeutic interventions (trauma-informed therapy, art therapy, mindfulness-based trauma therapy, etc.) lack contextual and theoretical conceptualization for detained children. They assume a hegemonic, colonial, universal, and individualistic description of traumatic experiences while they mystify the very existential differences that persist in general child-family separations due to familial discord and divorce, and generalize to all other sociopolitical tragic events that cause such trauma. The conceptualization of detained children's psycho-emotional experiences of trauma from a biopolitical and necropolitical approach is the first step for mental health professionals to develop systemic approaches and interventions for the purpose of healing and emancipation. Without really understanding how the state values certain bodies and easily disposes of others, we cannot truly understand how these bigger sociopolitical systems shape the trauma experienced during detainment.

Future Directions

Historically, the psychology field has focused on the internal world of the clients that it treats. However, by doing this, many psychological treatment models ignore the context that the problem exists within. This chapter hopes to motivate clinicians and any other practitioners involved in the treatment of detained children to look beyond a cognitive-individualistic way of thinking and acknowledge the ways a person's political experience may shape their existence.

As Ignacio Martín-Baró (1996, 25) once wrote, "Assuming a new perspective does not suppose, obviously, throwing out all of our knowledge; what it does suppose is its being made relative and critically revised from the perspective of the numerous majorities. Only from there will the theories and models demonstrate their validity or deficiency, their usefulness of uselessness, their universality or provincialism: only from there will the techniques that have been learned demonstrate their potential for liberation or subjugation."

During this time of mass detention, it is critical for all clinicians, policymakers, professionals, and advocates who work with children to understand the trauma and health risks that children and families face through pre-detention, detention, and post-detention—including experiences such as sleep deprivation, anxiety, depression, attachment wounds, suicidal ideation, and fear—to mitigate the severe and chronic effects of trauma experienced by these immigrant children and families. Clinicians have a crucial role in bringing attention and highlighting these dehumanizing practices and their health and mental health effects in order to stem the long-lasting damage being inflicted on this generation of children. The detention of a child inflicts profound short- and long-term harm, and its practices toward thousands of children as the standard and normal policy of the U.S. government should end. In the short term, practices in detention centers that deprive children of basic needs such as food and sleep should end immediately (Peeler et al. 2020).

The appropriate alternative to detention is to transfer children and families to safe community settings through proven culturally sensitive and culturally competent case-management approaches. Such approaches should ensure compliance with immigration proceedings and promote expanded access to health care, mental health, legal assistance, education, housing, and other essential services. With the transfer of children and families to community settings, trained clinicians and health care providers can play an integral role in caring for these children and families, including coordinating care across multiple service sectors. Experts in child development, pediatricians, child mental health clinicians, and family physicians will have significant roles in advocating and implementing such alternatives to detention centers and creating safe, appropriate, child-centered programs. It is also equally necessary to advocate and implement reparations to their post-detention that include a coordinated system that facilitates access to financial and medical needs and consistent access to education, mental health services, child care, interpretation services, and legal services.

The mental health field overall needs to reconsider how it views the trauma of detained children and their families. Without truly considering how some of our current models provide a shallow understanding of the suffering of migrant families, we can offer humane and progressive treatment for their wounds. Children arriving at the border have made distressing journeys, faced violence, and suffered severe physical duress before, during, and after their journey to and in the United States. We must rethink our approach to serving and treating these children, as their needs go above and beyond psychological wounds. In order for these children to truly be safe, we must advocate for the abolishment of any maltreatment and injustice at the hands of the nation's immigration detention system as well as create a new way to treat the trauma the system has inflicted on them.

The prevailing trauma models and the corresponding therapeutic approaches (such as trauma-informed therapy, art therapy, and mindfulness-based trauma therapy) currently lack the necessary contextual and theoretical framework to fully grasp the experiences of detained children. Western trauma theory operates under the assumption of a dominant, colonial, universal, and individualistic portrayal of traumatic experiences. This perspective tends to obscure the very real existential distinctions that persist in the ongoing, violent ordeals faced by Latinx children and their families during detentions and deportations. The conceptualization of the psycho-emotional trauma experienced by detained children, when viewed through a biopolitical and necropolitical lens, fundamentally contradicts the prevailing discourse on trauma in both research and practical applications.

The application of mainstream trauma therapy to detained Latinx children is largely ineffective. Looking at it from a Foucauldian standpoint, psychotherapy falls under the category of "technologies of self," which are meant to enhance the productivity of neoliberal individuals. It is primarily designed to govern biopolitical subjects, focusing on optimizing their well-being. However, it is not tailored to address the needs of necropolitical subjects, those whom the state does not prioritize for protection.

The Westernized psychotherapy system is not equipped to adapt, regulate, or safeguard individuals who are essentially stateless, like detained children. These children are subjected to the destructive forces of necropower, and the current psychotherapy apparatus is ill-suited to address their unique and dire circumstances.

The phrase "healing power of psychotherapy" represents the latest catchphrase used by the psychotherapy industry to emphasize its own successes. However, it's often more of an ideological proclamation, driven by what can be called the "psychotherapist-savior complex," rather than a genuine effort to bring about meaningful changes in individuals' psychological and social well-being. In other words, it's a slogan that tends to highlight the therapist's role as a savior rather than focusing on the actual impact on people's lives.

The current models of trauma therapy tend to individualize, pathologize, depoliticize, dehistoricize, and psychologize the experience of trauma. As Craps (2014) points out, this hegemonic approach to trauma discourse often acts as a kind of political soothing for those who are socially disempowered, which goes against the self-proclaimed ethical mission of the trauma field.

Martín-Baró (1996, 122), however, challenges the overly simplistic curative goal of psychologists. While he acknowledges its importance, he argues that psychotherapy, without addressing the underlying "traumatogenic structures," merely serves as a palliative measure that inadvertently supports the harmful political machinery. He further highlights that the trauma resulting from political violence is often entirely predictable and, unfortunately, may even be foreseen and planned (Martín-Baró 1996, 123). The dominant approach to trauma psychotherapy in essence reflects that the master's tools will never dismantle the master's house. Therefore, psychotherapy alone cannot and will not bring healing to Latinx children who are trapped in an ongoing state of injury.

References

Agamben, Giorgio. 1995. "We Refugees." *Symposium: A Quarterly Journal n Modern Literatures* 49 (2): 114–19.

Agamben, Giorgio. 2004. *Homo Sacer: Sovereign Power and Bare Life*. Stanford, Calif.: Stanford University Press.
American Civil Liberties Union (ACLU) 2018. "Family Separation by the Numbers." October 2. https://www.aclu.org/issues/family-separation.
Arendt, Hannah. 1958. *The Origins of Totalitarianism*. New York: Meridian Books.
Arendt, Hannah. 1998. *The Human Condition*. 2nd ed. Chicago: University of Chicago Press.
Becker, David. 1995. "The Deficiency of the Concept of Posttraumatic Stress Disorder When Dealing with Victims of Human Rights Violations." In *Beyond Trauma: Cultural and Societal Dynamics*, edited by Rolf J. Kleber, Charles R. Figley, and Berthold P. R. Gersons, 99–110. New York: Plenum Press.
Bhatia, Sunil. 2020. "#PGC2020 Sunil Bhatia: The Pandemic Is a Mirror: Race, Poverty and Radical Care in Times of Crisis." Keynote address, American University of Paris, May 29. Video of keynote, 42:50. https://www.youtube.com/watch?v=nsaYf46n9Hs.
Brabeck, Kalina, and Qingwen Xu. 2010. "The Impact of Detention and Deportation on Latino Immigrant Children and Families: A Quantitative Exploration." *Hispanic Journal of Behavioral Sciences* 32 (3): 341–61.
Bracken, Patrick J., Joan E. Giller, and Derek Summerfield. 1995. "Psychological Responses to War and Atrocity: The Limitations of Current Concepts." *Social Science & Medicine* 40 (8): 1073–82.
Briggs, Ernestine C., Lisa Amaya-Jackson, Karen T. Putnam, and Frank W. Putnam. 2021. "All Adverse Childhood Experiences Are not Equal: The Contribution of Synergy to Adverse Childhood Experience Scores." *American Psychologist* 76 (2): 243–52.
Butler, Judith. 1990. *Gender Trouble: Feminism and the Subversion of Identity*. New York: Routledge.
Butler, Judith. 2005. *Giving an Account of Oneself*. New York: Fordham University Press.
Butler, Judith. 2006. *Precarious Life: The Powers of Mourning and Violence*. London: Verso Books.
Butler, Judith. 2009. *Frames of War: When Is Life Grievable?* London: Verso.
Carlson, Vivian J., and Robin L. Harwood. 2003. "Attachment, Culture, and the Caregiving System: The Cultural Patterning of Everyday Experiences Among Anglo and Puerto Rican Mother-Infant Pairs." *Infant Mental Health Journal* 24 (1): 53–73.
Comas-Díaz, Lillian. 2007. "Ethnopolitical Psychology: Healing and Transformation." In *Advancing Social Justice Through Clinical Practice*, edited by Etiony Aldarondo, 91–118. New York: Taylor & Francis.
Cowan, Philip A., and Carolyn Pape Cowan. 2007. "Attachment Theory: Seven Unresolved Issues and Questions for Future Research." *Research in Human Development* 4 (3–4): 181–201.
Craps, Stef. 2014. "Beyond Eurocentrism: Trauma Theory in the Global Age." In *The Future of Trauma Theory: Contemporary Literary and Cultural Criticism*, ed-

ited by Gert Buelens, Samuel Durrant, and Robert Eaglestone, 45–61. New York: Routledge.

Dadras, Iman, and Manijeh Daneshpour. 2018. "Social Justice for MFT: The Need for Cross-Cultural Responsiveness." In *Cross-Cultural Responsiveness & Systemic Therapy*, edited by Shruti Singh Poulsen and Robert Allan, 1–20. Switzerland: Springer.

Devega, Chauncey. 2019. "Creator of Stanford Prison Experiment on Trump's Camps: It's How Nazi Guards Behaved." *Salon*, September 12. https://www.salon.com/2019/09/12/creator-of-stanford-prison-experiment-on-trumps-camps-its-how-nazi-guards-behaved/.

Field, Tiffany. 1996. "Attachment and Separation in Young Children." *Annual Review of Psychology* 47 (February): 541–61.

Foucault, Michel. 1978. *The History of Sexuality, Volume 1: An Introduction*. Translated by Robert Hurley. New York: Pantheon.

Foucault, Michel. 2003. *Society Must Be Defended: Lectures at the Collège de France, 1975–1976*. Translated by David Macey. London: Penguin.

Fox, Dennis, Isaac Prilleltensky, and Stephanie Austin. 2009. "Critical Psychology for Social Justice: Concerns and Dilemmas." In *Critical Psychology: An Introduction*, 2nd ed., edited by Dennis Fox, Isaac Prilleltensky, and Stephanie Austin, 3–19. New York: SAGE.

Goodman, Rachael D. 2015. "A Liberatory Approach to Trauma Counseling: Decolonizing Our Trauma-Informed Practices." In *Decolonizing "Multicultural" Counseling Through Social Justice*, edited by Rachael D. Goodman and Paul C. Gorski, 55–72. New York: Springer Science + Business Media.

Henrich, Joseph, Steven J. Heine, and Ara Norenzayan. 2010. "The Weirdest People in the World?" *Behavioral and Brain Sciences* 33 (2–3): 61–83.

Kagan, Jerome. 2011. "Bringing Up Baby: Are We Too Attached?" *Psychotherapy Networker*, March/April. https://www.psychotherapynetworker.org/article/bringing-baby/.

Keller, Heidi. 2013. "Attachment and Culture." *Journal of Cross-Cultural Psychology* 44 (2): 175–94.

Kornfeld, Elizabeth Lira. 1995. "The Development of Treatment Approaches for Victims of Human Rights Violations in Chile." In *Beyond Trauma*, edited by Rolf J. Kebler, Charles R. Figley, and Berthold P. R. Gersons, 115–31. New York: Plenum Press.

Langer, Marie. 1989. *From Vienna to Managua: Journey of a Psychoanalyst*. London: Free Association Books.

Layton, Lynne. 2005. "Notes Toward a Nonconformist Clinical Practice: Response to Philip Cushman's 'Between Arrogance and a Dead-End.'" *Contemporary Psychoanalysis* 41 (3): 419–29.

Lee, Erin J. 2003. "The Attachment System Throughout the Life Course: Review and Criticisms of Attachment Theory." December. http://www.personalityresearch.org/papers/lee.html.

Legg, Timothy J. 2020. "What Is Trauma? What to Know?" *Medical News Today*, June 3. https://www.medicalnewstoday.com/articles/trauma.

MacLean, Sarah A., Priscilla O. Agyeman, Joshua Walther, Elizabeth K. Singer, Kim A. Baranowski, and Craig L. Katz. 2019. "Mental Health of Children Held at a United States Immigration Detention Center." *Social Science & Medicine* 230 (June): 303–8.

Maiers, Wolfgang. 1991. "Critical Psychology: Historical Background and Task." In *Critical Psychology: Contribution to an Historical Science of the Subject*, edited by Charles W. Tolman and Wolfgang Maiers, 23–49. Cambridge, UK: Cambridge University Press.

Makariev, Drika Weller, and Phillip R. Shaver. 2010. "Attachment, Parental Incarceration and Possibilities for Intervention: An Overview." *Attachment & Human Development* 12 (4): 311–31.

Martín-Baró, Ignacio. 1996. "Toward a Liberation Psychology." In *Writings for a Liberation Psychology*, edited by Adrianne Aron and Shawn Corne, 17–33. Cambridge, Mass.: Harvard University Press.

Mbembe, Achille. 2003. "Necropolitics." Translated by Libby Meintjes. *Public Culture* 15 (1): 11–40.

Ndlovu-Gatsheni, Sabelo J. 2020. "Geopolitics of Power and Knowledge in the COVID-19 Pandemic: Decolonial Reflections on a Global Crisis." *Journal of Developing Societies* 1 (24): 366–89.

Newman, Louise K., and Zachary Steel. 2008. "The Child Asylum Seeker: Psychological and Developmental Impact of Immigration Detention." *Child and Adolescent Psychiatric Clinics of North America* 17 (3): 665–83.

Peeler, Katherine R., Kathryn Hampton, Justin Lucero, and Roya Ijadi-Maghsoodi. 2020. "Sleep Deprivation of Detained Children: Another Reason to End Child Detention." *Health and Human Rights Journal* 22 (1): 317–20.

Puget, Janine. 2002. "The State of Threat and Psychoanalysis: From the Uncanny That Structures to the Uncanny That Alienates." *Free Associations* 9D (4): 611–48.

Pyke, Karen D. 2010. "What Is Internalized Racial Oppression and Why Don't We Study It? Acknowledging Racism's Hidden Injuries." *Sociological Perspectives* 53 (4): 551–72.

Rothbaum, Fred, Karen Rosen, Tatsuo Ujiie, and Nobuko Uchida. 2004. "Family Systems Theory, Attachment Theory, and Culture." *Family Process* 41 (3): 328–50.

Rothbaum, Fred, John Weisz, Martha Pott, Kazuo Miyake, and Gilda Morelli. 2001. "Deeper into Attachment and Culture." *American Psychologist* 56 (10): 827–29.

Santos, Boaventura De Sousa. 2014. *Epistemologies of the South: Justice Against Epistemicide*. New York: Taylor & Francis.

Sidamon-Eristoff, Anne Elizabeth, et al. 2022. "Trauma Exposure and Mental Health Outcomes Among Central American and Mexican Children Held in Immigration Detention at the United States-Mexico Border." *Developmental Psychobiology* 64 (1): e22227.

Suárez-Orozco, Carola, Hee Jin Bang, and Ha Yeon Kim. 2011. "I Felt like My Heart Was Staying Behind: Psychological Implications of Family Separations & Reunifications for Immigrant Youth." *Journal of Adolescent Research* 26 (2): 222–57.
Summerfield, Derek. 2004. "Cross-Cultural Perspectives on the Medicalization of Human Suffering." In *Posttraumatic Stress Disorder: Issues and Controversies*, edited by Gerald M. Rosen, 233–45. Chichester: Wiley.
van der Kolk, Bessel. 2014. *The Body Keeps Score*. New York: Penguin.
van Ecke, Yolanda. 2005. "Immigration from an Attachment Perspective." *Social Behavior & Personality: An International Journal* 33 (5): 467–76.
van Ecke, Yolanda. 2006. "Unresolved Attachment Among Immigrants: An Analysis Using the Adult Attachment Perspective." *Journal of Genetic Psychology* 167 (4): 433–42.
Venta, Amanda, Cassandra Bailey, Alfonso Mercado, and Cecilia Colunga-Rodríguez. 2021. "Family Separation and Attachment in Young Adults Who Were Once Left Behind by Caregiver Migration." *Psychiatry Research* 302 (August): 114039.
Wilkinson, Sue. 1997. "Feminist Psychology." In *Critical Psychology: An Introduction*, edited by Dennis Fox and Isaac Prilleltensky, 247–64. Thousand Oaks, Calif.: SAGE.
Young, Allan. 1995. *The Harmony of Illusions: Inventing Post-Traumatic Stress Disorder*. Princeton, N.J.: Princeton University Press.

CHAPTER NINE

Alternatives to Detention

A Faith-Based Response

REVEREND DR. SAMUEL ARROYO

"Pastor, where is the church?" These were the pleading words of a New Jersey Families Belong Together rally attendant after I gave a passionate faith-based speech condemning the actions of the Donald Trump administration on separating immigrant children from their families. The question stopped me in my tracks. The inquiry was much deeper than just wondering why more people of faith were not present at the rallies and other demonstrations around migrant children's rights. The question really was: what concrete steps is the church taking to address the immigration crisis in this country?

Throughout the previous chapters, we have seen how social scientists, activists, lawyers, and civic nonprofit organizations are navigating social justice issues around child migrants in detention. The question, "Where is the church?" is an invitation to faith-based communities to reflect on how they can get involved in advocating for migrant children not only through passionate speeches but through concrete initiatives that put into practice foundational teachings of the Christian faith, such as love, compassion, and liberating hope to those who are under an oppressive system. A faith community that practices these teachings in concrete ways can create spaces that could lead to systemic changes.

The work for immigrant justice is at the heart of the Christian faith. From beginning to end, the Bible tells story after story of individuals or groups of people who for a variety of reasons—such as hunger, political and social persecution, family ties, a personal calling, or pursuing a better life—leave the land where they were born and venture into foreign lands. In response to these biblical narratives, congregations and faith-based organizations today have opened their doors to offer a safe space for immigrants in their communities. These faith communities and organizations that have made it their mission to witness God's love for the immigrants who live in their communities are moved by fundamental biblical teachings and a deep sense of justice. They seek to give hope to the immigrant community by creating spaces where their basic rights as human beings are valued and protected. These spaces are created with the conviction that immigrants have the right to live and to work, to keep their families together, and to feel safe, protected, and free, both physically and spiritually.

On the other hand, faith communities have also faced social and cultural challenges to their advocacy work from organizations, individuals, and elected officials who argue that immigrants pose a threat to national security. Sometimes these challenges come from other faith communities that have adopted an anti-immigrant approach. Churches are often influenced by the social, economic, cultural, and political ideologies that are dominant in their countries, and churches in the United States are not exempt from this influence. Faith communities and other Christian organizations in America find themselves having to make choices between how the Bible teaches how they should practice their faith and how American culture defines the practice of their faith. Government officials have used this tension to justify some of their actions and policies under the pretext that they were placed in these positions of power by God to protect the best interests of the country. Because this is a "Christian country," they argue that protecting its interests also translates into protecting the "Christian values" of the nation.

For example, on June 14, 2018, then attorney general Jeff Sessions, to justify the implementation of polices that separate migrant children from their parents, appealed to the Bible. He paraphrased the letter of the apostle Paul to the Romans. He said: "I would cite you to the Apostle Paul and his clear and wise command in Romans 13, to obey the laws of the government because God has ordained them for the purpose of order. . . . Orderly and lawful processes are good in themselves and protect the weak and lawful" (McFarlan Miller and Shimron 2018). In the same press conference, White House press secretary Sarah Huckabee Sanders doubled down on this idea by saying: "It is very biblical to enforce the law" (McFarlan Miller and Shimron 2018). By making these claims, they justified as a biblical teaching the implementation of policies that separated migrant children from their parents and put them in cages.

Miranda Zapor Cruz (2020), a theologian who specializes in theology, religion, and society, explains that "politicians using Scripture and Christians responding in this way is one manifestation of biblicism, a deeply flawed understanding of the doctrine of Scripture that insists on the strictest biblical literalism." In simple words, biblicism is a narrowed viewed of Christian Scriptures, where the Bible alone is the authority and rule of life and any other influence or source of knowledge outside it is deemed as outside the rule of faith. Zapor Cruz (2020) goes on to say that "at best, biblicism reduces the inspired and authoritative Word of God to a compendium of disconnected verses that can be referenced, quoted, cited, or ignored from one situation to the next." Zapor Cruz warns of two dangers of biblicism that are important to highlight. The first one is that biblicism makes it easy for politicians to abuse the Bible for their own benefit, and second, biblicism can lead Christians to succumb to Christian nationalism. Christian nationalism is the idea that for a person to fully represent what it means to be a citizen, they should uphold the Christian values of the dominant cultural group. When politicians use Scripture in the way that Sessions and Huckabee Sanders did, people of faith can fall into the trap of supporting actions that contradict fundamental Christian values. For Christian nationalists, the use of Scripture is important "because they believe Christian identity is intrinsic to American identity and must be restored or protected" (Zapor Cruz 2020). For both the biblicist and the Christian nationalist, seeing a politician quoting Scripture could signify that the said politician is a God-appointed leader who has the Christian faith and will defend American Christian values.

This form of biblical interpretation can also be exploited by people of faith who believe that immigrants are dangerous and therefore should not be allowed to enter the country. This has led many Christians to support policies that criminalize and oppress immigrants, even when these systems oppose what the Bible and Christian tradition teach about the right attitude toward immigrants.

The Bible, Liberation Theology, and Immigration

People of faith who engage in immigrant advocacy know the importance of helping immigrants feel welcomed and safe. Differing from the biblical literalists mentioned previously, these organizations have a liberative approach to the way they interpret Scripture and how they practice their faith. While liberation theology is associated with Latin American theologians such as Gustavo Gutierrez, Ignacio de Ellacuria, and Leonardo and Clodovis Boff, this theological method of reflection and biblical interpretation expands to a wider group of people around the world. This includes Black liberation theology, queer liberation theology, feminist liberation theology, Asian liberation theology, and more. Liberation theologian Clodovis Boff (1996, 1) explains how this approach "is an integral theology, treating all the positivity of faith from a particular perspective: that of the poor and their liberation." This means that liberation theology reflects on all aspects of traditional theologies. At the same time, liberation theology is not interested in the mere reflection or abstract understanding of these teachings of the Christian faith, but it seeks to operate positive changes in oppressive systems.

Liberation theology flips the script on how to do traditional theology, where now the theologian's faith is confronted with the realities of their own history, politics, socioeconomic and cultural realities, and how these systems oppress minorities and the poor. These theologians seek to understand how God is acting in their present moment in history and what is their responsibility as people of faith.

Boff (1996, 2) goes on to say that "the basic viewpoint of the theology of liberation . . . is the givenness of faith; its secondary, particular viewpoint . . . is the experience of the oppressed." Liberation theology seeks to give us an understanding of the historical processes that lead to the oppression of certain groups of people and implementing concrete and practical ministries that will work toward their liberation. For the liberation theologian, this is not an academic exercise but a full immersion into these oppressive systems. The best and only possible way for the theologian to fully practice faith from this perspective is by listening, standing by, and advocating with and for those who are being oppressed. People of faith who engage in this advocacy work will not only have knowledge of what the Bible teaches about immigration but will spend time listening to immigrants, learning about their stories, and finding ways to lift them up in ways that they can thrive in their new environment.

It is under this lens that people of faith who practice advocacy for immigrant rights engage Scripture. Bringing with them all the weight of what is happening at the U.S. borders, especially when it comes to the detention of children, the question of what the proper response to this crisis is becomes more urgent. The Bible offers a rich tradition of advocacy for immigrant rights that can serve as guidance for faith practitioners in their advocacy work.

The Bible consistently advocates for welcoming and caring for immigrants in local communities. The terms *strangers* and *sojourners* are widely used in the Bible to capture the difficulties of being an immigrant in a foreign land and how the people of God are to respond when interacting with them. Christian ethicist Miguel De La Torre (2009, 131–32) describes how these strangers and sojourners are captured in the biblical narratives and how the people of God are commanded to welcome them:

> Aliens live in an in-between space—in a land to which they were not born, yet a land where they now live and work. As such, the alien is "foreign," different from the native-born due to language, customs, history, and traditions. As such, the alien lacks the benefits and protection ordinarily provided to those tied to their birthplace. Vulnerable to those who profit from his or her labor, the alien derives security from the biblical mandate of hospitality.

This vulnerability that De La Torre is talking about forces immigrants to live in constant fear for their lives and for the lives of their loved ones.

The Old Testament, known as the *Tonakh* by the Jewish faith tradition, contains at least thirty-nine verses commanding God's people not to mistreat or oppress immigrants. Welcoming and caring for immigrants became an integral part of God's covenant. Leviticus 19:33–34 says: "When a resident foreigner lives with you in your land, you must not oppress him. The resident foreigner who lives with you must be to you as a native citizen among you; so you must love the foreigner as yourself, because you were foreigners in the land of Egypt. I am the Lord your God."[1] Not only immigrants were to be welcomed but treated in the same way as those who are native citizens. To safeguard the just treatment of immigrants, the following laws were created:

> You must not oppress a lowly and poor servant, whether one from among your fellow Israelites or from the resident foreigners who are living in your land and villages. You must pay his wage that very day before the sun sets, for he is poor and his life depends on it. Otherwise

he will cry out to the Lord against you, and you will be guilty of sin. (Deut. 24:14–15)

Not paying an immigrant their wages was an injustice worthy of God's anger against the employer. Therefore, people should not "pervert justice due a resident foreigner or an orphan" (Deut. 24:19).

The prophets in the Old Testament had the responsibility to spiritually lead the people of God, especially when they were doing wrong against other people. They constantly rebuked those in power for the injustices that they were committing against immigrants. For example, the prophet Ezekiel said: "See how each of the princes . . . used his authority to shed blood. . . . They have oppressed the resident foreigner among you; they have wronged the orphan and the widow within you" (Ezekiel 22:6–7). Prophets addressed not only those in authority but also the community at large. The prophet Jeremiah said: "You must change the way you have been living and do what is right. You must treat one another fairly. Stop oppressing resident foreigners who live in your land, children who have lost their fathers, and women who have lost their husbands" (Jeremiah 7:5–6). While those in authority had the burden of responsibility to take care of those most vulnerable in their communities, civilians also bear responsibility to care for them.

Radical hospitality to the foreigners, orphans, widows, and those who are vulnerable was foundational to the type of community God wanted built. Luis Rivera-Pagán argues that the command to care for immigrants has two foundations. As mentioned previously, the first foundation comes from the fact that "the Israelites had been sojourners and resident foreigners in a land not of their own . . . therefore, be sensitive to the complex existential stress of communities living in the midst of a nation whose inhabitants speak a different language, venerate dissimilar deities, share distinct traditions" (Rivera-Pagán 2014, 95). The second foundation is that "the command of care towards the immigrant foreigner corresponds to God's way of being and acting in history: 'The Lord watches over the strangers' (Psalm 146:9a). God takes sides in history, favoring the most vulnerable: the poor, the widows, the orphans, the strangers" (Rivera-Pagán 2014, 95–96).

The Christian New Testament continues this theme of favoring the ethnic "other" and the socially vulnerable. The Gospel of Luke states Jesus's mission for humanity was to bring about liberation from all kinds of oppression. At the beginning of his work, Jesus was asked to read from the prophet Isaiah during one of the meetings at the synagogue. According to the Gospel of Luke 4:18–19, Jesus read:

> "The Spirit of the Lord is upon me,
> because he has anointed me to proclaim good news to the poor.
> He has sent me to proclaim release to the captives
> and the regaining of sight to the blind,
> to set free those who are oppressed,
> to proclaim the year of the Lord's favor."

After he read these words, Jesus said to those who were at the synagogue that he had come to fulfill what the prophet had said: to bring good news to the poor, to set those who are under oppression free. The Gospels, which recount the life of Jesus, portray Jesus encountering many people outside his religious tradition, especially Samaritans. Samaritans practiced a different religion than Jesus's followers and had their own places of worship outside Jerusalem. For this reason, some religious leaders rejected Samaritans and treated them as people outside the faith. They were not only strangers to each other but also enemies. This tension led to the dehumanization of Samaritans by some, to the point where they sought to prohibit any relationship between the two ethnic groups. However, Jesus, in line with the mission of liberation to the oppressed, formed good relationships with those seen as the "other." In the Gospel of John, Jesus speaks with a Samaritan woman who is portrayed as having a dubious reputation, something that was not well viewed by some religious leaders, his disciples included.

Jesus was asked by a contemporary religious expert what people needed to do to go to heaven. Jesus's response was to follow the law, but he also asked the expert if he knew what the meaning of the law was. This expert responded to him by saying: "Love the Lord your God with all your heart, with all your soul, with all your strength, and with all your mind, and love your neighbor as yourself" (Luke 10:27). Jesus said to him that his response was right. In the Jewish tradition, this is a traditional response to that question because it summarizes what was written in the Old Testament. The fulfillment of God's commandments is to love God and to love the neighbor. However, this expert of the law did not end the conversation with this philosophical statement. Instead, he asked Jesus, "Who is my neighbor?" In other words, who are we supposed to love and how? It is in this context that Jesus tells the story of the Good Samaritan. In this story, two fellow Israelites who had religious authority chose to ignore a man who was assaulted and left for dead on the road. It was a Samaritan, a stranger and enemy that the Israelites thought was a not true follower of God's law, who fulfilled God's law by showing love and care to a person who belonged to a different ethnicity.

Not only did Jesus cross ethnic boundaries, but he also identified with the oppressed. In Matthew 25:31–46, Jesus tells his followers that whenever they help "the least of these," they are helping Jesus himself. In this passage, the least of these are the sick, the naked, the imprisoned, the thirsty—in other words, people who are living on the margins of society. Jesus is not only identifying with "the least of these" in a philosophical and sympathetic way. Jesus is telling his disciples that he is one of them. Jesus is the immigrant who crosses borders and needs shelter, water, and food. Those who reject the immigrant are rejecting Jesus himself.

In his interactions with the Samaritans and his direct identification with those who are being oppressed, immigrants among them, Jesus commands an attitude of mercy and acceptance. Biblical scholar M. Daniel Caroll R. (2020, 97), in his book *The Bible and Borders*, says that "Jesus' actions and attitudes transcend cultural identity; they also help define what it means to be his follower." Caroll (2020, 97) writes:

> Jesus directly confronts the identity question through what he says and does with Samaritans. Even as he continues to live as a Jew, Jesus lays aside his culture's exclusionary mores and negative feelings toward Samaritans. Jesus chooses what is more important: the Samaritan's value as persons and the potential of their faith. Jesus gives worth, hope, and direction to a woman who has had a rough life; he heals a leper and brings him joy and a future.

Welcoming and helping immigrants is the expected attitude in Scripture. Faith communities that engage in advocacy for immigrants use these scriptural teachings as a foundation for their work.

An Ethical Response to Migration

Throughout this chapter, we have done a short survey of what the Bible says about migration and the tension that exists within churches on how to respond to the present crisis. Unfortunately, one of the failings that people of faith have is the tendency to respond to social issues from abstract moral viewpoints that in most cases serve only to ease their minds rather than create true social transformation. Miguel De La Torre (2009, 61) says that "many Christians respond in words to the inhumane conditions forced upon the dispossessed when it is much more important to respond in deeds, in actions, in praxis. When a moral Christian life is reduced to individual piety or virtues, it often fails to result in Christian action." As mentioned previously, practicing a theology that seeks to bring liberation to those who are being oppressed involves closely engaging the people who are living on the margins.

An ethical response to migration moves beyond sending thoughts and prayers to concrete actions that will bring social and spiritual transformation. This is based on a foundational doctrine of the Christian faith that teaches that each person is created in the image of God and therefore is of sacred worth. This means that the immigrant deserves to be treated with all the dignity of a person of sacred worth. For this reason, Jesus said to his disciples, whatever you do to "the least of this, you are doing it to me."

This Christian perspective of immigration conflicts with the common belief that immigrants are valued only according to what they can bring to local communities. For many years they have been seen as cheap labor for farmers and as the people who provide services, such as cleaning homes or mowing lawns, cooking, and washing dishes. In the current anti-immigrant rhetoric, they are seen as undesirable, people who are coming to kill and rape: in other words, people to fear. This rhetoric that often invokes Christianity through biblicism fails to address the theological doctrine of the image of God inherent in each person. People of faith engage in immigrant advocacy to reverse this negative rhetoric against immigrants and seek to lift their sacred worth.

Faith communities and organizations have tremendous power to effect social change. During the 1980s, thousands of immigrants from Central America were fleeing from their countries and seeking refuge in the United States. They turned to congregations, who initially gave them humanitarian help and even advocated for them in court. When in court, these people of faith realized that immigrants were not being treated fairly, so they decided to declare their churches as sanctuaries where these immigrants could have refuge from persecution. Some decades later, in 2006, a new network of faith communities worked to form what is now known as the New Sanctuary Movement (NSM).[2] Sanctuaries are spaces where people can find refuge. Through this movement, some churches opened their buildings so immigrants could feel safe and protected. Scholar and advocate A. Naomi Paik (2020, 103) says that "at minimum, sanctuary provides a ground floor for survival and a strategy of resistance for targeted peoples like immigrants under deportation orders." When churches become a sanctuary, they provide spiritual refuge to immigrants and a place where they will be safe.

Other faith-based organizations have been established to provide aid to immigrants crossing the borders. One of these organizations is No More Deaths.[3] This is a volunteer-based organization that provides food, water, and medical aid to immigrants who have crossed the border into the Arizona desert. Similarly, Humane Borders is an organization led by people from many faith traditions, and as stated on its website, its mission is to "save desperate people from a horrible death by dehydration and exposure and to create a just and humane environment in the borderlands."[4] This organization has set and maintained dozens of emergency water stations across the U.S.-Mexico border. The General Board of Church and Society of the United Methodist Church, whose offices are in the only faith-based building on Capitol Hill, is one of the leading faith-based organizations working for immigration policy changes in Washington, D.C. These organizations are doing important and much-needed work in our borders, but there is only so much they can do. The injustices committed against immigrants at the border, especially against detained children, make this an urgent matter, and faith communities have great advocacy power to make changes in immigration policy. Equally important, faith communities can create spaces where immigrants can feel safe and protected. In the narratives that follow, we will hear from two faith-based organizations that engage specifically with the issue of young migrants in detention. Viator House of Hospitality, which operates in the tradition of the Clerics of St. Viator, has provided a unique alternative to immigration detention for young men. Its sister organization, Bethany House of Hospitality, is supported by communities such as the Benedictine Sisters of Chicago, the Felician Sisters of North America, and the Order of Carmelites. These faith-based communities provide inspirational models of how the church can work toward justice for young migrants.

Part 1. Watching Unaccompanied Minors Flourish: Hospitality as an Alternative to Detention

Father Corey Brost, C.S.V., and Brother Michael Gosch, C.S.V.

"If we see you again, we will kill you."[5]

According to Lewis, that was the soldiers' clear message when they released him.

At the time, Lewis was sixteen and living with an older brother in his West African nation's capital, selling jeans at a market during the day and studying English and math at night. He joined a protest one fateful day to demonstrate against the government's human rights abuses—and quickly experienced the abuse firsthand when he was beaten and jailed.

After his brother secured his release, Lewis stayed in hiding until his brother could raise enough money to fly him to South America, from where he would start a long and dangerous journey *alone* on foot, boat, and bus to the U.S.-Mexico border.

Nearly five years later, Lewis started another journey—much shorter and more hopeful. This journey was less than fifteen minutes by car—in fact, by his car. It took him from Viator House of Hospitality to his new apartment, where, as a college student with asylum, he settled in with two roommates to continue his path toward a nursing career.

Lewis's journey from violence to safety and opportunity in the United States is a common story at Viator House, where he lived for more than two years with more than twenty other young men from more than ten nations seeking asylum in the United States.

Opened in January 2017, Viator House is a "game-changer" for unaccompanied minors fleeing to our nation, according to an attorney who works with them. Though we also offer hospitality to some young adult asylum seekers who arrive at our border after age eighteen, most of our participants arrived at the border as unaccompanied minors. And at Viator House, instead of being transferred to adult detention or temporary shelters after "aging out" of federally funded programs for minors at eighteen, unaccompanied minors find opportunities to grow intellectually, emotionally, and spiritually while finding jobs that allow them to save for the future and send money home to desperate relatives.

The contrast is stark. Instead of being jailed in a cell or dropped off at a temporary shelter to "celebrate" turning eighteen, young men accepted to

Viator House celebrate with a private room and a birthday cake surrounded by peers who know what they've been through.

As of March 2024, 113 young men from twenty-seven nations had called Viator House home. Our mission at Viator House is to accompany young immigrant men seeking asylum in the United States. We don't "do for" our participants. We "do with" them, helping them explore their options in life and offering advice as they, not we, make decisions about their lives.

Rooted in the Catholic tradition, especially in the biblical passages quoted by Rev. Dr. Arroyo, Viator House is a concrete example of how people of faith can bring, as we say, "hope, healing and opportunity" to young people struggling in our cruel and broken asylum system. Viator House reflects the values of the Clerics of St. Viator, a Catholic religious order founded in France in the nineteenth century to educate children in poor, rural areas—children systematically forgotten then as young asylum seekers are systematically forgotten now in our nation.

Though inspired by both our biblical tradition and our Viatorian traditions, Viator House is also unique because of our reverence for non-Christian traditions. We make it a priority to connect each young man living with us to the faith tradition of his choice and have built strong partnerships with area churches and mosques as well as a Hindu temple and Sikh community to ensure that our participants can attend services when they choose to do so. With special dinners and gifts, we celebrate all the faith holidays represented by the young men living with us. Meanwhile, we have formal partnerships with twenty-two area churches, mosques, and synagogues that support us with volunteers living out the teachings they hold dear in their faith traditions. Finally, we have built a volunteer interfaith asylum advocacy team that meets regularly to explore how the Viator House Community can advocate at all governmental levels for a compassionate asylum system.

Our participants' journeys from the border to us starts when they encounter border authorities. After encountering unaccompanied minors seeking asylum in our nation, authorities transfer them to youth immigrant programs funded by the Office of Refugee Resettlement (ORR), which is part of the Department of Health and Human Services (HHS). There, case workers try to reunite the minors with family members already living in the United States. If they have no family members living here, or the family members don't participate in the ORR vetting process, the minors remain in the program until they turn eighteen. On their eighteenth birthday, minors without family sponsors have little or no options. Before 2021, these minors would be transferred to adult detention centers. Now, attorneys working with them tell us that—other than temporary shelters—there are few programs in the nation that will provide housing for them, but none of them offer young men the housing and wraparound services offered by Viator House.

Most young men come to Viator House after being "released on recognizance" (ROR) by Immigration and Customs Enforcement (ICE). That happens because we have sent a letter to immigration through their attorneys explaining our program. Being granted "ROR" changes everything for young immigrants seeking asylum. That means they are free and can, for the first time in years for some, relax and dream about the future.

The narrative in the next section outlines how Viator House impacts the lives of young men who sought asylum in our nation as unaccompanied minors or young adults twenty-two years old or younger. They have fled their home countries after experiencing horrendous violence. Some had family members killed by cartels, extremists, or soldiers. Some were kidnapped by gangs or beaten and detained after demonstrating against their government. We don't know the reason each participant fled home. That's for them to tell us if and when they are comfortable. Our only job is to offer them hospitality that provides hope, healing, and opportunity. This chapter includes quotes from men who have called Viator House home, men we call "participants" because we invite them to "participate" in programming that will help them build lives in the United States. It also highlights how we integrate principles for trauma-informed care into our program.

First Contact: Invitation to Opportunity

Some of our participants have told us that the final weeks in ORR shelters before they turn eighteen can be terrifying. They don't know where they might live if they have no sponsors ready to receive them. It is generally during this time that we first learn of a young man preparing to "age out."

Raul escaped gang violence in Central America. He was held hostage by a cartel in northern Mexico until his family paid ransom so he could cross the border. He had spent almost eighty days in an ORR program when his eighteenth birthday approached. At that time, in 2018, ORR was automatically transferring unaccompanied alien minors (UAMs) with no sponsors to adult immigration detention centers when they turned eighteen. "First when they told me [about going to jail]. I can't believe it. [It was] the first time I was crying in front of someone. Because I don't want to go into the jail," Raul said. "I cried for a long time. It was really hard."

Gibril escaped a brutal military in his West African nation and then traveled from Africa to South America to the U.S.-Mexico border for safety. He had spent almost six months in an ORR program before his eighteenth birthday and faced the prospect of adult detention. "It's scary," he said. "You can't imagine how . . . scary it is. [Jail is] something that you never thought would happen to you" after escaping to the United States for safety.

Like most of our participants, we first met Raul and Gibril in their final weeks in an ORR program. As mentioned, a few men have come to us after we've helped secure their release from adult immigration detention centers. But, generally, our first contact happens when a young man is in an ORR program and his attorney reaches out to us, asking us to interview him for possible placement. Before the interview, we research what we can about the young man's history in ORR placement or in detention to ensure that we can meet his needs. We are unable to serve young men with medical, emotional, or behavioral problems that require constant supervision or on-site medical care.

During the interview, we outline life at Viator House, which includes opportunities for school, work, learning English, and practicing the faith of their choice but requires participants to live respectfully with young men from around the world. We also invite the young man to share what he is comfortable sharing about his hopes, dreams, and reasons for coming to the United States.

If the young man wants to live at Viator House, we then appeal in a formal letter to immigration authorities, asking them to release him on recognizance on his eighteenth birthday. Almost always immigration authorities authorize the young man's release because he has a safe place to live. Unfortunately, that is not always the case because of the discretion given to authorities signing off on the release. Only a few times, however, has our request been denied.

The final hours before being released can be torturous for the young people involved. Raul said he thought he was going to jail until two hours before he was able to move into Viator House. "During the night [before] I couldn't sleep because I was waiting to go to the jail," he said. He also remembers the immense relief he felt when an ORR case worker told him he was approved to live at Viator House.

Gibril visited Viator House with an ORR official, days before his birthday, but also didn't know if he'd be released to live there until his actual birthday. Like Raul, he said he did not sleep the night before. He also remembers the relief he felt when he was approved for release. "You get different emotions [then]," he said, adding that he felt like "I got the beginning of my life again."

First Day: Freedom and Safety

Abdul, who escaped violence in East Africa, remembered that fear and the relief that followed when he was released and spent his first day at Viator House. He also remembered how our staff greeted him when ORR officials brought him to our front door. He recalled how comforting it was to be treated like "a brother" by the other guys in the house right away. As a Muslim, he also said he quickly felt at home when he was presented with a Muslim prayer rug and Holy Qur'an.

The welcome and first day are critically important at Viator House. We emphasize to a new participant that things have changed, that now he is free and once again has "agency"—the ability to make his own decisions. Indeed, we greet Viator House participants with a key to their private room and a front-door code that allows them to come and go from the house as they please.

We work hard to immediately show a new participant that he is important to us. Signs on his room door and in the kitchens welcome him. Staff stop what they are doing to offer a handshake and explain their role. A welcome basket in his room includes a picture dictionary and a gift card to buy some new clothes, in addition to bedding and hygiene supplies. He receives an immediate tour, during which other participants offer personal greetings as well, sometimes in his home language.

We also ask the young man if he wants to practice a specific faith tradition—and offer him resources he needs for that as well as promises to connect him with a local faith community. We've seen how young men grow and heal when they have the opportunity to practice the faith of their choice.

Perhaps the most symbolic moment of a new participant's first day is after his first dinner, which is cooked for him by staff or another participant if he doesn't know how to cook. That moment comes after staff have gathered as many other guys as possible to celebrate the new participant's eighteenth birthday with singing, a cake, and a group picture, which he receives a copy of as evidence that he now "belongs" to a community of hope, healing, and opportunity.

Raul's first decision after being welcomed at Viator House was to call his brother. "I was excited," he said, remembering he told his brother that "I am going to call our parents. I am free."

That evening's birthday party was important to him as well. In fact, it was a first in his life. "It's the first time I celebrated my birthday.... ever, ever, ever," he said.

Finally, the private room offered him emotional space that he remembered badly needing. The day Raul moved into Viator House was also the day he learned that his cousin in Central America had been murdered by gang members. So the private room offered him space to deal with the day's conflicting emotions. "Finally," he remembered thinking, "I can laugh by myself, cry [by myself]. I feel safe."

Gibril offered similar memories. He remembered that the case manager who interviewed him was waiting for him when he arrived. He said he felt "happy and blessed.... People were friendly. They welcomed me and showed me around the house, told me that I was free." He said he had "never met people who welcomed [him] like that." He said he also remembers "thanking God about it."

Additionally, he said that the birthday celebration "was super good," adding that he couldn't remember the last time he celebrated his birthday. Because of the persecution his family faced back home, "nobody was thinking about that."

The First Week: The Chance to Belong Again
The first week at Viator House for a participant begins a journey that can lead him to learning the skills he needs to live successfully and safely outside Viator House. It also is filled with reminders that he is safe and part of a community that cares.

During the first two days, he has two important meetings. The first is with his case manager.

His case manager first discusses the house covenant, which is a set of basic expectations that includes everything from our curfew to how to respect other participants and staff members. But the most time a case manager spends with a new participant during that first week is on long-term issues. The case manager identifies a participant's legal, educational, medical, and psychological needs, and then explores how to access community resources to help meet those needs.

We work with two legal nonprofit organizations that offer free services to young asylum seekers. We also work with nonprofit organizations that specialize in providing free medical and psychological care. In addition, several local medical professionals donate their time and expertise. Three nurses and a medical doctor are always willing to consult on the phone and even visit the house to evaluate a participant's health.

In addition to medical and mental health care, a big focus is on providing educational opportunities. We partner with two alternative high schools that offer immigrant youth the opportunity to learn English and earn a high school diploma. Since many of our participants have had little if any formal schooling, we also partner with local English as a second language (ESL) programs and education specialists so we can tailor educational opportunities to the specific learning needs of each participant.

In fact, one volunteer who is a retired education professor set up an in-house ESL program and worked with other volunteers to provide tutoring resources. Finally, we have more than seventy volunteers who help the participants at Viator House, many as tutors, helping participants with everything from basic English to college-level math.

The second important meeting a new participant has during his first week at Viator House is with a staff member who takes him shopping. Most young men come with little or nothing, sometimes even without pants and shoes, just slippers and sweatpants. We decided when opening against providing our participants with used clothing, except for gently used coats and outerwear. We believe that concrete reminders of their human dignity help trauma survivors heal. So we show new participants they are "worth it" by allowing them to choose their clothes at a discount clothing store.

We then purchase a basic cell phone for a new participant, another way we provide safety and connections to people who care. The participant, as part of our desire to help him build skills for life outside Viator House, pays the monthly bill from a monthly stipend we offer until he can begin working.

We provide the phone for two reasons: First, safety. Our participants are new to the sprawling Chicago metropolitan area. We want to make sure they can be in touch with us at all times. Many of them attend school in Chicago's northside and must master the Chicago subway system. A phone ensures that a participant can call us if he gets lost or stranded. Early on, one of our Asian participants called from the far southside of Chicago, having gotten on the train going the wrong direction. We were able to calm him and redirect him. Several other times men have called us after finding themselves stranded when they missed a connection between the train and a suburban bus.

The second reason a phone is important is because it helps participants build and maintain human connections. With today's apps, our participants can stay in touch with family and friends back home.

We also provide each participant with a used laptop to help them maintain connections back home. But although laptops can help, phones are even more important. We have been touched deeply by the opportunities we have had to meet a participant's mother via a phone app and reassure her that her son is safe—and point out that it is our honor to host him. After the fall of Kabul, we accepted several eighteen-year-old Afghan men who escaped through the airport and experienced all the trauma that many of us saw on the national news. One of the most meaningful moments for one of our case managers was the opportunity to call the mother of one of our new Afghan participants in Kabul and reassure her that he was safe.

As the first days become the first week, a new participant settles into life at Viator House. Another key to helping him feel more and more at home is the work of our house coordinators. Two of our coordinators also came to our nation seeking asylum but as adults. That background helps them be even more sensitive to the needs of our participants.

House coordinators ensure that the young men learn important skills for daily living in the United States. Under their guidance, they learn to use everything from laundry machines to dishwashers to stoves and microwaves. New participants also become part of the house by doing chores under the direction of the coordinators. Though chores are still chores, we've found that participating in house upkeep helps build a sense of solidarity among our participants, who often volunteer to help each other or trade off chores because of scheduling conflicts.

Often, other participants play an important role in helping a new participant feel at home. We remember the pride a Bangladeshi participant took in teaching a new Bangladeshi participant how to cook. That became even more touching to observe during Ramadan, when our "veteran" Bangladeshi participant, a Hindu, awoke before dawn throughout the month to help his new friend, a Muslim, prepare his pre-fast meal for the day.

Raul had a similar experience. He remembered feeling welcomed after meeting another participant from his home country during his first day because that participant cooked his first meal for him. "He cooked eggs and beans with tortillas," he said. "He was so friendly."

Other participants also helped him feel at home during his first days, he recalled. Three Somali participants welcomed him by helping him cook and trying to learn Spanish. "I couldn't speak in English, but they tried to get me food," he said. Also, "they asked me how to say, 'How are you?' in Spanish," while teaching him some Somali words.

Gibril echoed Raul's comments about the environment he experienced early on at Viator House. "I was surprised [by] the way people treated each other and loved each other," he said, "even though they don't have the same background, [or are] from the same countries. They don't even speak the same language. But they all came together . . . [to] help each other."

Indeed, as Gibril and Raul recalled, bonds can form quickly at Viator House as the young men who have lived there for some time often take newer participants "under their wings" to make sure they know how to cook, clean, and do house chores. Again, the credit for all this goes to our house coordinators, who have been instrumental in creating a culture of "brotherhood" that eases that fear and uncertainty—a culture that new participants experience quickly and almost always buy into.

Short or Long Stays: Building a Foundation for Life

The early community building that takes place in the first days at Viator House helps set the tone for a participant's stay, however long that might be. Men can stay at Viator House as long as they follow our covenant and until they can successfully and safely move out. For some that means only one night or a few weeks until they can reunite with family.

After all the separation from family—and the fear that it must provoke—we take pride in helping a young man move on so he can await his legal proceedings with family, hopefully comforted by his own culture, language, and food. We remember a young Vietnamese participant's joy in finding that extended family from his home village lived about thirty minutes away from Viator House—and the sense of belonging he reported to us when we visited him a couple of months after he moved out.

As of March 2024, Viator House had reunited thirty-five young men with family, while more than fifty had moved on to live with friends or former participants. Many men have stayed with us for two years or more to attend school, find jobs, seek therapeutic help, and develop all the other skills they need to thrive away from Viator House. Since opening in January 2017, eighteen men have graduated high school, eleven have begun classes at a community college, and twenty-six have learned to drive.

At first, Raul only wanted to work to learn English and pay debts back home that his parents incurred to get him to safety. But soon, with the encouragement of his case manager, he decided, "I want to graduate high school." He graduated in two years and started community college, despite learning in his third language and having taken no high school classes in his home country. Thus, he became the first member of his family to graduate high school. In fact, before leaving home he also was the first in his family to graduate primary school.

What Raul accomplished speaks volumes about our house culture, which builds self-confidence in our participants and forms men from all around the world into a community of hope, healing, and opportunity. The key to that culture is the people who maintain it. Our staff of eleven and seventy-plus volunteers play that important role.

Here are some examples of how we build and maintain that culture. We recruit tutors who become critically important to participants attending high school or learning English. The reliability, compassion, and affirmation these tutors show keep our young men moving forward successfully in academic classes and language learning. They play an important role, as well, as cheerleaders when the participants feel like giving up as they wait years for their legal proceedings. The bravest tutors, however, have been our driving tutors, who have accompanied men from reading about the "rules of the road" to behind-the-wheel practice.

Raul said that his tutors did more than help with high school subjects. "They gave advice," he said, and have helped him "grow up." It was clear, he said, how much each tutor cared about him and wanted him "to be a success in the future."

Gibril, who also graduated high school and started community college while at Viator House, also praised the tutors who helped him. "They are so good, helpful," he said. "They do all their best to make sure you are getting what you need."

Like Raul, Gibril didn't expect to finish high school in the United States, though he had completed ten grades in his home country. But the tutors made all the difference as he studied in English, his third language. "I said, 'Thank God' I have people who help me . . . build my future."

Mentors play important roles in our participants' lives as well. Acting as guides, they help our participants navigate what it means to live, work, study, and build relationships in the United States. By welcoming them into their homes for family occasions and holiday celebrations, they fill a bit of the hole that must come from being so far from home.

Gibril said his mentor is like a father figure. "He is very good," he said. "We always talk about how I can build my future, how I can get a good career and make a foundation . . . for life."

Volunteer house assistants act as another important part of the Viator House family. They help with house chores and with transporting these young men to and from work or school while also providing friendly faces who are available for cooking questions, a game of cards, or an impromptu tutoring session. Most are adults who have raised children. And because of that, they sometimes become house "moms" or "dads." But some house assistants are young adults who develop rich relationships with participants around shared interests like music and sports—or shared complaints about school.

Community activities are also important ways that we build house camaraderie and remind participants of their inherent self-worth. We gather as many participants as possible to celebrate each birthday with a song and a cake. We celebrate each U.S. holiday with special meals. We also celebrate the holidays of each faith tradition present in the house and make sure that participants have the opportunity to explain at the meal why the celebration is important to their faith tradition. Finally, we have gathered participants for interfaith prayer or ritual to support a participant who has lost a loved one to death back home.

Gibril recalled how Viator House welcomed his Islamic background. Since opening, almost half of our participants have been young Muslims from Africa or Asia. Gibril said that celebrating Ramadan with Muslims and non-Muslims "surprised me. Non-Muslims don't celebrate with Muslims in my country." But that made the holy month even more meaningful for him. "When the other faiths join you in your faith, celebrating your holy day," he said, "you feel more important in that group."

Service is also an important part of our house culture. On a monthly basis, we invite participants to serve the community with staff members. We have packed food for hungry children abroad and delivered food to people living in tent cities in Chicago. We also maintain a garden each summer that grows produce for local food banks.

Raul, whose mother passed away while he lived at Viator House, said he likes serving others because he "learned from my mother. My mother was a woman who [helped] anyone. Everyone. If she has one piece of bread," he said, "she can share it."

He said that his desire to help others will also guide his future. "I want to help a lot of people, maybe in my home country. Maybe I can help other children," he said. "Because I know where I come from. Viator House has helped us go to school. That's why I want to help others in the future."

Gibril's mother, who died before he fled his country, played a similar role in his life. "For me, my mom was always about that," he said. "She was always in service to people." In fact, he said service seems to reunite him with her. "When I go help [others], the whole day I am with my mom." His mother's commitment to service also has inspired his desire to be a nurse. "For me, it is a better way to work with people, in a way to help them," he said. "It is a way to give back to the community."

Finally, we memorialize all these events with photos. Each participant receives a small photo album when moving into the house. He then receives a group photo after taking part in a special event with other participants. In addition, we enlarge some of these photos and hang them in our common areas. We hope that creating "new memories" and posting symbols of belonging can compete with the painful memories that forced our participants to flee home and those they've loved or lost.

As might be obvious, work opportunities and the development of work skills also play a critical role in the Viator House culture. Jobs are an important way Viator House participants build self-confidence. They also allow our men to send money home to family members who can't afford things like medical care, education, or even basic housing.

Asylum seekers can work legally in the United States, though the wait for a work permit can be long. Getting and maintaining that first U.S. job can be a challenge. While we don't guarantee jobs, we do help our participants search for them and learn successful work skills. We often work with their employers as participants learn what it means to be a good employee.

A job can radically transform a young man. Take Raul, for example. A staff member took him on his first job search soon after he arrived at Viator House. As they walked into a fast-food restaurant to ask about the job, Raul stood back, expecting the staff member to ask the manager if she was hiring. The staff member gently refused and encouraged Raul to do that, especially since the manager spoke Spanish. After he timidly asked if there was a job, the manager quickly offered him one.

Jump ahead two years and you find a different, more confident Raul. The restaurant promoted him to manager and promised him a raise. Raul took the promotion and the added responsibilities. But when the promised wage increase didn't materialize, Raul, on his own, promptly found a job at the higher wage at a different restaurant. The first restaurant liked him so much it recruited him back and granted him the wage increase. Raul was clearly different. That difference shows the confidence a job and Viator House mentors had on him.

Unfortunately, however, there also are employers who hire young immigrants to take advantage of them. That's another reason why the support Viator House offers a participant is important. Several years ago, a Viator House mentor recalled a story about a discussion he had with the participant he was mentoring.

The participant, a Pakistani, was working at a South Asian grocery store. He disliked the job and told his mentor that he wanted to quit. But, he told his mentor, he knew that U.S. law prohibited him from quitting until his boss found a replacement worker. Obviously, that is not U.S. law. The owner, however, thought he could keep our participant working by lying—and provoking fear that his asylum case might be in jeopardy if he quit. Thank God for our mentoring program and this participant's trusting relationship with his mentor, who assured him that he could legally quit. And quit he did.

For Raul, work has helped him build confidence and help his family back home. He has sent money to help his parents buy food, purchase seed for farming, and seek doctors when they are sick.

Gibril agreed. "The first freedom is work. If you are working, you're free. You feel better," he said. "You fill yourself. I am doing something for myself. You feel independent and more important because you are helping back home."

The opportunity to work, build job skills, and help family members back home is as important as education, therapeutic intervention, and mentoring when it comes to building and maintaining a culture that builds hope, healing, and opportunity. But house conflicts and participant bad decisions can also help build that culture—depending on how we respond to them.

To maintain our culture, it is important that men respect staff decisions and not use illegal drugs. They can use alcohol if they are twenty-one and use it responsibly away from the house. But we are careful not to react when men don't meet these expectations. Rather, we need to respond. There is a big difference. A reaction can be a quick decision based on emotion or the desire to "stop" a behavior. It can quickly lead to an ultimatum like "stop this or find a new place to live."

Instead, we ask ourselves, "what trauma is the drug use medicating and how can we invite a young person to find different ways to soothe the trauma?" Or we might ask another question if a participant seems unwilling to cooperate, like "what traumatic experience might the request have triggered and how can we be sensitive to that trauma going forward?"[6]

Choosing to respond rather than react doesn't mean we don't challenge participants' inappropriate behavior. It just means the challenge we offer and how we offer it incorporates a sensitivity to the trauma they've experienced.

Nonetheless, a few participants have left Viator House after struggling repeatedly to follow our covenant. Because of their trauma, we believe, they were unable to regularly treat other participants and staff with respect. We have not forced any participants to leave. But after discussions about the importance of the covenant for everyone at the house, a few participants decided to live with friends they've developed in the area. Even then, however, we have offered them limited case management for a period of time after they move out.

Moving On

Our goal at Viator House is to prepare young men seeking asylum to live safely and successfully away from Viator House. But moving into an apartment can be quite a challenge for a young adult immigrant with no credit history or experience living in an apartment. For this reason, Viator House established a second-stage housing program.

The second-stage housing program recognizes the challenges our men face when moving out and devotes staff and financial resources to address those challenges. We pay special attention to the challenges they face in the following areas:

- *Apartment searches and rental applications.* A case manager and/or Viator House mentor working with a participant will help the

participant look for suitable apartments and complete the necessary application. If necessary, Viator House also acts as a personal reference, though not a financial guarantor, for the participant seeking the apartment.
- *Financial planning.* A case manager or a mentor walks a participant through a budgeting process, helping the participant identify the expenses he will incur and compare them to the income he can expect. That can lead to good discussions about what to buy and when to buy it.
- *Group living.* Sometimes a small group of participants plan to move out together. We've discovered that intentional discussions about how the participants plan to share expenses and chores are critical before the group moves. A Viator House social work intern even developed a community-living agreement that each "roommate" signs as part of those discussions.
- *Moving expenses.* Because of generous donors, Viator House has a fund that can award a participant moving into second-stage housing up to $3,000 for first-month rent, security deposit, and furnishings. Such grants provide a big hand up, even if the participant has savings.
- *Ongoing case management/mentoring.* Finally, living means learning. So, often we discover the ongoing guidance our participants need only after they have moved out of Viator House. For that reason, our second-stage housing program offers case management and mentoring for a year after a participant moves out. A community-living agreement might look good after an initial discussion. But what happens when one roommate hasn't cleaned his dishes for a week? A case manager or mentor can step in and help participants negotiate the situation. Expenses might seem to be covered. But what happens when an old car needs unexpected repairs? A good discussion can follow with a mentor who has been through that and who can possibly introduce the participant to a reliable mechanic.

So "moving on" is not necessarily a smooth process for a young man seeking asylum in the United States, even after a few years at Viator House and after he has graduated high school, started college, and successfully maintained a job. It can be frightening. It can trigger the trauma from that difficult and lonely journey each man first made as a kid who had to flee thousands of miles from home on his own. For that reason, our second-stage housing program can be an important bridge to life after Viator House.

The Viator House model is the alternative our nation should embrace as it welcomes the thousands of unaccompanied minors who flee to our border annually. It reflects the national values that we claim to hold dear—values enshrined in our asylum law that call us to offer a home to people fleeing persecution.

Viator House is an investment into the lives of young men who come to our nation as gifts to our nation, with talents that can enrich us. For instance, Lewis, a gentle young man who fled West Africa as a frightened teen and who had little schooling there, has started a community college program that will train him as a nurse. This investment pays off for all of us.

But perhaps Gibril's comments sum it all up. "Viator House is a place where you can come and get a foundation for your life, something you weren't expecting or something you lost before," he said. "It's also a house where so many beautiful hearts come together, always willing to help."

Part 2. What About the Women?

Sister Patricia Crowley, Sister Kathlyn Mulcahy, Darlene Gramigna, Sister Stella Akello, Jessica Alaniz, and Emily Ruehs-Navarro

In the midst of the political chaos and immigration upheaval of 2017, Viator House of Hospitality had recently opened its doors as an alternative to adult migrant detention for young men. A Catholic Sister, retiring from leadership in her own religious community, had begun work as a volunteer at Viator. While working one day, she overheard another volunteer asked one of the Viator cofounders, "What about the women?" The Sister responded, "I could help with that."

A month later, she reached out to her email list of fellow Sisters, inviting them to a meeting. Twenty Sisters gathered to learn about the situation and the fate of young immigrant women and detention in the United States. Over the course of 2017, the Sisters founded a counterpart to Viator House of Hospitality. They wanted to create a place that would serve as an alternative to detention for young women aging out of the Office of Refugee Resettlement shelters and to welcome young mothers seeking to prevent their children from experiencing family detention. In 2017, the Sisters incorporated, found a house to accommodate ten young women, secured funding from religious communities of women, and hired staff. Bethany House of Hospitality (BHH or Bethany) successfully opened at the end of October 2017 with one woman from Somalia who several years later was granted asylum. Since 2017, Bethany House of Hospitality board of directors, staff, and funders recognized the complexity of women's experience in the asylum-seeking process and expanded the organization's services to welcome expecting mothers, women with children, transgender women, and older women.

BHH is what its name says—a house of hospitality with a goal of welcoming young women seeking asylum into a home with other young women from different countries. On the Southside of Chicago in a stately Chicago graystone with stained glass windows, a multi-ethnic staff offers a loving presence twenty-four hours a day, opportunities for education, counseling, legal assistance, and support to help young people move into independent living and thrive in a new country. Collaborative relationships with other entities such as Viator House of Hospitality, the National Immigrant Justice Center, the Young Center for Immigrant Children's Rights, and Heartland Health provide vital community connections to this vulnerable but resilient population. A board of women religious, an advisory board, a core of volunteers, and mentors all work to provide what each of these young women needs to grow and to heal from past traumatic realities and attain the new life for which they longed.

This chapter was written as a collaboration between staff and board members of BHH, past and present residents, and sociologist Emily Ruehs-Navarro. Members of the BHH community wrote short vignettes that illuminate the work of BHH; these vignettes were then presented to Ruehs-Navarro, who worked collaboratively with the leadership to sort and analyze the themes of the stories. These vignettes are presented in their entirety throughout this chapter, although names and identifying information have been changed. Taken together, the stories speak to the needs that BHH addresses, particularly for young women migrating alone, mothers with children, and LGBTQ migrants; they provide evidence of the traumas caused by migrant detention; and they provide an opportunity to reflect on changes that still need to be made.

Reaching All Women

Migration historically was framed as an issue of men, and it was only in the past several decades that women began to be centered in migration research and policy. Girls make up around a third of unaccompanied young people (an increase over the past decade), and given that they are the numerical minority, they are often overlooked in the broader conversation (Office of Refugee Resettlement n.d.). Similarly, research shows that LGBTQ-identified migrants are certainly present among the unaccompanied migrant population—but specific data are hard to come by (see Tenorio, this volume). Estimates of transgender adults in migration detention are around 1 in 500 detainees (Luibhéid and Chávez 2020). Existing research on the experiences of transgender Latinx individuals has exposed the negative social, economic, and health implications for this population, which experiences ethnic-based-discrimination, transphobia, and cis-sexism (Abreu et al. 2021).

Young women migrants are particularly vulnerable to the various violences of migration, before, during, and after the migratory journey itself. Gendered violence, along with economic distress, environmental changes, and political and community violence, is often the impetus for young women's migration (Ruehs-Navarro 2022). Sexual assault or domestic violence in the home country may very well be the final push factor that drives many young women's decisions to migrate. During migration, women, especially young women, are vulnerable to exploitation and assault, by smugglers, criminal actors, and police and government officials. In fact, many of the women at BHH report that they received birth control before leaving, with the expectation that they would be assaulted. Then, upon arrival and apprehension, women in detention facilities remain vulnerable to the same sexual and gendered exploitation by U.S. Border Patrol agents and guards (Kriel 2020). They further lack appropriate medical services, particularly for pregnant women (Ellmann 2019). These young women also face incredible obstacles as they begin their new lives. They often arrive with a misleading vision of idealized life in America and are again traumatized when they realize the difficult life faced by immigrants in this country.

Similar vulnerabilities are present among LGBTQ migrants, particularly transwomen. Indeed, sexual and gender identity can be the impetus for migration; it creates vulnerabilities during the journey, and the U.S. system of detention is even more ill-equipped to respond to the needs of these migrants. Young trans migrants find that detention centers misgender them and refuse to place them in a same-gender setting. Worse still, reports suggest that violence against trans migrants by both guards and other detainees is rampant (Luibhéid and Chávez 2020).

When BHH formed, we knew we wanted to serve young women migrants. However, it became clear quite quickly that the parameters defining the population needed to be flexible. Indeed, early on, the leadership was faced with the question of whether their services should be extended to individuals who did not fit into the initial criteria, particularly transwomen, mothers with children, and women who were in their late twenties. After some debate, the leadership agreed that we needed to be flexible with the residents' various identities. Indeed, we took to heart lessons learned from intersectional feminists who have argued for decades that social service agencies must understand the various social locations that intersect to create particular vulnerabilities (Crenshaw 1991). Young immigrant women who are trans, who are mothers, and who do not fit into traditional understandings of youth and adulthood are no exception. The fact that the leadership of BHH has embraced this flexibility is one of the keys to our success thus far. However, the welcoming of this flexibility has come with its challenges.

In the following section, we detail the stories of several individuals who have spent time at BHH. These stories collectively demonstrate the damaging impact of the current detention system and show how alternative programs can help repair and minimize harm.

Responding to Complex Identities

BHH was initially created to provide a space for young women who age out of detention. However, the workers at BHH quickly discovered that the age-out process is not cut-and-dry, and the realities of transnational migration mean that many migrants are unable to prove their age to border enforcement. BHH thus became a place that met a need when young people's ages and identities were in question.

> Imagine you are eighteen years old and have spent fully half of your life searching for a safe and welcoming place to call home. That is Elizabeth's reality. She fled her home in Central Africa at nine years old with her mom, dad, younger brother, and sister, seeking to escape a brutal civil war described as "the bloodiest war since World War II." The family landed in a refugee camp where it was evident, even to a

child, that they were not welcome. A year later Elizabeth accompanied her father to Brazil, where they hoped to establish a home and reunite the family. She went to work braiding hair to earn money to help reunite their family sooner; however, they lost contact with the family back in the refugee camp. (Searches through the Red Cross have not found any trace of them to date in refugee camps or anywhere else.) Forced to uproot again, Elizabeth and her father made the long and treacherous journey north, mostly on foot, through eight different countries. Their goal was to reach the United States, with the hope that the rest of the family might find their way there and be reunited. Then tragedy hit: Elizabeth's father drowned crossing the Río Grande. Elizabeth arrived in the United States—alone and as one of thousands of unaccompanied children at our southern border. Elizabeth was sixteen years old by this time, but because she was tall and had no documents to verify her age, border agents believed she looked like an adult. Because of this, Elizabeth was sent for a dental exam, where X-rays were used to determine there was "at least a 75-percent probability that she was 18 or older" and she would be sent to adult detention. (A practice viewed by many as both unethical and unscientific [Laniado, Wright, and Seymour 2022].) As a result of this exam, Elizabeth was sent to adult detention for eight months. A caring Child Advocate lobbied for her to be sent to Bethany House of Hospitality instead. There she was able to take high school classes, make friends, and begin working as she continued to wind her way through the asylum process. Eventually, Elizabeth did receive asylum and began working as a certified nursing assistant. Unfortunately, to date, her family has not been located.

Elizabeth's experience of her age being in question is not unique. In countries throughout the world, the day and year of birth are not exactly recorded or a person has lost or fled without a birth certificate or other identity documents. Similarly, it is not uncommon for young people to carry false documents as a way of crossing international borders. However, as cases at BHH have shown, these documents end up creating further complications upon arrival to the United States.

Rose came from the horn of Africa, escaping from the violent upheaval in her own country at age seventeen. However, in order to be able to cross the border in her own country, Rose obtained false documents stating that she was over age eighteen. Upon arrival to the United States, she was sent to adult detention because the documents she presented said she was over eighteen. The officers who interviewed her rudely confronted this age discrepancy. Through several days of not eating much due to her religious restrictions, she became quite ill. Finally another officer intervened, they realized she was under eighteen, and she was transferred to a children's center. Upon her eighteenth birthday, Rose was released to a family friend in a small town halfway across the country. The bus ride there was frightening due to her poor English skills. After that situation did not work out due to violence in the house, she left on her own and ended up in a shelter in Chicago and eventually connected with Bethany House. She remains in BHH today, where she is working to support her family in her home country.

While questions of age can seriously influence a young person's path through U.S. custody, questions around gender identity can be even more fraught. As previously stated, the system of detention in the United States is severely ill-equipped to respond to the needs of trans migrants and, in fact, can cause tremendous harm to the safety and well-being of these migrants. When leadership at BHH decided to accept transwomen alongside cisgender women, they learned quickly the importance of providing a space that truly meets the needs of a wide range of residents.

Yessica was a transwoman living in Guatemala. She had faced continual harassment due to her gender identity and decided to seek asylum in the United States. She entered the country at the Calexico Station, where she was placed in a short-term holding facility. Soon after, she was turned over to a male federal detention facility, despite clearly and consistently identifying as a woman to the immigration agents. Yessica was transferred once more, although officials did not tell her where they were taking her, and she felt extremely unsafe in the facilities. One night, guards awoke her in the middle of the night and demanded that she sign a voluntary departure agreement. She refused, but they still put her on a plane that night back to Guatemala. She spent a month in Guatemala in a shelter and was able to connect again with her mother. Fortunately, an attorney in the United States was also working on her case and was quickly able to connect with her again while she remained in Guatemala. The attorney worked to identify the reason for Yessica's deportation, and after a month of investigation, the U.S. government was obligated to fly her back to the United States for her immigration hearing. At this point, Yessica connected with BHH, where she lived as a resident for a year while her asylum case processed. During this time, she helped sponsor her younger brother to the United States and has been instrumental in opening an LGBTQ home for new immigrants.

Responding to Inhumane Policies
In addition to finding the BHH could respond to the needs of young migrants who do not fit into normative understandings of age, gender, and life course, BHH also found itself in a position to respond to the particular tragedies created by the Trump administration. One of these policies was the Migrant Protection Protocol, which required migrants to wait in Mexico while their asylum case was pending.

> Carlota was originally from Guatemala, and Xiomara was from El Salvador, but the young women's lives connected while they waited for nearly two years in a Mexican tent camp on the border with the United States. At the time, Carlota was pregnant, and although she had traveled with her younger sister in order to escape an abusive family situation, she had been separated from the sister at the border. Carlota and Xiomara learned very quickly that the camp was incredibly unsafe: many people had been robbed of the little they had, kidnapped, or simply "disappeared." Tragically, Xiomara was exploited, sexually assaulted, and kidnapped twice during her stay. Eventually, the young women connected with a Baptist pastor who ran a shelter on both sides of the border; he was able to connect the women to BHH. Their tenacity and resilience have served then well during their time at BHH. Xiomara has a marvelous creative talent and is a tremendous asset to the community of women living together at BHH. Carlota gave birth to a healthy baby girl and named her Bethany. Carlota is also looking forward to being reunified with her little sister, once she turns eighteen.

Another policy that BHH has responded to was the so-called family separation policy.

Francisco was only fourteen months old when he crossed the border with his mother, María, to seek asylum in the United States. The mother and son hoped to be reunited with their father and husband, who already lived in the United States. It was months before the government would officially announce its "zero tolerance" policy of family separation at the southern border. Yet, though they crossed at a border crossing and asked for asylum in a process legal under U.S. and international law, María was charged with illegal entry and sent to a detention facility. Francisco was transferred to the custody of the Department of Health and Human Services as an "unaccompanied child." He ended up in a foster care home in the Chicago area for almost seven months. Nearly a month after then president Trump signed an executive order to rescind the family separation policy, Bethany House of Hospitality received a call asking if the organization could be a reunification point for Francisco and his mother. María was brought from a Texas detention facility to Bethany House. Francisco arrived with the woman who had been caring for him. A tearful reunion ensued, as Francisco clung to the woman who had been caring for him for the last seven months. He no longer recognized his own mother. Francisco and María spent two days at Bethany House, getting to know each other again, before Francisco's father arrived to take them home.

Bethany House of Hospitality was an essential facility in responding to the horrors of the family separation policy, although as the preceding story illustrates, family separation causes irreversible damage. However, whether or not this particular policy is in place, the staff at BHH has found that the very use of detention facilities can cause family separation regardless of explicit separation policies. The story of a South Asian family explains one such scenario.

Fleeing violence and the threat of human trafficking at home, four young sisters made a nearly year-long journey from South Asia, to Brazil, and finally to the United States. Their grandmother had helped fund their airfare to Brazil, and the girls supported each other throughout the perilous journey. By the time the sisters arrived at the border, two were considered "unaccompanied minors" at ages sixteen and seventeen, while the other two were considered adults at ages eighteen and twenty. The family was thus separated; the youngest two were placed in a facility under ORR custody and the older two were sent to adult detention. However, soon after, the seventeen-year-old aged out of her facility, where she was able to connect to BHH (with assistance from the Young Center for Immigrant Children's Rights). She was happy to be released but desperately missed her younger sister as well as her older siblings. Within a few weeks, attorneys helped in naming her the guardian of the sixteen-year-old, which allowed the youngest girl to be released to BHH as well. The two oldest girls remained in adult detention for many more months and faced an imminent threat of deportation. However, with some quick and shrewd legal work, BHH was able to sponsor the girls in order to avoid deportation. Eventually, all four sisters were released from the various facilities and reunited at BHH.

Providing the Luxury of Time

Much of the migration journey and the legal process for status is a game of time. Sometimes, time stretches on for months and years, and young people who are in detention for significant lengths of time may feel desperate for release. On the other hand, policies such as the rocket docket have worked to decrease time spent processing cases, often leading to situations in which decisions are made too quickly, with not enough time for migrants or attorneys to adequately weigh their options. The stories of young women at BHH demonstrate the importance of time, space, and nonrestrictive settings for allowing young migrants to understand and choose the best options available to them. Indeed, stories of young people at BHH demonstrate the failure of U.S. officials to adequately explain the options available to young migrants and lead to irreversible action that the better-informed young person would not have chosen.

> Aline was a seventeen-year-old girl from Brazil who was held in a facility with her two-year-old child. Her detention stretched on for months, and she found the conditions, especially with her child, unbearable. Out of desperation and a desire for freedom, she agreed to sign a "voluntary departure document," permitting her deportation. However, as she awaited this deportation, she turned eighteen and was transferred with her child to BHH. Once at BHH she was able to see the true pos-

sibilities of life in the United States, and stated mournfully to a staff member: "If I had only known of this alternative, I would have held out and not signed those voluntary departure documents." Unfortunately, it was too late for her, and although it took a full six months for her voluntary departure to be processed, Aline and her son were eventually deported.

In contrast to Aline's story, where the decision for voluntary departure was made in circumstances that felt coercive, the following parallel story shows how voluntary departure decisions can be made with more understanding and thoughtfulness, when given the time and space to truly understand the options available.

Like Aline, Sandra was seventeen years old, and mother to a four-month-old daughter. With her husband and baby, she had walked most of the way to the U.S. southern border from Brazil. At the border, she had been separated from her husband, who was placed in adult detention, while Sandra and her child were placed in a children's facility. Although Sandra missed her husband, she was grateful to have her baby with her. As her eighteenth birthday approached, she learned that she would age out of the children's detention. She was filled with worry: What would happen to her and her baby? Where would they go . . . or where would they be sent—together or apart? Sandra had an uncle in New Jersey, so arrangements were being made for her and the baby to go and stay with the uncle on her eighteenth birthday. Just three days before her birthday, however, a lawyer who was in communication with the uncle came to tell Sandra that the plan had collapsed. The uncle could not take them because he didn't want to attract ICE attention to the family, as there were many undocumented people in the household. Sandra spent a sleepless and tearful night fearing she would be separated from her child if she was sent to adult detention (housed in a local county jail). The next day the lawyer said she had called Bethany House of Hospitality and they would take Sandra and her baby. Sandra was thrilled to have a safe place to stay for herself and her child. However, her husband was deported shortly after her arrival at Bethany House. The baby was ten months old—almost ready to take her first steps—when Sandra chose voluntary departure and returned to Brazil to join her husband. She said she would be forever grateful to Bethany House for offering a welcoming home to her and her child.

As this story suggests, models such as BHH provide space, time, and environments that are noncoercive for young migrants to truly explore their options. Whereas Aline greatly regretted her voluntary departure, Sandra felt that she has been given a true choice while remaining at BHH.

A Faith-Based Response to Asylum Seekers
As workers and community members have come to learn about the stories and detention histories of the young women at BHH, the stories reveal that detention in all its forms is traumatic. Young women at BHH are clear about harmful experiences with Customs and Border Protection (CBP), ORR, and ICE detention facilities and immigration laws that do not consider the complexity of migration in the lives of women. The stories that young women at Bethany tell further illuminate the trauma of detention, make a strong case for the presence of alternative options, and help the staff, board of directors, and funders at Bethany make programmatic decisions that represent the needs of immigrant women.

While the U.S. immigration system is broken and in need of a total overhaul, the picture is not entirely bleak. Bethany House of Hospitality demonstrates that community-based alternatives to detention are both possible and realistic. They are significantly less costly than detention, and, more importantly, they prepare women to thrive and contribute to U.S. society.

In the first six years of BHH, more than ninety-five women and thirty-five of their children have experienced a safe space and respite in their journey to a new life. They have found friendship, support, and encouragement. Most have completed high school or GED studies. Some have begun college. Almost all of them aspire to service-oriented professions—medical, legal, counseling, or social work—recognizing those who have supported them on the journey and wanting to give back by supporting other vulnerable persons in their journey. In one instance a former guest at Bethany House, now a staff member, purchased a home and transformed it into a second stage of independent living to women moving out of Bethany House.

Bethany House of Hospitality provides a community-based alternative to detention. It is far from perfect but it is a step in the right direction. However, this housing model alone does not solve the much larger systemic problems, which include the need for legal representation for all, funding for more assistance programs for asylum seekers, creating a special division to protect the most vulnerable young people, and thinking globally about the U.S. role in the destabilization of many sending countries.

At BHH, we have a faith-based mission to support young immigrant women as they seek independence in a new country. We practice compassion, we center human dignity, and we recognize that we are all deeply connected. For this reason, we believe there is an imperative to ease the suffering of the current system while fighting for larger structural changes.

* * *

As the stories of Viator House of Hospitality and Bethany House of Hospitality show, faith-based activism is essential in today's work to provide justice for detained migrant youth. These communities demonstrate that there is a strong imperative in various faith traditions to assist migrants, and there is also an incredible foundation of resources and manpower in these communities to exert tremendous influence and create unique solutions to the current crisis.

Notes

1. Leviticus 19:33–34 (New English Translation). All biblical quotations in this chapter come from the New English Translation, Bible Gateway, accessed August 27, 2022, https://www.biblegateway.com/.

2. For a more detailed history of the NSM in the United States, see Paik (2020).

3. For more information about the No More Deaths organization, visit its website, accessed August 30, 2022, https://www.nomoredeaths.org.

4. Humane Borders / Fronteras Compasivas, accessed August 30, 2022, https://humaneborders.org.

5. Viator House participants are quoted in this chapter. Before including their quotes, they were interviewed by Fr. Corey Brost. Before publication, they reviewed the content to ensure that the quotes accurately reflected their commentary. We have changed their names to protect their identity.

6. Our staff has been trained in the principles of trauma-informed care, following the model promoted by the Buffalo Center for Social Research (n.d.).

References

Abreu, Roberto L., Kristen A. Gonzalez, Cristalis Capielo Rosario, Gabriel M. Lockett, Louis Lindley, and Sharrah Lane. 2021. "'We Are Our Own Community': Immigrant Latinx Transgender People Community Experiences." *Journal of Counseling Psychology* 68 (4): 390–403.

Boff, Clodovis. 1996. "Methodology of the Theology of Liberation." In *Systematic Theology: Perspectives from Liberation Theology*, edited by Jon Sobrino and Ignacio Ellacuria, 1–21. Maryknoll, N.Y.: Orbis Books.

Buffalo Center for Social Research. n.d. "What Is Trauma-Informed Care?" Accessed February 27, 2024. https://socialwork.buffalo.edu/social-research/institutes-centers/institute-on-trauma-and-trauma-informed-care/what-is-trauma-informed-care.html.

Caroll R., M. Daniel. 2020. *The Bible and Borders: Hearing God's Word on Immigration*. Grand Rapids, Mich.: Brazos Press.

Crenshaw, Kimberle. 1991. "Mapping the Margins: Intersectionality, Identity Politics, and Violence Against Women of Color." *Stanford Law Review* 43 (6): 1241–99.

De La Torre, Miguel A. 2009. *Trails of Hope and Terror: Testimonies on Immigration*. Maryknoll, N.Y.: Orbis Books.

Ellmann, Nora. 2019. "Immigration Detention Is Dangerous for Women's Health and Rights." Center for American Progress, October 21. https://www.americanprogress.org/article/immigration-detention-dangerous-womens-health-rights/.

Kriel, Lomi. 2020. "ICE Guards 'Systematically' Sexually Assault Detainees in an El Paso Detention Center, Lawyers Say." ProPublica, August 14. https://www.propublica.org/article/ice-guards-systematically-sexually-assault-detainees-in-an-el-paso-detention-center-lawyers-say.

Laniado, Nadia, M. Lindsay Wright, and Brittany Seymour. 2022. "The Use of Dental Radiographs for Age Estimation of Unaccompanied Migrant Minors: Scientific and Ethical Concerns." *Journal of Public Health Dentistry* 82 (3): 349–51.

Luibhéid, Eithne, and Karma R. Chávez, eds. 2020. *Queer and Trans Migrations: Dynamics of Illegalization, Detention, and Deportation*. Urbana: University of Illinois Press.

McFarlan Miller, Emily, and Yonat Shimron. 2018. "Why Is Jeff Sessions Quoting Romans 13 and Why Is the Bible Verse so Often Invoked?" *USA Today*, July 16.

Office of Refugee Resettlement. n.d. "Fact Sheets and Data." Accessed July 18, 2022. https://www.acf.hhs.gov/orr/about/ucs/facts-and-data.

Paik, A. Naomi. 2020. *Bans, Walls, Raids, Sanctuary. Understanding U.S. Immigration for the Twenty-First Century*. Oakland: University of California Press.

Rivera-Pagán, Luis N. 2014. "Xenophilia or Xenophobia: Towards a Theology of Migration." In *Essays from the Margins*, 84–103. Eugene, Ore.: Cascade Books.

Ruehs-Navarro, Emily. 2022. *Unaccompanied: The Plight of Immigrant Youth at the Border*. New York: New York University Press.

Zapor Cruz, Miranda. 2020. "Slap Some Scripture on It! The Theological and Political Dangers of Biblicism." Blog, December 28. https://mirandazaporcruz.com/slap-some-scripture-on-it-the-theological-and-political-dangers-of-biblicism/.

CHAPTER TEN

A Practitioner's Case Study of Immigrant Children's Artistic Narratives of Resistance

SILVIA RODRIGUEZ VEGA

During an exercise titled "Newspaper Theater," in which students identified a news article they selected as important and used theater to re-create the issue and think of solutions, twelve-year-old Daniel volunteered to show his drawing of what he thought to be the most important news story.[1] Daniel quickly stood up from his chair and loudly proclaimed, "My problem is Donald Trump, we really hate him!" Soon after, Jorge echoed, "Yeah, the problem is Trump is being racist and not letting immigrants come in by building The Wall . . . oh and he is trying to start a WWIII with North Korea!" Some kids nodded in agreement and others laughed while pointing their hands like machine guns. As an outspoken and energetic student, Daniel often gets in trouble while in class. Daniel is undocumented. He immigrated from El Salvador to reunite with his mother when he was ten years old. His friend Jorge is a second-generation Mexican American whose mother is a U.S. citizen and father is a permanent resident. Although both Daniel and Jorge live different legal realities due to their documentation status, they shared similar concerns regarding the president of the United States at that time, Donald Trump. The class provided an outlet for children's resistance—resistance to racial animus, state-sponsored violence in the form of migrant child detention, and the often silent violence that comes with being an undocumented child in the United States.

Here, I aim to provide a case study that can help practitioners like artists and activists use art to respond to the violence of detention by creating spaces for conversation, reflection, and healing that center children's narratives, art, and experiences. I highlight the experiences of children of immigrants in Watts, California (a neighborhood located in South Central Los Angeles), and how they resist narratives of anti-immigrant sentiments that during this time focused on the forty-fifth president of the United States. However, Trump in this case is a proxy for many other aspects of immigrant children's lives, such as the dangers and fears of detention and deportation practices. Since this research took place during the Trump administration, the art narratives directly resist Trump, but this piece is not only about Trump. Rather, children's hyperfocus on Trump is an attempt to resist what he represents. That is, immigrant children are resisting the most vile, racist, and xenophobic sentiments that already existed in our society and pervaded our immigration system. Not only do children have important and critical opinions about the Trump presidency, but they offer society hope in the creation of alternative realities, endings, and ways of seeing that challenge anti-immigrant narratives in the country. More specifically, I present Mexican and Central American children's narratives on resistance and resilience regarding Trump's political agenda and Twitter/media declarations to show the resilience of youth, particularly through educational, artistic, and anecdotal means. This chapter provides literature about immigrant children related to policy, educational outcomes, and artistic expressions. The methods section explains the site for this project and the development and implementation of the theater curriculum. Finally, I organize the findings by art form and conclude with implications for art practitioners, researchers, and teachers.

At the time of this writing, we are living under the Joe Biden administration, but some of the experiences faced by children in this study have not changed for the better. Currently, President Biden has waived numerous environmental protection laws to continue the plans set forth during the previous administration to build a wall twenty miles long between Mexico and the United States near the Rio Grande Valley region in Texas (Sullivan and Edmonds 2023). As was the case during the Trump administration, under Biden, migrants are still not allowed to seek asylum in the United States. Under new policies, asylum seekers looking to get to the United States must first apply for asylum in whatever country they cross into first. Further, for those who qualify, the process has also been made harder with a new digital application program being the avenue where migrants must file their application for asylum, which has proven inaccessible and difficult to use (Sasani 2023).

Immigrant Children During Moments of Heightened Animosity Against Immigrants

Approximately 5.3 million children living in the United States have undocumented parents (Yoshikawa, Suárez-Orozco, and Gonzales 2017). Demographers estimate that by 2040, one in three children will live in an immigrant household (Passel 2011). Despite the increasing numbers of immigrant children, and the economic dependency the United States has on this generation for the future, anti-immigrant policies targeting undocumented adults at the national and local level continue to impact children in harmful ways (Yoshikawa 2011; Dreby and Adkins 2012). In Arizona, immigrant communities have felt the heavy-handed immigration enforcement implemented by the Barack Obama administration, which deported more immigrants than any other administration before him (Nava 2014; Szkupinski Quiroga, Medina, and Glick 2014). Then Trump's presidency effectively upended the asylum process and continued to transform the immigration system by making legal entry into the United States nearly impossible for many, especially Mexicans and Central Americans. In fact, the Trump administration's efforts to curb undocumented immigration were constantly contested by the Supreme Court and federal judges across the United States (Verea 2018; Batalova, Fix and Greenberg 2019; Montoya-Galvez 2020).

We already know that deportations create detrimental outcomes for children vis-à-vis familial disintegration. Even when children do not experience deportation, they fear for the security of their family (Dreby 2012). Additionally, children often conflate immigration agents with local law enforcement, resulting in a fear of any public official. Likewise, children tend to assume all immigrants are undocumented, even seeing themselves as undocumented despite having U.S. citizenship (Dreby 2012; Dreby and Adkins 2012). Occasionally, children reported not knowing what happened to their own parents when they have been separated by immigration enforcement (Capps et al. 2007). Consequently, the everyday experiences for children are met with questions such as how will I get to school, who will I live with, and how will I get fed, which are also compounded by the psychological effects that may result in fear, distrust, depression, anxiety, and financial instability (Ayers 2013). On a day-to-day basis, caregivers reported frequent crying, loss of appetite, sleeplessness, clingy behavior, and increased fear and anxiety (Capps et al. 2007; Trisi and Herrera 2018). Given the myriad challenges and barriers for immigrant children, supportive and humanizing spaces found in schools and communities become essential to survival.

Education, Family Support, and the Role of Perseverance

Educational institutions have historically served as the primary point of assimilation and acculturation for immigrant young people, namely American Indian boarding schools and Japanese internment camp schools (Tuck and Gaztambide-Fernández 2013; Briggs 2020). In the current political moment, when it comes to the academic well-being of immigrant children exposed to immigration raids, for example, teachers reported that children often missed school and were seldom able to concentrate when they attended, resulting in the slipping of grades (Chaudry et al. 2010). The consequences of detention and deportation can affect children's abilities to transition into healthy and productive adolescents. For instance, the undocumented 1.5-generation—young people brought to the United States as children—describe coming into adulthood like waking up to a nightmare (Gonzales 2011). As children, they experience inclusive access to public education, but as adults they are often denied participation in jobs, higher education, and other privileges like driving, traveling, and voting (Abrego 2006; Gonzales 2011).

However, when a child is undocumented, there are more challenges to schooling. Legal status impacts every aspect of the ecological development of young people from health, cognitive, educational, socio-emotional, engagement, labor market, and more (Suárez-Orozco et al. 2011). Coupled with the risk factors of living in poverty and inadequate education, children in immigrant families come of age as they receive a series of societal messages about their cultural, ethnic, and racial group. These messages can be seemingly positive although still detrimental to students. For example, Asian American and Asian students are often perceived as "smart" and "hard-working," perpetuating the "model minority myth" (Lee 1994; Lechica Buenavista 2018). These messages, while they can be interpreted as neutral or benign, ultimately advance ideologies of white supremacy. For others, they can be overtly negative, such as the racist perceptions of all Latina/o children being "illegal." Through societal treatment, media representations, and political sentiments, this social mirroring can influence children's identities in either detrimental or positive ways (Suárez-Orozco 2000). When the social mirror reflects negative images, "adolescents may find it difficult to develop a flexible and adaptive sense of self" (Suárez-Orozco, Todorova, and Qin 2006).

Hence, being undocumented can cause serious risks to any person's well-being, particularly during a time of high anti-immigrant sentiment. Although undocumented status has significant consequences for young people, scholars have noted the optimism present in high school and college students to make their dreams of attaining a college degree possible, despite the many obstacles and challenges (Abrego 2006; Abrego and Gonzalez 2010; Perez et al. 2010; Gonzales 2011). It is also important to note that although undocumented status poses risks for young people's development, it is also a site of resistance and resiliency where young people form alternative ways of living, learning, and overcoming obstacles (Pérez Huber 2017; Muñoz 2018). However, as the next section demonstrates, learning about young children's lives in nuanced ways can sometimes be challenging when relying on interviews alone.

Art Epistemologies

Traditional forms of qualitative research such as interviews have traditionally been better suited for adults and youth, but not so for children, prompting an increasing interest in using art to communicate with preadolescents (Driessnack 2005; Crivello, Camfield, and Woodhead 2009). As children's drawings serve to make meaning out of the world around them, it is important to understand that children's art is based in physical movement and visual awareness (Kellogg 1969). Some scholars have seen the value of art in research and have incorporated it into their methodology. For example, visual arts methods like PhotoVoice, drawings, and performance have been especially useful for children who have experienced traumatic events in their lives such as illnesses, war, and abandonment (Johnson, Pfister, and Vindrola-Padros 2012). By conducting mixed-method studies that incorporate drawings into longer family interviews and ethnographic work, some scholars have used art therapy to understand views on immigration and family formation. However, most have not centered the art created by their participants.

Paul R. Smokowski and Martica Bacallao (2011) create "cultural maps"—drawings with roots in spatial studies—to complement the interview data they have from bicultural children in the United States. The drawings and interviews express the confusion and dilemmas that children face navigating two worlds, whereas the maps help young people express how they can coexist in two locations at once. Similarly, Joanna Dreby and Tim Adkins (2012) use children's drawings as complementary components to the mixed-methods study. For example, children in this study drew family members, and how they imagined life in the United States, illustrating children's notions of how their parents live. Recent studies have highlighted the importance of making music, particularly for immigrant children and refugees in Australia. For example, Kathryn Marsh (2017) posits that art activities for marginalized children are important in creating social inclusion, identity construction, and cultural maintenance of bicultural kids. We know that art education is crucial in schools, particularly for its positive effects on the development and education of marginalized children (Hudson 2020). Considering the research that shows art can be especially helpful for disenfranchised youth, it is concerning that there are massive cuts to arts funding, and particularly in public urban schools, which serve most disenfranchised young people (Shaw 2018).

Methods

This reflexive case study draws on research from 2015 to 2017, when two cohorts of students participated in an after-school weekly theater class I designed and taught. It is important to note that during this time, the country was going through the 2016 U.S. presidential elections, and by the second year of the study, Donald Trump was in his first year in office. The students in my class were all in sixth grade, designated as English-language learners (ELLs) and/or still working to pass the state's grade-level standardized English exam. As part of my doctoral research on immigrant children and art, I chose to partner with the sixth-grade ELL class of newly arrived students, often labeled or perceived as the "difficult" class by the teacher and school administrators.

My study took place in the Watts neighborhood, located in South Central Los Angeles. Historically, Watts has been predominantly an African American community. Then, in the 1980s, the area experienced a demographic shift (Behrens 2011). Currently, Watts is a Mexican and Central American immigrant-receiving community in South Central Los Angeles. Watts was an important site for this research, as a low-income community that often lacked art classes and programs. Watts also has a past of poverty, police brutality, job scarcity, and inadequate food and housing (Diver-Stamnes 1995). Contemporary scholars call this lack of fresh food a "food desert" (Lewis et al. 2011). Children growing up in Watts today confront the same issues their predecessors faced in the 1960s and 1990s. Given these realities, children in the area experience housing, food, and educational insecurities in their daily lives. Coupled with overpolicing, violence, and immigration issues, these stressors can have detrimental consequences for children's development. These stressors are also evident in the school environment.

Although labeled an arts academy, a few years prior, the school did not have art classes. As a new elementary school, some of the challenges they have faced included community violence, changes in school administration, a steady increase in the number of foster care youth, and mothers dying prematurely due to cancer. The school was 95 percent Latina/o, many of whom were recently arrived immigrants, and an even larger proportion were second- and third-generation youth. My class was particularly geared toward children of immigrants and focused on learning about their unique experiences through their stories, drawings, performances, and interviews. I also collected pre- and post-evaluations where the children expressed their thoughts and feelings about their school, community, peers, and families. The program culminated with a school-wide performance where family members and friends were invited to attend.

I visited the sixth graders during their regular class time and conducted observations prior to teaching and working with the students. Once the curriculum was created, I made a callout to any student in the sixth-grade class who was interested in joining an after-school theater class focused on important societal issues. A total of thirteen Latina/o students joined the first year: eight boys and five girls. All had immigrant parents and five had migrated to the United States themselves. We began each class talking about issues in the school and community, such as gangs, littering, environment, and bullying. However, almost every conversation turned to immigration. As I mentioned, during the fall of 2016, the country was undergoing the first presidential election with a woman candidate, Secretary of State Hillary Clinton. This topic inspired many thoughts about the election. Children had many other viewpoints and perspectives about the election, including opinions on Donald Trump, narco leader El Chapo Guzman, and police violence.[2]

Throughout the class, the most pressing and persistent themes discussed were Trump's remarks about Mexican immigrants as "rapists" and the proposed plan to build a wall between the U.S.-Mexico border, made during his 2016 presidential bid speech.

The second year of the theater class, the entire sixth-grade ELL class came to theater once a week for an hour. Over the course of the year, we added after-school rehearsals for the final performance. While there were many challenges in having a large class of thirty-one students, there was more diversity in family countries of origin, including Mexico, Guatemala, El Salvador, and Honduras, as well as students from multiple generations in the United States (i.e., newly arrived to fourth-generation immigrant). One of the most important reasons for including the entire class in the theater program was to ensure more girls participated, resulting in a total of eighteen girls and thirteen boys. As the weeks progressed, girls and shy boys started to come out of their shells and began to work on projecting their voice and presence. Although many of the children were born in the United States, and U.S. citizens, there were constant conversations about Donald Trump's unexpected presidential victory. Every week we met, children shared news and personal stories that involved immigration, deportation fears, the U.S.-Mexico wall, and other foreign policy concerns, including relations with North Korea and Russia.

Once we had common concerns to discuss, I introduced image theater (Boal 2000).[3] Students made statues based on the issues that continuously came up in the class. Each student used their body as a canvas and collectively created images that gave life to their stories, concerns, and ideas for possible solutions. Once we had the images created, we activated the images through *actos*.[4] For both years, the final performance was inspired by children's stories and concerns for immigration issues and President Trump. We collaboratively created a story and once our storyboard was complete, children volunteered to play certain roles and came up with lines, including jokes and punchlines. For the final performance, we installed a large projector above the stage that showed the drawings children created; below that, children performed the same story. Parents especially appreciated the images projected; even though they did not all speak English, they could understand what was happening by following the drawings of the plot. As the next section demonstrates, children had many ideas expressed through their imaginative use of art. The main concern they noted every week was

Trump—what he said on the news, the policies he was quickly changing, the wars that could start, and the way immigrant families might be impacted by his deportation-focused plan.

Narratives of Resistance

This section describes the ways children used self-portraits, drawings, theater performances, and storytelling to resist Trump's twitter claims and anti-immigrant proposals. Through these artistic mediums, children expose the fears they have about society, like wars, the border wall, detention, and deportation. They propose alternative possibilities that keep their families united and safe. Ultimately, they are able to develop resilience that would help them cope with difficulties in their lives.

The following example describes how students expressed their concerns in class during a brainstorming activity for drawings for their journals. One morning during a drawing activity, I asked students to draw what they saw on the news or what concerned them. Sergio, who was eleven years old, shared, "[Trump] might like, he could start a war—he could come here and send our families back to our country and we're going to stay—like we're going to stay alone with maybe—how do you call it? An orphanage and with another family." Sergio's drawing revealed that he is mainly concerned with Trump. The image included Trump, North Korea, and "the wall." Sergio shared that he was afraid of the future—the uncertainty of what might happen makes him think the worst. Although this sixth-grade class has students from mixed-status families, which can include parents with and without legal status, Sergio echoed what many of his classmates felt—a fear of being separated from their families. These themes of family separation fear are evident in the following artistic examples.

Self-Portraits

The examples in this section are taken from students who participated in both the painting and theater classes. The first is Diego, who at thirteen years old has decided that he wants to be a professional soccer player. Through a curriculum that centers students' dreams and future aspirations, they get to create a self-portrait that will be permanently installed in the school. Diego decided that if being a soccer player does not work out, then he will be a basketball player or maybe even a football player, although soccer is his first love.

Throughout the theme of the drawing in figure 10.1, Diego demonstrates the importance that sports have in his life. However, the image is strongly juxtaposing Diego's goals by including the face of President Donald Trump. Trump's face has a harsh red cross near the eye but takes up most of the face. This political symbolism informs the viewer of Diego's strong dislike of Trump or what he represents.

Next to the drawing was a description of the art. Diego wrote:

> My name is Diego and I want to be a soccer player and stop DONALD TRUMP from sending immigrants and stop being racist. I'm 13 and when I'm a soccer player, a pro one, I wanna donate my money to hospitals and donate my hair to kids that have cancer. I wanna help others, homeless that lost their jobs and their house, people that can't leave weed, drugs. I'ma help them get a new life and a family. I'ma teach my kids to not mistreat others to help people and to not think they are more than others. To respect others even tho they don't have a job and smell nasty. Homeless are still people and they are like us and need to respect them or let them be.

Diego has many intentions to help others and commit to a variety of causes, yet one of his primary concerns is to stop Donald Trump, something he feels simultaneously responsible for and capable of doing. Diego specifically highlights two issues with the president. The first is the racism he believes Trump embodies, and the second is the possibility of sending immigrants back to their countries of origin. Diego came to the United States from El Salvador with a *coyote* when he was ten.[5] His mom shared that they were separated for a period of two years. She worked very hard to save money to bring him to the United States, but she could only save $1,000 because she was being exploited by her employer as a live-in nanny. She had to ask all the people she knew to lend her money to bring Diego. Ultimately, she collected $10,500 to pay the *coyote*. When Diego made it to the United States, she was so happy to be reunited but had to work long hours for an entire year to pay back all the money she owed. When reunited with his mother in Los Angeles, Diego was happy but had a hard time learning English and would spend a lot of time alone while his mom worked. Although Diego and his mom have been together in the United States for three years, she is constantly worried that

A Practitioner's Case Study of Immigrant Children's Artistic Narratives 293

she could be pulled over for a traffic violation or any other reason that can result in detention and deportation.

During the art class, children loved embodying other people. They would put on fake mustaches, act like they were driving, going to work, or pretend to be a mom. Children also took on roles of power, like portraying the president, military people, bosses, or police officers. One of the many students who resonated with this role-playing was eleven-year-old Marla. Marla was one of the girls who really developed her voice throughout the course of the class. She began the class as a very shy student but volunteered for theater games and icebreakers.

FIGURE 10.1 Diego's self-portrait.

This motivated other girls to participate and be more outspoken. One day during a theater activity, students started talking about violence in their communities. Marla volunteered to play the role of a cop, something only boys had wanted to do. Later, I learned that Marla wants to be a police officer when she grows up but not just any police officer—a *nice* police officer.

When it came time to make the self-portrait (see figure 10.2), Marla personified a police officer holding sunglasses to her face as well as a police hat. Although she is wearing a Dodger's baseball team T-shirt and jeans, she brings in more police enforcement symbolism by standing in front of a Los Angeles Police Department (LAPD) car. Yet contrasting the police car and the accessories is a large thumbs-up-giving Donald Trump with a red denied sign on his face. The large letters next to him say, "We CAN STOP Donald Trump" with the STOP in large red letters. The image of Donald Trump and the statement of stopping him take up as much space on the portrait as Marla does. This image powerfully suggests that to Marla, stopping Donald Trump is part of her identity, equally important as becoming a police officer. For Marla, stopping Donald Trump is almost like her first duty. Donald

Trump takes up space and importance in her personal life, so much so that she must include him in her self-portrait. The artist information statement next to Marla's picture read:

> My name is Marla and I am 11 years old. I will be talking about my portrait. My portrait is about me being a nice police officer. What I mean by that is me stopping DONALD TRUMP FROM SEPARATING FAMILY! Another reason why I want to be a police officer is because it has always been my dream job. I also am doing my dream job because I want to help the community.

FIGURE 10.2 Marla's self-portrait.

Again, we see that the only time Marla capitalizes anything is when she is making a statement about Donald Trump, to stop him and to stop him from separating families through detention and deportation. It is uncertain if she is talking about Trump separating other people's families or if she is referring to her own family. Although the specific family is unknown, the importance of keeping families united is evident and transmitted even with great urgency as part of her own identity. Likewise, it is necessary to look deeper at the career she has chosen. It is interesting to note that she adds the word *nice* before police officer. This implies that there is a difference between "nice" and "mean" police officers. Although she does not talk about police violence, police brutality, or the role that police officers have in her community, her use of the word *nice* posits a criticality about police officers.

Theater

Figure 10.3 is of twelve-year-old Julio, but as he dons a yellow wig he becomes Donald Trump for our play "Los Niños Inmigrantes" or "The Immigrant Children." In this play, Julio (as Trump) parades along the San Diego–

A Practitioner's Case Study of Immigrant Children's Artistic Narratives

FIGURE 10.3 Julio and the wig.

Tijuana border to check out the place where he wants the wall to go up. There, he confronts three children who are crossing the border to reunite with their parents in Los Angeles. As they are crossing, the *coyote* stops the journey when he sees Trump at a distance. As the children and the *coyote* observe Trump, they see Obama enter the scene and begin a conversation with Trump about the wall. The most important part of the play happens here, when Trump gets irritated by the dust at the border and has a powerful sneeze that makes his wig fly off his head. At that point, the audience uproars with laughter and disbelief. Julio (as Trump) enjoys this moment, when he feels that the satire created by the play takes power away from Trump. As the laughter subsides, Trump no longer seems as scary as before. This is the power of art.

For the second year of the class, Trump was also a central character. In the play "Trump vs. Immigrants," Camilo, age twelve, enters the stage during

FIGURE 10.4 Trump vs. immigrants.

the time the main characters of a family are watching the news on TV (figure 10.4). Camilo now plays the role of President Trump, who stands on a chair to make an announcement about the wall for the media, as the family turns around in the background so as to "exit the scene." The audience then sees Camilo stand tall with his hands behind his back to transmit notions of authority and power. In that scene, he declares that the plan for building the wall is underway and the wall will be finished in a month. When he is done talking, he jumps off the chair and the family turns around as the news anchor finishes the news segment that the family was watching. In this play, the role of the media is key. In the scenes with the family, the television is always on, and when the news comes on regarding immigration and Trump, the family gathers attentively around the television. These are the grand entrances of Camilo as Trump, who looks confident and unfazed by the booing that comes from the audience every time he steps on stage.

In this scene, the family is worried that the dad has been detained or deported. Even the dog refuses to play catch because he is depressed. The story recounts how Diego, the main character, is motivated to take action and confront Trump. Diego decides that the next day he will go to school and organize his classmates to march to the border wall and confront Trump. Students at his school are motivated to take action by what they see on the news and the racist teacher who wears a "Make America Great Again" hat in class. As they make their way to the border with their signs and banners they confront Trump, who is giving a speech. The play ends with two "Men in Black / CIA agents" coming to announce that the ballots were wrong and that Trump is actually not president, yet neither is Hillary Clinton. To everyone's surprise, the CIA brings back President Obama for a third term while government agents carry Trump away as he kicks and screams and the audience enthusiastically claps.

Drawings

Of all the issues that children discussed as concerning during the election and Trump's first year of presidency, the building of the U.S.-Mexico border wall received the most attention. Aside from being afraid to be separated from their family members or for their parents to be detained, children did not want a wall to be constructed. The existence of the border wall meant to the children that they would never see family members on the other side who live in Mexico or Central America. To others, they were worried that if a wall existed, more people would die on the border when trying to cross. One of these sentiments made its way to a theater prop that Camilo, eleven years old, made during one of our improvised skits. Camilo's family has been in the United States for two generations before him, starting with his grandparents, who migrated from Mexico. Camilo speaks Spanish and is worried about Donald Trump's policies because he feels that although he has papers, he can still be targeted for being brown. In one of the theater activities, he assumed the role of Trump and debated others who acted like Hillary during the election. The debate they chose focused on who was going to pay for the wall. As Camilo was making his arguments for why Mexico should pay for the wall, he paused the entire performance and ran to get a piece of scrap paper. He came up with a contract (figure 10.5), or, as he called it, "the

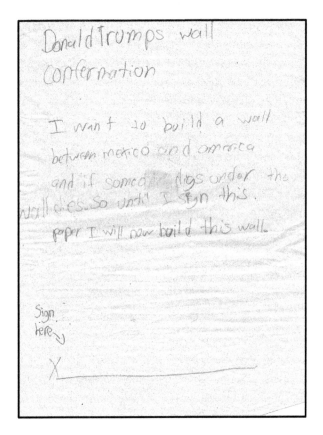

FIGURE 10.5 "Donald Trumps Wall Confermation."

confirmation" of the wall, titled "Donald Trumps Wall Confermation." The accompanying description reads, "I want to build a wall between mexico and america and if someone digs under the wall dies. So until I sign this paper I will now build this wall." The bottom of the page has an "x" and a line that is labeled "sign here."

To Camilo, the wall serves as a divider not only between nations but also between life and death. He does not see the wall as a tool that will ultimately stop all immigrants crossing into the United States. Rather, he thinks of ways immigrants can outsmart the wall; as he suggests, people can dig under the wall, but he also believes that people can die attempting to dig under. He also believes that signing a piece of paper can make this wall happen, without any other approval from other parts of the government like Congress. The power

A Practitioner's Case Study of Immigrant Children's Artistic Narratives

that Trump holds as president is paramount in their eyes. Although they may not know about the judicial process, they are keen to Trump's performance of certainty and authority when he speaks. Camilo goes on to play the role of Trump in our final performance for the entire school and family. Here, he uses the same word choices that Trump does and the same confidence in having all the power and the last word on any matter.

The first year I taught this class, in 2016, students, like the rest of the nation, were incredibly consumed by the election. Often, children were appalled by the statements Trump would make. At the same time, there was an excitement about the possibility of the first woman president of the United States. Other students were saddened that Barack Obama was no longer going to be president. The next image (figure 10.6) describes one student's thoughts about the election in 2016. I asked everyone to draw what they wanted to happen in the election, including who they wanted to win. Lalo, age eleven, drew this image and wrote a statement for it that read, "Trump lost the election and hillary won. Trump lost because no one likes him only a few people like his wife and his son." In the image, both characters are stand-

FIGURE 10.6 Trump lost the election and Hillary won.

ing with arms on their waists, in what looks like a powerful pose. Yet Trump has a deep dark frown with bloodshot eyes and dark circles around them, positioned slightly behind his opponent. Conversely, Clinton looks pleasant and is smiling. Behind them waves a great big American flag.

Discussion

In various contemporary social movements, children have become the spokespeople against injustice (Rodriguez Vega 2015, 2018, 2023). Young people have taken on this new and difficult role due to the extreme dehumanization of adults and communities of color. Like Sophie Cruz, who ran up to the pope to deliver a letter asking for help for her undocumented parents (Walker 2015); or Katherine Figueroa, who was the first person to ask President Obama for administrative relief for her parents, who were in detention for more than three months (Rodriguez Vega 2015); or nine-year-old Zianna Oliphant, who spoke on CNN asking for an end to police brutality and the killings of Black people (CNN 2016). To understand what is occurring in our society, we must look to the concerns of young people who courageously confront the challenges of our time. Art and theater help us understand children's complex thoughts and fears regarding detention and deportation, while allowing them a way to process their fears. My work suggests that educators and researchers should include artistic and expressive methods when working with children and develop new methodologies that include performative and visual tools, not only for the candid and descriptive information they produce but also for the meditative and reflective properties of the art-making process. These methods are particularly powerful for working with children who are shy, learning a new language, or have experienced trauma in their lives. As a precautionary measure to not retraumatize children, it is essential that school administrators, teachers, researchers, and practitioners be in contact with a school psychologist and have resources available for families and children who might need more professional assistance with matters of mental health.

Although children in Watts were and are experiencing fears of familial separation, art ultimately allows them to cope in empowering ways. We know that arts programs help boost student academic performance and interpersonal development, and critical thinking skills (Shuler 1996; Southgate and Roscigno 2009). *What does it mean when art programs are being cut at disproportionate rates in schools where the majority of students are Black and Brown?* During the time of this study, Trump and Secretary of Education Betsy DeVos released a budget to cut $27 million in arts education programs (Brown et al. 2017), and later Trump threatened to terminate the National Endowment for the Arts (NEA) (McGlone 2020). Although the budget for arts was secured, it is imperative that policymakers consider the importance of art programs for Latina/o/x, immigrant, and other vulnerable children. Unfortunately, when it comes to immigration, the Biden administration has not kept all promises made to end migrant detention at the border, and in fact many would argue it has gotten worse. When it comes to art, in 2022 President Biden increased the budget of the National Endowment for the Arts by $27 million; however, schools in inner-city communities continue to face a scarcity of arts programs. To refuse to consider the importance of arts education is an overt act of neglect for our children and the future of the country. The narratives of resistance to detention, deportation, and family separation are powerful and can have a profound impact on the resources needed for this quickly changing and frightening world. Through their critical analysis of media, rhetoric, and policy, children who create art resist the ways their lives are deemed disposable by the Trump administration and others. As such, practitioners like artists and activists can help children of immigrants respond to detention and deportation fears in ways that develop resilience, which they can harness in future moments of political repression.

Notes

1. All names are pseudonyms and all information is used with youth, parental, and institutional review board approval.

2. Joaquín Archivaldo Guzmán Loera, more popularly known as "El Chapo," is considered one of the most powerful drug traffickers in the world from the Mexican state of Sinaloa. During the time of this study, El Chapo was captured by the United States in Mexico and extradited to New York City. Later he was sentenced to lifetime imprisonment.

3. Image theater uses the body to create sculptures or frozen images that can represent issues facing the participants or viewers. Through the molding of images/bodies, participants can gain depth and visual understanding of those issues. Images can also be made to represent solutions to problems people might be trying to solve. There is also a way to activate images by adding voice or sounds to each of the frozen participants. Those on the outside looking at the image can treat it like a gallery of sorts, where you can pay attention to the way people create body positions, dynamics, facial expressions, and relationships between other images or frozen statues.

4. An *acto* can be defined as a "short, improvised scene dealing with the experience of its participants" (Huerta 1977, 46). Although popularized in the United States by El Teatro Campesino, *actos* are not unique to Chicanxs. The *acto* should inspire an audience to social action and express the thoughts and lived situations of the people. According to Valdez (1971), the most important part of an *acto* is not the ideas of the artist or individual but the social vision of the community.

5. *Coyote* is a term used to describe a person who helps undocumented immigrants migrate into the United States.

References

Abrego, Leisy J. 2006. "'I Can't Go to College because I Don't Have Papers': Incorporation Patterns of Latino Undocumented Youth." *Latino Studies* 4 (3): 212–31.

Abrego, Leisy J., and Roberto G. Gonzales. 2010. "Blocked Paths, Uncertain Futures: The Postsecondary Education and Labor Market Prospects of Undocumented Latino Youth." *Journal of Education for Students Placed at Risk* 15 (1–2): 144–57.

Ayers, Esther. 2013. "Is There Trauma and Resilience in Adolescents Who Experienced Immigration Raids? An Annotated Bibliography of Research." *Senior Honors Theses & Projects*. http://commons.emich.edu/cgi/viewcontent.cgi?article=1328&context=honors.

Batalova, Jeanne, Michael Fix, and Mark Greenberg. 2019. "Millions Will Feel Chilling Effects of U.S. Public-Charge Rule That Is Also Likely to Reshape Legal Immigration." Migration Policy Institute, August. https://www.migrationpolicy.org/news/chilling-effects-us-public-charge-rule-commentary.

Behrens, Zach. 2011. "Maps: A Quick Look at the Changing Demographics of L.A., 1940 to the Present." PBS SoCal, January 24. https://www.kcet.org/socal-focus/maps-a-quick-look-at-the-changing-demographics-of-la-1940-to-the-present.

Boal, Augusto. 2000. *Theater of the Oppressed*. New York: Pluto Press.

Briggs, Laura. 2020. *Taking Children: A History of American Terror*. Oakland: University of California Press.

Brown, Emma, et al. 2017. "Trump's First Full Education Budget: Deep Cuts to Public School Programs in Pursuit of School Choice." *Washington Post*, May 17.

Capps, Randy, Rosa Maria Castaneda, Ajay Chaudry, and Robert Santos. 2007. *Paying the Price: The Impact of Immigration Raids on America's Children*. Washington, D.C.: Urban Institute.

Chaudry, Ajay, Randolph Capps, Juan Pedroza, Rosa Maria Castaneda, Robert Santos, and Molly M. Scott. 2010. *Facing Our Future: Children in the Aftermath of Immigration Enforcement*. Washington, D.C.: Urban Institute.

CNN. 2016. "Girl's Speech Inspires City of Charlotte After Shooting." https://www.cnn.com/videos/us/2016/09/30/zianna-oliphant-charlotte-city-council-sot-lemon-tonight.cnn.

Crivello, Gina, Laura Camfield, and Martin Woodhead. 2009. "How Can Children Tell Us About Their Wellbeing? Exploring the Potential of Participatory Research Approaches Within Young Lives." *Social Indicators Research* 90 (1): 51–72.

Diver-Stamnes, Ann C. 1995. *Lives in the Balance: Youth, Poverty, and Education in Watts*. Albany: State University of New York Press.

Dreby, Joanna. 2012. *How Today's Immigration Enforcement Policies Impact Children, Families, and Communities: A View from the Ground*. Washington, D.C.: Center for American Progress.

Dreby, Joanna, and Tim Adkins. 2012. "The Strength of Family Ties: How U.S. Migration Shapes Children's Ideas of Family." *Childhood* 19 (2): 169–87.

Driessnack, Martha. 2005. "Children's Drawings as Facilitators of Communication: A Meta-Analysis." *Journal of Pediatric Nursing* 20 (6): 415–23.

Gonzales, Roberto G. 2011. "Learning to Be Illegal: Undocumented Youth and Shifting Legal Contexts in the Transition to Adulthood." *American Sociological Review* 76 (4): 602–19.

Hudson, Audrey. 2020. "Learning from a Young Indigenous Artist: What Can Hip-Hop Teach Us?" *Art Education* 73 (1): 18–22.

Huerta, Jorge A. 1977. "Chicano Agit-Prop: The Early Actos of El Teatro Campesino." *Latin American Theatre Review* 10 (2): 45–58.

Johnson, Ginger A., Anne E. Pfister, and Cecilia Vindrola-Padros. 2012. "Drawings, Photos, and Performances: Using Visual Methods with Children." *Visual Anthropology Review* 28 (2): 164–78.

Kellogg, Rhoda. 1969. *Analysing Children's Art*. Palo Alto, Calif.: Mayfield.

Lechica Buenavista, Tracy. 2018. "Model (Undocumented) Minorities and 'Illegal' Immigrants: Centering Asian Americans and US Carcerality in Undocumented Student Discourse." *Race Ethnicity and Education* 21 (1): 78–91.

Lee, Stacey J. 1994. "Behind the Model-Minority Stereotype: Voices of High- and Low-Achieving Asian American Students." *Anthropology & Education Quarterly* 25 (4): 413–29.

Lewis, LaVonna Blair, Lark Galloway-Gilliam, Gwendolyn Flynn, Jonathan Nomachi, LaTonya Chavis Keener, and David D. Sloane. 2011. "Transforming the Urban Food Desert from the Grassroots Up: A Model for Community Change." *Family & Community Health* 34 (January–March): S92–S101.

Marsh, Kathryn. 2017. "Creating Bridges: Music, Play and Well-Being in the Lives of Refugee and Immigrant Children and Young People." *Music Education Research* 19 (1): 60–73.

McGlone, Peggy. 2020. "Trump Budget Again Calls for the Elimination of Federal Arts Agencies." *Washington Post*, February 10.

Montoya-Galvez, Camilo. 2020. "2019: The Year Trump 'Effectively' Shut Off Asylum at the Border and Restricted Immigration." CBS News, January 5. https://www.cbsnews.com/news/immigration-2019-the-year-trump-restricted-legal-immigration-and-effectively-shut-off-asylum-at-the-border/.

Muñoz, Susana M. 2018. "Unpacking Legality Through La Facultad and Cultural Citizenship: Critical and Legal Consciousness Formation for Politicized Latinx Undocumented Youth Activists." *Equity & Excellence in Education* 51 (1): 78–91.

Nava, Erika J. 2014. "Federal Immigration Reform Would Help New Jersey's Striving Immigrants and Boost the State's Economy." New Jersey Policy Perspective, January.

Passel, Jeffrey S. 2011. "Demography of Immigrant Youth: Past, Present, and Future." *Future of Children* 21 (1): 19–41.

Perez, William, Roberta Espinoza, Karina Ramos, Heidi Coronado, and H. Richard Cortes. 2010. "Civic Engagement Patterns of Undocumented Mexican Students." *Journal of Hispanic Higher Education* 9 (3): 245–65.

Pérez Huber, Lindsay. 2017. "Healing Images and Narratives: Undocumented Chicana/Latina Pedagogies of Resistance." *Journal of Latinos and Education* 16 (4): 374–89.

Rodriguez Vega, Silvia. 2015. "From Barbies to Boycotts: How Immigration Raids in Arizona Created a Ten-Year Old Activist." *InterActions: UCLA Journal of Education and Information Studies* 11 (2).

Rodriguez Vega, Silvia. 2018. "Borders and Badges: Arizona's Children Confront Detention and Deportation Through Art." *Latino Studies* 16 (3): 310–40.

Rodriguez Vega, Silvia. 2023. *Drawing Deportation: Art and Resistance Among Immigrant Children*. New York: New York University Press.

Sasani, Ava. 2023. "Biden Administration Sued over Asylum Appointment App That 'Does Not Work.'" *The Guardian*, August 7.

Shaw, Ryan D. 2018. "The Vulnerability of Urban Elementary School Arts Programs: A Case Study." *Journal of Research in Music Education* 65 (4): 393–415.

Shuler, Scott C. 1996. "Why High School Students Should Study the Arts." *Music Educators Journal* 83 (1): 22–26.

Smokowski, Paul R., and Martica Bacallao. 2011. *Becoming Bicultural: Risk, Resilience, and Latino Youth*. New York: New York University Press.

Southgate, Darby E., and Vincent J. Roscigno. 2009. "The Impact of Music on Childhood and Adolescent Achievement." *Social Science Quarterly* 90 (1): 4–21.

Suárez-Orozco, Carola. 2000. "Identities Under Siege: Immigration Stress and Social Mirroring Among the Children of Immigrants." In *Cultures Under Siege: Collective Violence and Trauma*, edited by Antonius C. G. M. Robben and Marcelo M. Suárez-Orozco, 194–226. New York: Cambridge University Press.

Suárez-Orozco, Carola, Irina Todorova, and Desirée Baolian Qin. 2006. "The Well-Being of Immigrant Adolescents: A Longitudinal Perspective on Risk and Protective Factors." In *The Crisis in Youth Mental Health: Critical Issues and Effective Programs*, vol. 2, *Disorders in Adolescence*, edited by Francisco A. Villarruel and Tom Luster, 53–83. Westport, Conn.: Praeger.

Suárez-Orozco, Carola, Hirokazu Yoshikawa, Robert T. Teranishi, and Marcelo M. Suárez-Orozco. 2011. "Growing Up in the Shadows: The Developmental Implications of Unauthorized Status." *Harvard Educational Review* 81 (3): 438–73.

Sullivan, Eileen, and Colbi Edmonds. 2023. "Biden, the Border, and Why a New Wall Is Going Up." *New York Times*, October 6.

Szkupinski Quiroga, Selina, Dulce M. Medina, and Jennifer Glick. 2014. "In the Belly of the Beast: Effects of Anti-immigration Policy on Latino Community Members." *American Behavioral Scientist* 58 (13): 1723–42.

Trisi, Danilo, and Guillermo Herrera. 2018. "Administration Actions Against Immigrant Families Harming Children Through Increased Fear, Loss of Needed Assistance." Center for Budget and Policy Priorities, Washington, D.C.

Tuck, Eve, and Rubén Gaztambide-Fernández. 2013. "Curriculum, Replacement, and Settler Futurity." *Journal of Curriculum Theorizing* 29 (1): 72–89.

Valdez, Luis. 1971. *Actos*. San Juan Bautista, Calif.: Cucaracha Press.

Verea, Mónica. 2018. "Anti-Immigrant and Anti-Mexican Attitudes and Policies During the First 18 Months of the Trump Administration." *Norteamérica* 13 (2).

Walker, Jade. 2015. "5-Year-Old Girl Delivers Message on Immigration to Pope Francis." *Huffpost*, September 24. https://www.huffpost.com/entry/sofia-cruz-pope-francis_n_5603aea1e4b00310edfa1092.

Yoshikawa, Hirokazu. 2011. *Immigrants Raising Citizens: Undocumented Parents and Their Children*. New York: Russell Sage Foundation.

Yoshikawa, Hirokazu, Carola Suárez-Orozco, and Roberto G. Gonzales. 2017. "Unauthorized Status and Youth Development in the United States: Consensus Statement of the Society for Research on Adolescence." *Journal of Research on Adolescence* 27 (1): 4–19.

CONCLUSION

Toward a Decarceral Future

Reflections on the Practicability of Abolishing Migrant Child Detention

SARAH J. DIAZ

In a book titled *Kids in Cages*, a book that describes the harm and resistance experienced by migrant children in the U.S. immigration legal system, it seems fitting to end the dialogue with the consideration that there might be a better way. This chapter was developed through the thought partnership of immigration system–involved law students whose nexus to the issue informs this narrative.[1] This closing chapter invites the reader to explore components of the abolitionist perspective and reimagine a world in which migrant children are treated simply as children—worthy of love, voices respected, embraced in a system that seeks to both reduce the harm they experience and preserve their inherent human dignity. To do so, this chapter necessarily engages a dialogue about the propriety of considering the abolition of migrant child detention as not only a tool for but also the end goal of resistance to kids in cages.

A Note on Abolition

> Radical simply means "grasping things at the root."
> —ANGELA DAVIS, "LET US ALL RISE TOGETHER"

Abolition is defined as "the action or an act of abolishing (putting an end to) a system, practice, or institution."[2] Abolition has deep roots in the effort to end slavery, and the movement has been applied over the years as a form of critical resistance to inhumane practices generally connected to state violence—take, for example, the movement to abolish the death penalty, the movement to abolish prison systems, or the movement to defund the police (Davis 1983; Galliher, Ray, and Cook 1992; United Nations Office of the High Commissioner for Human Rights 2012; Kushner 2019; Ray 2020; Death Penalty Information Center n.d.). The state violence that persists exists as a postcolonial construct inextricably tied to racism.

Indeed, history demonstrates that "the triumph of hierarchy required coercive and persuasive forces to coalesce in the service of domination" (Gilmore 2022), and, while race is divorced from any biological basis for categorization, race has nonetheless underpinned constructs of domination in the Western world (Gilmore 2022). Since colonial times, race has been inextricably linked to systems of oppression, from slavery to Jim Crow, from the war on drugs to the mass incarceration and police brutality of contemporary society (Gilmore 2022). Abolitionists recognize that these systems are not broken; rather, "the system[s'] extreme racial disparities and daily dehumanization do not result from a glitch in the system but rather from the smooth functioning of a system designed to control and contain poor, Black, and brown people" (Sultan and Herskind 2020). Yet abolition is not merely concerned with dismantling oppressive systems. Instead, abolition is "an invitation into finding new answers to the problem of harm and into building new ways to prevent harm in the first place" (Purnell 2020). Abolition, looking forward, is "a long-term project and a practice around creating the conditions that would allow for the dismantling of prisons, policing, and surveillance and the creation of institutions that actually work to keep us safe and are not fundamentally oppressive" (Kaba 2017).

In general, abolition rejects reform and reformist strategies, which serve to maintain or expand "the reach of the system through social control or violence" (Detention Watch Network n.d.). However, abolition recognizes that some reformist strategies are, in fact, "abolitionist or transformative, moving us closer to liberation by chipping away at . . . incarceration" or other systems of oppression (Detention Watch Network n.d.).

To accomplish these ends, abolitionist theory thus requires the deconstruction of false narratives, the denormalization of violence, the reprioritization of human dignity, and the reimagination of a world in which our legal systems reduce harm rather than cause it. Abolition is the ultimate form of resistance—not one characterized by rebellion but instead a principled movement that pleads for equal treatment and mutual respect of all people moving through American socio-legal landscapes.

Abolition in the Context of Immigration

> Give me your tired, your poor, your huddled masses yearning to breathe free.
>
> —EMMA LAZARUS, "THE NEW COLOSSUS"

The contemporary narrative on our immigration system is that this system is a carefully crafted rule of law designed with purpose to be fair and have process. We are a nation of laws, and we are a nation of immigrants. If the law is broken, then the blame must be placed squarely on the immigrant who broke the law. All the consequences, then, of breaking that law are the natural result of the immigrant's actions. Living in the shadows, carceral detention, family separation, etcetera, are the appropriate consequences brought upon themselves for breaking the law—not getting in line.[3]

But what if the system is not a carefully crafted rule of law designed with purpose to be fair and have process? What if, instead, the system makes lawful entry a virtual impossibility (García Hernández 2014)? What if, by all accounts, the system serves to control and contain Black and Brown migrants (Kamasaki 2021)? What if the system is designed to create a permanent exploitable underclass of undocumented workers?[4] What if detention is not necessary to the immigration process but is instead a deeply lucrative business—the financial cost of which is born by taxpayers (Detention Watch Network 2011; Altman and Ascherio 2020; Bryant 2022)? What if the system actually abuses the rule of law to accomplish these nefarious ends, and the means by which these ends are accomplished exact extraordinary harm to humankind—just not *American* humankind? What then, does one do with the system?

There is significant existing literature that suggests that the immigration system manipulates the rule of law to accomplish racist, postcolonial ends (Detention Watch Network 2011; Gruberg 2015; O'Connor 2019). History is replete with examples of the creation of an underclass of exploitable Black and Brown Other. From the Chinese Exclusion Act to Operation Wetback and beyond, U.S. immigration law can be clearly viewed through the lens of containment and control of the racialized other—exploiting their labor while ensuring they cannot achieve full civic participation or rights.

Abolition and Migrant Child Detention

> Once groups are marked as "vulnerable" ... those groups become reified as definitionally "vulnerable," fixed in a political position of powerlessness and lack of agency. All the power belongs to the state and international institutions that are now supposed to offer them protection and advocacy.
>
> —LAUREN HEIDBRINK, "ANATOMY OF A CRISIS"

The focus on false narratives in this closing chapter relates specifically to what has been repeatedly stated, or, in other words, what has been learned about child detention. It is often explained that children are detained in the United States in order to protect them from the dangers of exploitation and abuse. Take, for example, the *New York Times* article "Alone and Exploited," which details the harrowing experiences of migrant children exploited for their work in extremely dangerous working conditions that often violate child labor laws in the United States (Dreier 2023). These articles paint a picture of the government (specifically the Office of Refugee Resettlement [ORR]) as a child welfare agency, abdicating its responsibilities and releasing children without regard for their safety.

As explored in "'I'm Not an Animal. I'm a Girl,'" this concept of vulnerability can tend to perpetuate structural violence. The narrative of child detention as child protection starts with the proposition that the laws triggering their detention *care* about the well-being of migrant children; that they are detained *for child welfare purposes, for their own protection, and to attend to their best interests.* This proposition is fundamentally untrue. Children, like adults, are detained by the Department of Homeland Security (DHS) pursuant to its authority to do so under immigration enforcement laws, not child welfare laws (Smith 2019, 2021). Children avoid transfer to Immigration and Customs Enforcement (ICE) custody only by virtue of the Flores litigation and the legal determination made under immigration laws with respect to the child's status as an unaccompanied child (Homeland Security Act 2002). Like adults, children are held pending the outcome of their immigration case. Like adults, some children may be released (adults via bond and children via family reunification or sponsorship). Like adults, children can be deported from custody even if they have family in the United States. Like adults, there is no best-interests assessment when sending them from custody back to their home country.[5] As we hear in the chapter "Emerging into

Darkness," on their eighteenth birthday, children are ushered off to county jail under the existing basis for their custody: DHS's authority to detain and deport. Unaccompanied migrant children are not detained in the United States for child welfare purposes; determinations about their release to family members are not subject to child welfare law and protections. Rather, migrant children are subject to detention as a component of the immigration law enforcement prerogatives of detention and removal. To call it otherwise confuses the objective of their detention.

Assuming, for the sake of argument, that children were detained for child welfare purposes or for their own protection, then it *must* be recognized that the United States acknowledges how harmful congregate care detention is for children. For years, advocates for children in the context of domestic child protection have sought to eliminate congregate care, and, starting in 2018, the U.S. Congress began actively defunding congregate care in the domestic child welfare context. The Family First Prevention Services Act was purposefully implemented with the intention of keeping children safely with their families "to avoid the trauma that results when children are placed in out-of-home care" (Child Welfare Information Gateway n.d.). This federal legislation was the direct result of researchers and advocates exhaustively fighting to explain how deleterious congregate care detention can be to children even for short periods of time. The very facilities that were shut down because American law and policy deemed them unfit for the development and well-being of American children were attempting to keep their doors open by gaining access to government contracts to detain migrant children. Detention is harmful to *all* children, not just American children. Child detention should not be the status quo in *any* system.

Denormalize Violence: The Known Harms of Migrant Child Detention

> No matter what it's called, a cage is still a cage.
> —SATSUKI INA, "A CAGE IS STILL A CAGE"

When using the phrase "kids in cages," one may only conceptualize the *hieleras*, or so-called ice boxes used by the DHS at the U.S.-Mexico border. However, a cage, as this book sets out and as abolitionists understand, need only restrict liberty to wreak havoc on a child's body, mind, and soul.

Unraveling the narrative that children must be detained for their own protection allows one to denormalize the violence exacted on migrant children through the immigration system and particularly with respect to their detention in congregate care. Children are harmed by detention—no matter what the facility is called (shelter, staff secure, residential treatment center) (Linton et al. 2017), no matter how long they are detained (Diaz and Vargas 2023).

> As an adult, I became a psychotherapist specializing in community trauma. From my professional training and experience, and from my own assessments of children held in family detention, I know the harm of childhood incarceration is deep and insidious. The trauma often manifests as hyper-vigilance, uncontrollable bouts of crying, sleep disturbance, and depressed mood. Incarceration also fractures the child's sense of self, leading to feelings of shame and humiliation that the child internalizes and then acts out on others. The chronic stress of mass incarceration can alter the child's developing nervous system to be over-sensitized to perceive threat; this hypersensitivity can lead to impulsivity, attention difficulties, mood swings, difficulties with intimacy and attachment, drug and alcohol addiction, avoidant behavior, and anger control difficulties—post-traumatic stress disorder, often misdiagnosed as anxiety or depression. I continue to have trauma-driven reactions from my own childhood incarceration. (Ina 2021)

This narrative is not unique. Studies indicate pervasive negative physical and emotional symptoms among detained children (Mares and Jureidini 2004; Lorek et al. 2009; Kronick, Rousseau, and Cleveland 2015; Linton et al. 2017). Research indicates that post-traumatic symptoms do not necessarily disappear upon release of the child from congregate care (Kronick et al. 2015; Linton et al. 2017). According to one study, "Young detainees may experience developmental delay and poor psychological adjustment" (Linton et al. 2017). And another explains, "Qualitative reports about detained unaccompanied immigrant children in the United States found high rates of posttraumatic stress disorder, anxiety, depression, suicidal ideation, and other behavioral problems. Additionally, expert consensus has concluded that even brief detention can cause psychological trauma and induce long-term mental health risks for children" (Linton et al. 2017). This research, and additional forms of the harm of detention, is borne out by previous chapters, especially "'Not Our Children.'" This research is entirely consistent with the research offered to support the Family First Prevention Services Act, which ended congregate care for American children. This level of harm is experienced across congregate care detention, not just detention by the DHS. Indeed, the research cited here is specific to the experience of unaccompanied child migrants in the care of the Department of Health and Human Services' (HHS) Office of Refugee Resettlement.

Migrant child detention is a form of legal violence that is normalized in American society because it is "embedded in the body of law that . . . purports to have the positive objective of protecting rights or controlling behavior for the general good, [and yet] simultaneously gives rise to practices that harm a particular social group" (Menjívar and Abrego 2012, 1387). While proffered as a mechanism to protect children, detention is plainly understood to cause harm (Committee on the Rights of the Child 2012; United Nations High Commissioner for Refugees 2017).

Harm, in this system, begets harm. Migrant children, fleeing trauma (often in the form of abuse or persecution), are met with state violence that invariably leads to more harm. Children are separated from caregivers at the border and placed in congregate care, where "any expression of this trauma can be used against a child, and—in certain circumstances—can be the basis for placing a child in an even more restrictive setting."[6]

Reprioritize Human Dignity

> Whereas recognition of the inherent dignity and of the equal and inalienable rights of all members of the human family is the foundation of freedom, justice and peace in the world.
>
> —UN DECLARATION ON HUMAN RIGHTS (1948)

Human rights law is built upon the foundational proposition that "all human beings are born free and equal in dignity and rights[; that they] are endowed with reason and conscience and should act towards one another in a spirit of brotherhood."[7] The plea that American legal systems respect human dignity is not an intangible request devoid of logical or legal underpinnings. Respect for human dignity belies the universal advancement of human rights across the world. Nearly every country besides the United States ascribes to human rights mechanisms with enforcement power.[8] Only in the United States (among some other countries in whose company we should not keep, as they are renowned for their human rights abuses) does the rhetoric of human rights (the rights of the people against their government) get mired in overtures for state sovereignty.

Human dignity is understood to be the bedrock of all human rights. Human rights exist to ensure each person's right to experience human dignity. For example, the UN Declaration on the Protection of All Persons from Being Subjected to Torture recognizes that "any act of torture or other cruel, inhuman or degrading treatment or punishment is an offence to human dignity and shall be condemned as a denial of the purposes of the Charter of the United Nations and as a violation of the human rights and fundamental freedoms proclaimed in the Universal Declaration of Human Rights."[9] Even the right to life contemplates, as central, the right to human dignity: "The right to life . . . concerns the entitlement of individuals to be free from acts and omissions that are intended or may be expected to cause their unnatural or premature death, *as well as to enjoy a life with dignity.*"[10]

The immigration system prioritizes law enforcement objectives that are often incompatible with respect for human dignity. The lucrative business of immigration detention makes centralizing human dignity a lofty goal.[11] Nonetheless, abolition of immigrant prisons must be the goal (Signer 2021). With respect to children, abolition of congregate care should be the goal.

Moreover, to effectively centralize the dignity of children, international law calls for the recognition of children's agency, demanding that states recognize "the capacity of the child to form an autonomous opinion."[12]

> In the case of young people in particular, a focus on vulnerability additionally ignores that children make decisions and that those decisions are influenced by a variety of factors and relationships (Caneva 2014; Heidbrink 2020). Discourses of trauma, exploitation, and risk produce young people's vulnerability, and thus, they are reliant upon the interventions of well-meaning (adult) professionals to guide their psychic and physical development into adulthood (Heidbrink 2014). The child victim in need of saving usurps power from the child and places it in the hands of the expert "to give voice" to victimised children. Thus, the very professionals intending to provide protection may render young people voiceless and agentless. (Heidbrink 2021)

To give dignity to migrant children, then, requires the provision of agency and the recognition that, while vulnerable, migrant children are still entitled to the full realization of their human rights. The realization can only be accomplished when caregivers reject the profound, long-lasting negative impact of detention on children's health, well-being, and cognitive development (International Organization for Migration, United Nations High Commissioner for Refugees, and UNICEF 2022). To do this requires a commitment to imagining a system that reduces such harm.

Reimagine a System of Harm Reduction

> We used to call 911 for everything except snitching. Now, we have not called in years.
> —DERECKA PURNELL, *BECOMING ABOLITIONISTS*

Some facets of American society are sewn so deeply into the fabric of American life that one cannot imagine what could happen if it did not exist. Defund the police? Abolish the border? At times it can be difficult to comprehend a world in which these structural societal elements do not exist. Yet, for nearly every purportedly "radical" call for abolition, there is a case study, a pilot, or a model that exists to demonstrate its effectiveness. Abolition of migrant child detention is no exception.

If Not Detention, Then What?

> Abolitionists reject the false choice of putting someone in a cage or doing nothing.
> —REINA SULTAN AND MICAH HERSKIND, "WHAT IS ABOLITION, AND WHY DO WE NEED IT?"

The movement to abolish migrant child detention is not a radical proposition. It does not even require the creation of a novel system. In fact, the abolition of migrant child detention (while the implementation may be imperfect) is already the commitment of Europe, with a significant number of European states having outlawed migrant child detention under their domestic law frameworks.[13] Abolition of congregate care detention is the stated goal for American children (U.S. Government Accountability Office 2015); HHS's own 2015 report indicates that "child development theory and best practices confirm that children should be placed in family-like settings that are developmentally appropriate and least restrictive. . . . Congregate care should not be used as a default placement setting due to a lack of appropriate family based care" (U.S. Department of Health and Human Services 2015).

Abolition of congregate care detention is the goal for American children and migrant children in Europe for extremely pragmatic reasons, not merely child protection. Research suggests that proposed alternatives to congregate care detention of children "have been shown to achieve up to 95 per cent compliance rates and up to 69 per cent voluntary and independent return rates for refused cases" (International Organization for Migration, United Nations High Commissioner for Refugees, and UNICEF 2022, 5). If care and integration are the goal, then there are significant "benefits of placing migrant and asylum-seeking children in foster care, including to learn the local language and have access to individual support and guidance" (International Organization for Migration et al. 2022, 5). All research suggests that "investing in appropriate care arrangements is therefore a more effective means of ensuring the protection and safety of children, keeping them off the streets while allowing them to develop more harmoniously, and at the same time ensuring a more effective approach to migration" (International Organization for Migration, United Nations High Commissioner for Refugees, and UNICEF 2022, 5).

The Council of Europe, of which nearly every single European country is a member state, has already laid out through Parliamentary Resolution the mechanics for the abolition of child detention for its member states (Council of Europe 2014). The Parliamentary Assembly has called on its member states to "introduce legislation prohibiting the detention of children for immigration reasons and ensure its full implementation in practice" (Section 9.3). The Resolution further calls upon state parties to "adopt alternatives to detention that meet the best interests of the child and allow children to remain with their family members and/or guardians in non-custodial, community-based contexts while their immigration status is being resolved" (Section 9.7). The Resolution calls for adequate resources to be committed to alternatives to detention (Section 9.8) and cites community placement through the Child-sensitive Community Assessment and Placement (CCAP) Model (Corlett et al. 2012) as the ideal implementation of alternatives to migrant child detention (Section 9.9). Beyond a foster care setting, community models include "open reception centres, accommodation within ethnic communities, shelters, as well as independent and supported accommodation" (Corlett et al. 2012, 73).[14] Again, while these laws and models may leave something to be desired in their implementation, they offer an opportunity to disentangle the notion that moving away from migrant child detention is a radical proposition. Instead, the resolution against congregate care child detention is a step toward abolition of a system that harms Black and Brown children.

These efforts are already underway in the United States. Borrowing principles from the international law and domestic child welfare systems, groups like the Young Center for Immigrant Children's Rights (2020) have literally already begun "Reimagining Children's Immigration Proceedings." Consistent with the chapter "Centering Children's Experiences," the Young Center proposal prioritizes principles that center the child's best interests and establish that no child should be held in congregate care, that immediate release is most appropriate, and that open community care settings or foster care placement should only be relied on as a measure of last resort:

> Release to parent. A parent has a constitutional right to the care and custody of their child, absent a judicial determination that the parent poses an imminent threat to the child's safety. . . . Therefore, immigration enforcement cannot separate children from parents unless these conditions are met. Parents who seek the release of an unaccompanied child from government custody will be required to submit evidence of their relationship with the child. They must also submit to a prompt search of state child welfare records to confirm that other children have not been removed from their care and that the parents' rights have not been terminated with respect to the child. . . . Absent concerns about the parent-child relationship or ongoing child welfare investigations of the parent, the child should be promptly released to the parent. . . .
>
> Release to other family or traditional caregivers. Consistent with the well-established importance of kinship ties and the role of traditional but non-parent caregivers for 50 children, children should not be separated from traditional caregivers as a matter of immigration enforcement. . . . Children will be promptly released from custody to other family members or traditional caregivers when a parent is not available or when a parent is available but unable to care for the child. . . .

> Home-based or small, community-based placements. During a brief window of government custody, the government will place children in home-based placements (short-term foster care) or small, community-based group homes (under 25 residents) as the norm, with limited exceptions.... Children will instead live in a home- or community-based environment [able to come and go]. If they are identified as having "behavioral" concerns (often related to the trauma they experienced in home country, on their journey, or by virtue of being separated from family) they will be place in a home where the caretakers have received training to care for traumatized children....
>
> Foster care: The government will continue to provide foster placements for children who have no parent, family member or family friend to step forward and care for them. These foster placements will be licensed and should be family-based, group homes, or 53 small shelter settings that are consistent with state child welfare standards. (Young Center 2022, 50–54)

The proposal essentially calls for the eradication of migrant child detention, consistent with international law, applying the detention of migrant children only as a measure of last resort.[15] The recognition of harm caused and the movement toward the abolition of migrant child detention has already emerged in various circles of the immigration advocacy world. Various authors in this book—including those who run Viator House of Hospitality and Bethany House—have already set out to centralize human dignity in their alternatives to detention. Noting the ancient, biblical roots of the call to protect migrants and refugees, faith-based communities have created spaces in which hospitality is offered as an alternative to detention. While alternatives to detention are an essential component of harm reduction, the abolition of migrant child detention should be the primary goal.

Conclusion

The elimination of migrant child detention, though only a step toward abolition, provides a tangible abolitionist outcome, a component of critical resistance to an oppressive, racist, and inhumane immigration system. The abolition of child detention does not change the fact that migrant children and their families, once reunified in the United States, still exist under an oppressive immigration state: the threat of detention, the threat of deportation, the total uncertainty of an outcome in an unforgiving system, the subjection to dangerous, underground labor conditions as a by-product of the system, etcetera (De Genova 2020). Nonetheless, abolishing migrant child detention ensures that we denormalize a practice known to cause harm to Black and Brown children. Abolishing migrant child detention centralizes the human dignity of all children, and it signifies a promise not to knowingly impair the incredible potential of all children, foreign and domestic. In short, it should not be an extraordinary request that America refrain from putting kids in cages.

Notes

1. Special thanks to Loyola law students Laila Alvarez (JD 2025), Juan Gonzalez-Martinez (JD 2023), Yessica Ramirez (JD 2024), and Oneida Molina Vargas (JD 2024) for their persistent, thoughtful education of this law professor on the topic of abolition, especially on abolition in the context of immigration. Their thoughts and contributions to this topic shaped this chapter. Thanks also to Loyola law student Meghan Scholnick for her research and other contributions to finalizing the chapter. Special thanks also to Dr. Lauren Heidbrink for her thoughtful feedback in the development of this chapter.

2. Oxford English Dictionary, s.v. "Abolition," accessed March 22, 2024, https://www.oed.com/search/dictionary/?scope=Entries&q=abolition.

3. The concept of legal violence incorporates the various, mutually reinforcing forms of violence that the law makes possible and amplifies. This lens allows us to capture the aggravation of otherwise "normal" or "regular" effects of the law, such as the immigrants' predicament that results from indefinite family separations as a result of increased deportations; the intensification in the exploitation of immigrant workers and new violations of their rights; and the exclusion and further barring of immigrants from education and other forms of socioeconomic resources necessary for mobility and incorporation. All these instances constitute forms of structural and symbolic violence that are codified in the law and produce immediate social suffering but also potentially long-term harm with direct repercussions for key aspects of immigrant incorporation (Menjívar and Abrego 2012).

4. For years, researchers and scholars have decried our immigration system as entrapping a permanent underclass of laborers ripe for exploitation by the agricultural corporate sector (Judis 2006; Salzman 2013).

5. At least, it is not required by law. In some instances, a few lucky children will be assigned a Child Advocate to represent their best interests to the court. In most other countries, a best-interests assessment is required to take any legal action impacting a child.

6. In ORR custody, children's trauma can manifest in multiple ways, as they may not have the tools, family or community contacts, or care they need to self-soothe or regulate their emotions. Sometimes, children experience grief over separation from family or because they learn of more violence afflicting their loved ones. ORR facility staff may characterize their behavior as aggressive or harmful to themselves or others, resulting in more restrictive placements (Young Center for Immigrant Children's Rights and National Immigrant Justice Center 2022).

7. Universal Declaration of Human Rights, GA Res 217A (III), UNGAOR, 3rd Sess., Supp No. 13, UN Doc A/810 (1948) 71, Art. 1. The epigraph to this section is from the UN Declaration's preamble.

8. Convention for the Protection of Human Rights and Fundamental Freedoms, opened for signature November 4, 1950, 213 U.N.T.S. 221, Europe. T.S. No. 5, http://conventions.coe.int/Treaty/EN/Treaties/Html/005.htm; Organization of American States, American Convention on Human Rights, art. 4(1), Nov. 22, 1969, O.A.S.T.S. No. 36, 1144 U.N.T.S. 123, http://www.oas.org/DIL/American_Convention_on _Human_Rights_7-22nov1969.pdf; League of Arab States, Arab Charter on Human Rights, May 22, 2004, reprinted in 12 *Int'l Hum. Rts. Rep.* 893 (2005) (entered into force Mar. 15, 2008) (hereafter Arab Charter); African Charter on Human and Peoples' Rights, June 27, 1981, 21 I.L.M. 59 (1982) (entered into force Oct. 21, 1986). For an English translation of the Arab Charter, see the University of Minnesota Human Rights Library, http://hrlibrary.umn.edu/instree/arabcharter.html.

9. Declaration on the Protection of All Persons from Being Subjected to Torture and Other Cruel, Inhuman or Degrading Treatment or Punishment, G.A. Res. 3452, U.N. GAOR, 30th Sess., Supp. No. 34, at 91, U.N. Doc. A/10034 (1976).

10. See Human Rights Comm., Int'l Covenant on Civil and Political Rights, General Comment No. 6: The Right to Life, P 3, U.N. Doc. HRI/GEN/1/Rev.1 (1994).

11. "ICE has increasingly incorporated guaranteed minimum payments into its contracts and agreements, whereby ICE agrees to pay detention facility operators for a fixed number of detention beds regardless of whether it uses them" (U.S. Government Accountability Office 2021).

12. Convention on the Rights of the Child, G.A. Res. 44/25, 44 U.N. GAOR Supp. No. 49, U.N. Doc. A/44/736, 6 (1989).

13. "The Assembly welcomes the promotion by some European countries of alternative solutions to the detention of migrant children. Such alternatives to detention, when implemented properly, are more effective and cheaper, better protect the rights and dignity of children and lead to better health and well-being for migrant children. The Assembly notes with satisfaction that a number of member States, including Belgium, Denmark, France, Hungary, Ireland, Italy, the Netherlands, and the United Kingdom, have taken steps towards ending the immigration detention of children. In these countries, migrant children are either not detained or there is a legal, political or practical provision for the release of migrant children from detention." Eur. Parl. Ass., Res. 2020, 9.1 (2014), http://assembly.coe.int/nw/xml/XRef/Xref-XML2HTML -en.asp?fileid=21295&lang=en.

14. Not to be confused with ORR shelters, the shelters mentioned here are not detention centers that call themselves shelters. Instead, children can come and go into the community, for example to attend community schools.

15. "Children should not be deprived of liberty, except as a measure of last resort and for the shortest appropriate period of time." Children's Rights International Network, October 31, 2014, comments on the draft of General Comment No. 35 on Article 9 of the ICCPR on the right to liberty and security of person and freedom from arbitrary arrest and detention, par. 18, https://www.ohchr.org/Documents/HR Bodies/CCPR/GConArticle9/Submissions/CRIN_Comments_GC35_ICCPR_article 9.docx.

References

Altman, Heidi, and Marta Ascherio. 2020. "Policy Brief: 5 Reasons to End Immigrant Detention." National Immigrant Justice Center, September 14. https://immigrantjustice.org/research-items/policy-brief-5-reasons-end-immigrant-detention.

Bryant, Erica. 2022. "ICE Is Wasting Millions of Dollars on Unnecessary Detention Beds." Vera Institute of Justice, July 20. https://www.vera.org/news/ice-is-wasting-millions-of-dollars-on-unnecessary-detention-beds.

Caneva, Elena. 2014. "Children's Agency and Migration: Constructing Kinship in Latin American and East European Families Living in Italy." *Childhood* 22 (2): 278–92.

Child Welfare Information Gateway. n.d. "Family First Prevention Services Act." Child Welfare Information Gateway. Accessed November 23, 2023. https://www.childwelfare.gov/topics/systemwide/laws-policies/federal/family-first/.

Committee on the Rights of the Child. 2012. "The Rights of All Children in the Context of International Migration." https://www.ohchr.org/sites/default/files/Documents/HRBodies/CRC/Discussions/2012/DGD2012ReportAndRecommendations.pdf.

Corlett, D., G. Mitchell, J. Van Hove, L. Bowring, and K. Wright. 2012. *Captured Children*. Melbourne: International Detention Coalition.

Council of Europe. 2014. "Resolution 2020: The Alternatives to Immigration Detention of Children." https://assembly.coe.int/nw/xml/XRef/Xref-XML2HTML-en.asp?fileid=21295&lang=en.

Davis, Angela Y. 1983. *Women, Race and Class*. New York: Vintage Books.

Davis, Angela Y. 1989. "Let Us All Rise Together: Radical Perspectives on Empowerment for Afro-American Women." In *Women, Culture & Politics*, 3–15. New York: Random House.

Death Penalty Information Center. n.d. "The Abolitionist Movement." Accessed November 22, 2023. https://deathpenaltyinfo.org/facts-and-research/history-of-the-death-penalty/the-abolitionist-movement.

De Genova, Nicholas. 2020. "Doin' Hard Time on Planet Earth: Migrant Detainability, Disciplinary Power, and the Disposability of Life." In *Waiting and the Temporalities of Irregular Migration*, edited by Christine M. Jacobsen, Marry-Anne Karlsen, and Shahram Khosravi, 186–201. London: Routledge.

Detention Watch Network. 2011. "The Influence of the Private Prison Industry in the Immigration Detention Business." May. https://www.detentionwatchnetwork.org/pressroom/reports/2011/private-prisons.

Detention Watch Network. n.d. "Ending Immigration Detention: Abolitionist Steps vs. Reformist Reforms." Accessed November 22, 2023. https://www.detentionwatchnetwork.org/sites/default/files/Abolitionist%20Steps%20vs%20Reformist%20Reforms_DWN_2022.pdf?fbclid=IwAR3d2ZpkMhzFz_1vQaTwyeKYU_Y9tkpaI3CROKw_LT0geyTWuNfmcQo5ilA.

Diaz, Sarah, and Oneida Vargas. 2023. "Denormalizing Harm to Migrant Children in the U.S. Immigration System: A Comparative Perspective." *Children's Legal Rights Journal* 43 (1): 1–20.

Dreier, Hannah. 2023. "Alone and Exploited, Migrant Children Work Brutal Jobs Across the U.S." *New York Times*, February 25.

Galliher, John F., Gregory Ray, and Brent Cook. 1992. "Abolition and Reinstatement of Capital Punishment During the Progressive Era and Early 20th Century." *Journal of Criminal Law and Criminology* 83 (3): 538–76.

García Hernández, César Cuauhtémoc. 2014. "Creating Crimmigration." *Brigham Young University Law Review* 2013 (6): 1457–1516.

Gilmore, Ruth Wilson. 2022. *Abolition Geography: Essays Towards Liberation*. New York: Verso Books.

Gruberg, Sharita. 2015. "How For-Profit Companies Are Driving Immigration Detention Policies." Center for American Progress, December 18. https://www.americanprogress.org/article/how-for-profit-companies-are-driving-immigration-detention-policies/.

Heidbrink, Lauren. 2014. *Migrant Youth, Transnational Families, and the State: Care and Contested Interests*. Pennsylvania Studies in Human Rights. Philadelphia: University of Pennsylvania Press.

Heidbrink, Lauren. 2020. "Anatomy of a Crisis: Governing Youth Mobility Through Vulnerability." *Journal of Ethnic and Migration Studies* 47 (5): 988–1005.

Heidbrink, Lauren. 2021. *Migrantidad: La juventud en una nueva era de deportaciones*. Mexico City: Centro de investigaciones Multidisciplinarias sobre Chiapas y Centroamérica, Universidad Nacional Autónoma de México.

Homeland Security Act, 6 U.S.C. § 279 (g)(2) (2002).

Ina, Satsuki. 2021. "A Cage Is Still a Cage: President Biden Must End Detention of Children and Families." *Time* magazine, February 21.

International Organization for Migration, United Nations High Commissioner for Refugees, & UNICEF. 2022. "Safety and Dignity for Refugee and Migrant Children: Recommendations for Alternatives to Detention and Appropriate Care Arrangements in Europe." May. https://www.unhcr.org/media/40217.

Judis, John. 2006. "Immigration Confusion: Illegal Substance." *New Republic Online*, April 6. Carnegie Endowment for International Peace. https://carnegieendowment.org/2006/04/06/immigration-confusion-illegal-substance-pub-18223.

Kaba, Mariame. 2017. "Marianne Kaba Offers s People's History of Prisons in the United States." *Intercepted* (podcast), May 31. Hosted by Jeremy Scahill. https://www.youtube.com/watch?v=qCvXRJFjZAA.

Kamasaki, Charles. 2021. "US Immigration Policy: A Classic, Unappreciated Example of Structural Racism." Brookings, March 26. https://www.brookings.edu/blog/how-we-rise/2021/03/26/us-immigration-policy-a-classic-unappreciated-example-of-structural-racism/.

Kronick, Rachel, Cécile Rousseau, and Janet Cleveland. 2015. "Asylum-Seeking Children's Experiences of Detention in Canada: A Qualitative Study." *American Journal of Orthopsychiatry* 85 (3): 287–94.

Kushner, Rachel. 2019. "Is Prison Necessary? Ruth Wilson Gilmore Might Change Your Mind." *New York Times*, April 17.

Lazarus, Emma. 1883. "The New Colossus." Poem inscripted on the Statue of Liberty. New York.

Linton, Julie M., et al. 2017. "Detention of Immigrant Children." *Pediatrics* 139 (5): e20170483.

Lorek, Ann, Kimberly Ehntholt, Anne Nesbitt, Emmanuel Wey, Chipo Githinji, Eve Rossor, and Rush Wickramasinghe. 2009. "The Mental and Physical Health Difficulties of Children Held Within a British Immigration Detention Center: A Pilot Study." *Child Abuse & Neglect* 33 (9): 573–85.

Mares, Sarah, and Jon Jureidini. 2004. "Psychiatric Assessment of Children and Families in Immigration Detention—Clinical, Administrative and Ethical Issues." *Australian and New Zealand Journal of Public Health* 28 (6): 520–26.

Menjívar, Cecilia, and Leisy J. Abrego. 2012. "Legal Violence: Immigration Law and the Lives of Central American Immigrants." *American Journal of Sociology* 117 (5): 1380–1421.

O'Connor, Kathleen. 2019. "The Business of Immigrant Detention." Unpublished book chapter. https://www.researchgate.net/publication/334126273_Chapter_5_The_Business_of_Immigrant_Detention.

Purnell, Derecka. 2020. "How I Became a Police Abolitionist." *The Atlantic*, July 6.

Purnell, Derecka. 2021. *Becoming Abolitionists: Police, Protests, and the Pursuit of Freedom*. New York: Astra House.

Ray, Rashawn. 2020. "Commentary: What Does 'Defund the Police' Mean and Does It Have Merit?" Brookings, June 19. https://www.brookings.edu/blog/fixgov/2020/06/19/what-does-defund-the-police-mean-and-does-it-have-merit/.

Salzman, Jason. 2013. "Building an Underclass of Workers." Institute for Policy Studies, OtherWords, July 24. https://otherwords.org/building-an-underclass-of-workers/.

Signer, Jordana. 2021. "Dismantling Detention: International Alternatives to Detaining Immigrants." Edited by Bill Frelick and Clara Long. Human Rights Watch, November 3. https://www.hrw.org/report/2021/11/03/dismantling-detention/international-alternatives-detaining-immigrants.

Smith, Hillel R. 2019. "Immigration Detention: A Legal Overview." Congressional Research Service, September 16. https://sgp.fas.org/crs/homesec/R45915.pdf.

Smith, Hillel R. 2021. "U.S. Customs and Border Protection's Powers and Limitations: A Primer." Congressional Research Service, November 30. https://crsreports.congress.gov/product/pdf/LSB/LSB10559.

Sultan, Reina, and Micah Herskind. 2020. "What Is Abolition, and Why Do We Need It?" Department of African American Studies, Princeton University, July 28. https://aas.princeton.edu/news/what-abolition-and-why-do-we-need-it.

United Nations High Commissioner for Refugees. 2017. "UNHCR's Position Regarding the Detention of Refugee and Migrant Children in the Migration Context." January. https://www.unhcr.org/us/media/unhcrs-position-regarding-detention-refugee-and-migrant-children-migration-context.

United Nations Office of the High Commissioner for Human Rights. 2012. "Moving Away from the Death Penalty: Lessons from National Experiences." October. https://www.ohchr.org/sites/default/files/Lists/MeetingsNY/Attachments/27/moving_away_from_death_penalty_web.pdf.

U.S. Department of Health and Human Services. 2015. "A National Look at the Use of Congregate Care in Child Welfare." March 30. https://www.acf.hhs.gov/cb/report/national-look-use-congregate-care-child-welfare.

U.S. Government Accountability Office. 2015. "Foster Care: HHS Could Do More to Support States' Efforts to Keep Children in Family-Based Care." October. https://www.gao.gov/assets/gao-16-85.pdf.

U.S. Government Accountability Office. 2021. "Immigration Detention: Actions Needed to Improve Planning, Documentation, and Oversight of Detention Facility Contracts." January 13. https://www.gao.gov/products/gao-21-149.

Young Center for Immigrant Children's Rights. 2020. "Reimagining Children's Immigration Proceedings: A Roadmap for an Entirely New System Centered Around Children." October. https://www.theyoungcenter.org/reimagining-childrens-immigration-proceedings.

Young Center for Immigrant Children's Rights and National Immigrant Justice Center. 2022. "Punishing Trauma: Incident Reporting and Immigrant Children in Government Custody." September. https://immigrantjustice.org/sites/default/files/uploaded-files/no-content-type/2022-09/Punishing-Trauma-Overhaul-SIRs-Report-Sept-2022.pdf.

CONTRIBUTORS

Sister Stella Akello, O.F.C (Orden Franciscanas Clarisas, Spain), is originally from Uganda and is currently the house coordinator at Bethany House of Hospitality, a program for young women seeking asylum. She works at Loyola Medicine, MacNeal Hospital, as a chaplain providing spiritual care to patients, families, and staff. She volunteered with the Interfaith Committee for Detained Immigrants. She earned her associate's degree at Malaga University in Spain, and she is now enrolled in a master's program in pastoral studies at Catholic Theological Union in Chicago.

Jessica Alaniz has worked with immigrant populations for more than ten years, dedicating time and energy to ensure everyone has access to equal opportunities and a better life. In the past, Alaniz has worked with Dreamers Clubs in the Chicago Public Schools to provide DACA and college assistance to students. Further, she served as a youth, peace, and justice program associate for the American Friends Service Committee. She has also created an Immigrant Activist Training Program to verse others in legal issues surrounding immigration while actively pursuing change. From 2018 to 2022, Alaniz was the case manager and associate director at Bethany House of Hospitality. Alaniz maintains a strong passion for immigrant rights and advocacy.

Aireen Grace Andal (she/her) is a global visiting fellow at the School of Geography, Politics, and Sociology at Newcastle University, UK. She did her PhD work in the discipline of Geography and Planning at Macquarie University, Australia. Her research pays particular attention to children and children's spaces and the importance of children as co-creators of knowledge.

The majority of her recent academic engagements involve children's play lives, with an emphasis on slum-dwelling communities. Her recent publications include topics in the fields of children's geographies and childhood studies, and she serves as a reviewer of journal manuscripts related to childhood research. Andal is a scholar for and with children and their spaces. Her academic life is devoted to making children's voices heard, their insights acknowledged, and their lives seen—matters that are hitherto often dismissed.

Reverend Dr. Samuel Arroyo received his Master of Divinities (M Div.) from Princeton Theological Seminary in 2009 and his PhD in theology from the Interamerican University of Puerto Rico in 2020. He is currently serving as the assistant director of Global Services and Latinx Programs at Princeton Theological Seminary. He has also served as associate superintendent for the United Methodist Church of Greater New Jersey and is currently part of the Conference's Board of Church and Society and its Immigration Task Force. In the spring of 2018, he served as co-chair of the Faith Communities Outreach Committee of the Poor People's Campaign in New Jersey, and later served as one of the Tri-Chairs for the whole New Jersey Campaign. Arroyo served as the Education and Outreach Fellow for Salvation and Social Justice, an organization that seeks to impact public policy in the state of New Jersey through a faith perspective. Through this organization, Arroyo worked on advancing racial justice to Black and Brown students in New Jersey public schools. His academic research has focused on the evangelism of Native and African enslaved people in Latin America during the sixteenth and seventeenth centuries. He highlights the injustices that enslaved people were subjected to with the excuse to "save their souls." Arroyo also analyzes the first two anti-slavery treatises written in America, by Friar Francisco Jose de Jaca and Friar Epifanio de Moirans. Arroyo believes his faith moves him to advocate for those who are oppressed in our society. He has been actively speaking at rallies and conferences in the state of New Jersey, advocating for immigrant rights, and opposing family separations, not just at the border but for the ones also happening all over the nation. One of Arroyo's goals is to help faith leaders in formulating a social moral argument for the poor and oppressed in their communities.

Father Corey Brost, C.S.V., is a member of the Clerics of St. Viator, a religious order of brothers, priests, and lay associates. He joined the order in

1987 and has served since then as a religious educator, classroom teacher, and high school administrator. He served as president of St. Viator High School in Arlington Heights from 2013 to 2016. He left with support from the Viatorians to work full-time as an advocate for immigrant rights and interfaith bridge building.

He currently is executive director of Viator House of Hospitality, a northwest suburban interfaith program that provides a home and services for up to twenty-five young men, eighteen to twenty-three years old, who've fled their homelands, are seeking asylum in the United States, and have no family to live with while they await their legal proceedings. He cofounded Viator House in January 2017 with another Viatorian, Br. Michael Gosch, C.S.V., who had the original inspiration for the project.

Lina Caswell Muñoz has a Bachelor of Arts in human services from Springfield College and a Master of Arts in sociology and social justice from Kean University. Caswell Muñoz completed high school in Colombia, where she emigrated from in 1997. Over the past twenty years, she served in Connecticut as an advocate for minoritized immigrant children and families and low-income Latinx communities for the Hispanic Health Council, the City of Hartford Office of Youth Development, the Refugee Assistance Center, and the Center for Children's Advocacy in Hartford. Caswell Muñoz worked as a sociology adjunct professor at several community colleges and served as a consultant for the Sisters of Charity of Saint Elizabeth Values Into Action college internship program, serving immigrant communities. Since 2012, she has served as a volunteer Child Advocate for unaccompanied immigrant children through the Young Center for Immigrant Children's Rights. In 2015, she began working as a volunteer advocate and board member for the Children's Emergency Medical Fund of New Jersey, representing chronically ill, uninsured, and underinsured immigrant children of mixed status and their families. She is currently the associate director for Children and Youth Services at Church World Service in Jersey City.

Marisa Chumil, LCSW, is a Child Advocate Program co-director at the Young Center for Immigrant Children's Rights. For more than a decade, Chumil has dedicated her work at the Young Center to directly serving and advocating for the rights and best interests of unaccompanied children, supervising Child Advocate cases in Chicago, consulting on cases nationally for all Young Center offices, and coordinating the program's work on international home studies and safe repatriation services. Prior to joining the Young Center, Chumil worked for nearly a decade in early childhood programs within immigrant communities, where she provided social services, implemented a social and emotional curriculum, and conducted mental health consultation for educators and families. She received her Master of Social Work and Bachelor of Social Work from Loyola University Chicago, specializing in migration studies and children and families. Chumil initiated her human rights career in Guatemala and El Salvador, where she worked in communities rebuilding after civil war.

Sister Patricia Crowley, O.S.B., served as a spiritual director, as a team member with the Ignatian Spirituality Program (ISP), and as board president of Bethany House of Hospitality (for young women seeking asylum in our country). She was the executive director for Deborah's Place and the Howard Area Community Center while working in the field of homelessness for many years in Chicago. As a former prioress of the Benedictine Sisters of Chicago, she was also the president of the Conference of Benedictine Prioresses and a board member of the LCWR (Leadership Conference of Women Religious). She earned her master's in catechetical theology at Manhattan College, New York, and her certification in spiritual guidance from the Siena Center in Racine, Wisconsin. During the past year, she had begun to lead short online series to help people learn the ancient practice of Lectio Divina. She passed away in October 2023, leaving behind a legacy of faith through action.

Iman Dadras, PhD, is an associate professor in the Couple and Family Therapy program at Alliant International University, Los Angeles. He is a Licensed Marriage and Family Therapist in the states of California and Minnesota. Dadras has provided psychotherapy services to marginalized populations with an emphasis on using a social justice approach. His main research interests are on critical consciousness of the psychotherapist, anti-oppressive psychotherapy, and psycho-political challenges of immigrant families.

Sarah J. Diaz, JD, LLM, is the associate director of the Center for the Human Rights of Children and faculty at Loyola University Chicago, School of Law. She has practiced at the intersection of child migration and human rights since 2005. Prior to joining academia, she served as the National Case Director for the Young Center for Immigrant Children's Rights and as legal counsel to migrant children in government custody at the National Immigrant Justice Center. Diaz teaches in the areas of immigration practice, refugee law, and human rights. Her scholarship focuses on the intersection of child migration and international law, including on the human rights of children in the context of international criminal, humanitarian, and public law.

Sandra Espinoza, PsyD, is a Licensed Marriage and Family Therapist in Los Angeles, California. Espinoza is also an associate professor and branch director at Alliant International University, Los Angeles. Espinoza has provided therapy to the undocumented community for more than ten years. Her research focuses on the long-term relational impact of deportation as well as the impact of sociopolitical systems on mental health. Espinoza maintains a private practice, where she provides therapy to the undocumented community.

Jacqueline Florian, MA, is a Licensed Marriage and Family Therapist who provides mental health services to children and families in marginalized communities. Her research focuses on the impact of separation and detention on the parent-child relationship. As a first-generation Latina, Florian is aware of the struggles that Latinx families face and has made it her goal to advocate for the BIPOC community. She is a doctoral student at Alliant International University, Los Angeles.

Brother Michael Gosch, C.S.V., is a member of the Clerics of St. Viator. He has worked as both an educator and a social worker in Illinois, Nevada, and Belize, Central America. Michael is a cofounder of Viator House of Hospitality and currently serves as its director of programs and housing. Prior to his work with Viator House, he helped establish two houses of hospitality for adult asylum seekers when he worked with Interfaith Committee for Detained Immigrants, now known as Illinois Community for Displaced Immigrants.

Darlene Gramigna is the former executive director of Bethany House of Hospitality for its first four and a half years. She has a Master of Social Work from the University of Denver and a Bachelor of Social Work from Southern Connecticut State University. She has previously worked as a program director on immigration issues at the American Friends Service Committee in the Chicago office. She has worked in the sanctuary movement with Central American refugees. She worked with Dreamers Clubs in the Chicago Public Schools to assist students with DACA and college applications. She has traveled extensively in Central America and worked as a social worker in Nicaragua.

Lisa Jacobs is a clinical professor of law with the Civitas Child Law Center. Jacobs provides subject matter expertise and technical assistance to jurisdictions working to improve the outcomes of youth and young adults "dually involved" in child welfare and juvenile justice systems, in collaboration with the Robert F. Kennedy National Resource Center for Juvenile Justice. Jacobs formerly served as program manager for the Illinois Models for Change Initiative, which was funded by the John D. and Catherine T. MacArthur Foundation to promote effective juvenile justice policy, practice, and programming in diverse jurisdictions across the state and nation. Jacobs currently serves as vice chair of the Illinois Juvenile Justice Commission, which is charged with advising the governor, the General Assembly, and other stakeholders on matters of juvenile justice law and policy. She is also a member of the Illinois Court Improvement Project Advisory Committee, convened by the Illinois Supreme Court to promote the continuous quality improvement of court processes in child welfare proceedings and to enhance and expand collaboration between the judicial branch, the Department of Children and Family Services, and child protection court stakeholders to improve child welfare outcomes.

Katherine Kaufka Walts is the director of the Center for the Human Rights of Children at Loyola University Chicago, School of Law. She earned her Juris Doctor from the University of Wisconsin and her Bachelor of Arts and Bachelor of Science from the University of Michigan. She began her career at the National Immigrant Justice Center, where she successfully represented survivors of serious crimes and human rights abuses in criminal and immigration legal proceedings. Observing that many of her clients were young people, she later joined the International Organization for Adolescence, where as its executive director she developed programs to advance the rights of children in the United States and internationally via services, leadership training, advocacy, and policy work. At Loyola University, she conducts research, teaches, mentors students, and continues to provide training and technical assistance to various stakeholders, including nongovernmental organizations and governmental bodies, on the experiences of migrant children and child trafficking victims.

Corinne Kentor is a 2023 American Council of Learned Societies Leading Edge Fellow with the Presidents' Alliance on Higher Education and Immigration. She earned her PhD in anthropology and education from Teachers College, Columbia University, in 2023. Her dissertation, "For Me, Us, and Them: Immigrant Families Pursuing Higher Education in Southern California," was recognized with awards from the National Academy of Education, the Spencer Foundation, and the National Science Foundation, among others. Her teaching and scholarship are highly collaborative, using ethnographic methods to investigate how policy shapes access to postsecondary opportunities for immigrant communities.

Jenn M. Lilly is an assistant professor in the Graduate School of Social Service at Fordham University in New York City. Lilly's work focuses on storytelling for social justice with youth populations using participatory, anti-oppressive, digital media methods. She believes in the power of digital media production for self-expression and social change, and primarily works with Latinx immigrant young people to share their stories and co-produce digital media focused on topics of concern to them. Before entering academia, Lilly worked in the nonprofit sector for more than ten years, developing and implementing culturally sensitive programs and policies for immigrant families, community organizing for immigrants' rights, and supporting Indigenous youth-led initiatives in Mexico and Guatemala.

Sister Kathlyn Mulcahy, OP, currently serves as executive director of Bethany House of Hospitality in Chicago (for young women seeking asylum). She served in pastoral ministry and formation work in Peru and then on the congregational leadership team of the Dominican Sisters of Springfield before coming to Bethany House. She earned her Master of Education at Clarke University and a certificate in cross-cultural ministry from Catholic Theological Union in Chicago.

Jennifer Nagda, JD, is the chief program officer for the Young Center for Immigrant Children's Rights, where her work focuses on children and youth in federal immigration custody. Her experience includes advocating for detained children in immigration court and before federal agencies; facilitating an intergovernmental working group that included the Departments of Justice, Homeland Security, and Health and Human Services; and authoring reports, testifying before Congress, and training judges and other advocates. She is a member of the American Bar Association's Commission on Youth at Risk and served on a Federal Advisory Committee in President Obama's administration. Nagda has held lecturer appointments at both the University of Chicago Law School and the University of Pennsylvania Law School. Before joining the Young Center, Jennifer was an attorney at the Mexican American Legal Defense and Educational Fund (MALDEF) and clerked for the Honorable James B. Zagel of the U.S. District Court for the Northern District of Illinois.

Vida Opoku was born and raised in a small village in Ghana. She sought asylum alone by fleeing to the United States as a teenager. Designated as an unaccompanied alien child by the Department of Homeland Security, Opoku was placed in the immigration detention system. She was released from detention in 2016 and won her asylum claim three years later before the immigration court. Surviving alone in the United States has been difficult, but Opoku has overcome immense obstacles through her determination, bravery, and the circle of advocates who supported her. Today, she attends Loyola University in Chicago and is expected to graduate with her master's degree in international affairs in fall 2024. Opoku graduated from Loyola University with a political science degree in May 2023.

Silvia Rodriguez Vega is an interdisciplinary scholar and assistant professor in the Department of Chicana/o Studies at the University of California, Santa Barbara. She is a community engaged writer, artist, and educational practitioner. Her research explores the ways anti-immigration policy impacts the lives of immigrant children through methodological tools centering participatory art and creative expression. Her first book, *Drawing Deportation: Art and Resistance Among Immigrant Children* (2023), argues that immigrant children are not passive in the face of the challenges presented by U.S. anti-immigrant policies. Based on ten years of work with immigrant children in two different border states—Arizona and California—*Drawing Deporta-*

tion gives readers a glimpse into the lives of immigrant children and their families. Through an analysis of three hundred children's drawings, theater performances, and family interviews, this book, at once devastating and revelatory, provides a roadmap for how art can provide a necessary space for vulnerable populations to assert their humanity in a world that would rather divest them of it.

Emily Ruehs-Navarro is an associate professor of sociology at Elmhurst University, where she teaches on migration, race, gender, and family. She is the author of the book *Unaccompanied: The Plight of Immigrant Youth at the Border* (2022). In addition to her academic work, Ruehs-Navarro has advocated for immigrant rights in various capacities, including as an English teacher in rural migrant camps, as a Child Advocate with the Young Center for Immigrant Children's Rights, as a case manager with Bethany Christian Services' refugee resettlement division, and as an interpreter with the Dilley Pro Bono Project.

Herlin Soto-Matute, MA, is an Associate Marriage and Family Therapist and a current doctoral student at Alliant International University, Los Angeles. Due to her experiences and struggles as an undocumented Latina alongside her parents, her therapeutic work and research focuses in working with Latine undocumented immigrant families by treating issues regarding trauma, immigration status, acculturation, and other barriers through a cultural, sociopolitical lens. She aims to advocate for BIPOC and underrepresented communities in and outside her work as a mental health clinician.

Luis Edward Tenorio is a PhD candidate in sociology at the University of California, Berkeley. His research focuses on the immigrant experience in the United States. In this work, he has conducted projects on the experiences of Central American unaccompanied youth in the United States as well as the socioeconomic mobility of immigrants who transition from being undocumented to lawful permanent residents across major U.S. cities. His research is funded by awards from the National Science Foundation; the American Sociological Association; the Institute for Governmental Studies, Center for Race and Gender, and Center for the Study of Law and Society at UC Berkeley; and the UC Center for New Racial Studies.

Jajah Wu is an attorney with Purpose Dignity Action, a harm-reduction NGO in Seattle that works to redivert individuals from carceral systems. She also works as an independent consultant in issues affecting unaccompanied immigrant children's rights. For nine years, she worked at the Young Center for Immigrant Children's Rights, as staff attorney and deputy program director. During her tenure at the Young Center, she also taught at the University of Chicago Law School's Arthur Kane Center for Clinical Legal Education. She is a graduate of the University of Chicago Law School.

INDEX

AAP. *See* American Academy of Pediatrics
AAPHD. *See* American Association of Public Health Dentistry
ABA. *See* American Bar Association
Abdul story, at Viator House, 259
abolition, 5, 20, 23, 77, 307, 319n1; alternatives to, 315–18; for answers to detention harm, 308; child migrant detention and, 310–11; Council of Europe Parliamentary Resolution on, 316; as critical resistance to inhumane practices, 308; as form of resistance, 308–9; HHS on congregate care facilities, 315–16; human dignity prioritizing, 313–15; in immigration context, 309; Lorde on, 18; Oluo on, 19; reformist strategies and, 308; state violence and, 308
ACLU. *See* American Civil Liberties Union
ADA. *See* American Dental Association
Adkins, Tim, 288
adult detention: children lack of identity verification and, 205–6; community-based housing programs and, 104, 206, 209, 214n15, 237–38, 317–18; cultural and linguistic challenges in, 204; lack of translator for health services, 204; sexual and physical abuse in, 204; threat to child and youth migrant mental and physical health, 203–4
advocacy: faith-based community immigrant, 247–48; liberation theology and migrant rights, 248–49; to reverse negative rhetoric against immigrants, 253; Young Center best-interests standard, 89
advocates, lessons for, 87; bigger facilities as not better, 95–96; child-centered proposals for change, 98–109; on family and community importance, 90–91; on government custody as not benign, 92–95; release and reunification service activation, 96–98; TVPRA authorization of HHS to appoint, 88–89; Young Center Child Advocates, 88–89, 110n4, 319n5
affirmative asylum, children in detention application for, 194
Agamben, Giorgio, 232, 234
age redetermination, in detention system, 211–12; adult misidentification and, 203–4; criminal treatment and, 204; DHS numbers on children placed in custody due to, 213n7;

age redetermination (*continued*)
DHS reliance on dental radiographs for, 189, 191, 198–200; *Garcia Ramirez et al. v. U.S. ICE* class action suit and, 190, 199; housing alternatives need for youth ages 17 to 21, 191; incarceration and, 20, 205, 206, 208–10; loss of legal protections given as UAC, 204; of Opoku, 197–98; racist and dubious legal grounds for, 190–91; release to jail, 197–98; transfer to adult detention, 194, 257; UAC status loss at, 191; USCIS on negative implications of, 195; Viator House ATD opportunities, 255–56; Wu on, 198–201

Aline story, at BHH, 278–79

alternative-to-detention (ATD) program, 206, 209; best candidates for, 210; BHH for women, 270–71; child experts and physicians implementing of, 238; community-based housing as, 214n15, 237–38; Council of Europe Parliamentary Resolution on, 316; faith-based community and, 245–81; flight risk mitigated by, 205; high appearance rates at hearings in, 210; ICE use of phrase for, 214n15; jail cost compared to cost of, 210; TVPRA on children aging out eligibility for, 209; Viator House as, 207, 210–11, 255–56

American Academy of Pediatrics (AAP), 105, 110n7

American Association of Public Health Dentistry (AAPHD), dental radiographs to determine age condemnation, 200–201

American Bar Association (ABA), on children at age of eighteen residual rights, 194–95

American Civil Liberties Union (ACLU): on average length of detention, 223; Yourdkhani representation for, 12

American Dental Association (ADA), on questionable use of dental radiographs, 199

American psychology, 229–30

"Anatomy of a Crisis" (Heidbrink), 310

Anderson, Benedict, 67

Angel Island, 8, 9, 213n13

anti-immigrant policies, of Trump, 3, 4

Antonio sexual and gender minority story, with Yaqueline, 183–86

Archard, David, 76

Arendt, Hannah, 232–34

arriving alien designation: *Flores v. US-CIS* on demeaning term of, 213n10; of Opoku, 204

art epistemologies, 287–88

arts education programs, Trump budget cuts for, 300–301

asylum seekers: Biden process of, 284; as disposable, 235

ATD. *See* alternative-to-detention

attachment theory, 22; application to detained children, 226–27; changes within attachment to caregiver, 224; child age and separation experience perception, 223; collectivist cultures and, 224–25, 226; continued effects from separation after parent reconnection, 224; critiques, 224–26; disrupted attachment to parent, 224; relational ruptures impact and, 226–27; separation and abandonment, trauma, depression feelings, 223; Suárez-Orozco, Bang, and Kim on separation and depression and anxiety, 223; Venta on attachment insecurity, 224

attorneys: for child migrant detention center closing, 4; immigration, 106, 205–6, 213n12; UC access to immigration, 106

Bang, Hee Jin, 223
Becker, David, 230
Becoming Abolitionists (Purnell), 315
Behavioral Systems Southwest, Flores detention by, 10
Berks County Residential Center, 13
best-interests standard: legal violence and incorporation of, 50, 53n19; negative connotations from family courts use of, 89; UN Committee on the Rights of the Child on, 53n20; UN High Commissioner for Refugees on, 61; Young Center advocacy for, 89
Bethany House of Hospitality (BHH), 23, 254, 318; agency collaborative relationships, 271; Aline at, 278–79; as ATD for women, 270–71; Carlota and Xiomara at, 276–77; Elizabeth at, 273–74; faith-based response to asylum seekers, 280–81; on family separation policy, 276–77; Francisco at, 277; human trafficking response from, 277–78; inhumane policies response, 276–78; luxury of time provision by, 278–80; reaching all women, 272–73; response to complex identities, 273–76; Rose at, 274–75; Sandra at, 279–80; transgender women at, 272, 275–76
Bhatia, Sunil: on American psychology and, 229–30; colonial psychology criticism by, 229
BHH. *See* Bethany House of Hospitality
Bible: immigration and faith-based community, 247–52; Jesus scriptural response to othering, 251–52; New Testament on oppression liberation, 250–51; Old Testament command for immigrant hospitality, 249–50; Sessions use for family separation justification, 246–47. *See also* liberation theology
The Bible and Borders (Caroll), 252

biblicism: leading to Christian nationalism, 247; politicians abuse of Bible for own benefit, 247; Sessions and Huckabee Sanders justification for immigrant policies and, 246–47
Biden, Joe: on alien and illegal terms replaced with noncitizen and undocumented, 7; asylum seeker process of, 284; child migrant detention policies and, 4, 15–16, 117; MPP temporary halt and termination, 15; NEA budget increase by, 301; Title 42 policy and UC entry allowance, 14–15, 48
biomedical and disease model of trauma, Young on, 230–31
biopolitics, 238; classical sovereign power and, 232; Foucault on, 232–33; ICE regulatory system and, 233; Mbembe on, 232, 233; psychological practice ignorance of, 237
biopower, Foucault on, 232–33
Black liberation theology, 248
The Body Keeps Score (Van der Kolk), 221
Boff, Clodovis, 248
Boff, Leonardo, 248
Bohrer, Ashley, 18–19
Briggs, Ernestine, 227
British Dental Association, dental radiographs opposition, 213n8
Brost, Corey, 23, 207, 210, 255–70, 281n5
bureaucratic processes, 20, 59–60; detention as purgatory in, 20, 66–68; identity and imagined community notion of Anderson, 67; long-term reform and short-term challenges in, 77–78; paperwork on, 61–62; shared representation importance in, 78–79; shift to children engagement in, 78; UC sense of belonging and, 67–68, 80

Bush, George W., 11
Butler, Judith: criticism of colonial psychology and trauma, 231; on grievability, 159; on individual protection or disposable, 236; on refusal and solidarity, 164; on strengths-based perspective and vulnerability, 144

"A Cage is Still a Cage" (Ina), 311
Carlota story, at BHH, 276–77
Caroll, M. Daniel, 252
catch-and-release policy, Bush end for migrant families, 11
CBP. See Customs and Border Protection
CCA. See Corrections Corporation of America
CCAP. See Child-sensitive Community Assessment and Placement
Center for the Human Rights of Children, 20
Central America migration: criminalization of, 208; faith-based community and refugees in 1980s, 253; reasons for, 6; research project of RMC and sexual and gender minority, 175–77; of sexual and gender minority, 173–87
child and youth migrants: CBP border intake facilities detention of, 10; DHS removed from care and custody of, 10; drivers for, 118–20; education, family support and perseverance role for, 286–87; Mbembe on children in cages as living dead, 235; multiple traumas for, 228; reasons for, 5–7; transgender and females sexual assault, 120; as vulnerable group needing protection, 143–44; Young Child Advocates one-on-one work with, 189. See also unaccompanied alien children; unaccompanied children

child-centered proposals for change, 98; to ensure small placements, 103–4; to keep families together, 99–100; to make communities the locus of services, 105–9; to prioritize family contact and expedite reunification, 100–103
child-family separation. See family separation
children: deaths in detention facilities, 14, 42–43, 254; deportation of, 310
children artistic narratives of resistance case study, 23; directed at Trump, 283–85, 289–97, 299–301; drawings, 297–300; family separation themes, 291, 300; image theater and, 290–91; methods for, 288–91; narratives of resistance, 291–300; "Newspaper Theater" exercise, 283; self-portraits, 291–94; theater, 294–97; Watts elementary school arts academy and, 289
children at age of eighteen: ABA on residual rights recommendation, 194–95; Flores Settlement Agreement and, 193–94; *Garcia Ramirez et al. v. U.S. ICE* on adult detention protection, 190, 199; homelessness and instability of, 194, 212n3; ICE and DHS of youth ROR, 190, 194, 257; limited protections terminated for, 194; Wu on system vs., 193–95; Young Center for Immigrant Children's Rights continued work with, 195. See also age redetermination
Children Entering the United States Unaccompanied: Section 1 document, of ORR, 65
children in cages: Franklin photo of, 14–15; Mbembe on living dead status of, 235; state-sanctioned, 21; treatment reimagination for, 221–39

Index 339

children of color: adultification in juvenile justice system, 38; juvenile justice system criminalization of, 37–38; othering of, 20; state-sanctioned violence against, 20, 33–36, 308. *See also* othering, of Black, Brown, Native children and youth
Children's Rights International Network, 321n15
Child-sensitive Community Assessment and Placement (CCAP) Model, 316
child welfare system: movement away from congregate care facilities, 104; ORR and, 310; othering in, 36–37; racialism in, 37; reactive policies of, 36–37
Chinese Exclusion Act (1882), 35, 208, 213n13, 309
Christian nationalism, 247
Cindy *testimonio* story, 159–65
classical sovereign power, biopolitics and, 232
Clerics of St. Viator values, at Viator House of Hospitality, 254, 256
Clinton, Hillary, 289
coercive medical practices, detention harm from, 20, 45–46
collective agency, for migrants, 120–21
collectivist cultures, attachment theory and, 224–25, 226
colonial psychology: Bhatia criticism of research and, 229; Butler criticism of trauma in, 231; Comas-Diaz on, 229; Summerfield criticism of psychiatric universalism and, 231
Comas-Diaz, Lillian, 229
Committee on the Rights of the Child, UN, on best interest standards, 53n20
communities: importance of, 90–91; in-person case management services access, 108–9; networks and coalitions in, 105–6; physical and mental health care access, 107; proposal for locus of services within, 105–9; service providers collaboration in, 105–6; UC children immediate access to immigration counsel, 106
community-based housing programs, 104, 206, 317–18; as ATD, 214n15, 237–38; high compliance rates and less cost than detention, 209
compulsory detention, 11
congregate care facilities: child welfare system movement away from, 104, 311; HHS on abolition of, 315–16; negative impact of, 104, 313
controlled outside world contact, in detention, 11, 15, 196
Corrections Corporation of America (CCA), T. Don Hutto Family Detention Center opened by, 11
Council of Europe Parliamentary Resolution, on abolition and ATD, 316
coyote, as person helping undocumented migrants, 178, 292, 295, 302n5
Craps, Stef, 230
credible fear interview with USCIS, of Opoku, 205, 213n9
criminalization: of children of color in juvenile justice system, 37–38; of migrants from Mexico and Central America, 208; in UC documents, 69
cultural and linguistic challenges, in adult detention, 204
cultural subjugation, 34
Customs and Border Protection (CBP): children in border intake facilities of, 10; children in cages audio from facility of, 3; in DHS, 10; on human trafficking and victim protection, 17; inhumane policies and detention by, 143; lawsuit against Trump administration on abusive behaviors of, 221; public outcry of temporary facilities of, 15; research on UC in-

Customs and Border Protection (CBP) (*continued*)
teraction with, 173; state-sanctioned structural violence of, 32–33, 144; statistics on unaccompanied minors increase, 5–6; temporary border facilities for 72 hours of, 17, 42–43; *testimonio* on vulnerable conditions for UC, 169; transfer to ORR facilities, 62; as TVPRA apprehending authority, 40; UC noninnocence and compromised treatment with, 70; UC terminology of, 7; vulnerability state in custody of, 165; Yaqueline molestation in custody of, 183. *See also* children in cages

Davis, Angela, 307
deaths, in detention facilities, 14, 42–43, 254
Declaration on Human Rights, UN (1948), 313
Declaration on the Protection of All Persons from Being Subjected to Torture, UN, 314, 320n9
Declaration on the Rights of the Child, 51n4
de Ellacuria, Ignacio, 248
De La Torre, Miguel, 249, 253
De León, Jason, 120, 121
dental radiographs: AAPHD condemnation of use of, 200–201; ADA on questionable use of, 199; British Dental Association opposition to, 213n8; DHS reliance on age redetermination with, 189, 191, 198–200; *L.B. v. Charles Keeton, et al.* on violation of, 200; Senn evaluation and age redetermination by, 200
Department of Homeland Security (DHS): arriving alien parole option by, 205; child detention under immigration enforcement laws, 310; children at age of eighteen ROR, 190, 194, 257; contracts with private detention centers and prisons for confinement, 209; enforcement-oriented detention of, 194; factors parole based on by, 205; ICE and CBP in, 10; on numbers of children placed in custody from age redetermination, 213n7; Opoku age redetermination by, 189; removal of child and youth migrant care and custody from, 10; transfer of UC to ORR, of HHS, 87, 256
Department of Justice, zero tolerance policy announcement by, 221
deportation: of children, 310; children as disposable in camps for, 235; family disintegration detrimental outcomes, 285; INS undocumented arrests and, 9; by Obama, 285
depression and anxiety, 10, 47, 200, 237, 285, 312; Suárez-Orozco, Bang, and Kim on separation and, 223; trauma and, 227
De Sousa Santos, Boaventura, 229
detained homemaking: affective results of, 186; state control and legal violence in, 174
detention: abolition and, 310–11; ACLU on more than 5 months before reunification, 223; affirmative asylum application for children in, 194; Agamben on children denial of political existence, 234–35; as bureaucratic purgatory, 20, 66–68; as choice, 41; compulsory and variable length of, 11, 40, 223; controlled outside world contact, 11, 15, 196; as form of deterrence, 4; function as boundary maintenance, 66; high rates of mental health outcomes from, 227; immigration law enforcement in, 311; international guidance on, 41; as

legal violence form, 40–41, 313; process of, 17, 21; Reagan on punitive deterrence of, 9; relational ruptures in settings of, 117–39; relationships of solidarity in, 164; social, emotional, behavioral difficulties from, 227; trauma from broken connections in transitions of, 118; trauma from inhumane conditions during, 228; trauma relationship with mental health and, 222; uncertainty role in experiences of, 118; UNICEF on prevention of UC, 41; Wu on working of, 196–97; youth-centered alternatives to, 209–10. *See also* adult detention; alternative-to-detention; family detention centers

detention, as form of state-sanctioned violence: in CBP processing centers, 42–43; forced psychotropic behavior modification and coercive medical practices, 45–46; prolonged and indefinite secure, 43–45; U.S. detention of UC, 40–42

detention facilities: children deaths in, 14, 42–43, 254; Franklin photo of children in cages, 14–15; ICE guaranteed payments to, 320n11; quality of care variance, 10–11; relationships built in, 121–22; Tornillo Tent Camp image, 14

detention harms: abolition for answers to, 308; Center for the Human Rights of Children on, 20; coercive medical practices, 20, 45–46; family separation, 20; harm reduction recommendations, 21; historical context to, 20; incarceration mental anguish, 20; long-term mental health outcomes, 40–41; short- and long-term, 237; trauma manifestations, 312; violence denormalizing and, 311–13

deterrence, detention as form of, 4
DHS. *See* Department of Homeland Security
Dreby, Joanna, 288
due process of law: immigration system violations of, 49–50; secure detention settings absence of, 44, 52n13

East Asian countries, othering from, 208
education: for child and youth migrants, 286–87; UC challenges in, 286
Elizabeth story, at BHH, 273–74
Ellis Island, 8, 9, 213n13
emergency intake sites, for UC, 16
epistemic violence: Bhatia on American psychology and, 229–30; De Sousa Santos on WEIRD system and, 229; Ndlovu-Gatsheni on detention and crisis of, 231
Estrella *testimonio* story, 148–59, 166
eugenics, 35, 36, 52n7

faith-based community: ATD for women, 270–81; Bible, liberation theology, and immigration, 247–52; Central America refugees in 1980s and, 253; challenges to, 246; Humane Borders, 254; immigrant advocacy, 247–48; immigrant hospitality of, 4, 23, 246, 249–50; on inhumane policies, 253; migration ethical response, 252–54; network for sanctuary, 253–54; No More Deaths, 254; NSM formation in 2006, 253–54; refugee resettlement and, 23; UC hospitality as ATD, 255–70. *See also* Bible
families: child and family relationship verification proposal, 99–100; children release to, 317; importance of, 90–91; proposal for child contact priority with, 100–103; reunification, 7, 40, 263

Families Belong Together rally, 245
family detention centers: Berks County Residential Center, 13; Hutto, 11–13; Karnes County Residential Center, 13; New Mexico converted law enforcement training center, 12–13; prisonlike conditions at, 12–13; South Texas Residential Center, 13
Family First Prevention Services Act (2018), 104, 311, 313
family separation, 24n1; BHH on, 276–77; as detention harm, 20; as detention violence, 20; forced racial subjugation in, 34–35; historical of mixed-status families, 47; impact of, 223; inhumane policies of, 168; under MPP, 48; normalized from nonlegal primary caregivers, 48–49; Sessions and Bible for justification of, 246–47; under Title 42, 14–16, 48; trauma feelings from, 223; Trump policy of, 46, 47, 117; Venta on psychosocial functioning influenced by, 224; under zero tolerance, 13–14, 47–48, 117; zero tolerance policy and, 13–14. *See also* parent-child separation
Federally Qualified Health Centers (FQHCs), 105
feminist liberation theology, 248
fictive kin temporary relationships, 118, 120–22
flight risk determination, for parole, 205
Flores, Jenny Lisette: Behavioral Systems Southwest detention of, 10; detention of, 9; federal, class-action lawsuit and, 10; guards dehumanizing treatment of, 10
Flores Settlement Agreement, for child migrant detentions, 310; government standards of care, 10; on least restrictive setting, 10; ORR services-oriented detention, 194; on UC under eighteen limited set of protections, 193–94
Flores v. USCIS, on arriving alien demeaning term, 213n10
forced sterilization, 35; *Madrigal v. Quilligan* on Mexican American, 52n7
Fort Bliss emergency intake site, 16
Foucault, Michel, 232–33, 238–39
FQHCs. *See* Federally Qualified Health Centers
Frames of War (Butler), 236
Francisco story, at BHH, 277
Franklin, Ross D., 14–15

gang violence: Estrella *testimonio* story on father and, 149; in Guatemala, 119; Raul escape from, 257
Garcia Ramirez et al. v. U.S. ICE (2022), age redetermination class action suit, 190, 199
gendered violence, toward women migrants, 272
gender identity, paperwork limited choices in, 73–74
General Board of Church and Society of the United Methodist Church, for immigration policy changes, 254
Ghana, Opoku from, 191–92, 196, 198, 202, 205–6
Gibril story, at Viator of Hospitality, 263–67; first day, 260; ORR and possible jail transfer, 258
Gomberg-Muñoz, Ruth, 120, 121
Good Samaritan story, 251–52
Gosch, Michael, 23, 207, 210, 255–70
grievability, Butler on, 159
group home, ORR placement type of, 63
Guatemala: gang violence in, 119; unaccompanied minors from, 5
Guatemala adolescents of Axel and Sebastian example, of relational ruptures, 5; CBP temporary detention

of, 118, 134–36; leaving home, 129–30; Mexico arrest and organized crime group, 118, 130–34; ORR long-term detention facilities, 118; reunification and aftermath, 136–37
Gutierrez, Gustavo, 248
Guzmán Loera, Joaquín "El Chapo," 289, 301n2

Halperin, Marj, 3–4
The Harmony of Illusions (Young), 230
harm reduction, for child migrant detention, 5, 18–20, 315
healing power of psychotherapy, ideology of, 239
Health and Human Services (HHS) detention system: on congregate care abolition, 315–16; family separation and, 47–48; migrant children at Southwest Indiana Regional Youth Village, 44; proposal for policies for child and family relationship verification, 99–100; psychotropic drug administered in, 45–46; Vincennes contract termination by, 44
health services, adult detention lack of translator for, 204
Heartland Alliance, ICC of, 196–97
Heartland Health, BHH collaborative relationship with, 271
Heidbrink, Lauren, 119, 310
Herskind, Micah, 315
HHS. *See* Health and Human Services
High Commissioner for Refugees, UN, on best interest of child, 61
Homeland Security Act (2002): ORR Unaccompanied Minors Division and, 10; on UC designation, 87; U.S. Code on UAC definition, 52n10
homelessness and instability, of children at age of eighteen, 194, 212n3
Homestead Temporary Shelter, of Caliburn International, 17

homo sacer, 234; detained children as, 236; individuals whose lives are unworthy of protection, 236
Huckabee Sanders, Sarah, 246–47
human dignity, abolition and prioritizing of, 313–15
Humane Borders faith-based organization, 254
human trafficking: assumption of UC involvement in, 70; BHH response to, 277–78; CBP on, 17
Hutto. *See* T. Don Hutto Family Detention Center

ICC. *See* International Children's Center
ICDI. *See* Illinois Community for Displaced Immigrants
ICE. *See* Immigration and Customs Enforcement
identities, BHH response to complex, 273–76
identity verification: adult detention from child lack of, 205–6; in ORR documents, 60, 63, 73–74, 80
Illinois Community for Displaced Immigrants (ICDI), 207, 208
image theater, 290–91, 301n3
immigrant hospitality, of faith-based community, 4, 23, 246; De La Torre on biblical narratives of, 249; Old Testament command for, 249–50; Rivera-Pagán on foundation of, 250; UC hospitality as ATD, 255–70
immigrants: children during heightened animosity against, 285–86; Halperin on support of, 3–4; Zimbardo on Trump stereotyping of, 221–22. *See also* migrants
immigration: abolition in context of, 309; biblical narratives of, 245–46; child detention under laws of, 310; lawful entry of noncitizen, 204–5; restrictive laws after 9/11, 208

Immigration and Customs Enforcement (ICE), 3, 310; age-out detention rates, 212n1; ATD phrase use by, 214n15; biopolitics and disciplinary system of, 233; CCA contract for Hutto Family Detention Center, 11; child and youth migrants detained at U.S.-Mexico border, 119; children at age of eighteen ROR by, 190, 194, 257; contracts with private detention centers and prisons for confinement, 209; detention facility guaranteed payments by, 320n11; in DHS, 10; on family detention facilities standards, 12–13; on family safety in detention, 18; family staging centers of, 18; *Garcia Ramirez et al., v. U.S. Immigration and Customs Enforcement* class action suit, 190, 199; lawsuit against Trump administration on abusive behaviors of, 221; paternalistic mission with migrants of, 17–18; research on UC interaction with, 173; residential centers for children and family, 17; routine strip searches of, 204

Immigration and Nationality Act (INA): on removal proceedings for UC, 87–88; SIJ status from state court finding, 110n2

Immigration and Naturalization Services (INS), undocumented arrests and deportation, 9

immigration attorney: children immediate access to, 106; of Opoku for legal status, 205–6; positive influence of, 213n12; role of, 106

immigration law enforcement: in detention, 311; DHS child detention under laws, 310; immigration system prioritizing of, 314; New Mexico converted training centers, 12–13

immigration system: due process violations in, 49–50; General Board of Church and Society of the United Methodist Church on policy changes to, 254; laborers exploitation and, 319n4; law enforcement objectives prioritizing, 314; Opoku reflections on, 211–12; rule of law manipulated by, 309; Trump and U.S. legal entry difficulties, 285

INA. *See* Immigration and Nationality Act

Ina, Satsuki, 311

incarceration, 20; age redetermination and, 209–10; children lack of document access, 206; DHS setting parole from, 205; immigration detention system racist, 208; parole, 205, 213n9, 213n11. *See also* jail; Opoku, Vida; secure detention settings

inhumane policies, 4, 208; abolition as critical resistance to, 308; BHH response to, 276–78; CBP detention and, 143; faith-based community on, 253; of family separation, 168; trauma from, 228

INS. *See* Immigration and Naturalization Services

institutionalization of children, Nowak on harm of, 110n6

Institutional Review Board (IRB), 176

International Children's Center (ICC): as NGO, 196–97; Opoku at, 195–96

international guidance: on child protection, 51n4; on detention, 41. *See also* United Nations

International Labor Organization, 51n4

IRB. *See* Institutional Review Board

jail: ATD program compared to cost of, 210; ORR release to, 197–98, 201–3, 257–58; parole allowing release from, 205

Javier sexual and gender minority story: with Stefano, 177–83; strategic reference to rules to gain favor, 177–78

Jesus, scriptural response to othering, 251–52
juvenile detention centers, 17; trauma and, 103; UC children in, 102–3
juvenile justice system: children of color adultification in, 38; criminalization of children of color, 37–38; ORR secure setting placement without hearing in, 52n13

Karnes County Residential Center, 13
Kim, Ha Yeon, 223
Kornfeld, Elizabeth Lira, 230

The Land of Open Graves (De León), 120
lawful permanent residence (LPR) status, for children of legal migrants, 72
Layton, Lynn, 229
Lazarus, Emma, 309
L.B. v. Charles Keeton, et al., 200
legal assistance, resistance through, 22
legal violence, 32–33, 319n3; best-interests standards incorporation and, 50, 53n19; child-centered system creation failure, 39, 49–50; child detention as form of, 40–41, 313; detained homemaking and state control, 174; in sexual and gender minority immigration interactions, 175, 186
legislation: Chinese Exclusion Act (1882), 35, 208, 213n13, 309; Family First Prevention Services Act (2018), 104, 311, 313; Homeland Security Act (2002), 10, 52n10, 87; INA, 87–88, 110n2. *See also* Trafficking Victims Protection Reauthorization Act
"Let Us All Rise Together" (Davis), 307
Lewis story, at Viator of Hospitality, 255
LGBTQ-identified youth, 272; in ORR custody, 22. *See also* sexual and gender minority
liberation theology: advocates of migrants rights and, 248–49; examples of, 248; Good Samaritan story, 251–52; of Gutierrez, de Ellacuria, Boff, L., and Boff, C., 248; on historical processes leading to oppression, 248; on oppression and immigrant treatment, 248, 250–51
liminal homemaking of UC: in ICE and ORR detention, 174; resistance expression in, 174; as search for belonging, comfort, safety, 174; sexual and gender minority and, 173–87; violence exacerbated by, 174
Lourde, Audre, 18
LPR. *See* lawful permanent residence

Madrid, Alison Jimena Valencia, 14
Madrigal v. Quilligan, class action suit for Mexican American women forced sterilization, 52n7
marginalized individuals, considered as disposable, 235–36
Martín-Baró, Ignacio, 237, 239
Matter of M-A-C-O, on immigration judges jurisdiction over UAC, 194, 213n4
Mbembe, Achille, 232; necropower and necropolitics of, 233, 235–36, 238–39
meaning-making process, of *testimonio*, 146
medical home, AAP on, 110n7
medical practices, coercive, 20, 45–46
mental health, 4; adult detention threat to child and youth migrants, 203–4; depression and anxiety, 10, 47, 200, 223, 227, 237, 285, 312; detention long-term outcomes of, 40–41; detention relationship with trauma and, 222; parent-child separation conditions, 47, 53n15, 227; posttraumatic stress disorder, 227, 228, 312; suicidal ideation, 41, 46, 200, 202, 227, 237, 312; UC equitable access to care, 107

meritocracy, in psychology, 229
Mexican migrants: child detention of, 8; criminalization of, 208; kidnap by criminal actors, 21; Trump disparaging of, 36, 52n8; U.S. Border Patrol to control entry from, 36; U.S. subjugation and disproportional state violence, 35–36; in Watts, 288–89
Migrant Protection Protocol (MPP), 276; Biden temporary halt and termination of, 15; family separation and, 48
migrants: collective agency for, 120–21; ORR, CBP and ICE paternalistic mission with, 17–18; relationships of solidarity, 164; sociality, 120–22. *See also* Mexican migrants
migration, ethical response to, 252–54
militarization, U.S.-Mexico border increase in, 120
mixed-methods study, Dreby and Adkins use of children drawings, 288
mixed-status families, historical separation of, 47
Moulder, Andrew J., 35
MPP. *See* Migrant Protection Protocol

National Association of Social Workers (NASW), 105
National Child Traumatic Stress Network (NCTSN), 105
National Endowment of the Arts (NEA), 301
National Immigrant Justice Center, BHH collaborative relationship with, 271
Native children: forced assimilation through government run schools, 34–35; infantilizing and saviorism of, 76–77
NCTSN. *See* National Child Traumatic Stress Network
Ndolvu-Gatsheni, Sabelo J., 231

NEA. *See* National Endowment of the Arts
"Necropolitics" (Mbembe), 233
necropower and necropolitics, of Mbembe, 233, 238–39; structural violence of, 236; on subjugation of life to power of death, 235
"The New Colossus" (Lazarus), 309
New Sanctuary Movement (NSM), 253–54
"Newspaper Theater" child artistic exercise, 283
New Testament, on oppression liberation, 250–51
NGOs. *See* nongovernmental organizations
9/11, restrictive immigration laws after, 208
#NoKidsinCages installations, 3
No More Deaths faith-based organization, 254
noncitizens: Biden term of, 7; DHS-ICE contracts with private detention centers and prisons for, 209; DHS processing and detention of, 209; immigration lawful entry of, 204–5; immigration laws permitting release of, 209; Trump Title 42 policy expulsion of undocumented, 14–16, 48
nongovernmental organizations (NGOs): ICC as, 196–97; ORR contracts for UC detention by, 196–97
noninnocence, in URM Program paperwork, 68; human trafficking activities assumption, 70; negative labeling of UC, 70–71; secure detention justification from, 71; UC criminalization in, 69
nonlegal primary caregivers, normalized family separation from, 48–49
Notice of Rights, in ORR documents, 80n3
NSM. *See* New Sanctuary Movement

Index

Obama, Barack: immigrant deportation by, 284; U.S.-Mexico border UC increase and, 13

Office of Refugee Resettlement (ORR): on children ages 0–13, 7; child welfare system and, 310; constant surveillance sense in, 178, 186; contracts with NGOs for UC detention, 196–97; custody procedures of, 66; goal for UC release to sponsor, relative, or family friend, 197; law on children transfer within seventy-two hours, 10, 42, 87; LGBTQ-identified youth stories, 22; migrant children referral numbers in 2022, 16; paperwork guiding daily practices of, 20; proposal to expedite evaluation of UC family relationships, 99–100; refugee admission and resettlement policy, 196; release to jail, 197–98, 201–3, 257–58; relocation of sexual and gender minority youth, 181–82; research on UC interaction with, 173; secure setting placement without juvenile justice system hearing, 52n13; services-oriented detention of, 194; on teens ages 14–17, 7; on telephone calls of children with family members, 101; transfer of UC from DHS to, 87, 256; UC placement assessment by, 62; unsubstantiated gang allegations and secure detention setting by, 52n12. *See also* Unaccompanied Children Program

Office of Refugee Resettlement (ORR) facilities, 62; activists protests at, 15; characteristics of, 17; group home, RTC and shelter care, 63; inappropriate behaviors and incident reports in, 179; Opoku at ICC, 195–96; public outcry over permanent, 15; RTC, 63; sexual abuse and hiring practices at, 15; Shenandoah Valley Juvenile Center contract revoked with, 43–45; Southwest Key organization, 15; special needs care, 63; trauma manifestation in, 319n6; UC average stay of 102 days at, 40; youth safety concerns, 15

Old Testament command for immigrant hospitality, 249–50

Oluo, Ijeoma, 19

Opoku, Vida: affidavit of birth receipt, 206; age redetermination by ORR custody experience of, 22, 197–98; arriving alien designation of, 204–5; borderlands experience, 191–93; community-based housing program search for, 206; credible fear interview for parole with USCIS, 205, 213n9; DHS age redetermination of, 189; from Ghana, 191–92, 196, 198, 202, 205–6; immigration attorney for legal status of, 205–6; interview without translator at U.S.-Mexico border, 192–93; lack of proof of identity, 206; in ORR custody at ICC, 195–96; ORR release to jail, 197–98, 201–3; placement in cage in warehouse, 193; reflections on immigration system, 211–12; release from adult detention, 207–8; sent to Chicago, 193; successes of, 211; Wu assignment as Child Advocate for, 189

oppression: Jesus identification with, 252; liberation theology on, 248; New Testament on liberation from, 250–51; Old Testament on immigrant treatment and, 249–50; sociopolitical context of, 222

The Origins of Totalitarianism (Arendt), 234

ORR. *See* Office of Refugee Resettlement

ORR Guide to Eligibility, Placement and Services for URM: Section 2 documents, 65
ORR URM Policy Guide: Record of Posting and Revision Dates documents, 65, 80n2
othering: defined, 31–32; dehumanization and demonization from, 32; Jesus scriptural response to, 251–52; through ORR paperwork, 20; Western trauma model and suffering, 231
othering, of Black, Brown, Native children and youth: in child-serving systems context, 36–38; in child welfare system, 36–37; deconstruction of, 50–51; dehumanization and history of state-sanctioned violence facilitation against, 20, 33–36, 308; from East Asian countries, 208; in juvenile justice system, 37–38; rhetorical devices and, 75
othering, of migrant children: family separation as state-sanctioned violence, 39, 46–49; harm reduction and state-sanctioned violence dismantling, 50–51; legal violence and child-centered system failure, 39, 49–50; normalization of state violence in, 39; state-sanctioned violence and, 31–32, 39–40
Othering and Belonging Institute, powell of, 51

Padilla-Rodriguez, Ivón, 9
Paik, A. Naomi, 254
parent-child separation (traumatic separation): lasting developmental effects of, 46, 227, 312; mental health conditions from, 47, 53n15, 227
Parliamentary Resolution, of Council of Europe, on abolition and ATD, 316
parole, 213n11; allowing release from jail, 205; ATD program and, 205; flight risk determination for, 205; Opoku credible fear interview before USCIS for, 205, 213n9
paternalistic mission: with migrants, 17–18, 72; between UC and service providers, 71–74
peer interaction: research absence on UC and, 173; socialization source, 173; social vulnerabilities exacerbation through, 173; surveillance to report bad behavior, 179
perpetual liminality state, of sexual and gender minority, 187
physical health care, UC equitable access to, 107
Physicians for Human Rights study, on adult detention lack of translators for health services, 204
political subjects, UC as, 79
posttraumatic stress disorder, 227, 312; as Western concept, 228
powell, john a., 51
Pratt, Richard, 34–35
professionalism in document language, 73–74
psychiatric universalism, Summerfield on, 231
psychological practices: attachment theory and, 22, 223–27; ideological tool of, 228–29; ignorance of biopolitics in, 237; Martín-Baró on, 237, 239; for trauma response, 22
psychological violence, sociopolitical context of, 222
psychotropic behavior modification, in detention, 45–46
Purnell, Derecka, 315
Pyke, Karen D., 29

queer liberation theology, 248

racialism, 308; age redetermination dubious legal grounds, 190–91; in-

Index 349

carceration in immigration detention system, 208; in U.S. child welfare system, 37. *See also* othering, of Black, Brown, Native children and youth
racial subjugation, 33, 36; forced family separation and, 34–35
RAIC. *See* Refugee, Asylum and International Operations
Rapid Deployment Inc., Fort Bliss emergency intake site maintenance by, 16
Raul story, at Viator of Hospitality, 263–67; first day, 259–60; ORR and possible jail transfer, 257–58
Reagan, Ronald, 4, 9
reformist strategies, abolition and, 308
Refugee, Asylum and International Operations (RAIO), 213n5
refugees: Agamben on stateless condition of, 233; from Central America in 1980s, 253; as disposable, 235; faith-based community on resettlement of, 23; ORR for resettlement of, 196–97; URM Program of ORR documents, 65, 80n2; Western medical model and trauma of children, 232. *See also* Office of Refugee Resettlement
refusal: Butler on, 164; resistance and, 164–65, 167; structural violence and, 164–66
relational ruptures, in detention settings: attachment theory and, 226–27; fictive kin temporary relationships, 118; Guatemala adolescents of Axel and Sebastian example, 5, 118, 129–37; migrant detention multiple contexts, 137–39; migrant sociality and fictive kin, 120–22; secure attachment affected by, 223–24; study methods for, 122–26; youth migration drivers, 119–20
release on recognizance (ROR), Viator House appeal for release to, 257, 258

release term, in rhetorical devices, 76
Relief for Migrant Children (RMC), research project on sexual and gender minority and, 175–77
research: absence of UC peer interaction, 173; art epistemologies in, 287–88; Bhatia criticism of colonial psychology, 229; on CBP, ICE, ORR interaction with UC, 173; of subaltern *testimonio* narratives, 146–48
residential treatment center (RTC), ORR placement type, 63
resistance, 23, 143, 169; abolition as form of, 308–9; as act oppositional to power, 145; CBP detention context, 145, 168–69; child and youth migrant everyday acts of, 145–46; of Cindy, 163–65, 166; Cindy *testimonio* story of, 159–65; confrontational overt acts of, 45; Estrella *testimonio* story, 148–59, 166; through legal assistance, 22; liminal homemaking expression of, 174; nonviolent acts of, 166; pretending to not understand English as, 157; refusal and, 164–65, 167; to separation and threat of solidarity, 158; through service provision, 22; solidarities as forms of, 167–68; solidarity among migrants as form of collective, 168; survival through subtle everyday, 21; *testimonio* research subaltern narratives, 146–48; in vulnerability condition to challenge power, 144, 145, 146, 165; youth organizing initiative for, 147. *See also* children artistic narratives of resistance case study
reunification: cultural responsive and strength-based approaches in, 102; family, 7, 40, 263; proposal for expediting, 100–103; service activation for, 96–98

rhetorical devices in UC descriptions, 60, 74–77
Rivera-Pagán, Luis, 250
RMC. *See* Relief for Migrant Children
ROR. *See* release on recognizance
Rosen, Karen, 225–26
Rose story, at BHH, 274–75
Rothbaum, Fred, 225–26
RTC. *See* residential treatment center

Sanchez, Juan, 15
sanctuary: faith-based community network for, 253–54; Paik description of, 254
Sandra story, at BHH, 279–80
saviorism ideal: rhetorical devices and, 76; in Western psychotherapy, 239
Schmidt, Susan, 79
secure detention settings: absent due process of law, 44, 52n13; designed for adjudicated delinquents, 43; HHS detention system and, 44; ORR guidelines loose interpretation for placement at, 52n12; as ORR placement type, 63; ORR unsubstantiated gang allegations for, 52n12; prolonged and indefinite, 43–45, 52n14; reasons for custody in, 43; remote locations of, 45; Shenandoah Valley Juvenile Center, 43–44; state-sanctioned violence in, 43; Vincennes, 44
self-responsibilization, in psychology, 229
Senn, David, 200
service provision: resistance through, 22; Schmidt on, 79; UC assumed relationship in, 71–74
servitude, of othered Black, Brown, and Native children, 34
Sessions, Jeff: Bible justification for family separation, 246–47; on zero tolerance policy, 13–14

sexual abuse: in adult detention, 204; at ORR facilities, 15; of sexual and gender minority, 175; of transgender child and youth migrants, 120; of women migrants by smugglers, 272
sexual and gender minority: background on, 174–76; humanitarian protection claims, 174; hyperaware of surveillance of, 178; immigration protections and, 173; legal violence in immigration interactions, 175, 186; limited peer relationships in detention, 178–79; literature absence on experiences of, 173; ORR relocation of, 181–82; perpetual liminality state of, 187; RMC study data and methods on, 175–77; sexual abuse of, 175; social erasure of, 173; Stefano and Javier story, 177–83; symbolic violence and, 174–75; UC liminal homemaking and, 173–87; U.S. discrimination against asylum admission of, 174; Yaqueline and Antonio story, 183–86
shelter care, ORR placement type of, 63
Shenandoah Valley Juvenile Center: abuse claims at, 43–44; ORR contact revoked with, 45
Shiloh Residential Treatment Center, psychotropic drugs administered at, 46
SIJ. *See* Special Immigrant Juvenile
slavery, abolition deep roots in end to, 307
Smokowski, Paul R., 287–88
smugglers and *coyotes*, 178, 292, 295, 302n5; women migrants sexual assaults by, 272
sociality, of migrants, 122; fractured relationships constrain of, 187; ORR detention challenges to youth, 179; Vogt on collective agency in, 120–21; Wheatley and Gomberg-Muñoz

on collective agency in, 120, 121; of Yaqueline and Antonio, 183
socialization pattern, of UC, 178
social justice, trauma-informed care promotion of, 222
"Society Must Be Defended" (Foucault), 232
sociocultural aspects of family, attachment theory and, 225
sociopolitical context: Agamben on sovereign power and, 234; Layton on dissociation of clinical from, 229; of psychological violence and oppression, 222; Wilkinson on psychology ignoring of, 229
solidarity: Butler on, 164; vulnerability and, 163–64
South Texas Family Residential Center, 13
Southwest Indiana Regional Youth Village (Vincennes): HHS contract termination with, 44; as original secure contractor for HHS system, 44; SWAT team attack on migrant children at, 45
Southwest Key organization, 15
sovereign power: Agamben on, 234; biopolitics and classical, 232
Special Immigrant Juvenile (SIJ) visa, 70; INA on state court finding, 110n2; status for abandoned, neglected children, 194; UC adultification for, 72–73
special needs care, ORR placement type, 63
Stanford Prison Experiment, of Zimbardo, 221, 222
stateless individuals, Arendt on, 233–34
state of exception, Agamben on, 234
state-sanctioned violence, 223; abolition and, 308; of children in cages, 21; against children of color, 20, 33–36, 308; community arts program on, 23; family separation and othering of migrant children, 39, 46–49; history of othering and dehumanization against children of color, 33–36; othering of migrant children harm reduction and dismantling of, 50–51; in secure detention facilities, 43; structural violence as form of, 32–33, 144; systemic detention of migrant children and youth, 40–46
Stefano sexual and gender minority story: contemplation of voluntary departure, 180; on helpless feelings in liminality of detention, 180; hyperawareness of surveillance, 178; intimacy display challenges with Javier, 180–81; Javier in, 177–83; ORR one-on-one observation, 182; ORR separation from Javier by relocation, 181–82; Stefano apprehension by CBP, 177; Stefano at ORR shelter in New York for five month, 177; Stefano from El Salvador, 177; Stefano gay orientation difficulties, 177
strip searches, ICE routine, 204
structural violence: CBP state-sanctioned, 32–33, 144; of Mbembe necropower and necropolitics, 236; refusal and, 164–66; vulnerability discourse and, 144, 166, 310
Suárez-Orozco, Carola, 223
subjugation, in U.S.: Black, Brown, Native children abduction and forced assimilation, 34; Black, Brown, Native children eugenics and forced sterilization, 35; around citizenship, 33–34; civic participation exclusion, 35; cultural, 34; dispossession of land, resources, and rights through, 34; Mexicans disproportional state violence, 35–36; racial, 33–36

suicidal ideation, 41, 46, 200, 202, 227, 237, 312
Sultan, Reina, 315
Summerfield, Derek, 231
supervised/conditional release program, 209
Supreme Court cases: *Flores v. USCIS*, 213n10; *Garcia Ramirez et al. v. U.S. ICE*, 190, 199; *L.B. v. Charles Keeton, et. al.*, 200; *Madrigal v. Quilligan*, 52n7; *Tape v. Hurley*, 51n6
survival, 21, 22

Tape v. Hurley (1885), on Chinese children public school attendance, 51n6
T. Don Hutto Family Detention Center (Hutto): ACLU representation of Yourdkhani, 12; activists minor reforms for, 12–13; CCA opening of, 11; Yourdkhani detention at, 11–12
temporary border facilities, of CBP, 17; deaths in and due to detention in, 42–43; seventy-two hour placement at, 10, 42, 87
temporary influx shelters, of ORR: Homestead Temporary Shelter, of Caliburn International, 17; Tornillo Influx Facility, of BCFS Health and Human Services, 17
temporary relationships, survival through, 21
testimonio: Cindy story of, 159–65; digital research project of, 147–48; Estrella story of, 148–59, 166; features of, 146; as meaning-making process, 146; policy and procedure need shown in, 168; research project of subaltern narratives, 146–48
therapeutic treatment, depoliticizing of, 222
Title 42 policy, of Trump, 14–16, 48
Tornillo Influx Facility, of BCFS Health and Human Services, 17

Tornillo Tent Camp image, 14
Trafficking Victims Protection Reauthorization Act (TVPRA) (2008), 110n1, 199; authorizing HHS to appoint Child Advocates, 88–89; CBP as apprehending authority for, 40; on children aging out eligibility for ATD programs, 209; least restrictive setting requirement by, 190, 197; ORR care 2020 average length of time of 102 days, 40; U.S. detention with family reunification goal, 40
transgender child and youth migrants: punishment and violence exacerbation for, 175; sexual assault of, 120; Yaqueline experience as, 183–86
transgender women, at BHH, 272, 275–76
translators: Opoku U.S.-Mexico border interview without, 192–93; Physicians for Human Rights study on lack of health services, 204
trauma: Becker and Kornfeld on Westernized discourse of, 230; biomedical and disease model of, 230–31; Briggs on, 227; from broken connections in detention transitions, 118; child and youth migrants multiple, 228; defined, 227; from detention inhumane conditions, 228; detention relationship with mental health and, 222; family- and community-based setting healing to, 104; family separation and child feelings of, 223; high rates of mental health outcomes, 227; juvenile detention center placements and, 103; long-term effects of, 227; manifestation in ORR facilities, 319n6; manifestations from detention harm, 312; powerlessness as trigger for, 103; during premigration, 228; social, political, cultural context of, 228

Index

trauma-informed care, 281n6; social justice promoted by, 222

trauma therapy, Craps on, 239

traumatic separation. *See* parent-child separation

treatment reimagination, for children in cages: attachment theory and, 223–27; biopolitics, necropolitics and detained children destiny, 232–37; future directions, 237–39; importance of understanding detention trauma and health risks, 237; mainstream trauma therapy ineffective for, 238–39; trauma and child detention, 227–32

Trump, Donald, 42; anti-immigrant policies of, 3, 4; arts education programs budget cuts, 300–301; children artistic narratives of resistance directed at, 283–85, 289–97, 299–301; disparaging of Mexican migrants, 36, 52n8; family separation policy of, 46, 47, 117; humanitarian outcry on immigration policies of, 221–22; lawsuit against administration for CBP and ICE abusive behaviors, 221; threat to terminate NEA, 301; Title 42 policy for migrant expulsion, 14–16, 48; Zimbardo on immigrant stereotyping by, 221–22

T visa, 70–71

TVPRA. *See* Trafficking Victims Protection Reauthorization Act

UAC. *See* unaccompanied alien children

UC. *See* unaccompanied children

unaccompanied alien children (UAC), 7, 60; age redetermination loss of protection for, 191, 204; asylum officer initial jurisdiction over, 212n2; Homeland Security Act, U.S. Code definition of, 52n10; *Matter of M-A-C-O* on immigration judge jurisdiction over, 194, 213n4; ORR transfer to adult detention or jail, 257–58

unaccompanied children (UC): Archard on Western view of, 76; CBP, ICE, ORR interaction research, 173; CBP statistics on increase in, 5–6; criminalization in documents on, 69; dangers of voyage to U.S., 203; toward dignified immigration for, 77–78; documentation of infants as, 223; education difficulties, 286; from El Salvador, Guatemala, Honduras, 5; emergency intake sites for, 16; faith-based community on hospitality as ATD for, 255–70; in juvenile detention centers, 102–3; long-term reform and short-term challenges for, 77–78; mental health equitable access to care, 107; ORR assessment for placement of, 62; ORR contracts with NGOs for, 196–97; as political subjects, 79; removal proceedings of, 87–88; SIJ visa and adultification of, 72–73; socialization pattern of, 178; TVPRA processing procedures for, 40; U.S. detention of, 40–42; U.S.-Mexico border increase of, 13

Unaccompanied Children Program of ORR, key administrative documents and legal resources, 7; child-friendly document versions, 78; Children Entering the United States Unaccompanied: Section 1 document, 65; documents for providers, sponsors, and health care providers, 64; documents for UC requirement procedures, 64; double standard narratives of vulnerability and non-innocence, 68–71; identity verification in, 60, 63, 73–74, 80; method-

Unaccompanied Children Program of ORR (*continued*)
    ology for study of, 61–62, 66; Notice of Rights in, 80n3; ORR Guide to Eligibility, Placement and Services for URM: Section 2 documents, 65; ORR URM Policy Guide: Record of Posting and Revision Dates documents, 65, 80n2; professionalism in document language, 73–74; rhetorical devices in UC descriptions, 60, 74–77; trivial bureaucratic processes in, 59–61, 77–80; UC and service providers assumed relationship, 60, 71–74; UC portrayal related to accommodation and release, 60
Unaccompanied Minors Division, of ORR, 10
Unaccompanied Refugee Minors (URM) Program, of ORR: documents for, 65; ORR Guide to Eligibility, Placement and Services for URM: Section 2 documents, 65; ORR URM Policy Guide: Record of Posting and Revision Dates documents, 65, 80n2
undocumented migrants, *coyote* as person helping, 178, 292, 295, 302n5
UNICEF. *See* United Nations Children's Fund
United Nations (UN): Declaration on Human Rights in 1948, 313; Declaration on the Protection of All Persons from Being Subjected to Torture, 314, 320n9; Declaration on the Rights of the Child in 1959, 51n4; Universal Declaration of Human Rights, 314, 320n7
United Nations Children's Fund (UNICEF), on UC detention prevention, 41
United States (U.S.), 203; child welfare system racism in, 37; detention of UC, as form of state-sanctioned violence, 40–42; discrimination against sexual and gender minority admission to, 174; history of othering in, 33–36; human rights abuses in, 313–14; othered Black, Brown, Native children servitude in, 34; racism in child welfare system of, 37; Trump and U.S. legal entry difficulties, 285. *See also* subjugation, in U.S.
United States Citizenship and Immigration Services (USCIS): affirmative asylum application and, 194; *Flores v. USCIS* on arriving alien demeaning term, 213n10; on negative implications for age redetermination, 195; Opoku credible fear interview for parole, 205, 213n9
Universal Declaration of Human Rights, 314, 320n7
URM. *See* Unaccompanied Refugee Minors
U.S. Border Patrol, 1924 creation of, 36
USCIS. *See* United States Citizenship and Immigration Services
U.S.-Mexico border: child and youth migrants detained by ICE at, 119; Estrella *testimonio* story of desert at, 149–50; Humane Borders and, 254; ICE detention of child and youth migrants at, 119; increasing militarization of, 120; Lewis travel from South America to, 255; migrant continued containment at, 117; Obama and increase of UC at, 13; Opoku experience at, 191–93; traumatic event during premigration, 228; U.S. Border Patrol to control entry at, 36

Van der Kolk, Bessel, 221
variable length, of detention, 11, 40, 223
Venta, Amanda, 224

Viator House of Hospitality, 281n5, 318; Abdul at, 259; age redetermination opportunity of, 255–56; appeal for ROR by, 257, 258; as ATD program, 207, 210–11, 255–56; BHH collaborative relationship with, 271; Brost and Gosch as founders of, 23, 207, 210, 255–70; candidate interview by, 258; Clerics of St. Viator values at, 254, 256; culture maintenance and, 264; employment opportunities and, 266–67; family reunification, 263; first day of freedom and safety, 259–60; first week case management and shopping, 260–63; Gibril at, 258, 260, 263–67; Lewis story at, 255–70; moving on from, 268–70; promotion of community and service in, 265–66; Raul at, 257–60, 263–67; resident phone purchase, 261–62; reverence for non-Christian traditions, 256; short or long stays at, 263–68

violence: Central America migration impacted by community and political, 6; denormalizing and detention harms, 311–13; in detention facilities, 20; epistemic, 229–31; legal, 32–33, 39–41, 49–50, 53n19, 174, 313, 319n3; liminal homemaking exacerbation of, 174; political and power structures evolving into, 222; psychological, 222; structural, 32–33, 144, 164–66, 236, 310. *See also* state-sanctioned violence

visa: SIJ, 70, 72–73, 110n2, 194; T, 70–71

visual arts methods, 287

vulnerability: Butler on strengths-based perspective and, 144; in CBP custody, 16, 169; resistance to, 144, 145, 146, 165; solidarity and, 163–64; structural violence and, 144, 166, 310; in URM Program paperwork, 68–71; women migrants and LGBTQ, 272–73

Watts, elementary school arts academy in, 288–89

Western, Educated, Industrialized, Rich, Democratic (WEIRD), 229

Western society: Agamben on state of exception in sociopolitical order of, 234; Archard on UC view of, 76; attachment theory paradigm development, 224–25; Becker and Kornfeld on trauma discourse of, 230; detained children failure from trauma theory of, 238; medical model failure to comprehend refugee children trauma, 232; othering and trauma model of suffering, 231; posttraumatic stress disorder as concept of, 228; Pyke on psychology meritocracy and self-responsibilization in, 229; saviorism ideal in psychotherapy of, 239

"What Is Abolition and Why Do We Need It?" (Sultan and Herskind), 315

Wheatley, Abby C., 120, 121

Wilkinson, Sue, 229

women migrants: feminist liberation theology, 248; gendered violence toward, 272; LGBTQ vulnerabilities, 272–73; smugglers sexual assault of, 272. *See also* Bethany House of Hospitality

Wu, Jajah: on adult detention dangers, 203–7; on age redetermination, 198–201; on detention for children, 196–97; on eighteen-year-olds vs. system, 193–95; Opoku Child Advocate assignment of, 189; as Young Center for Immigrant Children's Rights attorney, 189

Xiomara story, at BHH, 276–77

Yaqueline sexual and gender minority story: with Antonio, 183–86; gender confirmation surgery decision, 186; molestation in CBP custody, 183; need to feel safe for, 184; ORR staff removal from Antonio, 185; sociality attempts at expense of gender identity, 185; transgender identity of, 183–86

Young, Allen, 230–31

Young Center Child Advocates: advocacy and accompaniment of, 98; appointment of, 88, 110n4; court appointment of, 319n5; one-on-one work with child and youth migrants, 189; TVPRA authorization of HHS to appoint, 88–89

Young Center for Immigrant Children's Rights, 20; best-interests standard advocacy by, 89; BHH collaborative relationship with, 271, 278; on child immigration proceedings revision, 317–18; continuation of work with children at age of eighteen, 195; ORR facility request for Opoku Child Advocate, 189; staff of, 110n5; Young Center Child Advocates appointment by, 88, 110n4

Yourdkhani, Kevin: Canada family re-entry granted to, 12; Hutto detention of, 11

youth-centered alternatives to detention, 209–10

youth organizing initiative, for resistance, 147

zero-sum framework, in rhetorical devices, 75

zero tolerance policy, 277; Department of Justice announcement in 2018 for, 221; family separation under, 13–14, 47–48, 117

Zimbardo, Philip: Stanford Prison Experiment of, 221, 222; on Trump stereotyping of immigrants, 221–22